KT-153-223

*To Carol
with love, admiration
and great gratitude
from Ann + Ewen
April 2016*

McINTYRE'S PARCEL OF FINE RED HERRINGS

Ann J. McIntyre

*see especially
Chapter 11*

Cover photographs:
Main picture: Siccar Point, Berwickshire, Scotland
Insets: Donald holding a copy of Shakespeare's Macbeth on
                     Dunsinane Hill, Perthshire, Scotland
                   Seaver Science Laboratory for Biology and Geology,
                     Pomona College, Claremont, California

i

First published 2014 by FASTPRINT PUBLISHING of Peterborough, England.

www.fast-print.net/store.php

McINTYRE'S PARCEL OF FINE RED HERRINGS

Copyright © Ann I McIntyre 2014

All rights reserved

No part of this book may be reproduced in any form by photocopying
or any electronic or mechanical means, including information storage
or retrieval systems, without permission in writing from both the
copyright owner and the publisher of the book.

The right of Ann I McIntyre to be identified as the editor of this work has
been asserted by her in accordance with the Copyright, Designs and
Patents Act 1988 and any subsequent amendments thereto.

A catalogue record for this book is available from the British Library

ISBN 978-178456-039-3

An environmentally friendly book printed and bound in England
by www.printondemand-worldwide.com

Mixed Sources
Product group from well-managed
forests, and other controlled sources
FSC   www.fsc.org Cert no. TT-COC-002641
© 1996 Forest Stewardship Council

PEFC Certified
This product is
from sustainably
managed forests
and controlled
sources
PEFC
PEFC/16-33-415   www.pefc.org

This book is made entirely of chain-of-custody materials

*I dedicate this book to our beloved son, Ewen
and to our many wonderful friends all
around the world.*

*"In laughter lurks beauty,
content, and the love that it lends;
In laughing lies duty,
the lighting of life for our friends;
though the flood follows after,
its ripple once launched cannot cease;
Old laughter, dear laughter
Lives with us, our love-day and peace."*

from the poem *Laughter* by Geoffrey Winthrop Young

A Parcel of Fine Red Herrings

A life of learning, love and laughter
Donald B. McIntyre
1923 - 2009

On Monday next will be Published,
By J. DICKSON, and the other Booksellers of Edinburgh,
in one volume 4to, illustrated with copperplates,
VOLUME FIRST OF
THE PHILOSOPHICAL TRANSACTIONS
OF THE
ROYAL SOCIETY OF EDINBURGH.

Extracts from The Edinburgh Advertiser, 1788

RED HERRINGS.
A PARCEL of FINE RED HERRINGS, to be fold
in barrels, at JAMES M'INTYRE's, New Quay,
Leith.

Contents

Preface

Michael Mayne, one time Dean of Westminster Abbey writes: *"Often it is through the healing power of memory, a reliving of the past in the present that our fragmented selves find a unity. In recollection, one of the great gifts of old age, by combining memory and imagination, we are able to recreate our lives."* The editing and compiling of this book has been another of Donald's extraordinary gifts to me.

In October 2009, when Donald was no longer with us, one of my first challenges was to decide how to do justice to the great wealth of material in Donald's study. His parents had kept his letters from his childhood, from his travels and his decades at Pomona College and, wherever I turned, another file and box revealed texts of yet more of his own work. This treasure trove from a long and - in a sense - pioneering life, could neither just be stored nor discarded. So now, almost five years on, here is my pot-pourri selection about his life and of his work accompanied by generous contributions from some of his many friends. The book dovetails and expands upon Donald's own website: *http://www.mcintyre.me.uk*

Throughout this editorial adventure, I have come to know many of Donald's friends in a different context and have also made new and wonderful contacts. I am deeply grateful to Leslie Thomson, our friend and adviser, whose foresight and vision introduced me to Gilbert and Johanna Summers. Gilbert, though he never knew Donald in person, has worked tirelessly and patiently as my Editorial Coordinator and "Guardian of the Manuscript" and, so *in absentia*, Donald has become his friend too. Gilbert has given generously of his time and many skills; he has graciously tolerated my technical shortcomings and has buoyed me along so that this venture has been a huge learning experience, both nostalgic and yet joyful, for me. Gilbert's wife, Johanna, has played an important role in designing the cover of the book and helping me in many ways. My friend, Meg Cowie, as an Assistant Editor, has encouraged me endlessly with her love and enthusiasm for the project and by generously sharing her many practical skills.

I am grateful to students of the cheerful Edinburgh years in the 1950s. My thanks go to Paul Gilmour of Tucson, Arizona, USA and to David Mackenzie, Canberra, Australia for their reminiscences and contributions; to Charles Waterston, Edinburgh, for his careful attention to detail, his remarkable memory and his kindness to all three of us over many years; to the Baikie, Rutledge and Weiss families, and to Jennie Clerk, daughter of Bob Clark of Auckland, New Zealand, all of whom have generously sustained our long-term and treasured friendships.

Very many thanks to Donald's students of his Pomona years and for the encouragement and generous support from the Pomona College stalwarts of today - Eric Grosfils, Marjorie Harth, Lori Keala, Donald Pattison long with the Emeritus faculty members Martha Andresen, Nicole and Catalin Mitescu, Robert Woods and our dear friends Don and Ann Zenger.

It has been a pleasure to work long-distance with Keith Smillie of Evanston, Alberta, Canada who painstakingly and patiently has worked, re-worked and edited the computing chapter. I appreciate too the support of Dennis Dean of Evanston, Illinois and of both the Iverson and Hui families.

To name but a few of our incredibly generous and helpful Scottish friends, I thank and salute Iain and Patricia Brown, Arthur and Jean Bruce, Norman and Margaret Butcher, Jeremy Duncan, Eddy Durkin, the librarian who kindly catalogued all of Donald's library, John Mackay, faithful friend to Donald to the very end; David Mackie, art historian and consistently loving supporter to all three of us; Colin and Diana Nowell - caring friends who, time without number, kindly bail me out from my innumerable computer crises. I am grateful to our local friends – our immediate neighbours - Derek Burns, Denis Munro and Bertie and Patricia Robson - and my very special supporters and companions - Margaret Meade and Magdalene Sacrianie.

My deep gratitude and love to my brother-in-law, Ranald McIntyre and his family with whom I share so much in reminiscence and in laughter, and, of course, to our son, Ewen whose good cheer, (most-of-the-time) patience and great determination teaches me so much.

Ann McIntyre, Perth, Scotland,
August 2014.

In the quiet before cockcrow when the cricket's
Mandolin falters, when the light of the past
Falling from the high stars yet haunts the earth
And the east quickens, I think of those I love -
Dear men and women no longer with us.

And not in grief or regret merely but rather
With a love that is almost joy I think of them,
Of whom I am part, as they of me, and through whom
I am made more wholly one with the pain and the glory,
The heartbreak at the heart of things.

I have learned it from them at last, who am now grown old.
A happy man, that the nature of things is tragic
And meaningful beyond words, that to have lived
Even if once only, once and no more,
Will have been – oh, how truly – worth it.

Dear Men and Women (in memory of Van Wyck Brooks) (abridged)
by John Hall Wheelock.

★★★★★

"I am not going to try to comfort you", Spangler said, "I know I cannot. But try to remember that a good man can never die. You will see him in the streets; you will see him in the houses; in all the places of the town. In the vineyard and orchard, in the rivers and the clouds, (…the rocks and the stars…) in all the things here that make this world for us to live in. You will feel him in all the things that are here out of love, and for love, all the things that are abundant and the things that grow. The person of a man may leave – or be taken away – but the best part of a good man stays. It stays forever! Love is immortal and all things are made immortal through love."

The Human Comedy by William Saroyan

★★★★★

Introduction

In 2003, Alan Fyfe, Editor of "The Edinburgh Geologist" came to our home in Perth to interview Donald. I am grateful to have permission to reproduce this article from the Edinburgh Geological Society's Issue no.40, 2003.

Red Herrings by the Barrel

Alan Fyfe, Editor of the Edinburgh Geologist interviews Donald McIntyre

Donald McIntyre might be called the "Father of the Society" having been a Fellow for sixty years. I went up to see him in Perth, to chat and carry home a few stories to share with readers. I soon learnt that he has an amazing propensity for going off at all sorts of tangents as he talks, though the story always comes around full circle to the point of it all. He knows this himself and the title of this article stems from a lecture that he gave to the Royal Society of Edinburgh in 1986 during a celebration of the Enlightenment. After a long and apparent deviation from the main subject, in which he had read from The Edinburgh Advertiser of 1788 a brief mention of the publication of the first volume of the Transactions of the Royal Society of Edinburgh, he found another announcement: **"Red Herrings – a parcel of fine red herrings, to be sold in barrels, at James McIntyre's New Quay, Leith"**. *Laughter rocked the auditorium! Read on and see what I mean.....*

Editor: Donald, the Society records show that you are the longest-serving Fellow of the Society. I thought that readers of *The Edinburgh Geologist* might be interested in hearing something about you and your life and the people that have influenced you especially at the start of your career.

Donald: My father's father came originally from Balquhidder but he moved to Edinburgh and worked for the paper-making business of Bertrams of the Sciennes. My grandfather on my mother's side was a doctor in Morningside and went on his rounds in a horse and carriage. When he got a car, and it must have been one of the first in Edinburgh, the groom who looked after the horses became the chauffeur. When he washed the car he spoke to it as he had to the horses! I mention these things to show how much has changed – these were before my time but not much before my time.

My father, at the beginning of the [First World] War, joined up in the Horse Artillery. There are pictures of him with the horses; they actually went into battle with horses in France. And then he was shipped to the Mediterranean. They were in port for a long time in Alexandria and the officers (he was then a sergeant in the RA) got fed up and went to town – you can just imagine the situation. What happened was the ship sailed without the officers. They were sailing to Gallipoli, so these officers had essentially deserted in the face of the enemy. They could have been shot; it wasn't a question of a reprimand, it was something more serious than that. So he was the senior person in the group and he was actually commissioned in the field in Gallipoli. After the war he decided to become a minister so he took his degree in Edinburgh and his first charge was in Callander. We later came to Edinburgh to Morningside High Church, which is now the Churchill Theatre.

So when did you first develop an interest in geology?

When war broke out we were on holiday in Rothiemurchus. We always went to the Highlands and I was accustomed to climbing hills. My brother and I were at Watson's but my father decided that it would be unwise for us to go back to Edinburgh so we moved into digs in Grantown-on-Spey. That was a fantastic experience! I was in the Cairngorms virtually every weekend, so I knew those hills well. One of my friends was evacuated to Grantown to be billeted as an evacuee. His host had been a teacher and I got to know him. He was very interesting. He knew about the Gaelic place names of the hills and he told me about – I'll call it geology but he didn't use that word.

He gave me the memoir of the explanation of the sheet that covered that western part of the Cairngorms – Mid Strathspey and Strathdearn. Hinxman was one of the main authors of the sheet. As you can imagine, two thirds of it concerned itself with the 2V of the amphiboles, which meant nothing to me but, and this is the very important thing, about a third of the memoir was on the glaciation. And by golly, that was well done! I could see the ice coming down the Spey. Near Kincraig, there are two streams that come down from the Monadliath and turn at right angles to run almost horizontally for a while before turning to run down once again. This was at the height of the ice – and so you know I could see the ice level. And there are numerous ridges coming out of the Cairngorms with V-shaped notches in them. This was because the ice coming down the Spey went up into Glen More and pushed up into glens such as Glen Einich and the Lairig Ghru, so instead of the ice coming down as you would expect, the ice was pushing up and there were corrie glaciers higher up. The water drained right round Glenmore and when it came to one of these ridges, it cut a V-shaped notch. And I could see these V-shaped notches – I knew them well! And of course there were the great gravel deposits at the mouths of Glen Einich and the Lairig Ghru with crescentic moraines that were crescenting the wrong way. It was absolutely fantastic to me. It really turned me on.

And did that encourage you to study geology?

Well, at that time and for a while, a long while afterwards, geology was a three-year degree – you did mathematics, physics and chemistry first. So when I went to Edinburgh University, I was enrolled as a chemistry student and that meant that classes were predetermined. There was no question for example of taking a class on philosophy of science or the history of science – ridiculous – but that was the way it was. Now, in our mathematics class – you know, in those days one of the great things was that the professor taught the elementary class in every subject. That's a marvellous tradition and ought to be kept up in every Scottish university. Well, Sir Edmund Whittaker was the professor of mathematics and he was famous as a cosmologist as well as being a pure mathematician. The mathematics department at that time was in Chambers Street and we sat there at benches. I was beside a man (we always happened to sit in the same place; I don't know whether that was de rigueur but that's what happened) and this was Sandy Renwick. Later on, he became Director General of the International Geological Congress. He'd been educated in the south of England. Anyway, he was there and he had yellow gloves and a cane and wore a monocle. He must have been the last of the Great Colonials, absolutely the last, probably fifty years later than anyone else. Anyway, Sandy Renwick hadn't risen to these heights when I knew him in the maths class.

He told me that he intended to do geology. "Geology," I said, "what's geology?" He told me something about it because he'd done geology at school and I thought "this is interesting". Now, the Director of Studies was Robert Campbell, Reader in Petrology and acting head of the geology department when I first took a class. Professor Jehu was ill. So I'd seen Robert Campbell before signing up for mathematics, physics and chemistry in my first year. When I went back to register for the next year, I asked him about geology and he was delighted and (it wasn't very difficult) talked me into taking geology.

So your move to geology was mainly because of your love for the Cairngorms?

Oh absolutely! That's right – and I knew that other hills were not the same as the Cairngorms. So then I was a student in Edinburgh, a second-year student taking chemistry and geology. I had the beginning class from Robert Campbell in my first term and in my second term from Dr. Finlay who was the palaeontologist and Alec Cockburn. The staff consisted of the Professor, which when I went there at first was Thomas J. Jehu, and Robert Campbell, Reader in Petrology, and R.M. Craig, who taught Economic Geology, and T.M. Finlay, who taught Palaeontology, and Cockburn who was the Assistant – when he did his PhD on the geology of St Kilda, he lived there with the St Kildans. He told me a lot about that. And another interesting fact is that his son was called Ewen. He was named for the Ewen who was the St Kildan with whom Dr. Cockburn lived when he did his PhD – that was an interesting connection. Our son is called Ewen and the only Ewen I knew before was a boy who was named for a St Kildan.

Cockburn taught nearly every subject. He would do the diagrams and all that kind of thing – now that's an interesting thing – you know, there was no photo-copying of any sort at all, no Gestetners and everything had to be written in chalk on the board. That was the way that Cockburn taught in the geology department in my time. He would spend hours on the blackboard putting in coloured diagrams of cross-sections of the Moine Thrust. Hours – then after the class, a lab boy would come in with a bucket of water and a cloth and wash the whole thing off.

In my third year, that was 1943, Arthur Holmes took the chair of geology. That made a big difference to the Department. I was in his class for Advanced Physical Geology and in his introductory lecture to that class, there were three students. I was one – and one of the famous Norwegian geologists, the top Norwegian geologist of that time was Holtedahl and his son was at sea when the Germans invaded Norway, so he didn't go back. He came to Scotland and was in uniform when he came to Holmes's lectures. The third person wasn't a geology student. He eventually became the Secretary of the Communist Party of British Guyana. Anyway, the three of us sat there and Holmes gave the most lucid lectures from notes which he had in front of him, mainly of course from the draft of his Principles of Physical Geology. I kept very careful notes from Arthur Holmes's lectures (I later gave them to the special collections at Edinburgh University.) I did that for only one other lecturer and that was Professor Kendall of Chemistry, and it's an indication of the way that he lectured and the way in which I responded to his lectures.

You know, the staff had all been there for so long – two had been students there. Campbell had been an assistant to Geikie and went fishing with Benjamin Peach. He would tell me stories about Peach in the field – from being a contemporary really – Campbell smoked a pipe – it was a straight pipe which hung from his teeth. The only instruments we had were petrographic microscopes – with great glass bell jars over them. And Dr. Campbell would come in and go to show me something under the microscope. He'd take the big glass bell jar off and he'd be talking while he was doing it, which he could do holding a pipe in his teeth. He'd be looking at me as he was doing it and then he'd say: "what a mess on this microscope, what have people been doing here?" But all the time it was the ash from his pipe. Of course he was fantastic in old style Rosenbuschian petrology – absolutely fantastic. Well, that might give you something of a flavour of what it was like. My teachers talked to me – and some of the classes were one on one – about people like Hutton. If Hutton had arrived, I wouldn't have been surprised!

Then you joined the staff there when you graduated?

Arthur Holmes wanted me to join the staff as petrologist when Robert Campbell retired but the first vacancy was going to be R.M. Craig, the Economic Geologist. Dr Finlay was the first to retire. So Holmes turned to Glasgow which was a palaeontological school. Gordon Craig was the last student of A.E. Trueman and the first student of T. Neville George. And so he and I were invited to lunch with the Holmes's... so I was at Gordon Craig's interview. Maybe I was to be there just to make it easier for him, somebody not as old as his grandfather! And Gordon can still tell you what we were served. Anyway Gordon then came on the staff and Holmes had to find something for me to do for a year before R.M. Craig retired.

Now, you see, the granite controversy was at its peak; the discussion waxed very hot on the origin of granites and, as you can imagine, the reason for that was that we didn't know enough, we couldn't know enough. The presidential papers by H. H. Read for example, who was the President of this and the President of that, were on the origin of granite and migmatites. Well, Holmes wanted me to find out more so he sent me to work with Wegmann, who had published an important paper on the origin of migmatites in Geologische Rundschau. He sent me to Switzerland, which was a fantastic opportunity. Unfortunately, I was just too late to know Argand, who had just died but Wegmann had taken the chair and he gave me Argand's coat to wear and, for my birthday, he gave me a little box of Swiss cigars, they were the last ones that Argand had, with a little pencil with Argand's teeth marks on it – they were like holy relics. Argand of course did some great work on the structure of the Alps and of Asia. In fact he shows continental drift in his 1926 paper. He shows why the Himalaya are high because India is going down underneath.

Now, Wegmann was an extremely difficult person. I hadn't been there very long (it would be a matter of days) before we set off for the field, where he was doing his fieldwork in the Valais, the High Alps. There were people in Neuchâtel who were taking bets as to how long I would last because nobody else had ever lasted with him because he was so difficult. To give you an idea of what was involved; we went by train, of course, and Post Bus. When we got into the train, we sat facing one another beside the window. And I said to him, "Now, Professor Wegmann, I have tried to read up on your work," because Holmes had told me nothing about it, you see, "and I know that there's a particular thing that you talk about as the B-axis. But I haven't been able to figure out exactly what a B-axis is. I know it's a very crucial part of your work, but can you tell me what a B-axis is?" He looked at me – "what kind of moron has Holmes sent me?" He never answered questions by giving an answer, he asked another question. He always did that and his question was, "Well, tell me, here's an ash tray. It's fastened here just below the window. Why is the B-axis of that ash tray parallel to the B-axis of the train?" Now seeing that I'd asked what the B-axis was, that wasn't so easy, so I looked at this thing and I could see that it was hinged at the bottom and that was the only kind of axis that I could see. But the trouble was that that was parallel to the length of the train while the axles of the train were at right angles. Now, the question was "why were they parallel?" so I had obviously missed something. "Well, Professor Wegmann," I said, "I'm sorry, I don't understand." He was very annoyed – "what kind of person have I got here?" and he answered that with another question, "If the B-axis of the ash tray weren't parallel to the B-axis of the train, how could you empty the ash-tray without turning the train upside down?"

After I got back, I told this to some of his students and they laughed till they were sore. But nearly a year later, near the end of my time there, the French Association for the Advancement of Science met in Geneva and I was asked to give a talk – which I did in French, which surprises me now, but anyway, I gave a talk at Geneva and after that there was a field trip through the Jura Mountains.

I went with Wegmann and others on this trip and we ended up going by train through the tunnel from Besançon to Neuchâtel. Wegmann got me to sit by the window and look at the geology in the cuttings as we went past while he was talking to his colleagues who were going further on to Berne and Geneva... they were all talking in Swiss German and I didn't understand a word that they were saying. And they were getting more and more heated in controversy – Wegmann was getting quite angry and he was going on and he finally turned to me and said, "Well, we'll hear what M. McIntyre has to say on this question." And I thought, "what on earth is this?" and he said "Why must the B-axis of that ash-tray be parallel to the B-axis of the train?" And I said, "Oh. Mr. Wegmann, that must be a very complicated question because the first answer that comes to my head seems so simple. It must be more complicated than that." And he said, "No, come on, tell us!" and I said, "Well, if the B-axis of the ash tray weren't parallel to the B-axis of the train, how could you empty the ash-tray without turning the train upside down?" I said this because I knew the answer. Well it turned out that some of his students were sitting right behind us and they were hearing this whole thing. They were nearly in hysterics, because they knew that I had no idea why that should be the answer, but Wegmann said, "That's the sort of tectonics we teach in Neuchâtel!"

And that gives you an idea of the kind of situation. After that, I came back to Edinburgh and was taken on in the inappropriate position of Economic Geologist, of which I knew very little. But what I did worked out quite well: I taught what I knew. For example, I'd really learned about stereographic projections in Switzerland. Some of my students were from the Heriot Watt working for a BSc in mining. They had all sorts of complicated underground mining surveys that they had been given as problems and I solved these problems very easily with a stereographic projection because, you know, I was the first to publish a stereographic projection showing a fold axis determined from the normals to the bedding planes. It was first done in a paper in 1929 by Wegmann but he was doing it with imaginary data, but I published in the QJGS (Quarterly Journal of the Geological Society) the first actual data where a fold axis was determined in that way in the paper between Grantown and Tomintoul which was published in '51. So I was able to show these mining students how they could solve their problems quicker than the teachers could make them up.

Anyway, this was the kind of thing I was doing and teaching. Then in 1951, the British Association for the Advancement of Science met in Edinburgh. It was a big meeting – Edinburgh was considered a very important place for a meeting and there hadn't been one there for many years. Holmes should of course have been the main host but Holmes was a very shy man, so he and Mrs Holmes left Edinburgh and went to Donegal for field work while the meeting took place in Edinburgh. I had to take his place. I arranged a field trip to the Highlands for the distinguished foreign visitors, Anders Kvale of Norway, H W Fairbairn of M.I.T. and Frank Turner of Berkeley.

That field trip was very successful, and Turner invited me to go in '52 to Berkeley and bring some of the marbles from Strathspey with me, because I knew their context and he wanted to use the information that he and David Griggs had obtained by experiments; Turner did the microscopic work, on twin lamellae and showed how the crystals deformed. You see, the trouble with quartz was that all you can measure optically is the c-axis, whereas with calcite you've got planes of cleavage, planes of lamellae, twin lamellae in three dimensions. And of course it's easier to deform calcite than quartz. Turner and Eleanor Bliss Knopf had published a series of important papers in the Bulletin of the Geological Society of America on the experimental deformation of marble. So I went to Berkeley for the summer of 1952. Well, immediately I met some fascinating people there because Berkeley was one of the great geological institutes of the world at that time, the people that were there were an absolutely fantastic group – I am tempted to tell you more about them but perhaps it's beside the point! Although it influenced me, of course, about the possibility of going there permanently because of that environment – that was very important too but we'll leave that aside as well.

I hadn't been in Berkeley very long before Turner left for the International Geological Congress in Algiers. But before he went, he gave a wine-tasting in my honour at Berkeley. He knew all the people that mattered in Berkeley and at Stanford, and Californian wine was just taking off. Let me backtrack. When I was in Switzerland I was indoctrinated to the art of wine tasting because Argand had been a professional wine taster. Well, Wegmann taught me. Now, you're a geologist so you'll understand this. Bowen worked on fractional crystallisation. What Wegmann said to me – well, he put me on to kirsch to start with, because he said "Beginners should start with kirsch because it's easy." What you're doing is fractional distillation, you see. There's a certain fraction distilling off at room temperature. Well, we know that, so what you need to do is to take the glass and smell the wine because you're getting that fraction. And then having done all you can with that, you'll take a little, just a little, and let it go down below your tongue and taste it with the tip of your tongue and then begin to work it round and it's getting warmer as it's going. Then let the vapours go back up your nose, so that you're being able to sense the different fractions as it's breaking up, all of which made sense to a geologist. So you start off with the colour and then you get the aroma; they call it aroma if it's a white wine and bouquet if it's a red wine, and then finally, he said, you work it round like a peasant eating bread and cheese, and then you allow some of this to go back down your throat and you get the "aftertaste" – you're doing a spectral analysis of it.

So you see That's how I was brought up in Neuchâtel! Of course I told Turner about these things when we were chatting because it was very much a matter of interest to me and I was sharing this information gladly with anyone who'd be interested – and he was very interested. So Turner had these people for the wine-tasting. The room was crowded with people. Many were Nobel Prize winners, and of course I didn't know any of them. At one stage I was in the corner of the room, speaking with a man who seemed to be on his own and so the obvious topic of conversation was to ask him what department he was in, was it Berkeley or was it Stanford? He turned out to be C.S. Forester, author of the Hornblower stories. I'd heard of them but I'd never read a single one. Moreover, the movie of *The African Queen* had just won all the Oscars – and I hadn't seen the movie – I knew so little I couldn't even pretend. I couldn't say, "well I liked it when the African Queen was crowned," because I didn't even realise that it was the name of a boat! Well, we got on famously! He came later to see me in Pomona College and we met up again in London, and Mrs. Forester took me to the vineyards when I was in Berkeley, we had a marvellous time. So this was the kind of party you're in, you know, I could have been with someone else and it would have been just as remarkable a story to tell you now, but that was it.

Now, what Turner did was he gave us all a little of this wine... "This is a new wine from Wente Brothers..." We all took this wine and we all did our best to savour it and then he gave us something else and what he'd done was he'd kept back some of the wine in each bottle that he had served and at the end he gave us some of that and which one is it? So there was an exam at the end of the tasting. Well, that made a glorious evening and then when things were coming to a close, he said, "Now Donald McIntyre is here and I've got a wine here that I particularly want Donald to tell us about." So I said, "well, what is it?" Of course he wasn't going to tell me – I was supposed to tell him, so I knew I was on the spot. This was like a geologist being told, "now, what do you make of this rock. I know where it came from – do you know where it came from?!"

So he came in from the far end of the room with this wine glass with the wine in it – it was a red wine and I said, "Wait a minute, Frank, That's not a Californian wine." Now that was based on the fact that it was extremely unlikely that he would give me a Californian wine, but I was right! So he stopped in his stride a wee bit and then he came closer and I said, "hold it up to the light" and he held it up to the light and I looked at it and I said, "It's a Swiss wine." So I said, "would it be all right for me to take the bouquet?" and as I did so, I said, "it's from the village of Auvernier... can I taste it?" And I said, "It is from the village of Auvernier and it's 1947." And he said, "My God" and he went and got the bottle and you see everyone in the room was stunned by this amazing display.

But the point was that I was in Switzerland in 1947. There are not many red wines in the Neuchâtel region but I knew that it was likely to be something that had a connection with Switzerland rather than France or Arabia or somewhere else, and that if it was a Neuchâtel wine then that's the one he would have got. He would have seen a Neuchâtel wine and thought "I'll get that for Donald". And I knew that Auvernier was the biggest producer in the region and it would have to be a good year both for quality and quantity before they would try to sell it in California and so I thought well, that was the best year for many years – the chances are that's what it is – and that's what it was!

I'd been back in Scotland for a year or so when I got a telegram from

Turner that the President of Pomona College had been asking who they could get to succeed Dr. Woodford who was going to retire. He had been there since the beginning – he had founded the geology department and it was essentially a one-man department. So the President had asked Turner for suggestions, obviously thinking of Berkeley people, and he recommended me and so he said, "Don't turn it down just because you've never heard of the place," which I really hadn't, "because we think it would be the right place for you and you are the right person for them."

You see, some people are better in a big university but the smaller university suited me. It's a different environment and I was free to do everything – anything – I worked on seismology: I did work on first motion of big earthquakes. I think I was the first to describe impact metamorphism, at Clearwater Lake in Canada!

I suppose that if you're working in a big place and you start doing that, you're treading on other people's toes!

Exactly! It's all a question of opportunity – and I'll have to tell you something about that in more detail. When I got the opportunity to get equipment for the department, I consulted a colleague in Physics who was working in ultra-soft X-rays and I said "What should I get?" He said, "You should get X-ray fluorescence because you can then make chemical analyses by physics instead of by chemistry," and I said, "Yes but the trouble is that the elements I'm interested in, the major constituents of rocks, are light elements like silicon and oxygen and aluminium." Well my colleague was an expert in ultra soft X-rays so we used X-ray tubes made by him and the result of that was our equipment went to Mars. We were the only department in the world that contributed to the Viking Landers. We had two field stations on another planet. And that was because I was given freedom!

We've talked about the start of your career and some of your interests. You were involved with the Scottish Mountaineering Club as well. Tell me about that.

I met Bill Murray at the New Year meet of the Junior Mountaineering Club of Scotland at Kingshouse Inn in 1945-46. He was there, together with Kenneth Dunn, who was at one time President in the JMCS. At that meet – well, Bill Murray had been a prisoner of war, captured at El Alamein and had gone through a pretty hellish time and had lost both weight and strength. He was only just getting back the strength to go up mountains. And his friends? He was exactly ten years older than me. Kenneth Dunn and Bill Mackenzie were about the same age. These men had gone through the war; they had been active mountaineers, but they had taken the first steps in business and got married just before the war. So they were not free to go and climb with him because they had years to make up – both in their work and in their personal lives. Bill decided not to go back into banking but to try to make a career by writing about mountains – and he was very successful. He was asked to write the SMC rock-climbing guide to Glencoe and couldn't do it on his ow. Well, he invited me to climb with him, which was a great privilege. He was the most renowned figure in mountaineering in Scotland, and weekend after weekend I'd take the train through to Queen Street Station where he would meet me with his ancient car. I had fantastic experiences climbing with him. Many of the things we did together are included in his second book *Undiscovered Scotland*.

In the end, I gave up climbing because I learned to go to the hills to look at the rocks, not from the point of view of climb-ability, but looking at exposures whether at the bottom of the hill or at the top of the hill. And you know sometimes I've thought that for somebody who really wanted to be a mountaineer, the best thing to do might be to become a banker. Then when you had time off, you'd be able to climb. Once you're a geologist, you can't do that. The best rocks may be down in the river at the bottom of the hill, rather than at the top of the hill. But I have no regrets. I have had some fantastic opportunities and I have tried to make the most of them.

In conclusion, Alan Fyfe wrote: *"There were other things that Donald wanted to tell me and he decided he would walk with me back to where I had parked my car. We talked more of his time in California and of his general philosophy to life, but what struck me most was the spring in his step as he walked. He is still making the most of the opportunities that life gives*

Chapter 1
Early Days

"The childhood shows the man as morning shows the day" – John Milton

"Life is so full of meaning and of purpose, so full of beauty (beneath its covering) that you will find that earth but cloaks your heaven. Courage, then, to claim it; that is all! But courage you have; and the knowledge that we are pilgrims together, wending through unknown country."

From a letter by Fra Giovanni on Christmas Eve 1513 – from Donald's father's papers.

Introduction

It was always Donald's understanding that he was named after his grandfather – Daniel! About 1845 when that McIntyre baby was baptised in the little stone church in the Highland village of Balquhidder, the minister, who was perhaps a Lowlander, asked the parents to tell him the child's name. As Donald's great-grandfather's first language was Gaelic, it seems that his softly spoken pronunciation of the name "Donald" was misheard as Daniel….and so he remained all his days! Two generations later that mistake was happily rectified when Donald was baptised in1923. His middle name, Bertram, acknowledged his grandfather's very good friend of Bertram's Engineering Works, Sciennes, Edinburgh.

In due course, Donald's father, Robert Edmond McIntyre, became the minister of a church in the Highland-edge town of Callander and it was there that Donald was born. On one occasion, while Robert was visiting a Mrs McIntyre – an elderly parishioner but not a relative – he found her in great distress. This woman, a Gaelic speaker, was deeply offended because a neighbour had called her a "tinker" (US – a hobo). To console and encourage her, Robert told her to open her Gaelic Bible at Matthew 13.v55 –and just to prove his point – he also directed her to Mark 6, v.32. Both biblical verses refer to "Jesus son of the carpenter" or "Jesus McIntyre" – what better connection could there be for our clan! (Scottish Gaelic Mac an t-Saoir means son of the carpenter.)

In the 1920s and 1930s when Donald was a child, life in Scotland was still very family orientated – simple and somewhat unsophisticated by today's standards. Meals were wholesome – often using home-grown produce and based upon porridge, broth, "mince and tatties" – (ground beef and potatoes) and superb home baking – girdle scones, drop-scones (pancakes) and rock buns! A sponge cake, made from scratch – cake mixes not yet invented – would be light as a feather and a rare and delectable treat. Children played outdoors, often roaming their neighbourhoods enjoying great freedom in an environment where everyone knew each other and fearlessly allowed their "bairns" to roam in freedom.

Many middle-class families employed bright young girls to come to live as servants in the family home. These country lassies would often be leaving their homes in the Highlands or islands for the very first time to seek employment with town-dwelling families doing housework and some childcare. These "maids" – as they were known – were a great source of pleasure, fun and learning to us young people. They had their own quarters in the family home, eating in the cosy kitchen "Upstairs/Downstairs" style – but always there ready and willing to help "their" family as best they possibly could.

In those pre-war days it was customary for town dwellers of some means to take their families on a month-long summer holiday. They would rent accommodation on country hill farms or at the seaside. Donald's father, for example, sometimes arranged "a pulpit exchange" for a summer month while fathers who were in business might choose to have a complete holiday for a week or more and thereafter would "commute" to work on a daily basis to the office in town and then return to the family each evening.

When the children were young, the McIntyres went on holiday on several occasions to Kincraigie, a farm just north of Blair Atholl on the southern edge of the Highlands. On one occasion Donald spent an afternoon on his own climbing the local mountain, Beinn a' Ghlo (pronounced Ben y Glow) some distance from the farm. On his return, he told the family where he had been: whereupon his father, astonished and almost disbelieving of this achievement in one so young, asked Donald to take him there the following day. Donald's ability and accuracy were quickly confirmed.

The Trio –Donald, Sheila and Ranald.

In recollection of those happy days, (see Red Herring introduction) Donald would often refer to a family walk up Glen Tilt when soldiers of the cavalry regiment The Royal Scots Greys trooped past them on their magnificent steeds. They were so resplendent in their full dress uniform and helmets that shone in the sun that Donald dreamt of the day when he would be old enough to join them. Although things didn't turn out quite that way, imagine our delight when shortly after Donald's retirement and our return to Scotland in 1989, the same regiment, by then called The Royal Scots Dragoon Guards rode through Perth on an official visit. With shining eyes and camera in hand, Donald ran through the streets alongside their procession and joyously relived that magic experience of his childhood.

Donald's first schooling was at a small private school in Giffnock, south of Glasgow. His class took part in a music competition in Glasgow. Donald was chosen as conductor of this group – because, as he would explain, he had shown no proficiency with tambourine, drum or cymbals! Nonetheless his prowess as a conductor made headlines in the newspaper next day. He had imitated a famous conductor of that time, Sir John Barbirolli. When their band's piece came to a grand finale, Donald whisked out a large red handkerchief and mopped his brow. This conductor's authentic touch was much appreciated by the audience.

Mary's sister, Donald's Aunt Annie, had two daughters – Annette and Ailsa – and their family sometimes joined the McIntyre family on holiday. Donald's mother especially loved to recall, with a chuckle, how, when Donald was about six years old – she had, delightedly, bounced into the boys' bedroom, where they were already tucked up into bed. "You have a real wee cousin!" she exclaimed. Donald, already half asleep, was very puzzled – "Whatever could this be? – a Rail-way Cousin!"

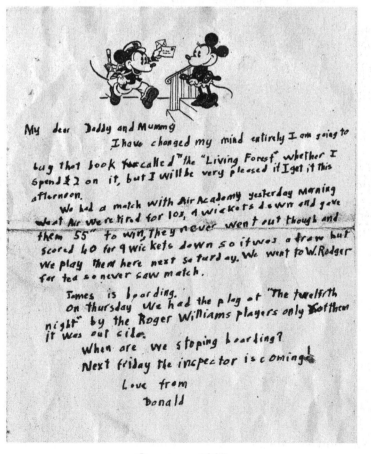

Ongoings, 1937

On 1937, on their father's appointment in Edinburgh as minister of Morningside High Church of Scotland, Donald and his brother, Ranald, were both enrolled at George Watson's College. This presented the boys with many challenges. At their first small school, Donald had learnt to write in script but, on arrival at Watson's College, he found that all the other boys were using joined-up cursive writing. Donald was assigned to a desk next to another pupil – Bobby Millar – and in an endeavour to master this more sophisticated form of writing as quickly as possible, Donald copied Bobby's cursive writing style as best he could.

As the boys were often asked to sign their names, Bobby and Donald B. McIntyre were both frequently penning the letter 'B'. To form that letter, Bobby made a downward stroke and then, continuing upward, without lifting his pen, he added two semi-circles, moving from bottom to top, to make a beautiful B. In common practice B is usually written by making one downward stroke, then lifting the pen to return to the top of that stroke and then adding two semi-circles on its right-hand side. Throughout his life Donald wrote the letter B the Bobby way! Sadly, Bobby never knew of the strong influence he had had upon Donald's penmanship. As I understand it, Bobby began to dabble in home chemistry experiments and, through making some tragic error, died as a teenager.

Prior to the declaration of World War II, it was anticipated that the boys would return to school at Watson's for the autumn term of 1939. Not appreciating the significance at the time, Donald, aged 16, realised later that he had *not* been assigned to enter Class "U" – the class designed for pupils considered to be academically strong enough to attend university upon leaving school!

★★★★★

Ruthless Rhymes

One of the delightful relics of Sheila, Donald and Ranald's happy childhood is the book, *More Ruthless Rhymes – Tales for Heartless Homes* by Harry Graham (1893-1936). From time to time and always with great hilarity, Donald would sometimes recite some of these gems to guests at our Claremont dinner parties – terrible tales of a bygone "non-politically correct" era!

Patience
When skiing in the Engadine
My hat blew off down a ravine.
My son, who went to fetch it back,
Slipped through an icy glacier's crack
And then got permanently stuck
It really was infernal luck:
My hat was practically new –
I loved my little Henry too –
And I may have to wait for years
Till either of them reappears.

Thoughtlessness
I never shall forget my shame
To find my son had forged my name.
If he'd had any thought for others
He might at least have forged his mother's.

From *When Grandmamma fell of the Boat – The Best of Harry Graham* with permission from Sheldrake Press publishers *of When Grandmamma Fell Off the Boat* 1986.

Not to be outdone, Donald's father composed his own Ruthless Rhyme. While on holiday at Kincraigie, the family visited The Falls of Bruar. As they walked beside the quickly flowing burn, their father entertained his children with a verse about Willie – a proverbial character of that era. Without hesitation, some 80 years on, Donald's brother, Ranald, still gleefully recites:

"Willie, at the Falls of Bruar
Made the population fewer.
Leaning further than he oughter
He fell right in to the water."

In the summer of 1936, when Donald's father "was filling the pulpit" in the village of Reay, near Thurso, in the far north of Scotland, the family and their friend Ena Hodge were all there together while the regular minister was away somewhere else.

A tale from that happy summer was of one misty evening when the children's mother insisted that she had seen a ghost on the road near the local cemetery. Great excitement all around! However, further investigation proved that though a phantom really did seem to appear, it proved to be an illusion caused by car lights dipping in and out of the hollows on the hilly country road – how disappointingly prosaic!

And there are many other memories – Ranald recalls how he and Ena experimented on taking up a stand on sinking sand and so narrowly escaped being swept out to sea!

Records of that special holiday include a little red covered book entitled "Autograph", where Donald aged 13, wrote:

> *"Yes this is my album,*
> *But learn ere you look*
> *That all are expected*
> *To add to my Book,*
> *You are welcome*
> *to Quiz it.*
> *The penalty is,*
> *That you add your Auto*
> *For others to Quiz."*

The first two – of the five – entries in Donald's book, speaks for itself:

> *"We shall remember*
> *When far from Reay.*
> *This fine September*
> *Bright sunny day.*
> *How we romped together*
> *And laughed and played*
> *In the sunny weather*
> *What hay we made!*
>
> *On rich and poor land*
> *The sunshine lay*
> *The wine brown moorland*
> *Stretches far away.*
> *The fields around us*
> *The skies above*
> *With Friendship crowned us*
> *And Peace and Love*
>
> *We shall remember*
> *In future years*
> *This fine September –*
> *And in our ears*
> *The brown burn flowing*

> *By Borlum Mill*
> *The soft winds blowing*
> *Off Katty Hill."*

Original by Henry Henderson

Some eighty years on, Henry Henderson is still well known locally as "The Bard of Reay".

Ann's version of family details

With his erect military bearing Robert Edmond McIntyre combined practicality with great kindness and understanding of the human condition; he was greatly respected for his pastoral ministry, his erudite sermons and profound scholarship were much appreciated as well as his skill – with a twinkle in his eye – to tell stories full of humour and fun.

At Robert's Memorial service in April 1961, his friend and parishioner, the Reverend Professor Norman Porteous gave an insightful and sensitive address. There is a familiar Donald ring about some of his observations:

"While modest to a fault, in actual fact Robert was a man of outstanding personality and of unmistakable originality of mind and this set its stamp upon all his work in the pulpit, not to speak of his personal relationships. and in his pastoral service he excelled where the need for his help was greatest and he gave himself then without stint and without reserve, no matter what the cost.... As a minister Dr McIntyre made his own choice of the things he knew he could do best and put his main weight into them...."

Professor Porteous continues "Dr McIntyre believed in preaching (*teaching*) and took his duty as a preacher (*teacher*) very seriously. He had an astonishingly fertile mind. There always seemed to be a number of subjects contending with each other for his choice and often in conversation, he allowed one illuminating glimpses of how his mind worked when he was thinking out a sermon. The best of his sermons were the simplest, when he focused our attention on some Bible incident or saying so that it reflected the everlasting Gospel – to borrow his own words.... 'as the sky mirrors its immensity in a fragment of glass and the stars that are beyond number shine back from the face of a wayside pool'....Here was God's plenty if we had the wit to see it and receive it."

In 1949 Robert was honoured to give the prestigious annual Warrick Lectures. His talks – *The Ministry of the Word* – were published in book form.

His unfailing interest, pride, pleasure and support for his three children is perhaps epitomised in that over the years, all Donald's letters to his family were so carefully preserved.

I recall with happiness my loving and supportive father-in-law and how special it was that he asked me to address him as Abu Donald – *Abu* – the Hebrew word for father.

Sadly, Ewen and his grandfather never met, but Ewen is proud that he bears his grandfather's initials (R.E.M.) and owns his grandfather's brief case marked with their shared initials.

Donald's mother, Mary – appropriately her maiden name was Darling – was truly unique – a little fairy-like person quick of body and mind with very blue eyes that twinkled mischievously. She was, as Professor Porteous commented, "a minister's wife *extraordinaire,* and when it came to bearing burdens, Dr. McIntyre had a rival in his wife. We think of them together, for they were indeed complementary to each other".

Throughout her long life Mary went out of her way to use her time and boundless energy to help and encourage whosoever crossed her path. Always eager to share adventures with her family and her many friends, Mary was a great companion to Donald whether walking together on the Isle of Skye, exploring Huttonian sites in the Scottish Borders or researching gravestones in Edinburgh cemeteries!

Mary's mother had died at the time of her sister's birth. Their father – Thomas Darling – was an Edinburgh doctor who visited his patients in a horse-drawn carriage. He married again but was on holiday with his teenage daughters when he collapsed and died at a Sunday morning service at Alvie Church, Kincraig, on Speyside in the shadow of the Cairngorm mountains.

In her later years Mary lived in a lovely south-facing flat in the centre of Edinburgh on the beautiful Victorian Eglinton Crescent. The Edinburgh Scottish Youth Hostel was just a few doors further along this street. From the large windows overlooking the street, Donald's mother would see young people passing by, burdened by their heavy backpacks. On occasion she would run down to the street and invite a young person or two to come to stay at her house – "It's much nicer than at the Youth Hostel!" she would tell them. Somewhat to our consternation, we know that several did indeed take up this offer! How very fortunate that no harm came of this spontaneous generosity from a kind but possibly rather lonely older person.

In her little Volkswagen "Beetle" car, Mary drove herself and her many friends numerous miles throughout Scotland. Sometimes she visited friends on the Hebridean island of Harris. On one such occasion, after her host had said a very long benediction prayer in Gaelic before a meal, Mary ventured to say: "Well, Murdo, I didn't understand a word of what you were saying." Without hesitation, came Murdo's laconic response…"I wasnae talking to you!"

Mary taught us another benediction – a brief one!

> *"We're aye asking*
> *And we are aye getting*
> *But we should be aye remembering Thee!*
> *Amen" (so be it!)*

★★★★★

Sheila – Mary and Robert's eldest child – was always extraordinarily dynamic, practical and articulate – to the point of sometimes being blunt and outspoken! There was never a dull moment when in Sheila's presence and – as I soon discovered – there was no hope of winning an argument with her! She was a voracious reader and also wrote some poetry. During the war she worked in a hotel in the Scottish Highlands and went on to became a driver for German clergy who ministered to their prisoner of war compatriots in camps all over Scotland.

After the war, Sheila, as sole carer, transformed the life of their cousin, Morag, who was disabled with muscular dystrophy and used a wheelchair. Together they led vigorous, interesting and generous lives in Reigate, Surrey, delving in depth into everything they undertook; charity work, sponsoring art and artists and much more. Undaunted by the challenges of ensuring wheelchair access wherever they went, they drove extensively around Britain and pursued their many interests with passion while supported by a lively and affectionate group of friends who had stamina enough to keep up with them!

All her days, Sheila was immensely proud of and devoted to her brothers, deeply loyal and generous to them and to her many friends but, at the same time, she challenged us all at every turn!

★★★★★

Ranald – as gifted with his hands as Donald with his head. After his years in the army, he enjoyed a spell as mechanic with Écurie Écosse, the Scottish motor racing team; he then went on to a career as a motor accident investigator. He and Barbara, his late wife, along with their three children, Fiona, Andrew and Judith, give Ewen much encouragement and support.

Ranald speaks for himself. Here is the text which he presented at Donald's memorial service on 30th October 2009 at the historic and beautiful St John's Kirk, adjacent to our home at Beaumont House in Perth.

Donald – my Big Brother

Big! Well, he was 963 days older than me! Donald, second child of the Reverend Robert E McIntyre MA DD and Mary McIntyre, was born in Edinburgh on15th August 1923.

As a minister of the Church of Scotland, our father, along with our mother, showed us the way through life…. consideration of others. Both our older sister Sheila and Donald were true to that all their days.

An early memory of life as sons of the manse in Giffnock south of Glasgow: Donald and I went to bed at the normal time, and we started our favourite game….. a pillow fight. Very soon feathers were flying all over the room, then we heard the voice of our father… "Boys go to sleep!" As soon as we heard that father was back in the study, the pillow fight restarted.

Our father was busy preparing his sermon for Sunday, and was not going to have interruptions. We heard him returning up the stairs, and saying in a loud voice "I told you to go to sleep".

We just had time to kneel down at our bedsides, and each with palm of hands together in prayer, but one eye open and looking at the door, said '…. And God bless Daddy, and make him a good wee boy'.

Yes, we were successful, as a defeated but smiling father retreated back downstairs. We did not dare start the pillow fight again, well not again THAT night.

Donald's first school was in Giffnock, near Glasgow, where there was a gem of a teacher, Miss Walker. The class was a mixed group of children, most with parents who were in business, doctors, lawyers, shop keepers. As it was December, Miss Walker said she would be telling them the story of Christmas, and proceeded to read.

However she noted that Donald was looking out of the window, and not paying any attention. She spoke quietly: "Donald, I am telling the story of Christmas". Donald's instant reply: "Yes, Miss Walker I know all about it!" "Oh! you *know*, Donald." 'Yes' Donald replied, "my father is in the business!" (Other children's fathers were shopkeepers; lawyers and accountants.).

When Donald and I went to Belmont House School at Newton Mearns, I was very proud to be his brother. Why? Well, he received a school medal for his boxing abilities. I say proud – but perhaps fearful would be a more accurate description! And then as a young man, Donald became an expert at ju-jitsu and always energetic and strong he took up mountaineering, skiing, rock climbing and excelled in them all.

One day Donald asked me if I would like to go up the lift on Arthur's Seat, Edinburgh. I had been up the hill before from the east side, but did not know about the lift. We set off from the manse about 6 am and arrived at the Kings Park (as it was known then) where Donald started walking at a brisk pace up the Radical Road, stopping at the quarry for me to catch up. As soon as I was near him, off he set up the rock face at some speed. Hanging on with just one hand and pointing to the various 'holds' he told me to "just follow" him. And then when I was about 10 or 15 feet up, Donald announced that I should "look down and you'll see where to place your feet". LOOK DOWN!!!!!…….. I just could not do that – not without falling off!

How I managed to get to the top I will never know, but I did, even as I discovered that 'The Lift' was the name of the rock climb! Yes, Donald summed up his pupils, and with his encouragement, he knew just how far they could be pushed with safety. (In those days you were only permitted to rock climb in that park prior to 8 am on a Sunday morning!)

At the beginning of World War II, Donald and I stayed at Grantown-on-Spey, going to school there. Donald was the leading man in the school play and in his final year was the School Dux – leading scholar!

As I was in the forces from 1944 to 1949 we did not see much of each other, but on release I used my 'de-mob' money to fly to Switzerland while Donald spent a year there. With his tuition we enjoyed great skiing days on long runs in the Davos area. Then Donald took up his post as Lecturer in Geology at Edinburgh University where he wasn't just an enthusiastic teacher, but was also learning to play the bagpipes. At first he practised in the basement of the Grant Institute until he realised he was noisy enough to banish himself to practising at Craigmillar Quarry! Our introduction to music had been early when both of us made bamboo pipes from scratch. Donald then went on to learn to play the trumpet and graduated to learning to play the bagpipes even practicing pibroch, known by pipers as "The Big Music". (I should add that soon after Donald's return to Scotland in 1989, he transcribed some of the notation of the most celebrated pibroch music into the computer. The College of Piping in Glasgow then used this most meticulous and exacting work as a teaching tool for young pipers.)

Following his year in Switzerland, Donald extended his enthusiasm to include the study of wines and in Edinburgh formed the Oenological Club in memory of The Oyster Club founded by James Hutton and his friends in the days of the Scottish Enlightenment. This modern version of that club met just once over a six-course dinner when a different wine was served with each course – it was a very happy but unrepeatable occasion!

Inevitably to some extent Donald and I lost touch during his thirty years in America. However, on the family's return to Scotland in 1989, it was as if the "missing" years had never existed.

And now I like to think that perhaps on the day that Donald died, 21st October 2009, he may have been greeted by the proud playing of Norrie Sinclair's bagpipe tune, "Professor Donald McIntyre!"

★★★★★

Chapter 2
Foundation Stones: Schooldays 1939-41

This darksome burn, horseback brown,
His rollrock highroad roaring down
In coop and in comb the fleece of his foam
Flutes and low to the lake falls home.
A windpuff-bonnet of fawn-froth
Turns and twindles over the broth
Of a pool so pitchblack, fell-frowning
It rounds and rounds Despair to drowning.
Degged with dew, dappled with dew
Are the groins of the braes that the brook treads through,
Wiry heathpacks, flitches of fern,
And the beadbonny ash that sits over the burn.
What would the world be, once bereft
Of wet and wildness? Let them be left
O let them be left, wildness and wet;
Long live the weeds and the wilderness yet.

Inversnaid by Gerard Manley Hopkins

In the 1970s, in the early days of computing, Donald pioneered a study with David Davies, Director of the Honnold Library of The Claremont Colleges. They analyzed and listed some of the unique words "created" by Gerard Manley Hopkins. They used this poem as part of their study.

Introduction

In April 2011, while gathering material for this book, out of the blue, I received a remarkable letter from someone I had never heard of before.

Ian Collie wrote: "I was interested in an article about your late husband in the Munro Society Journal, 2011. In the article, there is reference to a holiday the McIntyre family had at Tullochgrue, Rothiemurchus in September 1939. Tullochgrue was my home and I remember that the McIntyre family (who were there in the farm-house on holiday) came over to our summer house to hear over the radio the news that we were at war. Rev. McIntyre delivered a prayer. I was a boy of six, but the occasion is still clear, as is the recollection of my two brothers leaving within a few days for war service with the Lovat Scouts. I enclose a photograph of the farmhouse taken about 1955."

The McIntyre family were indeed on holiday on Speyside in September 1939, and when Donald and Ranald's parents learnt that, in war-time circumstances, the boys' school George Watson's College, in Edinburgh, was only able to offer students just half day of each day at school, (boys in the mornings and girls in the afternoons) they decided that it would be better for their sons to remain in the Highlands and to be educated full-time at Grantown Grammar School. This turned out to be a remarkably successful decision. They stayed with family friends in Boat of Garten and, during their first term in the north, not only did the boys greatly enjoy the freedom of the hills but also the novelty of travelling daily to Grantown on the local steam train. Soon it became evident that it would be more practical if they were living in Grantown itself and so became lodgers with the Paterson family who ran a well respected shoe shop.

Apart from the many obvious advantages in wartime for Donald and Ranald to remain in the Highlands and to attend full days at school, this decision turned out to have influenced Donald far beyond anything imaginable! In the small classes of the village school, many of the pupils having already completed their schooling at the legal age of 14 to work on their family farms, there was only a handful of pupils in the upper classes. The opportunities were many and varied. Donald took advantage of them all including playing a leading role in drama productions and, of course, being overjoyed to have easy access to the hills.

Ian Baikie, also evacuated from an Edinburgh school, became one of Donald's close friends. Both of adventurous spirit, they shared many wonderful experiences.

They particularly loved to row a boat on Loch Garten where, offshore, Ian sometimes painted the Highland landscape. On other occasions, Donald would play the bagpipes while they were afloat, absorbing the magnificence of their surroundings.

On stage – Grantown Grammar School 1940

Donald's high academic achievement at Grantown-on-Spey surprised everyone – not least himself! In 1941, Donald was the Harvey Dux Medallist of Grantown Grammar School, the school's top scholar of his final year there.

> *This August I came from Auld Reekie* (Edinburgh)
> *To this lovely wee place on the Spey,*
> *And I think it is all very pretty*
> *When I go for a walk every day;.*

The people of Grantown show kindness
To me and to all my wee friends;
We are all very happy to be here,
Till this dreadful old Nazi war ends.

> by Frances Johnston – Class of Primary V
> (a fellow evacuee from Edinburgh) from
> *The Grantown Grammar School Magazine –*
> *December 1939*

For that same December 1939 issue of the Grantown Grammar School
Magazine, Donald wrote:

A Day on the Hills

One fine morning, early in September this year, found me cycling over the very rough Glen Einich road. As I came close to the corner, known to some as "Windy Corner" or the "Summit", I pedalled faster, knowing what a magnificent view of Sgoran Dubh would burst upon me there.

This view soon came in all its grim grandeur, and, even in the brilliant sunshine, the Sgoran looked black and forbidding – but, after pausing a second, I pedalled on down the hill and soon found a place to leave my bicycle.

Starting off again, I walked onto the bridge, which carries the road over the burn, and there turned back, on the other bank, towards Carn Eilrig.

I stopped to admire the view. An eagle was soaring in and out of the black buttresses of the Sgoran in all his majesty. After watching him for a few minutes, I set off to climb a small ridge.

As I raised my head above this ridge I saw three huge hinds not one hundred yards from me. However, they soon scented me and made for the top of Carn Eilrig. I kept on up the steep slope and soon came to the top – much to the annoyance of the deer who ran down towards the Lairig.

After eating a few sandwiches on the top, I made across the moor for Braeriach. In an hour I reached the burn which runs down past the Coire Lochan. This Coire I found to be very deceptive, and I thought I should never reach the Lochan. I shall never forget the sight of the blue lochan with the waterfall coming from the very top of Braeriach.

At last I tore myself away from this gem of the mountains and renewed the climb on the Einich side of the Coire. I made up on two boys toiling up this, the most tiring part of the ascent. Together we reached the summit plateau, but, as they were going on to Cairn Toul, I parted from them – but not before I had had a look at their map. (I was carrying only a prismatic compass.)

I made for the Wells of Dee, and, after admiring the view of Cairn Toul, Ben Macdhui and the Garbh Coire, I made my way to the cairn which crowns the summit of Braeriach.

When I had dutifully laid my stone on the cairn I set off to make the descent by the Sron na Lairig, but, mistaking the way, arrived on the ridge between Coires Ruadh and Beanaidh

After I had gone down the ridge a bit I turned to look back, and there saw an eagle soaring up from the Garbh Coire above the cairn. Leaving all this I restarted the descent until the ridge ended in a cliff. Then I saw that there were some hinds in the Coire and that I was cutting off their retreat from it. Then they smelt me and made off. After that I soon reached my bicycle without event and it was not long before I was relating the experiences of one of my most enjoyable days before the crackling log fire.

D.B.M. IV

The Cairngorms, looking south.

Donald gives further glimpses of his life in Grantown-on-Spey.

Sunday 21st January 1940

You will be sorry to hear that I cannot find my report card anywhere, and that Mr Hunter is in hospital. Where my report is I do not know. Mr Hunter has something internal wrong and was going to have had an operation, but he has had treatment instead. There is a Miss Lindsey teaching mathematics instead now. I brought a petition to her to prove that all numbers are equal! However she said what was wrong was (roughly) that 0 is not finite. I have now proved that i) 0 is finite; ii) All numbers are equal; iii) there is no such numbers as + or − 00; iv) the universe is definitely finite; so I will see what she will say on Monday.

On Thursday night, we saw a very good performance of Graham Moffat's "A Scrape of a Pen". Skating has not been any good because of snow. Wednesday it was 2 degrees below zero. (Fahrenheit) (I think it was colder today)……..

Donald

P.S. Could you please find from the most reliable source the definitions of finite and infinite? D.B.M.

★★★★★

School in Grantown – March 1940
Here are my results:

History: 46% (out of 50 for total)
English: 68%
French : 50%
Algebra: 64%
Arith/Trig: 63%/ 74.3%
Geom: 96%
Science: 80%
Total: 295

Average = 295x100
450% = 66%

I made the biggest mess in the Algebra – for which I deserve to be thrown out!

I have been as busy, or busier, since the exams as before. For example, one day last week I spent 5 solid hours on history alone. It has mainly been history.

On Friday night I woke several times finding myself doing algebra problems – why algebra, I do not know – and got up with a headache★. So I determined to go for a cycle round about before dinner. I left at 10 o'clock, but found myself at 10:25 at Nethy Bridge, by 10:45 I passed the Boat (of Garten). I couldn't stop! And by 11, I was at Pityoulish! 11:15 Coylum; 11:40 Achagoichan!! The roads on Tullochgrue are terrible, truly terrible! Mrs McKinnon was in, but I could not wait long enough for Mr McKinnon's return, so at 11:50 I left the view there – lovely as it was – and at 12:10 made Aviemore – but could not wait to see Doshit – 12:35 I passed the Boat and at 1:25 arrived home – not bad! (By the main road it used be seventeen and a half miles to Aviemore).

On Tuesday Drummond came with us to see "Confessions of a Nazi Spy" and on Saturday we three saw "The Lion has Wings" – both very good.

We are wondering what the Easter arrangements are – we hope to go South but don't look forward to spending holidays here.

However, so long just now – Donald

★*Editor's note: Donald suffered from headaches throughout his working life – especially on Saturdays. On retirement the problem completely disappeared. As a small boy, it is reported that he named these unpleasant episodes as his "hay-ducks"!*

In May 1940 Donald wrote

"An all school expedition went up Cairngorm on Saturday. The boys left the square at 6:30. Ian Baikie, Norman Dow and I kept together. After waiting an hour and a half for the cars with Mr Wilson, some lady teachers, some girls and two men, at last they condescended to leave, but they went so slow that the trio led the way. None of the Grantown boys knew which hill was Cairngorm, let alone the way! It was funny, 3 Edinburgh boys leading the Grantown School expedition up the Cairngorms! After we got onto the ride, the others, everyone except Norman and I, ate.

The girls were in a separate party far behind. Then the rest dashed on ahead, but we went comfortably along the ridge. Although led by two older chappies, the rest went far off the ridge into Coire Cas (like idiots) and went much quicker than us, but I made Norman and Ian stick to the ridge and we had very easy, pleasant going. We were well ahead of the others when in sight of the cairn because I made the trio keep to the edge of Coire Cas, instead of, as the others, going too far over the back of the hill as you are apt to do and as the cairns lead. The others went very quickly, cutting over towards us and reached the cairn first. We were going the same speed as before and had no wish to reach the cairn first. We took 2 hours from Morlich.

After staying a silly time on the top, they decided to go down to the Shelter Stone but none of the trio wanted to go (I had rubber soles for one reason). They thought of Macdhui but I wasn't going there for the first time in a party! No fear! Then they thought of the corries and I volunteered. Ian and Norman went with the others. We went along the edge of the precipices and it was much better than the way we went last time. I was talking to Mr Wilson:

Mr W: Donald, That's Loch Etchachan
Me: Yes sir!
Mr W: Loch Avon is down there
Me: That's right, sir!
Mr W: You won't have been to the Shelter Stone have you Donald?
Me: Yes sir!
Mr W: When?
Me: A fortnight ago, sir!
Mr W: This way?
Me: No sir! The Saddle!
Mr W: Garbh Allt! Who took you to the Garbh Allt?
Me: Nobody, sir!
Mr W: I mean who went with you?
Me: No one, Sir!
Etc. etc. etc.

You MUST go along the TOPS of the corries. It is perfectly safe and is most super. You can't imagine it. Remember, Daddy, crawling out to Cairn Lochan? Well, it's as safe as houses! I went right round the cairn. Another chap, one of the Johnnies in charge and I left the others behind and I took him down the Coire Lochan path and we were down an hour before the others – just one wee shower but windy at top. We have had super weather except for a few days when there was thunder and rain. Not bad today. Warm, brightish intervals

No news, so cheerio....

From the Editorial of The Grantown-on-Spey School Magazine, December 1940 – when Donald was their Advertising Manager:

"In this our second war-time Grammar School Magazine, we hope many a former Grammarian on active service will find something to divert his mind from ever-present events......

Since the appearance of that last innovation, a war-time magazine, a Great Power has fallen, gallant smaller countries have been overwhelmed, a National Government has been formed, and the most important capital in the world wantonly attacked, but, as ever before, Britain stands determined...

Quite a few new names or monograms are to be found at the end of literary efforts. Don't be alarmed- we have no secret agents among us! These are the names of migrants from various parts of the British Isles....

Consistent with war conditions and the varied claims which our national effort makes on young as well as adult citizens, normal school activities have been well maintained during the past year.

In conclusion, we would wish all our readers "Bon voyage!" until next Christmas, when we hope to be able to offer a magazine in which falling bombs and burning homes are a thing of the past."

Another challenging expedition was reported in The Scottish Mountaineering Club Journal, vol.22, 1941. p.388-389

The Seven Highest Cairngorms in a Day

The seven highest Cairngorms have been climbed on Friday, 5th September of this year [1941] by two of the younger generation of Scottish mountaineers, Mr Donald B. McIntyre and Mr Ian Baikie (both round about eighteen years of age). Comparison may be made with summaries of previous traverses of the six and four highest Cairngorms respectively as recorded in the "Cairngorms Guide". Our young friends have most justifiably added to the six the "separate mountain Munro" Beinn Mheadhoin (3,883 feet), clearly higher than Ben Avon. The start of the expedition was at the Green Loch of Ryvoan where bicycles were left, but a kindly fairy took them across to the Lower Einich Bothy where they were a godsend to the party returning down Coire Dhondail from Cairn Toul the next evening.

The first night was spent in an open shed at the Avon bridge near the Allt an t-Sluichd. It will be noted that much time was spent between Ben Avon and Beinn a' Bhuird owing to an adverse conspiracy of darkness, cloud, aneroid, and lack of previous acquaintance with this section of the traverse. The total distance from the Avon to the Einich Bothy is about 30 miles and involves some 10,300 feet of ascent. The expedition lasted from 1 A.M. until 9.5 P.M. (sun times). We are sorry that limitations of space do not permit of printing a fuller account than a mere timetable, but we heartily congratulate the party on their enterprise and achievement. Apart from the clouding of the Eastern Cairngorms during the dark hours the weather was good.

Leave Avon bridge, 1 a.m.; Ben Avon, 2.50 a.m.; Beinn a' Bhuird, 5.40 a.m. ; Beinn Mheadhoin, 9.25 a.m.; Ben Macdhui, 10.50 a.m.; Cairngorm, 1 p.m.; Braeriach, 4.45 p.m.; Cairn Toul. 6.30 p.m.; Lower Bothy, Glen Einich. 9.5 p.m.

Sixty years on, Donald's commented on that memorable day on his website (www.mcintyre.me.uk) I was never interested in "bagging Munros"; i.e. climbing mountains listed by Sir Hugh Munro as separate mountains over 3,000 feet high; but what bothered me 60 years ago was that the SMC's Guide to the Cairngorms asserted that the six highest had twice been climbed in one day, despite the fact that, although undoubtedly higher than Ben Avon – Beinn Mheadhoin was omitted.

To correct this error – rather than to create a record – my friend and fellow schoolboy, Ian Baikie, joined me in climbing the seven highest Cairngorms in a day [5 Sept. 1941]. Having gone to the trouble to correct the obvious error, and despite the notice in the SMC's own Journal, both the SMC's Journal and Guide to the Cairngorms surprisingly continue to report without comment that the wrong six have been climbed again!

Ian Baikie

In 1963, while far away in California, it was a great shock and distress to learn that Ian had died of cancer of the throat, leaving his wife, Moira and their four small children – Anna, John, Robert and Duncan, all under eight years of age. Happily, they have all prospered and our families remain close. Moira, widowed for 50 years, died in January 2014.

Following Ian's untimely death, Donald wrote to Moira:

"Old Grantown memories – the botanizing…the study of Gaelic place names. The famous expedition when we climbed the 7 highest Cairngorms together (a feat still unequalled) and two days later cycled from Aviemore to Edinburgh – the searching out of the Golden Eagle and the following of deer over the high tops – and the "find" of Cairngorms on Ben A'an. My first experience of mineralogy….."

"The infinite pains that went into the selection of the best site for our 'lodge' near the old Glenmore Lodge – long before the days of the multitudes. We were lucky indeed. And Ian's designs for the building that was to go up there. Dreams of course but healthy happy ones and we were preparing for the work to come."

"The following poem by James Logie Robertson was brought to my attention years ago by Ian. Its title translates loosely as 'It isn't always raining'!"

It's no aye rainin'.

Non Semper Imbres

It's no aye rainin' on the misty Achils,
It's no aye white wi' winter on Nigour ;
The winds are no' sae mony sorrowin' Rachels,
That grieve, and o' their grief will no' gie owre.
Dark are Benarty slopes, an' the steep Lomon'
Flings a lang shadow on the watter plain ;
But fair Lochleven's no forever gloomin',
An' Devon's no' aye dark wi' Lammas rain.
The birks tho' bare, an' the sune-naked ashes,
Not always widow'd of their leaves appear;
The oaks cry oot beneath November's lashes
But not for all the months that mak' the year.
Comes round a time, comes round at last tho' creepin',
And green and glad again stand buss an' tree ;
E'en tender gowans, thro' the young gress peepin',
Rise in their weakness, and owre-rin the lea.
Thus Nature sorrows, and forgets her sorrow ;
And Reason soberly approves her way.
Why should we shut oor een against tomorrow
Because our sky was clouded yesterday?

Chapter 3
Town and Gown
Edinburgh University – 1941-
1954

The crags that fade and gloom
Starts the bare knee of Arthur's Seat;
Ridged high against the evening bloom,
The Old Town rises, street on street;
With lamps bejewelled, straight ahead,
Like rampired walls the houses lean,
All spired and domed and turreted,
sheer to the valley's darkling green;
Ranged in mysterious disarray,
The Castle, menacing and austere
Looms through the lingering last of day;
And in the silver dusk you hear,
Reverberated from crag and scar,
Bold bugles blowing points of war."

From a Window in Princes Street,
William Ernest Henley *1849-1903*

A University should be a place of light, of liberty, and of learning.

Benjamin Disraeli, 1873.

Student Years 1941-1947

Specific details of Donald's busy undergraduate years are sparse as he lived at home with his parents in the manse, as the church minister's house is called in Scotland, and, of course, was not writing to them on a regular basis, though his mother didn't think that was often enough! Nonetheless it seems remarkable how Donald's parents preserved his correspondence to them over many years and from many different environments.

Throughout his halcyon Edinburgh university years – both as student and later as lecturer – Donald shared his father's study. Robert E. McIntyre was a voracious reader and scholar. He built up an extensive library, much of which Donald inherited in due course. His father's breadth of literary interest and scholarship greatly contributed to Donald's own pleasure and wealth of literary and historical knowledge.

Donald's university life was rich on so many fronts. In 1941, though Britain was at war, Donald as a science student was exempt from military service. For his wartime contribution Donald enrolled and trained in rifle shooting with the University Army Cadet Corps led by Colonel Moffat. This contact evolved into a long and sustained friendship – indeed, Colonel Moffat and his family were active members of Morningside High Church where Dr McIntyre was the minister.

I recall tales of Donald's continuing pleasure in acting, following on from his success in the Grantown Grammar School plays. He joined the Edinburgh Gilbert & Sullivan Society as a member of the chorus and took part in a performance of "Iolanthe". He added Scottish country dancing lessons to his repertoire – nimble and neat of foot and elegant in kilt and formal Highland dress – a lovely pursuit that we enjoyed together in the early days of our friendship and later when we lived at Kinfauns.

Donald wasted no time in becoming a member of the Edinburgh University Mountaineering Club, quickly taking a very active role there. In 1946 he became their President, holding office as Secretary of the Scottish Junior Mountaineering Club and often spending his weekends in the hills. (See Chapter 4 – Mountaineering.)

In the mid-1940s, Donald learnt to play the bagpipes and was particularly drawn to pibroch – "the big music" for which he became renowned for his practice sessions late into the night in the basement at the University Geology Grant Institute. The pipes and/or his practice chanter were part and parcel of his travels. His teacher, Pipe Major Logie, led the Edinburgh City Police Band, and it was he played for us outside the church on our December wedding day when Donald, newly arrived from sunny California, would comment that the sun barely rose above the horizon on that wintry, misty Scottish day!

Discovering Geology

Donald often spoke of a fortuitous meeting. He was enrolled at the university as a chemistry major. In the autumn of 1941 after Donald had attended a morning lecture taught by the celebrated mathematician, Sir Edward Whittaker, he asked the student sitting next to him what plans he had for the rest of the morning. When **Sandy Renwick** described the geology class he was about to attend – a subject of which Donald had barely heard but to which Sandy had been introduced at high school – Donald decided to go along there with him – and the rest is history.

And a footnote which Donald loved to recount. At the end of the academic year 1941/42, Sandy Renwick failed his exams and, since it was war-time, he had no alternative but to temporarily abandon his university studies and be conscripted into the army. Fast forward to the autumn term of 1947. The war was over and Donald, who had all but completed his PhD thesis, was appointed lecturer in Geological Engineering. To his astonishment and amusement, on arriving to teach his very first class, who should be seated in the front row than Sandy Renwick, once more a student! (In due course, Sandy became Director General of the International Geological Congress and went to work in Malaysia – and the story goes that wherever he went, he always sported his bowler hat, yellow gloves, monocle and cane!)

Donald's school years at Grantown had given him a unique opportunity to explore and enjoy the Cairngorm Mountains. In one of his first geological papers while working toward his BSc degree, he put his hill-walking experience to good use. He often walked alone in this remote territory, rarely seeing anyone else and long before the days of modern technology.

The Scenery of the Cairngorms
DBM October, 1944

The scenery of the Cairngorms has a peculiar charm well known to the faithful who return year after year, drawn irresistibly by the misty tops. The scene is characterised by flat topped mountains and high summit plateaux ending abruptly in mighty precipices down which the mountain burns roar to the corries far below, for depth and not height is the secret of the Cairngorms.

The clear pure burns are a familiar feature and one drinks the water for pleasure, not just to quench the thirst. Follow one of these burns down from the hills after a long day's climbing and it will lead you to the low ground and the forest, where, standing on a rich carpet of cranberry and blaeberry, you can look back and see the hills framed by those magnificent old Caledonian pines which give character to the scene. The low ground, too, has its charm. If you have finished the day's climbing at Loch Morlich or Loch Einich, you will not need to be reminded that the lochs contribute in no small measures to the beauty of the scene.

Nature is a carver and the tools she uses are those familiar agents – wind, water, snow and ice; but she is a blind carver so the grain of the rocks guides the tools. The Highlands of Scotland are but the etched bones and roots of an ancient 'Himalayan' range long since razed to the ground. Yet how many of those who love the Highlands realise that those rocks have a history at all? The legend of permanent, unchanging and everlasting hills has gone. We must regard mountains not as dead and static, but as living and dynamic, as possessing a history, coming into being and passing out of being, being born and dying away, so that as time unrolls, history repeats itself not exactly as it was, but at a higher level, for life has worked a stage further in the interval. Mountains come and go – new ones being raised from the ashes of the old.

To view mountains with a scientist's eye will enhance and not detract from the appreciation and enjoyment of scenery. The imagination will be stirred in trying to picture those ancient seas, the snowy peaks, the fire and the ice, lack of which have been where the Cairngorms now stand for a short period of geological time and lack of which have helped to mould them in their familiar form as we see them today. In short, rocks are historical documents. What to a historian is a valuable papyrus is to a layman a scrap of waste paper.

Evidence of decay is all around. Every cliff has its scree slope; every outcrop is weathered and worn. Water percolates into the pores, freezes and disintegrates the rock. Wind and wave, rain and river, all are co-ordinated to bring about the downfall of the land, to reduce the mountains to sea-level.

Judging from the quantity of material carried to sea every day by the River Thames, the whole of the Thames basin will be brought to sea-level in some two million years. Yet there are rocks in the Thames basin 200 million years old (dated by radioactive methods). Rocks known to be over 1,700 million years old have been found above sea-level in

America. The explanation of this anomaly is that the crust of the earth is periodically actively elevated above sea level. Indeed, the difference between the figures quoted is such that the evidence of elevation can be regarded as definite as the evidence of decay.

By human standards uplift is slow, but examples of recent elevations are to be found. One example will suffice to show that elevation is a very real phenomenon and not just a figment of the imagination. The pillars of the so-called Temple of Jupiter Serapio, standing at Pozzuoli on the Bay of Naples, offered a curious riddle to the archaeologists. The lower and upper portions of the pillars were quite normal, but the middle part of each pillar was abundantly bored by the mollusc *Lithodomus* and shells of the creatures are still to be seen in the holes. The mollusc is commonly found in similar borings in rocks round the shores of the Mediterranean. The solution of the riddle is this: a great eruption of Vesuvius buried the lower parts of the pillars in a thick deposit of volcanic ash and subsequently the land sank so that only the tops of the pillars were above the waves. At this stage the middle parts of the pillars were bored by the shellfish, the upper parts being out of reach and the lower parts being protected by the ash. The rhythm changed; elevation followed subsidence; the ash was washed away and the temple left to tell its tale to those who have eyes.

All mountains must crumble to dust, but a practical man is entitled to ask what happens to the dust, for even the Cairngorms will give rise to a considerable quantity. Rock debris is driven downwards by gravity, rain, wind etc. till it reaches a water course and then it is only a matter of time before it is swept into the sea or deposited in a large estuary. Indeed, the roar of a Highland burn in spate is largely the rumble of the stones rolling downstream.

When the sea level is reached the downward flow of water ceases and the load of sediment is dumped on the flat plane of marine denudation! This fact is well known to Clydeside people who see dredgers continuously at work keeping the river open to shipping. In this way great beds of sand and mud are deposited one on top of the other, and if the area of deposition is one of subsidence a considerable thickness of beds may be accumulated. Pressure of overlying beds, heat due to deep burial in the earth, a cementing material left by waters draining through the deposits; each of these can transform the beds into solid rocks. Beds of sand become beds of sandstone; mud is transformed into shale or even slate.

If an area of deposition and subsidence becomes, through time, one of active elevation, then the beds of hardened sediments, the sandstones and the shales, are raised to form new land. Erosion begins, of course, as soon as the new land rises to within reach of the waves and the forces of elevation and the forces of denudation and decay join in a battle royal. The struggle reaches a climax when the growing mountains lose energy and decay gains the upper hand. Thereafter the mountains, aged in the fight, soon pass away. The wheel has turned a complete cycle; the cycle begins again.

Evidence that this cycle has recurred again and again in the past is seen every time we see sedimentary rocks "in the field". It is good for the imagination to try to picture the changing scenes implied by each exposure. How few have ears to hear the fascinating story so subtly told by every silent stone! How few have eyes instructed how to see!

While Ian Baikie, his friend of Grantown school days, was serving in the Royal Navy Donald sent him the following as an air-letter. It gives a sense of the remoteness of the highland terrain at that time and is a reminder that only in comparatively recent decades has the Cairngorm mountain plateau been opened up and made accessible to all.

5 November 1945

Another job which kept me busy recently was a lecture I was asked to give to a joint meeting of the J.M.C.S. (Junior Mountaineering Club of Scotland) and of the Edinburgh University Mountaineering Club. The subject was to be "The Cairngorms". And by old Harry, I missed you. All the time I was preparing for it I could not help feeling how good it would have been if we could have done it jointly – or at least prepared it and schemed it out together. For this reason you may be interested to hear what I did and you can consider what you would have done.

In the first place I had access to the Scottish Mountaineering Club slide collection, which although once very extensive has now woeful blanks due, I presume, to breakages. I supplemented these with half a dozen slides which I borrowed from the department, and I made one – a diagram showing corrie formation – for the occasion.

Here is a very brief account of the line I took – remember, very few in the audience had ever been to the Cairngorms and therefore the topographical names would be meaningless unless you took special care.

1. Purpose. To appeal to a group of hill lovers who are crazy about the Cairngorms and yet who are disappointed and cannot work up enthusiasm. Into which group will you fall, in other words what are the characteristics that appeal to the Cairngorm-lover and what are those which disappoint the people who go away willingly, (leave of their own accord) and will the characters appeal to me?

2. The appeal is chiefly to hill walkers and not to rock climbers. Some of the reasons, such as distance before you start climbing etc.

3. General idea of the layout as shown on the map. Unfortunately I did not have time to get a lantern slide made of a diagram-map. At this stage I mentioned all the place names which I would be using later (reducing these to a minimum) and showed their relative positions. From time to time during the showing of the lantern slides, I got the lights put on and went over the place names again.

4. I then showed Miss Martineau's water-colour of the Cairngorms from Kinveachy (*which has always graced the homes of our married life – Ed*) and spoke on first impressions – disappointment due to lack of peaks and foreshortening due to the difficulty of appreciating the distance of how far the hills are away – and on second impressions – appreciation of the scale and the feeling of depth rather than of height. (As you will appreciate, your grand-uncle's book was invaluable here.)

5. The features of the Cairngorms are due to the combination of a) plateau summits b) through valleys, like the Lairig c) corries, d) the great gravel-covered plains, now so beautifully wooded, which form the foreground to the view.

6. Next I said a word about the geological origin of each of these phenomena, and illustrated the remarks with a few lantern slides.

7. After all this introduction I began the systematic traverse of the Cairngorms and began by taking out the map and indicating our route. I showed one or two slides of somewhat distant view, first from Aviemore and then from Barrie's Grave and the Einich Road, taking care to point out Carn Eilrig in these. Having done this we went to the top of Carn Eilrig and saw Braeriach and the Sgoran (Sgoran Dubh Mor) from this viewpoint.

8. Next followed various slides of the Sgoran

9.   Coire Lochain of Braeriach at different times and different angles

10. The plateau of Braeriach

11. Coire Bhrochain with views of and from Cairn Toul

12. The Lairig Ghru. From Allt Druidh, the Pools of Dee and from the other side. There was not much choice here.

13. Slides of Macdhui and Loch Etchachan

14. Loch Avon and the Shelter Stone

15. Cairngorm

I tried to point out where the next view would be taken in relation to the previous slide so that everything linked up. I spoke with no notes and got quite carried away at times e.g. with the cave, the Shelter Stone and the Turriff Home Guard and me sleeping on top etc.

After I finished questions were asked for. These gave me a chance to deal with some practical points such as use of a bicycle; certain paths e.g. the zig-zag road, the usefulness of the knowledge that the heather line is at 3,000ft; the advantage of an aneroid, working from burn to burn (here I took some examples from our long trip) etc. etc. I was glad to say the meeting was a grand success. (It was an open meeting so there was as good turnout – also women) and we had to stop when the Synod Hall was supposed to be shut up for the night. I talked for 3 hours continuously! I really did miss you.

Little Jimmy Stewart of the S.M.C. said it was the most interesting lecture he had ever heard in the S.M.C. clubrooms. I have mentioned this at length because you would certainly have been "in on this" if you had been available.

By the way, Mr Grant wanted me to take drawing lessons at a night class in the Art College, but I fear they 'lead' it in the usual hopeless method i.e. set up a higglety-pigglety mixture of rubbish, ask you to draw it and then tell you, this isn't like that, which you know anyway. Disappointing. I shall begin another letter but in the meantime cheerio and best of luck / from Donald."

Loch Doon, 1945

In the summer of 1945 Donald worked in the area of Loch Doon, Galloway, south-west Scotland, doing research for his PhD degree. He spent a busy, warm summer in that area at Ballochbeatties, west of Loch

Doon and lived in the home of one of the local shepherds. He would often recall the stamina of these hardy country folk.

Donald wrote to his parents from Ballochbeatties, Tuesday 7th August 1945:

........The Sunday I arrived here was wet but a good week followed. After another bad weekend, another good week came and there were some scorching days. Gordon Parish cycled down from Edinburgh but broke his chain on the way so arrived here very late. Thursday and Friday were very hot and we did not go far. Saturday was wet again, but on Sunday we did a long trip (20 miles) with a 500 ft rock climb, and we came back by The Merrick. We dodged the rain all day but it was teeming everywhere around. We got a magnificent view from The Merrick including the Solway and the Lake District to the Isle of Man, Stranraer Bay, a long stretch of the Irish Coast, the Mull of Kintyre, Arran and the Clyde, the Cumbraes, Bute and the Highland hills. The sunset from the ridge was really glorious with Cairngorm blues, goldens, reds and scarlets – really very fine. After darkness fell we still had 6 miles of trackless bog and rocks to negotiate but we made good speed and arrived back at midnight. Gordon has spent 3 weeks in Skye, in Glen Nevis and on the Mamores but the thought that this was by far the best day of his holiday.

I am very comfortable here and well fed. Balloch Fishing Lodge is less than a quarter of a mile away and it is very well equipped. There are only 25 members and they pay an entrance fee of £24 and an annual subscription of £8. As you can imagine, it is very exclusive. I can get a boiling hot bath there (if the members are out!) and sometimes a bacon and egg tea or a bowl of lentil soup, the price of which is simply that I sit and listen to the grumbles and groans of the cook (who is really a very decent old soul) with a sympathetic ear for half an hour or so!

Ballochbeatties is a double herd. That is, there are two shepherds, a married man and a single man. Mr Miller (Fred) is the married man and he has 400 sheep, his brother-in-law, Tommy, is the single man and he has 300 sheep. Each has his own hill. The two kids Tommy (1) and Billy (3) are spoilt, I am afraid, and they are sometimes terrible howlers. The sole purpose of the screams being to get their own ways – and they generally succeed. You can imagine what it can be like when I tell you that Jean, the cook at the lodge, broke 3 dishes one day after the kids had paid her a visit!

Gordon left yesterday for Edinburgh. I am afraid that he would have a head wind to Ayr, but after that it would not be quite so bad. I think he got it dry, but it is wet and misty again today. Well, the post van will be any minute so I must stop, so cheerio, Donald.

Donald's PhD thesis on the geology of Loch Doon was never published, possibly because, at that time, many prominent senior geologists were arguing with great acrimony over the origin of granite. Donald always hated controversy and possibly, rather than prolonging and provoking further bitterness, he chose not to have the thesis published but preferred to move on to fresh fields and new geological challenges. Others continued to keep him posted about the granite topic.

In 1951 Donald received a D.Sc. degree from Edinburgh University. This was the outcome of his original research on the Dalradian rocks of the Scottish Highlands (including his beloved Grampians and Cairngorms). It was based upon his understanding of the principles of Alpine tectonic analysis and a direct outcome of his work with Professor Wegmann in Neuchâtel, Switzerland.

For further details of Donald's geological career see the Royal Society of Edinburgh obituary in the Tributes chapter.

Distinguished Teachers

When Donald went to Edinburgh University in the autumn of 1941, he enrolled as a student in the chemistry department, a connection which later led to the publication and presentation of Donald's first academic, scientific paper(1946) written in collaboration with **Arnold Beevers**, a distinguished crystallographer.

Donald often referred to this publication and in 2004, he wrote:

My first published paper, on the crystal structure of apatite and its relation to that of tooth and bone material, was written with the distinguished crystallographer Arnold Beevers. The paper was read to the Mineralogical Society, London, on June 7 1945 almost exactly 60 years ago.

Our work resulted from Prof Victor M Goldschmidt's request that we refine the structure of fluor-apatite. While visiting Edinburgh, Goldschmidt gave memorable lectures on how trace elements are selectively captured during the growth of crystals acting as three-dimensional fishing nets of exactly the right size. I believe he expected that – as we found – the size of the fluoride ion was critical to the structure of apatite. The work led to the publication of Beevers and

McIntyre (1946) "The atomic structure of fluor-apatite and its relation to that of tooth and bone material" Mineralogical Magazine, 27, 254-257. Most of our instruments (including computers and x-ray cameras) were made by Dr Beevers' own hands. In addition, I believe that ours were the first coloured illustrations published in the Mineralogical Magazine. Goldschmidt's interest in apatite was not a passing one. Among his several positions, Goldschmidt was appointed director of the Norwegian government's laboratory for the study of raw materials. He was particularly in a successful project to extract apatite for use in fertiliser. His outstandingly successful research was terminated by Nazi persecution of the Jews. In 1942, the Norwegian resistance arranged his escape to Britain. When I met him in Edinburgh in 1945, Goldschmidt was in a nursing home. The great scientist appeared to be in his late 80s. In June, 1946, he returned to his beloved Norway, where he died in 1947 at the age of only 59.

*****

In all that he accomplished, Donald never failed but to give credit to his teachers.

He had immense admiration for **Arthur Holmes** (1890-1965) who moved from the University of Durham to lead the Edinburgh University Geology department in 1942 – the very year when Donald switched from studying chemistry to become a student in the Geology Department.

Professor Holmes soon noted Donald's academic potential and Donald quickly recognised and appreciated a remarkably gifted teacher. Donald delighted in taking and transcribing very extensive and meticulous notes of all Holmes' lectures. On our return to Scotland in 1989, he gifted these, as a historical record, to the Grant Institute of Geology of Edinburgh University for safe keeping.

It was Professor Holmes who arranged for Donald to spend the formative year in Switzerland to study with Professor Eugene Wegmann and who, along with his wife, Doris Reynolds (1899-1985) – also an eminent geologist – shaped the early stages of Donald's career.

Such was Donald's admiration for Arthur Holmes, that he submitted Professor Holmes' name as a potential candidate to receive a knighthood in The Queen's New Year Honours, c. 1960. Since

Professor Holmes was of modest and retiring nature, perhaps he himself would not regret that this recognition didn't materialize.

Donald would often comment that, although Professor Holmes was such an inspirational teacher and writer, it was surprising to note how he rarely went "into the field". He never visited Siccar Point in Berwickshire – one of the most famous of the Huttonian sites – a mere 40 miles (64 km) east of Edinburgh! No one held that against him.

As a footnote, Paul Gilmour, Edinburgh geology graduate of 1958, points out the fact that Donald's work for his DSc degree, actually motivated Professor Holmes to investigate the style of tectonics in the Dalradian rocks in Northern Ireland and to make plasticine models of folded rocks. The object was to illustrate the existence of double folding by analogy between plasticine model forms and what is shown on geological maps. At least two papers on this topic were published in the Geological Magazine c. 1954-5. Thus the student had reversed roles and had become the mentor!

Over the years Donald always kept in touch with Mrs Holmes. One summer in the 1970s she came to London to spend a lively afternoon with our little family and Donald visited her at her home in Brighton on more than one occasion.

Dr. Alex Cockburn *played a special role in Donald's life. When he died on Sunday 8th March 1959, Donald wrote from Claremont, California to Mrs Cockburn:*

In a way it is odd for me to refer to such a dear friend as **Dr Cockburn** under so formal a title, but he well knew how much affection and respect stood behind the mode of address. I will never know all I owe to him but I can never forget what I know. I treasure little words of encouragement even when I was a beginning student and well remember the impact they had on me. Always it was to him that I turned for advice at moments of decision, and an abundantly sympathetic and wise counsellor he invariably was. How pleased I am that Ann knew him too and can share with me the memory of him whom we always call 'dear Dr Cockburn.'

. On my desk as I write, I have two books which were given to me when I left Edinburgh in 1954. On the title page of Chambers' *Traditions of Edinburgh*, over the characteristic and beloved signature A.M.C., there is the inscription "D.B. McIntyre, from one Edinburgh callant to another!" On the other, the first volume of John Brown's

'Horae Subsecivae': "Donald, from his friends at Ladysmith Road. Remember them in your leisure hours over a 'cuppa tea'." These I will treasure; these memories I will not forget.

When I heard the news of his death I took out the pipes and played a pibroch. He knew me and he knew that I would do this, but I thought to myself how he would smile and how he would come out with witty and pertinent quotations at the idea of his lament being cried on the pipes by an exiled "son-of-the-hammer' in distant California.

On 8 March 1959; Professor Holmes wrote a personal letter to Donald enclosing a copy his own appreciation of Dr A.M.Cockburn.

Professor Holmes wrote:

"This is mainly a spontaneous tribute to Dr Cockburn's flair for friendship and his real gift of sympathetic understanding and human kindness…..By his work on St Kilda, Dr Cockburn made a major contribution to the geology of what had been the least known of Scotland's ancient volcanoes. Nearer home, he found the volcanic history of the Pentlands irresistibly fascinating. Although he published few papers on this absorbing subject, it was not for lack of material and achievement but because he gave his time so unstintingly towards furthering the interests of his young associates. Barely a month ago, he told me that he hoped to retire at sixty in order to devote his remaining years to the completion of this vast project. Alas, it was not to be, but we who remain can appreciate the priceless worth of his unselfish devotion to the Grant Institute. Thoughtless of self advancement and never seeking for geological fame, yet his beneficent influence has already spread far and wide across the world wherever geologists who trained in Edinburgh are to be found."

In September of 1947 Donald set off to spend that academic year in Switzerland and his work for his D.Sc. degree was based on what he learnt there. In 1948 he was invited to return to the Geology Department to fill an unexpected role – Lecturer in Engineering Geology. One grateful engineering student of that era searched Donald out and came to visit him some sixty years later at our home at Kinfauns!

Letter from Doris Reynolds from Newry, Co. Down, 3rd July 1947:

Dear Mr McIntyre

…..Wegmann sounds very pleased that you are going to him. I feel sure it is the best thing for you to do. With all this curious oppositions rising, it will be well for all transformists to form a solid block.

If I were you, I would have your Loch Doon paper published through the usual channels. It is best at the start not to publish in an unusual way and cause senseless comment. Can I help you to get the paper completed? If you have time to rough-out from the thesis what it should contain I could get it into form for you, ready for publication. It could then be posted to you to see that all was well, and make any alterations and suggestions before going into final type. Anyway if there is anything I can do to help over this you only have to ask me. It would be a great pity to miss the field work with Wegmann and would also be a pity not to get your paper into shape quickly, and I will be only too glad if I can help in any way.

...I have had a letter from Rastall, by the way, saying that although he accepts granitisations he does not accept basic fronts, and wishes I had not mentioned them in my paper now in proof! I have written to him and drawn parallels with the animal kingdom. I wrote about bulls assimilating grass and turning it into beef, and manuring the land in the process. I am afraid Rastall will think I am mad. I shall post him a small specimen of a basic front when we get home.

I was quite pleased with B.C. King's paper in the last number of the Geol. Mag. It kept the argument going, in a way, by describing an unconformity as a barrier to granitisation.

The quarry manager at the gabbro quarry got two of his men to knock off some beautiful large specimens for me. They are large specimens with the billed edges of what were originally pillows running down the centre and showing how the grain size increases to both sides away from the fine material. He also got me some big specimens showing the contact of a basalt dyke with the gabbro to show in contrast with the gradation from fine to coarse in the pillows.

Well, all the best. Think out whether you cannot quite quickly rough out what your paper should contain so that I can help you with the good work.

Yours, Doris L. Holmes.

And a letter from Sir Edward Bailey, Edinburgh, sent to Donald at Neuchâtel, Switzerland, 27 December 1947

Dear McIntyre

Happy New Year to you! I was, of course, very glad to support your candidature for the Geol. Soc and look forward to much of interest from your hammer and microscope before I hop off this mortal coil. Mrs Holmes gave us a very fine exposition of her position on granitization. I have seldom listened to a better lecture. I'm afraid you would have been disappointed with the subsequent arguments put forward by those in disagreement with the speaker. I think it was generally felt that we had been given a good and helpful account of a difficult subject and that what was fitting at the close of the meeting was an expression of appreciation and thanks. Someone did ask what about Ben Nevis and Glen Coe. The question was not very intelligibly put, but I expect it meant "If the granites of Ben Nevis and Glen Coe are metamorphic rocks, why have they rhyolitic or andesitic selvages where quenched against the down-faulted contents of cauldron-subsidences?" I don't share your opinion that it is becoming more and more difficult to avoid the conclusions drawn by Mrs Holmes. I think there is, for instance, strong evidence against solid diffusion of the type she envisages having produced geological effects through distances as great as a meter.

I am very glad you find Wegmann so stimulating and look forward to learning a lot from you when you come back. I am groping forward with my tectonic attack on our own Highlands and ever-thankful for the help I got about 20 years ago from young Vogt, Rowe & Co.

I also remember that when I started 45 years ago my hope and aim was to establish and spread certain ideas of Peach about Highland geology. It was a great pain to find that I had to get him to confess that in most of these particular ideas he was mistaken. Today at the end of my run I have got on to his favourite of all – the Torridonian age of the Moines – and it looks as if in this, he was correct.

Please give my best wishes to Wegmann.

Yours sincerely, E.B. Bailey

Faculty member 1948-1954
Friendships and Fun at the Grant Institute, Edinburgh

In 1954, just before exams, David Mackenzie jests in 'Broad Scots' about the Geology Department lecturers – Alex Cockburn, Gordon Craig and Donald McIntyre.

"Man! what a burst o' high elation
Whan feldspathoid in close relation
Wi' quartz I spy. Whilk implication
I maun enquire
'Twill tak a deal o' explanation
Frae McIntyre

Yestreen while grubbin' in the glaur
I found a muckle dinosaur
Wi' heid than body bigger faur
At Girnal Craig
Richt gled am I noo I can daur
Dumfooner Craig

Whan dookin' in the Cambrian Sea
A landmass started chasin' me
The stanes he chucked sae craftily
Werena in imbrication
If Cockburn kent o' this there'd be
Some consternation.

But I've been ditherin' in a dwam
The morn they're giein' me an exam
At which they'll speir me hoo I cam
By this fule tale
My papers three stoot chiels will damn
An' forthwith fail"

David Mackenzie, March 1953

★★★★★

A fellow graduate student in the Geology Department working under Professor Holmes was **Ma Hsing-Yuan** from Peking – today's Beijing. He was one of the few Chinese students in Britain at that time and became not only a close friend of Donald but also of all the McIntyre family. Donald and Ma shared many geological and mountaineering expeditions both in Scotland and in Switzerland – and legend has it that on two occasions, Ma and Donald's mother went dancing together in Edinburgh! Ma returned home to China just a week before the outbreak of The Cultural Revolution and from then all contact with him was lost until 1983. In the interval Ma had carved out a distinguished career and became both Director of The

Geological Institute in Beijing and President of the Geological Society of China.

In 1948 Ma's paper "On the Occurrence of Agmatite in the Rogart Migmatite area, Sutherland, Scotland" was published in the Geological Magazine (Cambridge University Press). There he explains that "Agmatite (fragments of older rocks cemented by granite) was one of the new descriptive terms introduced by the late Professor J.J. Sederholm in connection with his life-long study of the Finnish migmatites."

Among Donald's many friends in 1948, **Harold Rutledge** (1920-1954) became part of the geological team working under Professor Arthur Holmes in the Geology Department at King's Buildings Edinburgh. Harold taught sedimentary petrology to undergraduates and related this to his war-time desert duties as part of the El Alamein campaign (mentioned below). His wife, Elma, recounts Harold's and Donald's pleasure in each other's company and in their shared geological experiences as teachers and field work leaders. Apparently, it was rare that either of them returned home from the department before midnight. It wasn't all work – Donald was often playing the bagpipes!

In 1952, Harold was appointed to a university post in Australia but was one of 33 passengers and crew who died aboard a BOAC Constellation which crashed and caught fire on landing at Kallang Airport, Singapore, on 13th March 1954. His son, Philip, born in the happy Edinburgh days, was Donald's god-son and is now a distinguished Edinburgh doctor.

In a tribute to Harold, Professor Holmes wrote of this tragedy: "Rutledge was an outstanding success as teacher and lecturer; clear and vigorous in style and able to inspire in his students the enthusiasm which he brought to all his interests. His main research work was concerned with the structure and petrology of part of the plutonic complex of Loch Doon, Galloway and its metamorphic aureole."

And, in a final and historic footnote about Harold Rutledge, Paul Gilmour, student of that happy era, recalls that during World War II, the 8th Army in North Africa had "go-ability" maps. Some of these were doctored and deliberately allowed to fall into the hands of the German commander, Erwin Rommel, because they were designed to forestall or frustrate a flanking movement at the battle of El Alamein. Harold was one of the military team which prepared these false maps.

(The maps more-or-less reversed or exchanged the areas of "go" and "no-go" desert.)

And there was **John Christie** who came from Edinburgh to join Donald in the Geology Department at Pomona College. In 1960 John moved on to consolidate his successful career at the University of California, Los Angeles (UCLA). (It is appropriate that in 2011 Donald and John's names have come together in the founding of The McIntyre/Christie prize within the Laidlaw-Hall Trust at the Edinburgh University School of Geosciences. This will be presented when "a student, in the opinion of the Exam Board, has produced a truly outstanding 4th-year mapping dissertation".)

A life-long friendship with **Gerhard Oertel** and his wife, Irmgard, also began in the Edinburgh days. In due course, Donald invited Gerhard to move from work in Goa to join him in teaching at Pomona College (1956-59). Gerhard then continued to build his significant and important geological career at UCLA.

Donald greatly enjoyed his friendship with **Lionel Weiss** (1929-2006), a fine geologist, intrepid sailor and adventurer, novelist and photographer, whom he met in Berkeley on his first visit to California in the summer of 1952. In due course, Lionel published four textbooks on structural geology. (*See Donald's letter in 2006 to Lionel's wife, Liv Weiss*)

Bob Clark (1921-1987) from New Zealand, who shortly after leaving Edinburgh became Professor of Geology at Victoria University New Zealand (in 1954) and convener of the Antarctic Research Centre, was another good and life-long friend. In 1952-54 their family lived in Edinburgh where their daughter, Jenny, was born. At the time, Bob was completing his PhD thesis on Arthur's Seat before going n to teach optical mineralogy. In 1953 Donald and his sister, Sheila, took the Clarks on a whistle-stop geological camping tour of Europe and arrived at Neuchâtel one happy afternoon to visit the Wegmanns – and, as it happened, with whom I was spending that joyous summer officially learning to speak French and helping spring-clean their home!

Jennie Clark, Bob's daughter born in Edinburgh but who lives in New Zealand, sent this description of her father and his work.

Bob Clark was born on 10 June 1921. He shared this birthday with Prince Philip. When the guns used to go off in Wellington in the 60s and 70s on the Duke's birthday we always had a family joke that it was for Dad! He died on 8 October 1987 and now has two permanent memorials. In the late 1950s he was offered the choice of having a glacier or a mountain named after him – both in the Ross dependency in Antarctica – this is the name for the NZ part of that continent. He chose a glacier – so the Clark Glacier it has been for the past 50+ years.

Dad did an amazing amount of research and work in Antarctica – as little kids Malcolm and I were very used to waving Dad goodbye as he spent every second summer on the ice (This went on from 1957 to 1975+.) Then in the 1990s we got the Clark volcano – or sea-mount. There is a lot online about this, as sea-mounts are very rich in sea-life, and Malcolm gets to visit the area regularly in our research vessel. Sometime in the next 1000 years it will break the surface and become a new land mass! Clark Island, anyone?

Geological expedition from The Grant Institute, Edinburgh University, 1954.

He and Donald were great friends, because they complemented each other so well. Dad had the pragmatism that typifies New Zealanders. He had what we call the number 8 wire mentality. Number 8 wire is the wire used in fencing here- I think the US 'equivalent' would be duct tape? I remember many American men were very keen on all the things they could create with duct tape (though they would have perhaps called it baling wire or haywire)? This commonsense was exemplified by, say, Sir Ed Hillary – whom, of course, Mum and Dad knew. New Zealand is still a very small country! If you don't know someone, a friend of yours does! Donald had the imagination and ethereal qualities of the Highland Scot. I remember Donald saying to me once that his head was in the clouds, but Dad kept his (Donald's) feet firmly anchored on the ground. I think that is a lovely quote that sums up their relationship.

In 1997, **Robert A. Lyall** *who graduated in Edinburgh in 1956 wrote from Chile where he worked for The Anglo American Corporation of South Africa:*

To put myself into perspective, I used to be one of those pale, nondescript young and (I hope) earnest faces amongst the thousands which have confronted you in the course of your long career in teaching geology.

You may forgive me for recalling two other, perhaps irreverent, little details from your own most interesting lectures which have stuck in my memory. In the crystallography lectures you seemed to have remarkably flexible arm joints. To be able to point along crystal axis directions from almost any angle! In a lecture which must have included something on the Great Glen Fault, you had a large rounded boulder form the fault plane, which had been broken in half, displaced about ten centimetres, and re-cemented. To demonstrate the forces at play, you took the boulder in both hands, and pulled violently in opposite directions, with your teeth clenched, until you were a bit red in the face! Message received!

The excursion you led for first year students to Siccar Point was one of the turning points. I still vividly recall your hunched figure, back turned to the gusts and drizzle, a lock of dark hair blowing in the breeze, reading the self-same passage which Tom has quoted – many of the phrases from Playfair's writings have stuck in my memory to this day. The first year, of course, was the one that made geology irresistible – Arthur Holmes's' lectures on Physical Geology were the highlight of the week for me – and his textbook became my favourite bed time reading."

Ann notes: Over the years I have been remarkably fortunate in having met so many of these key people of Donald's life. I met several of them for the first time on a magical, whirlwind tour immediately after our engagement in August 1957, just before Donald flew back to Claremont by way of a conference at the Dominion Observatory in Canada.

I was greatly touched to be warmly welcomed by Professor Arthur and Mrs Holmes, Dr Alex Cockburn and his wife and Sir Alexander Cross at Redgorton, Perthshire. Sir Alexander was Director of the Carnegie Foundation and instrumental in funding Donald's important year in Switzerland.

A much prized wedding present throughout our marriage was a gift from Doris and Arthur Holmes – two silver napkin rings engraved with the initials D on one ring and A on the other and which **Doris** *and* **Arthur** *Holmes had received at the* *time of their wedding. The rings graced our every meal throughout the 52 happy years of our marriage. A long time ago, Donald and I decided that the rings should, in due course, be passed to another D & A couple and they have found a good home with our lawyer and his wife – Donald and Anne Elliot, Perth, Scotland and who have accepted the challenge, in due course, to pass the rings to another D & A couple in the hope that that tradition may be carried for future generations!*

*Two students of the mid-1950 era remained in touch with Donald over the years becoming wonderful and supportive e-mail editors/friends to me – **Paul Gilmour** of Tucson, Arizona, USA and **David Mackenzie** of Chapman, Australia – both of them are full of fun and the source of a wealth of Grant Institute/Geology tales (see David's poem above.*

Paul recounts a true story…

A Tale of the Highlands and Islands

Many will recall the novel "Whisky Galore" by Compton Mackenzie. It became a film of the same name in Britain, though in the USA it was called "Tight Little Island." The film is based on the true story: a vessel named S.S. Politician, carrying a mixed cargo that included large quantities of whisky to the U.S., went aground in February 1941 by the Hebridean island of Eriskay.

When the locals learned the nature of the cargo, they liberated as much of it as possible before customs and excise agents arrived to take over what remained.

As it happened, two friends of Donald – Max and Libby Carman – visited Edinburgh in 1952 or '53. While they were there, they bought a used car and towards the end of their stay, planned a tour the Scottish Highlands following a route that Donald suggested by way of Assynt and Inchnadamph. Donald arranged to meet them in the Inchnadamph Hotel.

After dinner, the three repaired to the lounge where Donald produced a bottle of whisky. Perhaps inspired by the bottle, Donald regaled his guests with the story of the *SS Politician* and its cargo. As the evening progressed, Max picked up the bottle and, while casually examining it, he enquired:

"Donald, where did you get this bottle?"

"Gosh, I don't remember," Donald replied, "it might have been on

Skye – one time when I was climbing with Bill Murray. I seem to recall being surprised to see it in a local village General Store and Post Office where the owner gave me a good price. Why do you ask?"

Max: "Well.....this bottle came from the SS Politician"

Donald: "You mean... you think....or you know.....?"

Max: "I know,"

Donald: "How can you be so sure?"

Max:" Look at the bottom!"

He handed the bottle to Donald. There it was – moulded into the glass base of the bottle: "Federal Law Prohibits the Re-use of this Bottle."

Turning point

In 1951 Donald was enthusiastically involved with the first post-war International Conference of the British Association of Science. This took place in Edinburgh and was a great success. However, since Professor Holmes characteristically decided not to lead the geological field trip to the Scottish Highlands following that conference, he asked Donald to take his place.

Such was the success of that expedition that in 1952, Professor Frank Turner of the Geology Department of the University of California in Berkeley, invited Donald to spend the summer in Geology Department at the University of California. This was Donald's first experience of life in America and directly linked to Donald's appointment to the Geology Department at Pomona College, Claremont, California in 1954.

See overleaf for two historic photos.

The geologists Benjamin Peach and John Horne at the Inchnadamph Hotel, in Assynt in the North-West Highlands of Scotland. 1912. Donald McIntyre and Harold Rutledge merrily relive that occasion on the very same seat in 1951.

Berkeley, California, 1952

Letter to his parents, 23 July 1952

Thanks for the letter which arrived today (posted 19th July). You ask me to send you a little sunshine, so I take it you don't quite appreciate the weather situation here! At this time of year there is almost constant fogbank just off the coast. Every night (nearly) it comes in over the bay and over the Berkeley Hills and sometimes by midday it clears again. Tonight is the second time I have seen the stars since I arrived. The result of this situation is that it is never terribly hot here (rarely any hotter than it can get in Edinburgh) and it can be quite chilly. At this time of year the fog can even get damp, but it never rains and there has scarcely been any wind. It can of course get windy at other times. Last year in a freak gale (the worst since the Golden Gate bridge was built) the bridge swung 13 ft from its mean position on each side; when you remember that the cable weighs somewhere around one and a half tons per foot length! I have worn my jacket only twice – and I didn't really need it. Of course in the great valley parallel to the coast (between Sacramento and Bakersfield) on the other side of the hills there is absolutely no moisture and it is over 100 degrees every day in the shade.

The Arvin/Tehachapi earthquake caused some excitement in the geology dept which houses the seismology dept. too. It caused very little notice otherwise. There are 9 seismographs in Bacon Hall and I saw the records. We felt nothing here (4:30a.m.) but all the non-photographic seismographs broke their needles by shooting right off the record. It is reckoned the biggest 'quake since 1906 and it is lucky it missed any really populated area. I hope to pass that way in Sept, but I won't be near it before that.

I plan a trip to Los Angeles, Grand Canyon and Yosemite late in September. It will be a little cooler then and less busy too. Prof Turner is going to Algiers then so it will work in well.

I have got a great deal of work done and spend most of the time at the Dept. I have been working on a specimen of marble from Tomintoul and tonight I have completed the first draft of my account of it. In essence what I do is to make a very large number of measurements of the orientation of crystals etc. in the rock and then try to interpret the results in the light of experimental work which has been done in California. We are developing a technique and the real necessity of working here is for discussion of what precisely is worth measuring, and of course the interpretation. As this is an almost untouched field anything we do is new and worth publishing. The results are very satisfactory. Naturally in the course of this I am learning much in the way of technique which will be very useful later. Prof Turner is very different from Prof. Wegmann and he is very helpful indeed. I have also had several sessions of wine-tasting with the Turners and their friends!

More from Berkeley, California, to his parents, 9 August 1952

I have just sent Ranald a note to say how pleased I am with the colour photos which I have got of Bakersfield. More are still to come. My camera and meter were very good investments. Daddy, who dreamt that I lost my camera, will be relieved to know that I insured all my photographic equipment before I left home!

When we were in the Valley it was not so hot as usual and I was not unduly put out at all. Also we were mainly driving about in the University cars so it was not hard work. I really must say that Frank Turner has been extraordinarily good to me, and, of course he is very easy to get on with – unlike old Wegmann. I had a Chinese dinner with him and some friends in San Francisco a few nights ago. Excellent fare and very cheap.

Talking about prices, it is quite impossible to make comparisons by converting dollars to sterling. You have to reckon in terms of currency here or have a heart attack. Prices are all very high but wages are higher and taxes lower than at home so things balance out fairly well. I do alright and if I lived very carefully I could no doubt bring quite a bit home. I prefer, of course, to spend here, and especially I hope to travel a bit (Grand Canyon etc.) at the end of my stay.

For 6 weeks at I House I pay about $135.00 at about £45 simple exchange. This is for all meals (except Sunday evening) but means sharing a room. As I work at the Dept. this sharing is no disadvantage. It takes about 7 minutes to walk along. I House is a huge building and at the moment is inhabited mainly by school teachers taking summer classes and Latin-Americans learning English. Food is not bad and is served in cafeteria style.

The work on the marbles is going very well and I have learnt a great deal about techniques etc. Technically this will be a very valuable experience, and I will be able to use it right away in further work in the Highlands. So far as I can see, I shall be working in the lab here for another month and will then have a trip and return here for a few days before going to Boston for a very short visit.

To his parents on his 29th birthday, Berkeley, California, 15 August 1952

Last night I had dinner (Mexican style) with C.S. Forester and his wife. He is the author of the Captain Hornblower stories and of the novel "The African Queen" which made one of the films of the year. Very charming people; he plays the recorder so I took along my chanter and we compared notes. Mrs Forester has invited me to go north for a run someday next week. I haven't been north from here at all so I shall be very glad to see that part. Also next week Frank Turner, Theo Crook and I are going for a day to look at part of the coast somewhere north of San Francisco. Tomorrow I am going with some students to an Agricultural Show near Sacramento in the Valley; I am keen to see the Valley there but not very keen to see the show!

The work on marble is progressing very satisfactorily. I have finished working on the Tomintoul and Dulnain Bridge marbles and have begun on the Ord Ban sample. I am learning a great deal about general technique. Frank Turner leaves for Algiers (International Geological Congress) on 3 September and returns on the 25th or 26 Sept. During that time I shall complete my work, put in a trip – to the Grand Canyon especially – and meet him here when he returns to discuss the results and method of publication. I shall leave for Boston on the 28th Sept. So I shall have only a very short time there. This is my birthday but I am much more conscious of the fact that it marks the middle of my stay here and that the second half will probably go much faster than the first. By the way, the University is giving me $25.00 (about £8.10) for expenses on the Bakersfield trip. Of course I have no travelling to pay for.

To his sister Sheila from the cliffs above the Grand Canyon, 19 September, 1952

The Grand Canyon trip has been a really wonderful experience, and especially so for a geologist. This afternoon I visited a store with blankets etc. woven by Navajo Indians. You will be glad to know that I was overcome by their attractive colours and designs and recklessly bought a blanket for Luachmore. I am optimistically hoping that I can bring it in as a travelling rug since I won't have a coat when I travel home. It has a beautiful blue background and has a red and black Indian pattern on it and I think it will make a wonderful wall hanging. I am sure that you will like it. I was sorry not to be able to get a floor rug as well. *(In due course, this Navaho tapestry reverted to us and has graced our bedroom ever since – AMcI.)*

Before coming here I had a day with **Lionel Weiss** in his area at Barstow. The combination of American car and American roads enabled us to do the 450-500 miles comfortably in about 10 hours.

We slept out in the desert and I played my chanter in the dark – fortunately without attracting any rattlesnakes (which incidentally I heard several times today). Then we had 3 grand days in the E. and NE Mohave Desert with two Survey geologists. The last day we motored right through Death Valley (nearly 300 feet below sea level and often 130 degrees in the shade – and positively no water for nearly 100 miles).

I wonder if Ian is with you just now. If so, it will be interesting for him to try to picture me with my legs literally dangling over the Canyon – which is fading away in the dusk – and piping with the chanter, as I am about to do!

On learning of Lionel's death in 2006, Donald wrote to his wife, Liv.

Thank you for telling me that Lionel – my oldest surviving colleague and friend – passed away quietly beside you.

After the 1951 British Association Meeting in Edinburgh I led a small group including Frank and Esme and Gill on a geological field trip in the Highlands. As a result Frank invited me to spend the summer of 1952 in Berkeley. I stayed at the International House or Club where I had breakfast – my first meal in The United States. Lionel and a non-geological student – who were also staying there – escorted me. I remember their discussion about what to order. I thought it would be wise to follow their choice but to horror they both chose "a snail". I was thankful to discover this meant a "Danish pastry".

A couple of years later – when Lionel joined me in Edinburgh – we ended a very meagre lunch by ordering a "penguin", I think that Lionel was relieved to find that this was – and is still – a delicious chocolate biscuit!

During my stay in Berkeley I was delighted to visit Lionel's field-area in the Mojave Desert. I think I contributed a little to Lionel's study. We were also privileged to see wonderful geology in remote parts of the Desert under the guidance of Foster Hewett -- the distinguished authority on the area. I have a 35mm slide of Lionel and Foster Hewett opening beer cans on a grilling hot day.

I was fortunate to accompany Professor Byerley's students when they explored the San Andreas Fault after the Arvin Tehachapi earthquake – I don't know why Lionel wasn't along on that trip. I suppose he was just too busy, or perhaps space was limited in the car.

The Football season began in Berkeley just before I returned to Edinburgh in time for classes to begin. I was to meet Lionel for the opening game, but the crowd was too big at the gate and we were unable to go together. Needless to say I made nothing of the game! I was sure that players took off their helmets and tucked them in so that the other side would think they were carrying the ball! I remember asking Lionel later how many balls were in play!

Once back in Edinburgh I persuaded Professor Arthur Holmes to offer Lionel a Fellowship. Holmes agreed, but Lionel couldn't return to the UK without being compelled to do army service. So Frank Turner gave Lionel a job as a draughtsman to tide him over the critical dates. This turned out to have a happy result because it ensured that Lionel thoroughly understood Frank's paper. So when Lionel finally arrived in Edinburgh he brought with him familiarity with Frank's latest ideas.

From Edinburgh Lionel and I co-operated on research on the geological structure of the Loch Leven area near Glencoe in the Highlands. This was published as a joint paper in the Journal of Geology, but before it was finished I had left for Pomona and the work was more Lionel's than mine.

On my recommendation Professor Holmes offered my position to Lionel, but Lionel rejected the offer because he wanted more time for research. As a result Lionel earned an Edinburgh DSc on top of his English PhD.

At that time I was the only member of staff in geology to have a car. My revered and much loved teacher, Dr Cockburn, actually had a car but never travelled far from Edinburgh. He taught the students about the structural geology of the NW Highlands (where I took Frank and Esme and Gill and others) but he had never been there!

When I left Edinburgh I gave Lionel my car. It was a pick-up van that had been used in the North African desert during the war. Because I had taken students and friends – including Lionel of course -- on many geological trips – including to Switzerland and the Alps, all sorts of rock specimens etc had accumulated inside! So when Lionel attended the Graduation Ceremony he knew he needed black shoes – Prince Philip, as Duke of Edinburgh and Chancellor of Edinburgh University, officiated and proper dress was expected, so Lionel looked in the van where he did indeed find a pair of black shoes – so the day was saved! Of course I was in California and didn't participate!

I had permission to offer Lionel a position at Pomona – though I knew it wasn't the ideal position for him. But this was the trigger that let Frank Turner offer Lionel a full faculty position at Berkeley.

So Lionel returned to Berkeley. Nothing stays the same of course, and perhaps Lionel was not appreciated by Frank's successors as much as he had been by Frank himself. The good thing, of course, is that being in Berkeley he found you and enjoyed a very happy marriage.

I hope these memories of mine will help to fill in the story of the years before you knew Lionel.

And a postscript from Ann

Dear Liv – You are all so much in our thoughts as you struggle to come to terms with your new and unwelcome situation. We both grieve with you for a good and wonderful friend. Through Donald, I too knew Lionel a little in "the old days!" and after our marriage and before yours, Donald and I went to stay with Lionel on more than one occasion. We particularly remember a Thanksgiving dinner. Lionel was our host and invited Esme and Frank Turner and another couple. The occasion merited the sampling and sharing a bottle of 1815 vintage brandy. Esme, however, had some concerns that the contents of this unique and precious bottle might not be appreciated to the full by all the guests. In her flamboyant style and with great gusto, before the other guests arrived, Esme declared: "This brandy must not go down any unworthy throat!" Perhaps my throat too was in question, but in the event, we all enjoyed this rich and rare opportunity. And then, some years later there was the memorable time with you – Nicholas was little and Ewen just a few years old – when we shared Thanksgiving with you in Berkeley and that occasion included a visit to San Francisco and a beautiful autumnal walk. And there were visits together in Claremont…so many happy memories that sometimes seem so distant – and yet so fresh and always special.

Frank Turner and Lionel together were the authors of an important book: *Structural Analysis of Metamorphic Tectonites.* And, as well as writing several other geological books which are still available on the internet, Lionel was author of three novels.

On retirement in 1989, Lionel and his wife, Liv, set sail on their own yacht to make a four-year-long cruise to the Bahamas and around South America. They both described this as a life-defining experience. The McIntyres have indeed been – and continue to be – blessed with many friendships.

Over the decades, Donald never missed an opportunity to visit Siccar Point (photo: John McAlpin – November 2005).
The geology of Siccar Point and much more is explained in the book: James Hutton – The Founder of Modern Geology *by Donald B. McIntyre and Alan McKirdy, third edition published by National Museums of Scotland. ISBN 9781905267736*

Chapter 4
Mountaineering

Until one is committed,
there is hesitancy, the chance to draw back,
always ineffectiveness.
Concerning all acts of initiative (and creation),
there is one elementary truth,
the ignorance of which kills countless ideas
and splendid plans:
that the moment one definitely commits oneself,
then Providence moves too.
All sorts of things occur to help one
that would never otherwise have occurred.
A whole stream of events issues from the decision,
raising in one's favour all manner
of unforeseen incidents
and meetings and material assistance,
which no man could have dreamt
would have come his way.

I have learned a deep respect for one of Goethe's couplets:

"Whatever you can do, or dream you can, begin it.
Boldness has genius, power and magic in it"

The Scottish Himalayan Expedition
by W.H. Murray

Donald, Honorary President of the Perth Mountaineering Club, sets the scene himself in this article 'Magical Land of Hills'. It was published in the Millennium edition of the Perth Mountaineering Club Journal, March 2000 and is reprinted here with the Club's kind permission.

Magical Land of Hills

My first hill was Beinn a 'Ghlo, which I climbed about 1935 while staying with my family at Kincraigie in Glen Tilt. The Royal Scots Greys, mounted and splendid in full uniform, passed our door on their famous recruiting march from the Tay to the Dee. Though eager, I was too young to enlist, and exactly sixty years later I was too old when the Greys' successors marched through Perth to repeat their recruiting march through Tayside.

In 1939 we were on holiday at Tullochgrue in Rothiemurchus. I already knew the glens, all the paths through the forest, the lower hills, and had climbed Braeriach on my own. At the outbreak of war my brother and I were sent to school in Grantown-on-Spey, travelling on the old Speyside railway line and returning via Dulnain Bridge. Many weekends were spent in the Cairngorms – I then knew every nook and cranny. We slept both under and on top of the Shelter Stone, in secret caves in the upper part of the Nethy, or even in the luxury of a bothy in Glen Einich. We used Whymper's version of a "sleeping bag" by sewing up a blanket, and a friend in the rubber business made us impermeable sacks so that we slept out in any weather. In those days the hills were deserted; only once or twice did we meet soldiers practising mountain warfare, their mules transporting the field artillery. Once we found a dead golden eagle. We took his pinion feather and had it cut to match Winston Churchill's favourite nib. The great man said he would use it to sign the Peace Treaty!

The SMC guide to the Cairngorms reported that the six highest Cairngorms had twice been climbed in a day. We knew that this was wrong – Beinn Mheadhoin, which is higher than Ben Avon, had been omitted. Taking up the challenge, my friend Ian Baikie and I climbed the seven highest on 5 September 1941 (35 miles and 10,300ft of ascent in 20 hours – some of it in the dark and in the mist). The SMCJ (vol.22, 1941, p.388-9) duly recorded the expedition: "Our young friends have most justifiably added to the six the 'separate mountain Munro' Beinn Mheadhoin, clearly higher than Ben Avon. ... We heartily congratulate the party on their enterprise and achievement." Curiously, that notice has been ignored by later climbers and editors; for subsequent volumes of the SMCJ and the SMC Guide to the Cairngorms have continued to climb and name the wrong six mountains.

In Edinburgh I joined the JMCS, and was introduced to the joys of rock-climbing on the Salisbury Crags and the great cliffs of Ben Nevis under the tutelage of Freddie O'Riordan, Archie Hendry, and others. In the course of time I succeeded O'Riordan as Secretary.

The JMCS had its first postwar meet over Christmas 1945. Twelve members stayed at Kingshouse. Gordon Parish (who succeeded me as President of the re-created Edinburgh University MC), E.E. Gardiner, and I represented the Edinburgh Section. The SMCJ (April 1946) records that we took 10 hours to climb the Crowberry Ridge by Macgregor's ledge – "Much snow and the slabs icy" On our way back to the Inn we met a search party coming out to look for us! Kenneth Dunn was JMCS chairman (later I climbed with him in Glencoe and in Skye); the nine SMC members attending the meet included Bill Murray, Bill Mackenzie, Tom MacKinnon, and Douglas Scott; three of them later became SMC President, one Hon. President, and one Hon. Vice-President.

Bill Murray was recovering from three years in a central European prison camp. While a prisoner Bill wrote his classic 'Mountaineering in Scotland' on scraps of paper. After the Gestapo confiscated his work, he began writing all over again. One chapter describes A December Night on the Crowberry Ridge with Mackenzie and Dunn. It tells of their abortive attempt, in 1936, to make the first winter ascent of Crowberry Ridge by Garrick's shelf. Because *Mountaineering in Scotland* was not published until 1947, we did not fully appreciate that at Kingshouse in 1945 we were in the company of such illustrious pioneers! Bill had been released in April, and as his last climb had been on Buachaille so in June 1945 his first climb was The First Day on Buachaille – with Bill Mackenzie. Read the fine account in *Undiscovered Scotland*.

Attendance at that meet in 1945 changed my life. Before joining the Army, Bill had been a banker, but on his release he made a characteristically bold decision; he would make his living by writing about mountains. Moreover he had agreed that his first book would be one that would provide no income: he would write the SMC'S first guide-book to rock-climbing in Glencoe. But by then Bill's pre-war companions were mostly married and re-building their careers to make up for years in the Army. I was a student, and eagerly accepted Bill's invitation to be his assistant. Based with easy access to the SMC Library in Edinburgh, I dug out descriptions of climbs from the journals, but of course we spent as much time as possible in Glencoe. I regularly took the train to Queen Street, where Bill would meet me with his pre-war Morris eight. Sometimes I stayed overnight at his mother's house, but mostly we set off for the hills – usually to Lagangarbh. Sadly the hut-book for that period is missing.

Although our efforts were mainly devoted to checking descriptions of known routes, we occasionally made new routes. Some of these experiences are recorded in *Undiscovered Scotland'*; for example, a week in Glen Affric before the dam was built. His 'Winter Days in Coire nan Lochan' quotes from my own 'Winter Days on Bidean nam Bian' (SMCJ 1948), including our winter camp on the summit of Bidean, and SC Gully with H.W. Tilman, the leader of the last pre-war attempt on Everest.

In 'Night and Morning on the Mountains', Bill described our double traverse of the Aonach Eagach by moonlight in February 1947 under perfect winter conditions. I concluded my tribute to Bill at his funeral on 26 March 1996 with his description of the sunrise (SMCJ 1996).

Bill quoted Geoffrey Winthrop Young's 'Knight Errantry' on the title-page of *Mountaineering in Scotland*. That was my introduction to GWY's writings. His poems influenced me greatly; indeed my tribute to Bill began by quoting from the same poem:

"Ice-crowned castles and halls to test / steel with the ashen shaft"

Although GWY's *Collected Poems* was published in 1936 and long out-of-print, I wrote to the publisher and was lucky enough to get two copies. I copied out 'For Any Boy' for our son, Ewen, the day he was born. I was also much influenced by GWY's 'Mountain Craft', which I studied closely. GWY, a prominent member of the Alpine Club, lost a leg in the First World War (See SMCJ 1950, p.177-179 and GWY's *The Grace of Forgetting*). The *Collected Poems* ends with a moving verse from the poem, *Wind Harp*:

> *I have not lost the magic of long days:*
> *I live them, dream them still.*
> *Still am I master of the starry ways,*
> *and freeman of the hill.*
> *Shattered my glass, ere half the sands had run, –*
> *I hold the heights, I keep the dreams I won.*

GWY entered Cambridge University in 1894 and for many years he inspired and guided all Cambridge mountaineers. Just as Bill Murray was ten years older than me, so GWY was ten years older than George Leigh Mallory. In both cases an older man introduced a younger friend to mountaineering. Sandy Irvine, 16 years younger than Mallory, was selected for the Everest expedition of 1924 on the recommendation of the geologist and mountaineer Noel E. Odell. Why Irvine, rather than Odell (a far more experienced mountaineer) was chosen to attempt the summit is debated. Mallory admitted to GWY that Irvine's lack of experience was against him. Perhaps it was Irvine's skill with the finicky oxygen apparatus that won him the chance, but Mallory clearly regarded Irvine as a "splendid companion" and probably chose Irvine simply because he liked him – despite GWY's warning against inspiring "weaker brethren" to take risks beyond their experience. Mallory certainly knew the danger – he had failed on two previous Everest expeditions. At any rate it was on June 8, 1924 – when I was 10 months old – that Odell saw Mallory and Irvine "going strong" near the summit of Everest. It was Odell's opinion that "there is a strong probability that Mallory and Irvine succeeded" (*The Fight for Everest*, 1924). The recent discovery of Mallory's body encourages us to hope that the truth will finally be discovered. (*Editor's note.* On retirement in Perth, Donald and I came to know Irvine's sister-in-law and, at her family home, were privileged to read originals of some of Irvine's letters.)

I also had the privilege of meeting Geoffrey Winthrop Young when he spoke to the SMC in Edinburgh. Indeed it was on GWY's personal recommendation that I wrote to his publisher asking for his *Collected Poems*. I met Odell, first in the Cairngorms, then in Switzerland, and finally when he visited me in California. He wrote to me just before he died. Whenever I reflect on the many remarkable people that I have known through a shared love of mountains, I am reminded deeply how privileged I have been!

Through the initiative of its commandant, Group-Captain Lord Malcolm Douglas-Hamilton, the Air Training Corps converted Glenmore Lodge into a training centre for mountaineering. As President of EUMC and Secretary of the Edinburgh JMCS, I offered to recruit young mountaineers as instructors: I particularly remember Gordon Parish, Malcolm Slesser (SMC President, 1982-84), and H.Y. Ma, my fellow post-graduate geology student, who, as President of the Geological Society of China, invited me to Beijing in 1983. It was at Glenmore that I first met Odell. In the photograph of our group (now in SMC Archives) Odell and I are the only ones not draped in climbing ropes; we were about to leave for the Geological Society of London where I was giving a paper.

On one occasion Lord Malcolm and I were each leading cadets climbing in Coire Lochain, when Lord Malcolm fell, landing on the ledge where I was standing. I partly broke his fall. We had difficulty getting him off the hill – no mountain rescue then – and he ended up in Raigmore Hospital. (See ff 'A Climbing Adventure').

Later I sailed round Skye with Lord Malcolm, landing at Dunvegan where we were entertained by Dame Flora. We beat our way up to Talisker before sailing to Rum where Lady Bullough received us at Kinloch Castle. I often stayed at Allt Dearg, Lord Malcolm's cottage at Sligachan, and on one occasion we traversed the Cuillin Ridge, in sections, under fine winter conditions. Lord Malcolm was a member of a remarkable family. His eldest brother was the first to fly over Everest. Tragically Lord Malcolm and his youngest son, Niall, were lost in 1964 crossing Africa in a small plane; he was only 54. The remains were only found two years later.

Editorial note: *To the best of my recollection, Donald understood that, in World War Two, Lord Malcolm had played a significant role in leading the raid on the V-2 plant at Peenemunde, flying low across Germany in full moonlight. Although it is no longer possible to confirm the accuracy of Donald's conviction, Lord Malcolm's son, Alastair, states in his father's biography –* Lord of the Skies ISBN 978-1-4475-0624-9. published by Lulu,2011 – *that* "in April 1943 my father received news that he was to be posted to RAF Benson to what he described as 'The Squadron I hoped for'. He started his command of 540 Squadron at the beginning of May 1943 and during the year he was there, flying Mosquitos on photo-reconnaissance missions, he is reported as having given the lead to his Squadron by invariably picking for himself and his navigator the nasty deep-penetration missions right into the heart of Nazi Germany. There were, as has been said, "easier ways of passing the time than flying, in broad daylight, an unarmed Mosquito, loaded up with cameras and extra fuel, to the nerve-centres of the Fatherland, confronted by perhaps the most lethal defensive fighter force ever marshalled in modern war."

Among Donald's files is the Order of Service of Lord Malcolm's funeral in Inverness, 4 May 1965 where he was remembered "for his service to his country in peace and war; his high hearted endeavours for the people of the Highlands and Islands of his native land; his leadership for the young" as well as for "his zest for life, and spirit of high purposes mingled with light-hearted gaiety; the happiness he carried with him and spread around him; his gift of music and song, of laughter and friendship; his love of Nature in all her changing beauties, the mountain-tops and the ocean waves, above all the free wide regions of the air".

Donald continues "Other memorable days on the hills in the 1940s included the winter ascent of Crowberry Gully with Bill Murray and Malcolm Slesser (then a fellow member of EUMC and JMCS), and, again with Slesser, climbing the Torridon hills, which were far more remote then than they are now – when I first visited Assynt I arrived on a bicycle! I remember, too, a particularly fine EUMC meet at Steall.

1947 was a vintage year; I spent Easter at the CIC hut on Nevis with Bill Murray and others. After Bill and John Barford (Secretary of the BMC) left, Michael Ward and I had the hut to ourselves. (Michael was doctor on Hunt's successful Everest expedition in 1953). We climbed Comb Gully in its heavy winter condition. (Michael's account is in SMCJ 1950). A few months later Murray, Barford, and Ward were hit by falling rocks on the Ailefroide. I flew to Basle and made my tortuous way to Gap, where I found Bill and Michael still in blood-soaked clothes. Bill and Michael had fractured skulls. Michael had no idea who I was, and John Barford was dead. *(Editor note: a fuller account of this is given below.)*

From an early age I had found delight in my father's copies of Whymper's *Scrambles amongst the Alps*, Smyth's *Spirit of the Hills* and *An Alpine Journey*, a delightfully illustrated edition of Leslie Stephen's *Playground of Europe*, and in de Beer's *Escape to Switzerland* (1945). I envisioned the Alps as a fascinating paradise – "land of the silvery glacier fire, magical land of hills". My dreams were realised when in the summer of 1947, Arthur Holmes, the distinguished Professor of Geology in Edinburgh, dispatched me to Neuchâtel to spend a year studying the structure of the Alps. For the first few weeks I was joined by H.Y. Ma. Taking money out of Britain was strictly limited, and I couldn't afford a guide; besides I wasn't on holiday! Although I covered much of Switzerland and spent a lot of time in the mountains, my serious climbing was very limited.

I was fortunate to climb the Zinal Rothorn with a casual acquaintance who could afford a guide. When Malcolm Slesser visited, we climbed the Doldenhorn, but in appalling conditions – a thunderstorm knocked

Malcolm's ice-axe from his grasp and heavy rain made snow bridges suspect. Bill Murray joined me briefly in the summer of 1948; we attempted the Matterhorn, but were turned back before reaching the summit by a storm.

I did, however, learn to ski in the Jura, at Grindelwald, and at Davos, enjoying the famous runs under perfect conditions. I was particularly fortunate in being able to represent the Neuchâtel section of the Swiss Alpine Club in a course promoting ski-mountaineering. It was held in the Bernina Group, above Pontresina. We skied on glaciers, and were always roped; we carried ice-axes, crampons, and full rucksacks. We learned how to rescue a companion from a crevasse, and how to bring back an injured skier by making a sledge from his skis. We made ascents, of course, going as high as possible on ski, changing to crampons (which were new to me), and completing the climb in boots. It was a challenge because my companions were all members of the Swiss mountain troops. I was never fitter and I had fantastic pleasure on the last day when we crossed the long but easy ridge and swooped down to Silvaplana and St Moritz.

Returning to Edinburgh as a young lecturer, I was elected a member of the SMC Committee (1948-51), but my opportunity to climb became more and more limited. I skied with Arthur Cromar from Glenshee to Fealar Lodge in Glen Tilt, and with Malcolm Slesser in the Cairngorms and in the Jotunheimen, Norway.

Malcolm and I read with care Bill Mackenzie's 'The Snow and Ice Climbs of Glencoe' (SMCJ 1947), noting that "It is not suggested here that the use of crampons is necessary for Scottish winter climbs, nor yet that their habitual use is at all desirable here". Bill's opinion that "To rely on crampons before one has mastered the technique of using the ice-axe on steep snow-ice or ice is a great mistake" shows how much climbing has changed in fifty years. We were particularly fascinated with Mackenzie's article on 'Bad Weather and Bivouacs' (SMCJ 1946). Its subtitle, with notes on frostbite, chills, exhaustion etc made the subject irresistible. Mackenzie always knows what he is talking about, and, after several years with the Army School of Mountain Warfare, on this subject he is an authority. He assured us: "It cannot be too strongly emphasised that a snow hole is a very warm place to sleep in. ... A maximum of one and a half hours should give ample time to construct a snow cave". The diagrams are clear: we noted the sleeping bench and learned that the roof should be "high enough to almost stand up straight"; there should be a ventilator pipe and a chimney, and that "the door should be big enough to crawl through."

With these precise instructions in mind, we left my parents' home in Nethy Bridge on ski and chose a suitable site near the summit of Cairngorm. Being Hogmanay it was dark early, and we didn't use a light for fear of attracting a search party from Glenmore. Inspired by one of Mackenzie's diagrams, we used our skis to support a roof of large slabs of compacted snow. As a geologist I should have known better. "Nature abhors a vacuum" and when nature has fashioned a landscape, it will resist your efforts to change it. Dig a hole and nature will use its resources in attempting to fill it up. Drifting snow, like sand blown in the wind, will fill your hollow until equilibrium is restored. Snow trickled into our snow hole relentlessly through every crack and tiny hole. In those days we used newspaper for insulation, and we survived the night without undue discomfort. The snow hole wasn't quite as warm, however, as we had been led to believe. In the morning we skied from the summit of Cairngorm to Nethy Bridge and across the Spey, taking our skis off at the railway station at Dulnain.

Love for mountains led me into geology, but as the years passed my work left little time for climbing. In 1952 I was invited to spend the summer at the University of California, Berkeley, and two years later I accepted an invitation to head the Geology Department of Pomona College in southern California. My climbing came to an end when our son, Ewen, was born with cerebral palsy.

As protection against rattlesnakes, the boots I used in the Mojave Desert covered my calf. When I returned to Scotland in 1989 I told Alec Runciman I needed to replace them by boots suitable for Scottish hills. Alec asked what, from his large selection, I had in mind. When I responded "Nothing special, just a stout pair of boots with tricounis and hob nails", Alec exclaimed with an astonished expression: "You must be Rip Van Winkle!" True indeed and I knew then how out-of-date I had become. Shortly after its centennial, the SMC made me its first Honorary Archivist. Looking back over more than sixty years, I appreciate how very fortunate I have been. I owe unbounded gratitude to my many comrades of the hills.

In this short span
Between my finger-tips on the smooth edge
And these tense feet cramped to the crystal ledge
I hold the life of man......
......For what is there in all the world for me
But what I know and see?
And what remains of all I see and know
If I let go?

From *The Cragsman,* Geoffrey Winthrop Young

A Climbing Adventure

Shortly after our marriage, Donald's father wrote to Ann:

"Donald drove from Edinburgh to Glenmore Lodge with Lord Malcolm Douglas Hamilton on Friday evening 5th July 1946. They travelled in a Humber Super Snipe, touching 80 mph at times. They called in on a brief visit to Lord Malcolm's sister, Lady Margaret Drummond-Hay, at Seggieden, Kinfauns, near Perth, while on their way to spend some time training schoolboy cadets in the art of mountain survival.

We were surprised when Donald returned home to Edinburgh much earlier than expected. He said nothing to us his parents and left for Ballochbeatties (Galloway), to continue his Ph.D. geological research next morning."

In a letter to his sister, Sheila, this was Donald's account of that incident

On Saturday (6 July 1946) Lord Malcolm and I each took two cadets and went up to Coire an Lochain (Cairngorm). We climbed by different routes on the same buttress and the two climbs converged 150 feet from the summit.

Lord Malcolm, having arrived on the platform first, climbed the last pitch while I waited at the foot to avoid entangling the ropes. The pitch was steep but easy, and he was soon up and out of sight. He called on his second-man to follow. When about two-thirds of the way up, this second-man fell off without warning. The pitch was such that his whole weight came on the rope and he was swung out below an overhang. Lord M. was trying out a new rope (nylon) which was unusually slippery, and was wearing woollen gloves as the rocks were wet and cold. When the strain came, he was unable to check the rope, although he exerted a considerable braking force on the running rope. This saved the falling second-man from serious injury. Unfortunately, the second-man did not remain on the somewhat narrow platform, but bounced off thereby drawing out more rope than Lord M had in his hands for holding purposes. Thus the strain came directly on Lord M's waist, and as he had been unable to find a belay, he was catapulted clean over the pitch and fell 90 feet without touching the ground.

Fortunately, the jerk stopped his second-man who stopped on a sloping slab 10 feet below the platform. My first view of Lord M was when he came over the pitch. He was then quite clear of the ground and was coming down head-first with a great rushing sound. It reminded me of an underwater film of someone swimming down towards the camera. Fortunately, it was possible for me to run forward along the ledge and try to catch him. I was knocked over and I threw Lord M to the back of the platform where he landed on his third-man who was sitting with his back to the rocks. This man received the bulk of 15 stones descending a clean 90 feet drop. Fortunately, the third-man suffered nothing worse than a strained back. It was very fortunate that Lord M did not knock me off the ledge, for then we should each have dragged our parties with us and gone down at least 500 to 600 feet.

The whole thing could not have had less serious consequences than it did. There were no bones broken. I got the whole party to the top of the rocks and down to the Meadow of the Lurcher's Crag. I then sent my smallest boy back to Glenmore to bring out a stretcher, and Lord M's two boys back arm in arm giving mutual support. The fourth boy (my second-man) helped me to carry Lord M down to the path above the stable. The accident was at 2:30p.m. We got to the path at 5:15pm. The stretcher-party was up shortly afterwards and Lord M reached the Lodge at 8:15 p.m.

I spent the night with Lord M, washed him, and helped him to shave before he went to Raigmore Hospital, Inverness, in the morning. Both of his boys went up for X-rays, and I went to the hospital with them. One of the boys was to be kept in for a day or two, and Lord M a little longer. However, I see that he gave a speech in Inverness yesterday. So, after all, Lord Malcolm's "business in Inverness did delay him longer than he had expected". Needless to say, my boots were wet with getting the stretcher across the burn.

As it was not my "secret", I naturally could not tell anyone, hoping that (seeing there were no fractures) the matter would blow over without the press finding out. As he had to attend that meeting in Inverness yesterday, and as he appeared in a bath-chair, the news had to come out. I hoped it would be too old for the papers, but they wangled it in into their report of yesterday's meeting (11th July 1946) when Lord Malcolm attended the meeting to be adopted as the Liberal-Unionist candidate for Inverness for the Westminster Parliament.

Extract from a letter to Donald on 10ᵗʰ July 1946 from Lord Malcolm. It is written in pencil and is almost illegible.

"…I should like to thank you for all you did in first saving my life and those of the two cadets incidentally – and then for your stalwart work in bringing me down. It was altogether a grand job of work which I shall never forget and words are not adequate to thank you for it."

On 25 July 1946, while still in hospital, Lord Malcolm, wrote again:

"…..I have suggested to others that I could have held the rope had it not been nylon. It is quite possible that this is not so known. The rope may in this instance have come with a greater jerk than at the time I mentioned to you on the Minta Ridge. I have the impression that I was on both occasions holding the rope taut but not tight. It may well be that at the time of the accident the rope may have been temporarily caught in a crack and there may have been in consequence some slack between the cadet and the place where it was caught that would account for the rope running away so fast..

Anyway it all sums up that one must be really especially careful with nylon in particular in wet weather. These accidents are really most valuable provided one survives; the only snag is that things happen a bit too quickly for careful observation of just what did happen in detail."

In April 1960, Donald's father sent me further details:

"One really has to know the scene at close range to appreciate what was involved. I knew the area fairly well, but one day, when Donald and another family went up by the Lurcher's Crag to Ben Macdhui, we crossed the ridge and looked into the Corrie from the west – that is to say from the direction in which Donald, with the slight assistance of one of his young cadets, half carried, half dragged Lord Malcolm down to the 'Meadow' beneath.

We could just see where the mishap took place, but we saw better when Donald ran round the precipice top and dropped down by a gulley to the platform at the foot of the buttress and pointed to the 'details' which he mentions in the letters, that is – the buttress itself, the so-called 'Platform' which was just a narrow ledge sloping downwards to the Boiler Slabs which make this corrie conspicuous from afar, and the 'rise' up which he worked Lord Malcolm and the others and got them to the flat top of the cliff. That route is rough, steep and consists of loose rocks, any one of which might have come away under the pressure of hand or foot. Some of these he had to clear away to let the more-than-half-bemused Lord Malcolm get a footing. One big rock he had to manoeuvre past the cadet who hung downwards over a slope below the Platform, being held from crashing to the cliff foot by the rope still attached to him and now belayed by Donald above.

The task of getting these folk along the ridge and down the slope of the Lurcher's Crag was formidable, and was not eased by the fact that the lad who assisted him was a lightly-built stripling of a boy who was unfit to bear the dead weight of the heavy and badly damaged Lord Malcolm. Donald and he took Lord M's arms around their necks and let his feet more or less drag along behind."

Characteristically, Donald rarely spoke of this near-fatal accident and then only in the most casual of terms. And, by coincidence, when Donald retired in 1989 and our family came to make our home in Scotland at the hamlet of Kinfauns, Lady Margaret Drummond Hay's daughter – Nina Bowry and her family at Seggieden, turned out to be our neighbours and dear friends. Nina always enjoyed Donald's tales of her adventurous uncle.

★★★★★

The following article by Donald from The Scottish Mountaineering Club Journal, May 1948, is reprinted with permission.

Winter days on Bidean nam Bian

During the winter of 1946-47 my work gave me an opportunity for serious climbing, and I was peculiarly fortunate in entering the land of "ice-crowned castles " with W. H. Murray, a master of ice-craft and a patient teacher, as my guide. My debt to him may be repaid in part by encouraging others to venture on our Scottish hills in winter, there to know the intense joy and satisfaction of climbing on snow and ice.

One misty December day found us on Stob Coire nan Lochan at the top of S-C Gully. The steep, smooth rocks were encased in an armour of fog crystals, and overhung by tottering cornices left unstable by a recent thaw. From above it seemed that the visible part of the gully verged on the impossible, but I was assured that the main difficulties were hidden in the mist below. My companion's reminder that S-C was on our winter's schedule of climbs was frankly terrifying.

Two months later Kenneth Dunn, Murray and I laboured through deep, soft snow to Coire nan Lochan. From the corrie S-C looked sensational indeed; to me the 70-foot pitch was clearly on the wrong side of the vertical. When once we were in the gully, however, the first pitch appeared to be set at quite a reasonable angle.

My companions dug in, and with, "Well, Donald, it's all yours!" I was commissioned to "have a crack at it". By hard experience I have found that, although I may overestimate the angle of an ice-pitch while I am on it, I invariably underestimate the angle when below. The first pitch in S-C was no exception; half-way up, the ice actually bulged and cling-handholds had to be cut.

Cutting above the head is an occupation which tests the power of both body and will. Accurate placing of the steps is vital. Well-placed steps enable the cutter to stand easily in balance while he fashions the steps beyond. Poor steps initiate a vicious circle; the cutter is forced to move on before adequately constructing the steps above, and the tendency to move faster than one cuts is much easier to be aware of than to check. Even although cutting in relays, we took two hours to surmount that first pitch; as time did not permit us to continue, we resolved to return to the assault the following week-end. But south-west wind and thaw during the next week meant that S-C became impracticable.

On Saturday evening Murray and I halted at Altnafeadh and debated the relative merits of Lagangarbh with a fire and a high camp on Bidean. Although the night was anything but promising we chose the latter. It was a dark night with no wind, and toiling up Coire nam Beith was hot work; shirts were opened and sleeves rolled up. The cliffs were felt rather than seen. High on the mountain the snow became hard and we had to cut.

A chill wind swept over the summit as we pitched the tent beside the cairn. For a brief moment the peak rose into the clear frosty sky,

> *...at my feet*
> *Rested a silent sea of hoary mist.*
> *A hundred hills their dusky backs upheaved*
> *All over this still ocean; and beyond,*
> *Far, far beyond, the solid vapours stretched.*
> *In headlands, tongues, and promontory shapes,*
> *Into the main Atlantic.....*

Mount Snowdon section from *The Prelude*,
William Wordsworth.

The stars flashed bright in the absence of the moon. How small a summit for so large a mountain! A cloud-wave broke coldly over the summit, and with a shudder we dived into the warmth of the tent. It may be remarked that winter camping (with a high-altitude tent) is by no means uncomfortable, provided that ground insulation is achieved. On this occasion the tent fabric was rapidly sealed by a wind-proof layer of ice; outside, the ice-axes were thickly encrusted with delicate fog crystals. Once we were comfortably settled in our sleeping-bags, the crackling of the ice-skin as the wind shook the canvas and the strangely soothing noise of drifting snow were delightful to listen to; they kept us reminded of our airy situation. The morrow was a grand day of rolling mists and warm colours; a day that effectively dispels the common illusion that winter colours are only black and white. They were, in fact, more rich and varied than those of summer. "

After a week of frost, I rejoiced at the prospect of a further attempt on S-C, and the following week-end joined Murray and Dunn at Lagangarbh. We went to Coire nan Lochan that night in order to get an early start in the gully. The frozen loch, covered with snow, made an excellent camping site. The night was still.

Through breaks in the grey sky streamers of aurora were flickering. The towering cliffs seemed infinitely remote and awesome in their grandeur; their details were outlined in ice. He would be insensitive indeed who, looking on that scene, failed to understand why Byron asked,

"Are not the mountains, waves, and skies a part / Of me and of my soul, as I of them?"

That night, however, the weather broke; a blizzard came up from the east. S-C had to wait for another day. In the morning we saw the gully; the lower 250 feet was continuous ice:

Between those hanging rocks that shock yet please the soul.
Charming the eye with dread . . .
Horribly beautiful.

A fortnight later H. W. Tilman, who had come north to lecture on Nanda Devi, joined Murray and myself. We made an early start from Lagangarbh. The hills were in a happy mood; white clouds were herded peacefully by the west wind, and in S-C we were sheltered.

Murray avoided the first ice-pitch by very difficult rocks on the left, and a further run-out took him to the rock-belay below the 70-foot pitch. Tilman and I joined him and prepared for a long wait. Above us Murray traversed right, onto the ice-pitch, and looked up. A pause, and he cut up out of sight, using the short axe.

The gully walls rose steeply to imprison us. Ice-chips raced in a steady stream down the ribbon of ice and disappeared over the lip of the pitch below. They made a pleasant, tinkling, swishing sound as they went. The mist opened. The sun shone on the white crest of the Aonach Eagach, the lower slopes of which were rich brown. Cloud shadows moved leisurely. How pleasing was the blue of the sky above the white pitch and the black rock walls! A fleecy cloud rushed over the top, and, watching it, I nearly overbalanced. The mist closed in again, and we were conscious only of the pitch. For a long time the ice-chips still sped downwards; intermittently the rope ran out a few more inches.

The crux was at the very top of the pitch where an ice-bulge had to be removed before the staircase could be continued. The strain must have been cruel after so much one-armed cutting, but it is characteristic of great ice-pitches that they must be "forced".

Of another place Tilman wrote: "I will not guess at the angle for fear of being called a liar, but it seemed to me that a man with a long nose, standing upright, could have wiped it on the snow." I myself can affirm that on this pitch my nose did touch the snow, but whether this was due to the excessive angle of the pitch or length of my nose, I know not; one unkind critic has even suggested that perhaps I didn't stand quite upright. The ice-pitch surmounted, we moved together up to the cornice, which was small and gave no trouble.

What a joy to tread on the level summit! No longer now the need to place the feet precisely. After the confines of the gully, how vast the expanse of sky! The shades of blue and green in Loch Linnhe were superbly delicate, and lower Glencoe was bathed in warm and kindly colours. For long, hard hours the mountain had kept us, body and mind, to one single task. Released, we found our senses keener and our vision widened; we perceived new subtle harmonies in common things. The mountain had been gracious. We stood, not conquerors but by permission, on the summit; and we had tasted true joy – for surely to climb a mountain is to serve it.

★★★★★

Christmas 1946

In pencil, Donald wrote two postcards to his parents from Achnasheen, Wester Ross Christmas 1946. At the outset, he joined a meet of the Scottish Mountaineering Club.

Postcard 1

I arrived at Fort William on Friday as planned and trekked up Glen Nevis to Steall. It was quite dark coming through the gorge and with much ice was quite "interesting". A good fire waited and a meal was soon prepared. The hut has a wonderful situation with a fine view of the famous waterfall. Saturday and Sunday were wet; most of those attending the meet went off. Nobody climbed. Monday was perfect. We left the hut about 9 a.m. (Malcolm and I were the only people left) and had a good day on the Grey Corries i.e. the hills between the Nevis group and Loch Treig. We climbed Sgurr Choinnich Beag, Sgurr Choinnich Mor, Stob Coire an Easain, Stob Coire Claurigh (3858 ft) and Stob Ban. Altogether about 7 mile ridge walking mostly above 3000ft over crisp snow with magnificent views which occasional mist only enhanced e.g. we saw a good Brocken Spectre. We saw the sun set from Stob Ban and then had a long trek back to Steall.

After packing, having a meal and clearing out the hut we set out down Glen Nevis. We had intended spending the night at the Youth Hostel but as it was rather late we bivouacked in an open shed between Polldubh and Steall. 20 degrees of frost was registered in the district. Before dawn we started off again and had breakfast at Fort William.

Malcolm set off by motor bike. I got the 11:30a.m. Inverness bus. The roads were iced so Malcolm joined the bus at Fort Augustus where we had lunch.

Postcard 2

I am writing this on the Inverness-bound train. On Christmas Day Malcolm and I got the Torridon bus to an uninhabited cottage that I had been told of. It was very comfortable and we had a good dinner.

Menu:
Sardines on toast with peanut butter
Beans
Chicken with roast potatoes and gravy
Christmas pudding with semolina sauce and rum butter
Coffee with biscuits and cheese

On Thursday we climbed Liathach (3,456 ft) and had some step-cutting on the ridge. Although at times it was wet and it was more misty than not, the cloud effects were very fine. We were occasionally in the air and got superb views in glimpses.

On Friday we climbed Ben Eighe and although we got pretty wet, had quite an alpine day.

This morning we got the 9:45 a.m. bus to Achnasheen and caught the 12:30 Inverness- bound train. We will get the Fort William bus and will probably go to Kinlochleven for the night. We will climb tomorrow and go to Dalmally on Monday, returning to Edinburgh on Thursday.

I enclose my ration card for this week which will be overdue when you get it, but as the coupons are not dated, perhaps you can do something about it.

Cheerio, Donald.

Quotations abbreviated from Chapters 4 and 9 of Undiscovered Scotland *by W.H. Murray by kind permission of the owner, Anne Murray.*

Bill Murray, Donald's good friend, climbing tutor and companion wrote:

Chapter 4

"I had never been to Glen Affric never even seen a map of it, nor read as much as chapter. Rumours reached me of its being the most beautiful of all Scottish glens… I explained this sorry state of affairs to my friend Donald McIntyre, whom I met one morning in mid-April at Fort William.

To my great delight his frame of mind was much like mine. Glen Affric? Yes, he'd love to go there. But did he know anything about it? Well, only that Gladstone had once been taken to the end of Loch Beneveian and there been so affected by the view that he'd raised his top-hat."

From Chapter 9

"On one of those protracted May evenings, when the sun shines long and low up the fifteen miles of the glen and the white foam on the River Coe takes an unaccustomed sparkle, McIntyre and I crossed the ford below Coire nan Lochan. This undertaking was no light one. We were heavily loaded, the river was high and twenty yards wide, and our route lay over the tops of spray-splashed boulders, irregularly dotting the water in a long, curved line down-stream. Of all boulder-hoppers McIntyre is the most expert. He learned the art in the Cairngorms at the age of sixteen. Accordingly, while I dallied on the brink, searching for my non-existent courage, McIntyre gave his amazing display of animal grace. From boulder to foam-washed boulder he leapt like an antelope, but with the speed of a gazelle, coming down always at the right angle to make his instantaneous spring for the staggered stone ahead. His rucksack seemed to serve all the better for its weight to steady and ballast him. The exhibition must have given him a tensely thrilling enjoyment, because on reaching the far side he strolled off with studied nonchalance, not looking back, to signify that all this was a mere nothing. I smiled delightedly at his high spirits. I was duly impressed. I was even inspired to follow, like the common goat…

…The next morning was dry so we rose early…the sun was already warming the uppermost rocks of the East Cliff (Aonach Dubh) and every detail of its face was clear and precise in the hard morning light. We examined the rock intently…indeed we had no clear idea as yet what the qualities of the rock might be…then well to the left of the Bow, we saw the Bow-string – a long chimney starting about a hundred feet up the face. If we could reach it the route would go.

The leading of the Bow-string was to be McIntyre's work, his first essay on unclimbed rock, and so it was a great occasion. For the highest delight that rock-climbing offers is searching out one's own way on crags unknown to men – doubt of the issue, encounter with the unexpected, the sense of exploration.

…. (Later that day) McIntyre led the first half of the Quiver and I the second half. The rock had become exposed by the time we hauled ourselves on to the big platform on top. I looked up and confess to a twinge of conscience at encouraging McIntyre to face as leader the dire troubles in front. But I need not have worried. He is a geologist – the Ideal Geologist made flesh. Rock in any shape or form, at whatever angle, is the delight of his heart. He loves rock, in all circumstances. If he were ever about to fall off an overhang he would, just before parting company with the rock, draw his tongue over the surface to bring out the colour. I have observed him do this at other times and feel quite confident he would do it then.

'Your lead, Donald' I commiserated. 'Bad luck.'

Looking all the while keenly up at the cliff, he swung his waist-knot to the rear, and his mouth tightened. He was in good training, I reflected, watching the spare face and clear eye. That would help him much when his situation became hopeless and he had to come down; for such seemed the likely end to his efforts.... Both to the right and directly above, the drag was impossibly smooth. On our left, however a ledge ran diagonally up the wall for several feet...To this edge he slowly scrambled and vanished beyond. My heart bled for him, especially when the rope continued to run out for another score of feet...but still the rope ran out, and at no funereal pace.

'Come on!' came the distant shout. I picked my way to the edge, passed cautiously round and found myself on a smooth precipice. Running diagonally up and across, an unbroken thread of superb holds curved all the way to the top...If we met no difficulties neither did we feel disappointment. We were charmed."

"......The climbing was hard.....I was overjoyed when I reached the corner, and so was McIntyre judged by the sparkle in his eye as he lifted himself up out of space. "A severe!" he exclaimed. "On the first ascent," I agreed – "less another time". He took the lead and passed on to a second corner; his final move was an exit over the right wall, his body curved over thin air while he wrestled with awkward rock. We returned to our bivouac and supper. The cliffs across the ravine now wore a very different look to our appreciative eyes. The inscrutable visage of unknown crag in the morning had been transformed in a twinkling to a friendly and open face. 'Come back,' they said, 'often'."

First published in Undiscovered Scotland, *Dent, London 1951 and currently in print in the compilation:* Mountaineering in Scotland/ Undiscovered Scotland *Diadem London, 1980, presently available in trade paperback published by Baton Wicks, London, 1997 (ISBN 1-898573-23-9 © Anne Murray)*

This personal letter to Donald is probably the only full record of an accident in the French Alps (see Magic of the Hills *above)* Lochwood, 26 Aug 1947.

Thank you for your letter. I think you were very wise not to go up the Zinal Rothorn by any route, with or without a guide. And I do indeed wish I had been there. Providing that we have enough money left by next summer would you climb with me in the Alps? I really don't mind where, so long as you're there.

I was delighted with your father's visit, and that of your mother and Sheila. They got a good day – in fact for 6 continuous weeks no rain at all has fallen in the west highlands, and there has been bright sun every day at Lochgoilhead. It is an indescribably beautiful country in these conditions. Anyhow, a visit by your people, and especially Sheila, always bucks me up enormously. I feel happy and therefore look fit. But most of the time since coming home I have felt rather weary and my head has been apt to ache – not at all "painfully", but quite quietly.

Last Sunday I got Bill Mackenzie and Archie Macalpine, who used to be the strongest climbing team in Scotland in pre-war days, to lead me up the Crowberry by Greig's Ledge. It was a perfect day. Rocks were hot to handle. But I felt just as I did when led up my first rock-climb. The environment seemed strange and I felt the exposed bits. But later I began to take my holds well. One snag was that I couldn't look vertically up, nor turn to one side without a grating noise at the base of my skull, accompanied by pain. But the Buachaille gave me a gift – I met Martin Nichols on the Crowberry! He is the brain specialist at Killearn Hospital who is already beginning to steal Dott's thunder. He does the surgery, with the aid of a radiologist, a psychiatrist and sundry others. They do nothing but head injuries, tumours and the like. I made an appointment.

Today they x-rayed my head from every angle – about 12 photos. I have a bad fracture extending 4 inches from the left temple to the ear. It is still unhealed, but ought to close in another fortnight. The pain at the skull-base was due only to torn muscles. They were horrified at the medical inefficiency of the French doctors.

For 5 days after the accident my left eye was closed with congealed and clotted blood. The French doctors made no move to clean it until I insisted. The eye was then found to be suffused below the surface with internal blood-flow – one of the certain symptoms of skull-fracture. Yet even then they did not bother about an x-ray! Again, during these 5 days, in fact 8 days, the slightest sun touching my head caused dizziness and sickness. I told them, but they didn't even examine the head wounds. Michael, meantime, was only slowly recovering his memory, but even that was of no interest to them.

I don't think I ever gave you an exact account of the accident. Firstly, we had 10 days very hard climbing in very good weather (saving the Meije). On 20th July we bivouacked 3 days at 10,000 feet beside the Glacier Coste Rouge, below the north wall of the Ailefroide. While there we did the Coste Rouge Arete, which was last done by Peter Lloyd and Tony Dummet in 20 hrs with a summit bivouac. Thanks to a brilliant lead by Barford we got up in 12 hours. I did not enjoy this climb. It was most exacting. The summit view was wonderful, and the most extensive I've ever seen.

Thereafter we decided to do the Barre Noir of the Ecrins (a vs), and depart for Mont Blanc and the Innominata. This meant ascending the Glacier Coste Range to the Col Coste Range of the Ailefroide, then descending the far side to the Glacier Noir. We made the col at 9am on 23rd July. The descent lay down a 400 foot couloir with a bergschrund to the Glacier. Angle 45 degrees. No trace of stone-fall. Could normally be ascended at any time of the day. We put on crampons, roped, and started down – myself first, then Michael, then John. Almost immediately snow balled on John's crampons. He slid down. Michael drove in his axe and belayed. But he held the rope at the axe-head (!) and the leverage snapped his shaft at the middle when the jerk came. He was dragged off and they both came on my own axe-belay. The snow was firm, but not hard-frozen. When the strain came my axe was pulled from the vertical to the horizontal position, and then just came out. I was pulled off. But meantime we were all braking with our picks, and the combined effort brought us to a halt in 50 or 60 feet. Michael's balaclava had come off but stopped lower down. This was to save my own life in a few minutes time.

We continued down. We had gone down 200 feet when a great stone peeled of the wall of the Ailefroide. It came for us but we all dodged and it sailed into the bergschrund. John` called "Steinschlag!" and laughed. The next instant a score of big stones again fell from the Ailefroide. They came straight at us. I had just picked up Michael's balaclava and stuck it on my head. The next moment the party was struck and fell together. We whizzed down to the bergschrund. Then I felt a terrible wrench on the shoulders and found myself swinging in mid-air. I swung for 10 minutes, being hopelessly blind through dizziness and blood flowing into my eyes. Then after 10 minutes of frantic struggling I pulled myself to the top of the bergschrund, and realised that I had been jammed in a narrow lip of it. The others were below. No sign of life. I climbed 10 feet back into the 'schrund and found John on a narrow ledge. He was dead. He had been hit by a boulder on the right temple and his skull was smashed. I climbed down another 5 feet and found Michael. He was conscious and moving, but terribly gashed about the head. He too was jammed in a narrow neck of the 'schrund. After a long struggle I helped him to climb up to the top. His balaclava had saved me from even worse injuries than he had suffered himself.

We rested, then climbed down to the Glacier Noir. I couldn't tell how long we should last without collapse, the glacier was long and crevassed, and I was perversely carrying down my bergen despite the blood loss. Michael had utterly lost his memory. He didn't know what country we were in, nor with whom he had been climbing, nor what had happened. No matter how often he was told he immediately forgot and asked again. Then I saw a lone Frenchman on the other side of the glacier. He was heading for another easy pass to La Berarde. I blew my whistle, which I had carried for 12 years without ever using it. I used it now. He came over. He was an obviously efficient climber. I told him about the accident. I explained (what was obvious from the blood alone) that we were unsure of reaching Ailefroide village without help and guidance, and that John was dead in the bergschrund. He gave us a drink of wine. But he said very politely that he was bound for La Berarde, and therefore regretted that he could not descend with us. In short he couldn't have cared less, and went on his own way.

Michael and I descended alone in 7 hours, and then more or less collapsed. We were removed by ambulance to Gap. Before I did collapse I got the guides and instructed them precisely where to get John. This they did next day. He was brought down and buried at the village of Saint Antoine. The guides submitted a bill for 100,000 francs = £200.

The doctors stitched up Michael and dressed my own wounds. We got no further examination, and were not once washed during our stay of 10 days. They too could not have cared less. The nuns, however, were exceedingly kind to us and fed us well. But we were very glad to see you.

On reaching London I saw G.W.Y (Geoffrey Winthrop Young). He is going to ask Tony Dummett to be Secy. of the BMC. But T.D. may not agree.

Last weekend Douglas Scott led the most direct route up the waterslide of Weeping Wall. He found good small holds all the way – perfect rock. The slabbiness was pure deception. That East Face is a remarkable place. He classifies it as v.d. in rubbers with one severe move. Hamish Hamilton tried the unclimbed gully in Glen Etive. He drove in 9 pitons but failed to get up.

My book now comes out in 2 days – before you get this. They have given it the best quality production given to any Dent book since 1939. The binding is excellent.

Good luck, Yours, Bill.

Donald's Memorial Tribute to W.H. (Bill) Murray, OBE., Honorary President, Scottish Mountaineering Club, 26 March 1996

There is a region of heart's desire
free for the hand that wills;
land of the shadow and haunted spire,
land of the silvery glacier fire,
land of the cloud and the starry choir
magical land of hills;
loud with the crying of winds and streams,
thronged with me fancies and fears of dreams.

There are perils of knightly zest
fit for the warrior's craft;
pitiless giants with rock-bound crest,
mystical wells for the midnight rest,
ice-crowned castles and halls, to test
steel with the ashen shaft;
realms to be won by the well-swung blow,
rest to be earned from the yielding foe.

> *All that the wanderer's heart can crave,*
> *life lived thrice for the lending,*
> *hermit's vigil in dreamlit cave,*
> *gleams of the vision that Merlin gave,*
> *comrades till death, and a wind-swept grave,*
> *joy of the journey's ending -:*
> *Ye who have climbed to the great white veil,*
> *Heard ye the chant? Saw ye the Grail?*

[These stanzas are from 'Knight Errantry' in Collected Poems of Geoffrey Winthrop Young, published by Methuen & Co. Ltd, London. 1936.] The poem has 10 stanzas, of which these are numbers 7, 8, & 10. Bill used stanzas 7, 8,9, & 10 preceding the acknowledgements in Mountaineering in Scotland and he acknowledged Mr Geoffrey Winthrop Young's permission to reprint them.

GWY was born in 1876 and died in 1958. He was "one of the greatest mountaineers that Britain has produced". He lost a leg in the First World War.

Bill introduced me to GWY's poetry, which have had a profound influence on me. Although the *Collected Poems* of GWY was out of print, I wrote to the publisher and was fortunate in acquiring two copies.

I still have copies of two other GWY books: *Mountain Craft* (1920, which was my textbook) and *On High Hills* (1927). I gave Bill my copy of *The Grace of Forgetting* (GWY's autobiography).

A signed photograph of W.H. Murray had a special place in my father's study: the bearded, somewhat ascetic face of a man who had been an elder in my father's congregation. I gave Bill that picture of his grandfather.

I have several photographs of Bill, including his passport photograph dated June 47 – it was for his first post-war expedition to the Alps. One, with the hood of his anorak over his head, reminds me that Bill spent time at a Benedictine monastery.

I met Bill at the JMCS meet at Kingshouse in 45, a few months after his release from prisoner-of-war camp. I immediately started climbing with him on weekends through the great winters of 46 and 47. Bill waited for me at Queen Street station with his old Morris eight and gave me a camp-bed at his mother's house, which was then Bill's home. When Bill and his mother moved to Loch Goil, my sister stood in for me and scrubbed the floors. Unfortunately the water came through between the floorboards to the rooms below.

Bill was ten years older than me, and was like an older brother – or like a kindly master with a novice. I was keen to learn, and he to teach. His smiles at my struggles and enthusiasms come through whenever he writes about our comradeship. Of our week in Glen Affric, before the dam was built, he wrote:

"Having no plates we ate straight out of the pot, keeping pace with each other in spoonfuls. In its detail this way of feeding gives illuminated glimpses into a man's character. A valuable essay could be written on the subject, with a long and learned title."

O death, where is thy sting? O grave, thy victory?

In the summer of '47 I went to Switzerland to spend a year studying Alpine tectonics. On the point of leaving, I learned that Bill was in hospital after a serious accident in the French Alps. I flew from Edinburgh to Basel and made my tortuous way to Gap, where I found Bill and Michael Ward still in blood-soaked clothes. They had been climbing with John Barford on the Ailefroide when they were struck by falling rocks. Bill and Michael had fractured skulls. Michael – with whom I had climbed on Nevis – had no idea who I was. John Barford was dead.

When I visited Bill four years ago in the Vale of Leven hospital, he was gravely ill. He had little strength to speak, but he told me he was going to die. Indeed the doctors thought this very likely. Bill looked on death, and indeed on every eventuality, with a quite extraordinary composure. He knew no fear.

Sitting in a slit-trench at dusk waiting to be overrun by the 15th Panzer Division, Bill systematically destroyed everything of use to the enemy. He came across an address book: every name in it was the name of a mountaineer. He reflected on how much he had learned from these men, and been given by them, and thought how little he had been able to give in return.

Bill wouldn't want us to mourn *for* him! As an experienced mystic, he was confident that through death he would arrive at a higher level of perception and adoration.

Integer vitae scelerisque purus

*The man whose way of life is characterised by moral integrity,
and whose heart is pure,
needs not the weapons of lesser mortals …*

Bill exemplified the truth of Horace's words. He trained himself to develop Purity, Fearlessness, Truthfulness, Selflessness, Humility, and Love of all fellow creatures. Again and again Bill advised us that "Our search for beauty on the mountain has to be a conscious one. ... Wings do not grow of their own accord".

Describing his first ascent – The Cobbler – he wrote:"The rock had beauty in it. Always before I had thought of rock as a dull mass. But this rock was the living rock, pale grey and clean as the air itself, with streaks of shiny mica and white crystals of quartz. It was a joy to handle such rock and feel the coarse grain under the fingers. From that day I became a mountaineer."

A fellow prisoner-of-war encouraged Bill in meditation, which Bill continued to practice for the rest of his life. He also contributed two breath-taking articles to the SMC Journal: 'The Evidence of Things not Seen' in 1946 and 'The Approach Route to Beauty' in 1948.

"May it not be possible", he wrote, "by some practical method to help one's mind to grow in awareness of beauty, to develop that faculty of perception which we frustrate and stunt if we do not exercise? The answer is that growth may be given to the spiritual faculty as simply as growth and health are given to the body – by awakening it from slumber, and providing nourishment and then by giving hard exercise. In this work there is no static position; one goes on, or one drops back. Therefore, and above all – persist."

My mind fills with memories of being on mountains with Bill. A storm on the Matterhorn, and climbing SC Gully (joined by Tilman) were notable occasions. Another classic climb was Crowberry Gully jointly with Bill Murray and Bill Mackenzie. But there were two supreme days – or rather nights. The first was a winter camp on the summit of Bidean nam Bian, when on a moonlit night we found ourselves above the clouds.

"The most acutely difficult expedition to achieve on mountains in this country", Bill wrote, "is a moonlight climb in winter... The problem is to combine leisure with a full moon, a hard frost, and a clear sky...

Success needs patience, long and persistent patience... But at last the record frost of February '47 brought the long-sought opportunity."

In *Undiscovered Scotland* (Chapter 6 – Night and Morning on the mountains), Bill goes on to describe how we traversed the Aonach Eagach ridge from east to west, then from west to east, and waited on the summit of Meall Dearg for the dawn. For Bill "Corrie and mountain are the natural altars of the earth, to be used as such before one goes".

I was privileged to share the experience with him. Wearing our padded flying suits, we sat down facing east.

"We fell still. We drove from our heads every thought of self and simply observed the scene detachedly, allowing it, and nothing else, to flow into us." "We knew, as surely as men know anything on earth, that the implacable hunter had drawn close. One's ear caught the ringing of His footstep; and one's eye, *gleams like the flashing of a shield.*"

In *The Evidence of Things not Seen,* Bill wrote:

"Unlike the Lady of Shalott I failed to break the spell and gaze straight upon the ultimate reality; yet the hills that night were big with it; its signs unmistakable. It is this that mountaineers style the mystery of hills. Put more broadly, it is the mystery of my universe, where the forms of man or mountain may be likened to veils that reveal its being and yet mask the true essence." "Something in that night cried out to us: that the world was full of a Divine splendour, which must be sought within oneself before it might be found without: that our task was to see and know. From the deeps of the earth to the uttermost star above, the whole creation had throbbed with a full and new life; its music one song of honour to the beautiful; its Word, Holy, holy, holy, Lord God of hosts, heaven and earth are full of Thy glory ..."

"Sunrise opened the final movement..... The act of adoration had begun, for this was the sun's hour of morning song. In that we shared; for we could say to ourselves: We had stood as sure stars stand, and moved as the moon moves, loving the world."

> *The world is charged with the grandeur of God.*
> *It will flame out, like shining from shook foil.*

from *God's Grandeur* by Gerard Manley Hopkins.

"We had set out in search for adventure and we had found beauty. Thus we had found them both in their fuller sense; for in the architecture of hill and sky, as in great art and music, there is an everlasting harmony with which our own being had this night been made one. What more may we fairly ask of mountains?"

"The truth is that in getting to know mountains a man gets to know himself. That is why men truly live when they climb."

Bill concluded this account with these words: "We came down in the forenoon to a point about a thousand feet above the Glencoe road. We found a patch of sun-bathed turf, on which we curled up side by side. There kept running through my head, between waking and sleeping, a recently read verse:

> *Thou shouldst die as he dies,*
> *For whom none sheddeth tears;*
> *Filling thine eyes*
> *And fulfilling thine ears*
> *With the brilliance ... the bloom*
> *and the beauty," ...*★★★

This is precisely what Bill Murray did. And it's his wish for us.

★★★from *The Death of Meleager by* Algernon Charles Swinburne (1837-1909)

Chapter 5
Switzerland

Tis morn: with gold the verdant mountain glows;
More high, the snowy peaks with hues of rose
Far stretched beneath the many-tinted hills,
A mighty waste of mist the valley fills,
A solemn sea whose vales and mountains round
Stand motionless, to awful silence bound;

The Alps from Descriptive Sketches'
by William Wordsworth (1770-1850)

Note: Occasionally, from Neuchâtel on very clear days, the peaks of
the Alps can be seen piercing through "a mighty waste of mist".

Introduction

Just as Professor Holmes predicted, Donald's year in Switzerland was one of
several significant turning points.

In July 1947, on this – his very first expedition away from Scotland – Donald
left Edinburgh to travel to via Paris on a day so hot that people there were said to
be frying eggs directly on the pavement! Instead of squeezing bulky winter clothes
into a suitcase, Donald decided to simplify matters to travel wearing much of his
heavy gear. He too was almost fried alive!

The year was filled with new experiences. By coincidence, Donald's mother had
a distant cousin whose home was in Neuchâtel, so Donald spent the year living
happily in the Christens' home and came to feel very much a part of their family.
And others considered it be a remarkable achievement that, from the outset,
Donald enjoyed good rapport with Professor Wegmann – this was certainly not an
experience to be taken for granted!

Letters Home

Donald wrote to his parents while staying with Professor Wegmann at a
pension in the village of Zinal, 10th August 1947.

I have now been here for nearly a fortnight. What are my impressions of Switzerland? First, of all I think that it is neither so grand nor so wild as Scotland. The whole country is so cultivated and tamed! Even at an altitude of nearly 2,500m yesterday we could not drink the water of a burn because there were alps and cattle still higher up.

With the famous Valais (i.e. a section of the valley of the Rhone) I was definitely disappointed. No snowy peaks were to be seen; vineyards rose in tiers as high as the eye could see, and, of course, the river was grey with mud. Once at the level of the glaciers, however, it is as different matter, it is very magnificent. Indeed yesterday I thought that our view of the Dent Blanche compared favourably with that of the North-East Buttress of Ben Nevis in full winter conditions!

Food is arranged on a very different system from Scotland. At 7 a.m. we have petit dejeuner, which is tres petit! This consists of white coffee, two rolls and butter and jam. All in excellent quality, but, of course, here in Switzerland sugar is not taken with white coffee. I have become quite used to that now! As a matter of fact there are quite a few things to "get used to" but this does not take long. At first I thought the bread was very poor compared with ours, and I have not been impressed by the renowned cheese.

The first packed lunch that I had contained uncooked bacon and some terrible-looking meat. Having no cooking facilities I was about to throw them away when I was told that they were exceptionally good and concentrated, and moreover, were sufficiently cooked. I am now glad when I see them in my lunch!

In Neuchâtel we have a good lunch at 12:15. Here at Zinal we take packed lunch with us. Nothing is eaten until supper at 7 p.m. There is a good three course meal, always rounded off with fruit. In the food line, it is the abundance of fruit, the fresh butter and the jam which have impressed me most. This evening meal finishes the day for we go to bed very early in Switzerland. At Zinal I have been in bed by 9 p.m. every night!

Neuchâtel itself is a very pleasant, clean little town nicely situated on the steep slope down to the lake. There is a little harbour and besides some fairly large paddle steamers, there are numerous yachts, rowing boats, motor boats etc.

The buildings, especially the public buildings are very fine. Only as few of the larger houses have gardens but there are many beautiful, small public gardens. The houses are all shuttered because when it is hot, it is very hot. When I was in Neuchâtel the daily variation in temperature was about 70-100 degrees.

The shops are full of beautiful things but with very few exceptions, everything is much more expensive than in Britain, and I can see already that it will be only with difficulty that my money will last out a full year.

I do not find the people here to be so wonderfully polite as I had been told they were. In fact the habit of addressing everyone from Professor Wegmann to the scavenger as "Monsieur" may be democratic, "if everyone is somebody then no one's anybody!" There is no equivalent to our "sir". I have not found either that everyone is a linguist. Very few have more than French and German, and the majority know only one of these languages. I have found that this is so even at the train information offices and at customs.

I do not mean to imply that the Swiss are either impolite or dirty, for they are not, but for Swiss people in Britain to complain about the cleanliness of hotels and restaurants, and about the quality of the food and of the cooking – as I have heard them do – is quite ridiculous. I certainly have not found any of these things to be better in Switzerland than I would expect for the same price in Scotland.

Having given you some notion of my general impressions – which sound unfavourable simply because it is what you expect, but do not find, which impresses most – I will now try to tell you how I have spent my time.

I have already told you of my journey to Neuchâtel and of my subsequent trip to Gap *(where Bill Murray and Michael Ward were both in hospital after a mountaineering accident.)*

I arrived back in Switzerland on Friday 1st. What an extraordinary day the 1st of August is in Switzerland! Although it is the National Holiday everyone works as usual. In the evening speeches were made; the band played; flags were paraded; fireworks were everywhere; all the lights were on; and everyone was gay – not in a rowdy fashion. After listening to the speeches I went out in the lake on one of the boats with the Christens. There were hundreds of boats – big and small, and all with lanterns. The moon was full and was really yellow. The air was warm and quite still – apart from the noise of the fireworks! Colourful fireworks were going off contin-uously; some of the buildings in the town were floodlit.

The climax of the evening was at about 10 o'clock. The lights along the front were all put out and an official firework display began. The fireworks were mainly fire rockets which were fired in pairs, one from each side of the harbour. There was an amazing variety and the crowd in our boat positively gasped at the beauty of some of the rockets, and the boat was tilted over at 45 degrees to the landward side!

Everyone dispersed quietly and most people went to bed quite early. In the morning everything was as clean as ever and there was not a trace of the big bonfire beside the harbour.

On Tuesday 5th Professor Wegmann and I left for Zinal. We took the train to Sierre, changing at Lausanne. Unfortunately the train was half an hour late and our bus did not wait for us, so we had to spend the night in Sierre.

At 8:30 in the morning we got the bus to Ayer. There is a very stiff pull up (Zinal is 3,000ft above Sierre) which was managed by an amazing series of hairpin bends. Sitting in the bus I could see them all from the top-one. One bus every three years fails to arrive at its destination; fortunately it was not ours!

The buses have most remarkable horns; they sound just like the old post horns! Having climbed up into the Val d'Anniviers we found that more excitement was in store. Two tributary ravines have cut the most tremendous gorge and the road is cut out of the solid rock rounds the walls. This is the gorge of the Pontis. The road passes through tunnels from time to time.

The gorge of the Pontis passed, we had a fine view of the glaciers and of the high mountains. At Ayer the bus stops and we had to walk to Zinal; this takes about 2 hours if you are loaded. It is as pleasant path through the pines with nice views of the river. Zinal is quite a small place – I have sent you a card of it so you will have a good idea what it is like. This hotel is cheap (as hotels go) and somewhat crude, but the food is good and the beds are comfortable.

We have been out every day except Sunday and although we have never gone far as mileage goes, we have climbed up about 3,000 feet every day. We generally get very fine view of the Dent Blanche and the Weisshorn, and we saw the Matterhorn the other day. Professor Wegmann has not been too well recently so he does not expect to go above the snow-line this time. I hope that someone else will turn up so that I can get a day or two's climbing.

The geology here is very interesting and very complicated; it is most instructive to watch Prof. W tackle it. He has a good sense of humour and we get on well together.

Ma Hsing-Yuan, the PhD geology student from Beijing, China – was nicknamed "Henry" by Donald's sister Sheila. Donald usually referred to him as Ma – the Chinese word for horse – and in due course, we both came to know his daughter – Ma Li.

To his parents, 12 October 1947:

Henry's first words on arriving here were that he had been commissioned from everyone at home to find out what was wrong with me – I was criticising everything. Actually I simply recorded my (subjective) impressions (and stressed this in my letters). If I said that I found Switzerland more tame and cultivated than Scotland, I stated a fact; that is what I found. Incidentally, other people have said the same, but, though I am supported there in my judgment by others, that is irrelevant; I stated my impressions. In doing this I made no attempt to make absolute pronouncements: to say that because I found Switzerland to be less wild than Scotland, it was necessarily worse because of that, and that must agree with me.

If people don't want to hear my impressions then it saves me the bother of writing them. *(This is a sentence of some significance. Donald quickly sensed when he was not holding the attention of his "audience" and responded accordingly.)*

You ask about my research. Strictly speaking I am not doing any research at all, and I don't see any prospect of doing any in the immediate future. Apart from languages, my geological aims are

i.   To learn Professor Wegmann's techniques in tectonic (structural geology) analysis. This I have begun seriously and I am spending a lot of time on it.

ii. To learn more than I know already about optical mineralogy. The main thing here was the Fedorf stage and that is really accomplished already.

iii. To learn something first-hand about the geology of Switzerland. This involves reading but is mainly field-work.

iv.   To read as much as possible (French and German) on any subject on which there is literature in the geology library here which is not readily obtainable in Edinburgh.

Perhaps next spring, I might do some original work on tectonic analysis myself. Perhaps, too, I might go to Geneva or elsewhere to do some original work on optical mineralogy. If not I don't expect to do any research at all.

Letter to his mother, 18 November 1947

......Last Wednesday Professor Wegmann left for a short convalescence, and he may be returning at the end of the week. He hopes to start his lectures next week. Unfortunately for him the weather has been terrible since he left. All the depressions which you have had have come over here too, and they don't seem to have lost any force on the journey. The day he left the visibility was so extremely good as to be a bad omen; everyone tells me that it was the best visibility of the Alps for the year. You would have thought that they were only on the other side of the Lake. All the details were wonderfully clear, and the colours were wonderful also. At sunset the whole sky was flaming with bright reds.

Such superlatively clear atmosphere is always a bad sign for the weather and it broke good and proper on the Thursday. Since then we have had rain every day. Monday morning cleared up a little and it was quite cold also. But this did not last – a deep depression came up during the night and we have had our first snow here. I hear on the wireless that Britain has had snow too. Naturally it has not lasted at this altitude, and it is now raining and all the slush has melted away. Many of the Alpine passes were blocked however. The weather forecast speaks of more depressions on the way, so I think Professor Wegmann will return without having had a single decent day. Most unlucky, for he needed to get out for short walks.

On Saturday evening I attended the annual banquet of the Club Alpin Suisse, Neuchâtel section. It was well attended, but I was very sorry that Professor Wegmann was not here to have gone also. We gathered at 7 o'clock and the meal began at 7.30. It was good both in quality and quantity, and it was well served. Although I ate well I had to refuse second helpings; this amazed many of the people who were at my table, but I really think that several years of restriction feeding have decreased the size of my inside. Anyway this banquet will have stretched it out a bit.

The food stopped at about 9.15 and we remained at our tables to continue with the liquid part of the proceedings, and to be entertained by the more energetic members. There were several excellent recitations; specially outstanding were three of La Fontaine's fables, and a piece from Daudet. There was a pianist and a violinist present also and they played very well. I thought that they might have chosen pieces rather more jolly and bright, but what they did play was not too heavy.

At midnight the infirm members parted for their beds, and the remainder got down to the real business of the evening. I had made great friends with one of the members of the committee who was sitting next to me. I presented him with an excellent cigar.

At 2 o'clock the officials of the hotel informed us that the appointed hour had struck. After considerable delay we left. I was invited to join the president and certain other distinguished members in a continuation of the evening's enjoyment. About 17 of us gathered in the Cellar of one of the largest of the Neuchâtel wine-producers, where we were entertained "on the house". We spent a very pleasant "evening" there before the séance broke up at 4 o'clock. Sunday morning was still wet, damp, and miserable. I went to church in the morning with Monsieur Christen at 9.30!

Extract from a letter to his father, 3 January 1948

"I was interested in Harold Nicholson's article on English difficulties for foreigners, and M. and Mme Christen are now reading it. Although some of his points are excellent and I thoroughly agree with you that he exaggerates the difficulties. I have often discussed the question here. As it is compulsory to learn German in this part of Switzerland, and as most try to learn English too, the students here can speak with authority. I have found a unanimous decision that English is child's play compared with German (this is the French-speakers' point of view).

Needless to say the higher flights of any language are difficult, and English is no exception. However, I believe H.N.'s article would have been more balanced if he had pointed out where English was easy as well as where it is difficult No declensions of the articles, no genders (i.e. artificial ones) no agreement of adjectives. These are a vast simplification in comparison to French or German! Then think of the verbs: they have good points as well as bad, and there are irregular verbs in French and German – English has no monopoly. Think for example of this:

I had gone, we had gone, he had gone, you had gone, they had gone.

What more does anyone want? In French the "had" would have changed each time: and if the person was masculine or feminine, singular or plural, the "gone" would vary too!!

With regard to prepositions I agree that English is hard, but as you point out, so is French.

Pronunciation in English is very difficult – or so we usually think. But from the number of foreigners that can pronounce English correctly, I think that we are apt to exaggerate the difficulty. Moreover, the German pronunciation in English is also found exactly the same when the Germans speak French. In other words a German who finds English pronunciation difficult also finds the French equally difficult. The trouble is in him not in the English (or the French).

....At one of the talks we had during the evenings at Grindelwald (skiing course) the padre said that all wars were evil; a soldier called to defend his country could only say to God "have pity on me". I challenged him but he didn't understand my point and I didn't follow it up because it was only a red herring – however important a one.

I have discussed the same problem with the Christens; Mme. Christen is completely in accord with me. One can never say "God have pity on me for I am going away to sin". One must decide on each group of circumstances what is the right thing to do – and then do it. This appears very elementary and axiomatic to me, but I find that it's not everyone who is in agreement. What do you think?

In a country at war each man must decide whether pacifism or war is the right path for him. He must decide this for himself. Having chosen the right path he must then walk along it. One cannot say "War is wrong in all circumstances. I am attacked; I must defend myself; God have pity on me for I have decided to sin."

I enclose 2 New Year cards. One I bought and didn't use; the other I received from the hotel at Zinal. In Switzerland they do these things very nicely. Have you ever heard of a British hotel sending out cards like that?!

Letter to his parents 10 February, 1948

"The main purpose of this letter is to tell you about a German geologist who has gone to Glasgow for three months by mistake! The mistake was that he didn't go to Edinburgh. He chose Glasgow because it is nearer Mull and Skye.

Last night at Professor Wegmann's I met Professor and Mrs Hans Cloos from Bonn. Cloos is, in my judgement, by far the best geologist in Germany. He told me that his assistant at Bonn, Wilhelm Bierther, has gone to Glasgow for three months. He couldn't stay longer because his family of three couldn't be left longer than that in Germany, and it was not possible to take them with him to Scotland.

Cloos and his students have been working on intrusive granites; i.e. on granites that have become sufficiently plastic after their formation to become mobile under pressure. There is therefore a mutual interest between his school and Edinburgh. On the other hand, Bierther worked in Greenland before the war on rocks of the same kind as we have in Skye, Mull, Ardnamurchan, etc., and as Mrs Holmes has been working on in Ireland. That is why he chose Scotland, but he made a big mistake not to come to Edinburgh.

I have already written to Mrs Holmes to tell her about Bierther and I hope that she will write to him. Will it be possible for him to get a shake-down at the manse if this should prove necessary? I will write him to tell him that this may be possible to arrange; if it is, would you please drop him a note to the Geology Department, Glasgow University, to tell him so. If he does come it would be valuable for him to meet any of the prisoners who are still in Edinburgh; I am sure that they would be interested to meet a German who has been living in Germany.

The Christens have just heard from Zermatt. The chalet for their summer holiday is going to be pretty expensive and they haven't decided whether they will take it or not. With regard to whether you should come over here in the summer, I should say definitely yes. But where to, is another matter.

By the way, I am glad to hear that the food that Ranald took home was still in an eatable condition after such a long time. Since Ranald left there has been a new decrease in rationing. Butter and milk and sugar are now off. Bread is about the only rationed food now, but I find that the ration is as much as I can eat.

The weather has remained very "soft" and the prospect of skiing on the Jura seems to be fading away altogether. January was the warmest ever recorded in Switzerland However I will get a week in the Bernina at the end of March. That is high so there will be certainly snow there. Incidentally, Monsieur Bengereull of the University is arranging a trip to the Rosablanche (3,300 m.) above Martigny at the end of this month. I hope that the weather will be good, for the view of the Pennine Alps from there should be splendid.

I was told that a lot of snow had fallen on the Jura on Saturday and that the weather report was sunshine. On Sunday morning I left on the 7.09 train to find that it was raining and misty and no snow.

I had to come back by the next train, so it was rather a waste of time. I have finished a draft of my lecture on granite and I have given it to Professor Wegmann to read. I don't know whether it is what he wants or not for it is not to a geological audience and yet he wanted it detailed.

Letter to his parents – 28 February 1948

Many thanks for your letter of the 25th. Thank you for looking up the etymology of pudding for me, and also for sending the difficult spelling words. The Christens are very interested in the list; Monsieur Christen got 6 out of 10 right, which I thought pretty good!

The weather has been extraordinarily fine for the last few days; although the south wind has been trying to set in, it has not been strong enough to do so yet. I am glad that it is not too cold with you. I am glad to hear that you have good news from the returned Germans; if the cold is bad as they are here, the living conditions will be terrible.

Perhaps it would be as well if, as you suggest, you approach Dr Peddie about my finances to find out whether any increase could be allocated. One never knows, and he might say right away either yes or no which would settle the question one way or the other. The cost of living is certainly higher here than it is at home, and I have spent £16 on transport during the last six months. This figure is really very high when you take into account that I have used cheap rates whenever possible.

Then, too, the climbing things that I bought in August were quite essential for work in the Zinal region, and if I hadn't had already considerable climbing equipment, the cost would have been a good deal more. In my application to the Exchange Control unfortunately I didn't keep a copy of this – I made no allowance for any equipment, or things like shoe repairs etc which are anything but cheap. Nor did I allow for books and maps, or even mapping paper, pencils, mapping pens and all the numerous other accessories which add to the cost of things.

Thank you for the news that I can always draw money from Mme Penard. This will make it certain that I can last the time whatever happens. Incidentally the travel costs will not be a whit less this summer; they will almost certainly be very much more. Last summer I couldn't understand many of the things that I was looking at – I mean understand from the highly technical Wegmannian point of view which I am here to learn. Now my eyes are opened a good deal wider and by the summer there will be a tremendous lot for me to do all over the country. Another point is that travelling about is usually much more expensive than staying in one place for the reason that the hotel charges vary with the time you are there. Of course, now that I am a member of the CAS I hope to save a good deal by using alpine huts.

I don't think I will go to the International Congress. The cost of staying in London will probably be prohibitive and I think that I will learn more by being in the field, either here or at home. The only advantage (and it is certainly an important one) is the opportunity to see the famous geologists from all over the world. From the point of view of the Exchange Control, I will be eligible for £35 more as a tourist. But, if they are increasing the tourist allowance (at present it is zero), I don't see why they can't increase the allowance for people who are working here. Incidentally nearly all the young English students here spend three or four times what I do, so there are always ways and means. Well I am sorry that I have filled another letter with financial topics, but it seems to be necessary.

I have no other news about my lecture on granite except that it will be given at Neuchâtel, Berne and Lausanne for sure. Prof Wegmann has given me back my draft and I have only a few excisions to make and then I will be ready when he is. However I don't think it will be before the middle of April at the soonest.

I am amused that you have been taken up by the postmark on my letter to Annette. Gibraltar is the name of the corner of Neuchâtel as Churchill is in Edinburgh. It was at the post office there that I posted her letter. Ranald knows the place – it is on the way to the Institute.

You happen to mention that you don't know what it is that I am doing as far as work is concerned, so perhaps I should explain. This I cannot do in any detail (for proof of this see the letters written to Henry [Ma of Beijing] – Sheila tells me she has already seen some of them!) One reason for this is not because of the intrinsic complication of the work, but simply that the study of folds etc is three dimensional in outlook and this is notoriously difficult to describe in two. When I get back there will be a good deal that I can explain quite easily although to do so by letter would be nearly impossible.

In the first place Professor Wegmann is one of the very few geologists who has studied structural geology as a science. Nearly everybody thinks that tectonics (ie the architecture of the earth, and in particular of mountains both modern and ancient) is a subject that any petrologist, palaeontologist, or stratigrapher can do in his spare time. For example no palaeontologist would dare to do any microscopic crystallography, for he would realise that he doesn't know very much about it. But he would never stop to think that tectonics is also a subject as complicated in its higher branches as is petrology. In fact that there are techniques to be learnt and difficulties to be overcome is simply not realised. Noel Odell (Everest etc) calls himself a tectonician because he wouldn't dare to call himself either a palaeontologist or a petrologist.

The fundamental principle in Wegmannian tectonics is the conception of a fold axis. Fold a piece of paper into an arch and the line that traces the top of the arch ("the line of highest points") is the axis of the fold. Push your hand across the tablecloth and you will see how the fold axes direct themselves at right angles to the direction of push. This elementary concept, which is the turning point of all serious structural studies and without which the structure of the Alps would still be a mystery, you will not find in a single textbook that I know of.

Make a fold out of a piece of paper and hold it so that the axis is not horizontal. Now imagine that you are looking, not at a piece of folded paper, but at the folded strata of a mountain chain. Imagine further that a river has cut a deep valley through the fold at right angles to the axial direction, You will then see that if you have examined the fold in one valley wall, and if you have measured the axial direction and dip in the field, you will be able to project the fold on to the other side of the valley and predict the outcrops there even if you had never visited it, or if it was completely covered with scree.

While I was at Zinal, Professor Wegmann found a small exposure of a very important contact, and I was very sorry we didn't have more of it, and better exposed. Professor Wegmann took a measure of the axis of the fold, and the following day led me to the other side of the valley right to the spot where the same contact was most beautifully exposed.

At the time I didn't understand what he had done and I thought that it was nothing less than miraculous – yet I don't think that I was any "dumber" than most geologists of the non "Wegmannian type" would have been.

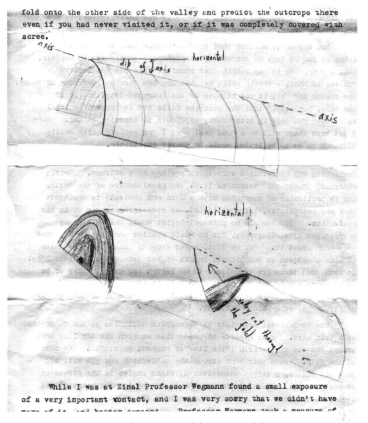

Sketch 1 from Donald's original letter.

That example will show you the way in which the concept of the axis can be important. It is obvious that for economic work (e.g. tunnels) it would prove invaluable. From the point of view of my old friend the granite, the best way of explaining the importance is by telling you what Prof. Wegmann did in Scandinavia. Just as he did in Zinal, there he was able to predict what structures were likely to be present in a region as yet unvisited. And, sometimes when he arrived in these areas at a later date he found the structure – but preserved in the heart of a granite massif. It is obvious that a magmatic granite could not show a continuity of structure like this with the surrounding sediments which it had intruded. There is a structural pattern which is continuous irrespective of the nature of the rocks traversed.

The classic example of the use of the axis is the unravelling of the structure of the Alps by Emile Argand, Professor Wegmann's teacher who was Professor here at Neuchâtel.

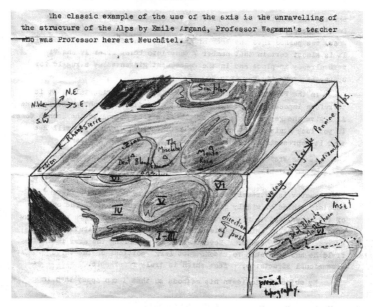

The classic example of the use of the axis is the unravelling of the structure of the Alps by Emile Argand, Professor Wegmann's teacher who was Professor here at Neuchâtel.

Sketch 2.

In the block diagram the upper face represents the geological map of the main part of the Pennine Alps. The right-hand side-face shows the axial direction for the region. This was determined by taking many measures directly in the field. For example the measure that I described Professor Wegmann as taking at Zinal was one of these. As a matter of fact his object at Zinal was to measure hundred of axes, wherever they could be found. Zinal is probably one of the most complex regions of the whole Alps, and very serious work will have to be done before the fine details become clear. But in the block diagram Argand did not take into account local variations of the axis, but employed an average for the whole region. This is a first approximation.

Using this axis he projected the upper face of the block onto the front vertical face. He therefore got an esquisse of a section through the Alps to a depth of several miles. From this section he could read off the structure of the Pennine Alps, and also the history of their origin. For example it is clear that they are made up of large recumbent folds which are "rooted" in the S.E. (See the inset showing the relation of the present topography to the massif of the Dente Blanche.) Furthermore you can see how the massif V (the Monte Rosa) was pushed into the back of massif IV (the Grand St Bernard). It is almost certain that number V came into being after IV and VI were already in place and in the consequent gigantesque struggle for space, it drove its way into number IV.

In the French Alps the axis is mostly about horizontal. It is therefore impossible there to construct a similar section. The Pennine Alps give the key to the whole of the Alps from Vienna to the French coast. If you look again at the upper face of the block diagram you will see that it represents a distorted picture of the actual section.

It was Professor Wegmann who developed these methods to the study of the highly complex Scandinavian regions where there are no high valley walls to give you sections as in the Alps. Moreover this flat country is extremely complex for there are many many different mountain chains of widely differing ages all superimposed one on top of the other, and to make matters worse, some parts are transformed into granite, and this granite has locally become sufficiently soft to intrude the rocks above. Nevertheless by measuring the axes in the field he has been able to reconstruct large portions of the three dimensional structures, a feat which is truly remarkable.

My object is to learn his methods so that I can apply them in Scotland. This has been no easy matter because Professor Wegmann is notorious here as a poor teacher. For him everything is so simple that he cannot conceive that any explanation is necessary. And what is more he is liable to become annoyed if he is questioned, for he is extremely temperamental and requires careful handling. Krank (a Finn who is Professor of physical geography here and is an excellent geologist) worked with Wegmann in Scandinavia many years ago and he tells me that Professor Wegmann has changed. He is really two individuals in one, and the proportions have changed. Sometimes it is hard to believe that he is the same person as he was an hour ago.

When I went to Zinal I knew very little about the general structure of the Alps, less about the geology of Zinal, and nothing at all about his methods, or his object in working there. Naturally I expected him in the evening to give me a short resume, to give me my geological bearings. Although he was always a most agreeable person to spend an evening with if we were discussing the relative merits of Marc and Kirsch, if I attempted to extract some geology from him he changed at once and it was impossible to continue with the subject. If he did attempt to enlighten me it was by way of analogy. His analogies are extremely good if you understand the whole position, but as a means of explanation they simply leave you more mystified than ever.

I now know that the structures at Zinal are the most complex in the Pennine Alps, and probably equal to any anywhere, so you will realise that I was rather lost. Fortunately in retrospect I can now learn a lot from that trip, but the great part was so much over my head that it was completely lost. And the annoying thing is that even in five minutes he could have explained the significance of the concept of the axis and I would have had the key. But he really isn't a teacher.

When I started work here in Neuchâtel I started with the Jura. The latter consist of folds of a relatively simple type, and there are several good sections into their interior provided by some of the rivers near here that out transverse valleys across the range; the work consisted essentially of constructing profiles (i.e. sections) across geological maps which, of course, did not show the axes directly. The object was to be able to read the axes from the map by the relation of the beds to the topography, and then to make the projection onto a vertical plane to get the section. I did three of these, in increasing difficulty before Christmas.

After doing these I began to get a much better idea of what it was all about and was ready for something more serious. Accordingly, the next exercise that I got was to draw a hypsometric map of the Hauenstein region. That is, a map showing the contours of the surface of a particular geological stratum. The result is a map which shows the folds just as a topographic map shows hills and valleys. The Hauenstein is in the Jura to the south of Bâle, and it was very well mapped some years ago. My map is based on the data of the old map. In other words it was an exercise in interpretation of a geological map.

When I came here first I expected to be given a piece of research of my own to do. Indeed Professor and Mrs Holmes also were quite astonished that Professor Wegmann didn't find me even a small problem to tackle. However I can see now that before I could reach that stage a rigorous training was necessary. I still believe that if Prof Wegmann had been a good teacher I could have made very much faster progress, but all the same there are some things that don't really become part of you until they have had a chance to soak in through a considerable period of time. At present I am interpreting the maps of others; but in every case they are first class maps. Most have taken anything from five to twenty years of fieldwork by experts to prepare. Obviously it would be quite impossible for me to do anything like that.

When I am finished with this training I will be able to read a map like no-one in Britain. This moreover means the acquiring of the ability to evaluate a map, ie the quality of its workmanship. This training allows one to appreciate the significance of every little detail on the map, and to see at once where the critical regions are. Thus in reviewing the maps of others one can take all the data from the old map and really appreciate it, and also see where it is necessary to go in the terrain to collect the critical evidence that has been missed by the other people because they didn't appreciate the significance of it.

Although the Hauenstein map was only an exercise the results are rather interesting. I can hardly claim to have been very original in its construction, but at the same time one cannot produce a map like that in an afternoon. It is therefore of some interest and we have had several copies made. I have sent two copies to Henry, one for himself and one for the department. If you see him you could ask him to show it to you if you are interested. Other copies have been sent to Professor Cloos at Bonn, and to Professor Glangeaud at Besançon.

That being finished successfully, Professor Wegmann thought that I was ready to begin on the Alps, where the structures are much more complicated than the Jura, but where there are enormous vertical exposures. An alpine geological map contains an enormous amount of information that requires a real craft to read. I am working on the massif of the Dent Blanche. If you look at the stereogram you will see that the Dent Blanche massif (vi) is like a cake sitting on top of iv (the Grand St Bernard). My object is to construct the contours of that surface of contact, ie of the base of the Dent Blanche massif. This is not confined to the area on the stereogram but is continued also to the south west.

I have already finished with the part that is in Switzerland and I am ready to begin on the Italian maps as soon as I get them. One complication is that they are to a different scale from the Swiss. I have already learnt an enormous amount from this exercise, and I feel much more confident of returning to Edinburgh with a really good and well-based knowledge of tectonics. There was a time when I began to think that I was wasting my time and the Carnegie money.

When the Dent Blanche map is finished it will be even more valuable than that of the Hauenstein, and it will have a fairly wide interest.

I hope that this more or less satisfactorily answers your query as to my work.

Monsieur Christen has just received confirmation of his chalet at Zermatt for August. It is a wonderful chalet (belonging to Faber the pencil manufacturer), and has a magnificent situation to the south of Zermatt, with a splendid view of the Matterhorn, and of the Zinal Rothorn etc., etc. Donald.

Note: Paul Gilmour, Edinburgh graduate of 1952, wrote to me in 2012:

"All these geological principles were passed to Donald through Maurice Lugeon, Emile Argand, Eugene Wegmann, to Donald McIntyre and many students, beginning with Paul Gilmour (1952); John Christie, John Howkins and David MacKenzie (all class of 1953) and Martin Kuersten (1954) and, no doubt, many others who followed during Donald's long teaching career in California and elsewhere."

I must close now. It is already Monday and the centenary of the Republic. On the 1st of March 1848 the Neuchâtelois threw off the Prussian overlordship by a bloodless revolution. (Incidentally this will give stamps posted today a special value provided that there is a lift today. I will post them at the GPO just in case, and you could give the stamps to Annette or someone who collects.)

It is a perfect spring morning with the Lake as calm as a mill pond; but unfortunately the Alps are in a haze. This morning began with a salute of guns, but I lost count of the number for they were fired so slowly (perhaps they were hundred year old guns), but they didn't fire a hundred shots. After that the church bells throughout the Canton were rung for half an hour, but I heard only the Roman Catholic church opposite as I couldn't be everywhere at the one time.

Today is not going to be a very great day. The present generation is enfeebled compared with their fathers. They consider it is too cold at this time of year to celebrate a revolution and the celebration will be in July. The revolutionaries marched across the Neuchâtel Jura, waist deep in snow, and finished by taking the château.

Letter to his parents, Neuchâtel, 23 March 1948

Many thanks for your letters which were waiting for me when I returned on Saturday night. It is certainly extraordinarily good news to hear that Sir Alexander Cross has arranged for his trustees to grant me £100; it certainly will make all the difference to the rest of my time here. I have received a very kind personal letter from him and to which I am replying this morning.

Well, I am now back from an extraordinarily interesting trip to the Bernina. I left Neuchâtel at 6 o'clock on Sunday the 14th and took the same route as Ranald knows by Zurich as far as Landquart. From there I continued south to Chur where we branched off for the Albula Pass to the Upper Engadine. It was a very interesting journey through splendid scenery, high mountains, deep gorges, etc. etc. At one part the railway climbs so steeply that there are a whole series of spiral tunnels one above the other. I arrived at Pontresina at about 2 o'clock in the afternoon and, after joining the other members of the party, we set off for the hut.

The first five miles were extremely pleasant for a sledge took our skis and rucsacs. The route went up the Roseg Valley, the view of which from Pontresina you can see in one of the enclosed postcards. Although there was snow still on the ground it was thawing for the sun is now very hot. Nevertheless there was still sufficient to make the walk through the trees very beautiful. Incidentally we passed the Engadine ski-jump on the way.

Another postcard that I have enclosed shows the view of the Sella Group and the Roseg Glacier from the valley. It is taken a short distance below where the sledge took our rucsacs. Although the peaks don't look very spectacular in the photograph they are still about 8 miles away. These peaks form the Italian frontier and rise to 3,600 m. After marching on ski to the foot of the Roseg Glacier we turned left on to the Tschierva Glacier and made our way up to the hut.

Another card shows the view of the hut and the Piz Roseg (3927 m) taken in summer. Naturally when we were there it was possible to ski on the moraine. Unfortunately I couldn't get a card of the Piz Bernina itself. It is immediately to the left of the Piz Roseg and in full view from the hut. However, I enclose a card of the Piz Bernina taken from the other side and which resembles quite closely its appearance from Tschierva.

There were about 18 of us on the course and we had two guides. For the exercises we split up into two groups, one with each guide. When we were roped we roped in groups of three, and, as it was a course to "develop the practice of ski and ski touring in high mountain, and the formation of chefs de cordée" we all took turns of leading, and the guides were never in front. The food was excellent, both in quality and quantity and we didn't need to occupy ourselves at all with that. Unfortunately, to begin with I suffered a little from the altitude and couldn't eat much. Fortunately, however, that passed after a day or two and towards the end I was feeling very fit indeed. Part of the reason for the effect of altitude was that to be free to go to the course I had been working very hard (e.g. up to midnight at the Institute).

The camp was not intended to be a rest camp and we went at it every day and all day. Generally we got up at 5 o'clock and the evening discussion of theory usually finished at 10 o'clock.

On the first day we spent the morning by traversing the glacier and by demonstrations of the way to rope up for skiing where there is danger of crevasses. In the afternoon we went up the glacier and were given an introduction to crevasse technique. Various people fell into crevasses so that we could see how to get them out. After that we descended again to the hut roped together. As you can imagine, the skiing was very different from Davos. There were no tracks, it was always fresh country, the snow was often extremely hard and extremely steep, there were the dangers of crevasses and rocks, we always skied with rucsacs, with ice-axes, crampons etc., and when you are roped together it is essential that everyone turns at the same time and doesn't fall!

The second day we made the ascent of Piz Morteratsch (3754 m). I enclose a post card which shows the bit we did to the summit after leaving the skis, but it doesn't do justice to the imposing mass that forms the peak. We left the skis at about 3100 m and did the rest with crampons. The weather wasn't very great with a good deal of mist and wind. Nevertheless we saw something of the nearer view, although nothing of the distant mountains. I enclose a postcard of the view of Piz Bernina, Scerscen and Roseg from the summit of Morteratsch. It is a summer view, so you can imagine how fine it was when I was there.

After returning to the skis we crossed to the col at the foot of the summit peak of Piz Tschierva (3564 m). The others went to the top all the way on ski, for it is an easy mountain. As the man I was with had a headache with the altitude, we didn't go to the top. On the Wednesday we set off in pretty thick weather for the Piz Glüschaint. We descended the Tschierva glacier and negotiated the first ice-fall of the Sella glacier, but after that we decided that it would be impossible to continue to the summit. Accordingly we descended to the Coaz hut for lunch, and after that returned to the hut. Normally in the Alps if the weather isn't really good no one climbs at all. So even to do the Morteratsch under the conditions that we did, and to go out at all on the Wednesday is considered a pretty good show.

Although we got plenty of theory on the course, it was not confined to that. For example we got instruction on how to make a sledge out of a pair of skis and transport an injured man on it. Immediately after we went up to the Tschierva glacier, each party chose a victim, made a sledge out of his skis and transported him back to the hut. An interesting experience!

In the afternoon we crossed the glacier for crevasse practice. Roping in threes it was for everyone in turn to ski into a crevasse and for the others of the party to hold him, and then to get him out. It gave occasion for much joy, for some people didn't like the idea of ski-ing headlong into the void, so it was necessary to give them some material assistance!

On the Friday we were blessed with a glorious day. We climbed Piz Glüschaint (3600 m). A long ski trek over the glaciers, including a part where we had to carry the skis for a considerable distance; a climb on crampons with plenty of concealed crevasses, and finally a delightful scramble along quite a long rocky summit ridge. The latter gave many of the people some difficulty, but by Scottish standards it was very easy and wholly delightful. The view was superb. In the west we could see distinctly the Grand Paradiso, the Monte Rosa, the Matterhorn, the Dent Blanche, the Mischabel Group, the Bernese Oberland, the Tessin, the Tödi Group, the Säntis Group, the Scesaplana, the Silvaplana, the Bergell, the Bergamasque, the Adamello and the Dolomites. Incidentally, we were on the Italian frontier so it was the first time that I was in Italy. We could also see the village of Sondrio in the Val Tellina, over 10,000ft below. From a geological point of view it was worth coming to the course for that one view alone. The whole chain of the Alps was spread out "from end to end". And also the details of the geology of the eastern Alps as developed in the Bernina Group itself were especially clear from that view point. If I had wanted to see this by myself the cost would have been very much more than it was by going on the course, for being an official course of the CAS, guides, food, and hut charges were a minimum.

On the Saturday we left the hut at 6.30 a.m. and took our rucsacs down to the Roseg Glen where they were to be collected by sledge for

Pontresina, and ultimately for Saint Moritz. After that we climbed Piz Corvatsch (3456 m; or 5000 ft of ascent). On ski it is possible to develop a beautiful rhythm for the ascent, and I must say that usually I prefer the ascent to the descent, which is rather unusual. Indeed when it was my turn to go first I was actually told that people liked to be behind me because of the rhythm. Thus a climb of 5000ft was not in any way a strain. Incidentally the weather kept magnificent all day, and the views were beyond description.

From the top of the Piz Corvatsch we descended on Saint Moritz. The snow was perfect (fresh powder without any tracks), the sun was broiling hot, for once we had no sacks or other equipment, and the slope down to Saint Moritz is 6000ft long. I enclose a card of Saint Moritz which shows the Piz Corvatsch and the descent. The remaining two cards show the Piz Languard group to the east of St Moritz and the Piz Julier Group. These I have enclosed for geological purposes.

At 4pm we got the train to Zurich. I had an interesting talk about geology with some of the party on the way back in the train. As I was able to demonstrate beautiful axes from the train window as we went through the Albula Pass it made it easy for them to follow.

The train arrived in Neuchâtel at half past midnight on the Saturday night. The weather has kept fine with beautiful colours in the lake although the depression tried to break in last night. It is very warm and I have seen a great difference in the flowers and trees in the short time that I have been away. In another week the leaves will all be out. When Madame Christen saw me after I came back she thought I was ill. The reason was that I have been well sunburnt and the shadow of my sunglasses is quite clear round my eyes!

Just before returning to Scotland, Donald enjoyed a holiday with the Christen family in Zermatt staying in "a wonderful chalet to the south of Zermatt" This was a splendid finale to his time in Switzerland and from there, Donald set off on his journey home to Scotland.

This proved to be quite a learning experience which Donald would often refer to with amusement. Since he was seriously financially strapped at that time, Professor Christen kindly suggested that he lent Donald his personal rail ticket to provide him with a substantial discount for his travel to the Swiss border. However, Swiss Rail is ever famous for its efficiency and its experienced ticket collectors not easily fooled! Donald's possession of this special ticket was considered highly suspicious especially when the ticket collector kept addressing Donald over and over again as "Monsieur Christen". But that was also his saving grace, for the ticket collector, cleverly checking in the local Swiss telephone directory, found the listing "M. Christen, teacher of English"! Nonetheless, not prepared to face further embarrassment, Donald fled from the train at the next station and remained ever after convinced that a life of crime and deception was not for him. Sherlock Holmes, Colombo and Swiss rail officials were ever his heroes!

And another tale. Toward the end of his time in Switzerland Donald was asked to give a lecture in Germany. Although he had become fluent in French, Donald never learnt German so he decided to make his lecture as understandable as possible for a German audience by using English words of Teutonic origin. At the time, the lecture seemed well received and understood, but, nevertheless, it was a comical surprise for Donald when, on a return visit to Bonn a few years later, he was congratulated on the excellent talk that he had given in German!

I was incredibly fortunate – and thereby hangs many another tale – to have spent the summer of 1952 with Monsieur and Madame Wegmann in their home and later some months with the Baer family in the nearby village of St Blaise. Unlike Donald, on my arrival in Neuchâtel, amidst the vineyards, views of the distant Alps and by the lake shining in the sun, I was convinced I had arrived in heaven. And better still, very soon after, Madame Wegmann and I accompanied Professor Wegmann, his assistant (and Donald's good friend), Jean-Pierre Portmann and five students to the Alps for a week's stay in a chalet high on Mont Nouble above Sion in the Valais, where gentians and Alpine roses were strewn at my feet. And there it entertained the students to tease this extremely naive young woman with their outrageous tales. I recall that of the dari – a mythical Alpine animal that has two short legs on one side of its body that facilitates its walking on a steep mountain side! In due course, the Wegmanns, the Baers and the students all came to be dear friends. I was fortunate to be able to make several brief return visits to Neuchâtel while working for two years as a translator – thanks to contacts by way of the Baer family – for The International Union for the Conservation of Nature in Brussels. (1955-57).

On our marriage in December 1957, Jean Paul Schaer, one of those students, gave us a beautiful book "Le Vignoble Neuchâtelois" (The vineyards of Neuchâtel): His description is given overleaf

A. D. McIntyre, en souvenir de l'evocation de noble bouteilles!
En ces jours de Noel 1957, je fais le voeux
que votre vie soit aussi clair qu'un vin d'Alsace
Aussi parfumee qu'un Moselle
Aussi moelleuse qu'un Graves
Aussi equilibree qu'un Gevrey-Chambertin
Aussi genereuse qu'un Châteauneuf du Pape
Et aussi riche que votre meilleure bouteille.

J.P.Schaer

To A and D McIntyre evoking the memory of magnificent wines!
At this Christmas time, 1957, I wish for both of you
That your life shall be as clear as a wine from Alsace
As fragrant as a Moselle
As gentle as a Graves
As balanced as a Gevrey-Chambertin
As generous as a Châteauneuf du Pape
And as rich as your very best bottle.

A geological trip to Switzerland in 1953
David Mackenzie, Edinburgh University graduate 1954

In the spring of 1953 my lecturer in petrology and structural geology at Edinburgh University, Donald McIntyre, invited me and two fellow students, Bill Brown (sadly now deceased) and Donald Smith, to accompany him on a geological trip to Switzerland in late summer that year. Donald had enthused me as a schoolboy in 1949 to take up geology. I was then in second year geology, as were my colleagues, but in the third year of a BSc (Hons) degree as decreed by the Edinburgh system of the time.

Donald had studied at Neuchâtel in Switzerland as a postgrad in 1947-48 under the distinguished Swiss geologist Prof. CE Wegmann. He intended to use the trip to gather photographic material to illustrate a proposed book on Alpine structural geology. The combination of great relief and deep tunnels through the Alps mean that they are the most comprehensively geologically known of the world's fold belts and a text book for any practical geologist.

We left Edinburgh in August 1953 in Donald's squat little blue Morris 10 Tilly van. It was a military surplus radio van with an enlarged body with small side and rear windows behind the front cab. There were two dickey-type seats in the back and some storage space. It was pretty cramped with four on board plus luggage and camping gear for over a month on the road.

Throughout the trip we camped in one biggish tent and cooked on primus stoves. Our safety precautions may not have been of the best because Donald Smith recalls putting his foot on the spout of a fuel can which had ignited while trying to light a stove. There were virtually no camping grounds in France or Switzerland at the time so we had to ask local farmers if we could use a field or an orchard to camp for the night. Alpine meadows were temptingly green but hazardous as invariably there was a cow byre higher up the slope contributing fluids to the sward. I doubt one could camp like that today. At this distance in time it is difficult to recollect exactly where we camped each night on our extensive figure-of-eight tour around the country. Donald always had a persuasive way of smoothing out permission with locals.

My recollection of meals is hazy but I think we had a fair bit of tinned food which was high quality (as were most things in Switzerland). The trip was a gastronomic delight especially for cheeses, breads, pastries, cold meats and fruits.

The trip was done on a shoestring. British currency regulations limited one to £25 in currency to be taken out of the country. My passport shows that I supplemented the cash allowance by £35 in travellers' cheques. Thus we had about 10 pounds each per week for petrol, food, ferries, chairlifts, mountain railways and extras like maps, guidebooks and souvenirs.

That first night we camped in a field beside the A1 near Retford, Notts. The second day took us through London to the Dover-Calais ferry, where I made my first contact with a native French speaker, a customs officer, who stamped my passport 7 August 1953. Despite over five years of high school French I was hopelessly floundering with the language. During the war we had no contact with colloquial speech. By the second night we were in a small walled field near Péronne on the Somme. There I had my first and last attempt at driving Donald's van. Abject failure resulted as it bucked and reared under my total lack of clutch control. Just as well Mr Morris of Oxford built well. At some stage on the third day we stopped to admire the magnificent façade of Reims Cathedral of Notre Dame. The long drive across France continued until we stopped somewhere near Épinal for the third night.

These long days behind the wheel must have been hard on Donald as none of us students could drive. By day four we crossed the Swiss border between Delle and Boncourt in the rolling green Jura Mountains. Some geology at last as we viewed in road cuttings near Moutier the classic rounded anticlines and synclines in – surprise – Jurassic limestones. These rocks had been rucked up well in front of the Tertiary geological turmoil of the Alps as Africa pushed against Europe in a great mountain building event. From the lookout at Le Chasseral (elevation 1607m) we looked SE across the flat Swiss Plain to the northern front of the Alps which we were to explore later. At peaceful Neuchâtel we camped in an orchard. I bought a Shell 'Carte touristique de la Suisse' 1: 400 000 on which I traced our route in Biro. That map is the basis of this account.

In Neuchâtel we took afternoon tea in the garden of the geology department with Donald's mentor Prof. Wegmann and his gracious wife. We were introduced to the distinctive greenish-tinged Neuchâtel wine, described, as Donald Smith recalls, as having the colour of 'pelure d'oignon' (onion skin). The introduction to wine for us students was something very special for which Donald Smith says he is eternally grateful.

From Neuchâtel we headed east across the Swiss Plain into rolling country around Bern which is formed of sandy and pebbly debris washed down from the uprising Alpine chain in the late Tertiary and referred to as 'molasse'. In places the molasse is overridden by the remains of huge folded rock sheets many tens of kilometres across called nappes which slid northwards from the uplifted basement to the south. At Willisau we diverted to a viewpoint near Menzberg (elevation 1016m) where we could get a good view of the 4000m plus peaks of the Bernese Oberland to the south.

When trying to identify the distant Bernese peaks we got talking with a passing Swiss farmer who was accompanied by his stunning blonde daughter, the immediate focus for us 20-or-so year old males. Bill put on his best schoolboy German and boldly asked the farmer "What time can I see the Jungfrau (jung Frau) in the morning?" We doubled up at the 'double entendre' of the question and never let Bill forget it.

We continued to Luzern where we walked as so many do across the medieval covered wooden bridge over the Reuss at the outlet of the Lake of Lucerne (elevation 434m). Luzern lies near the geographic centre of the country and the serious work of observing and trying to understand the geology of the Alpine nappes was about to begin with a southerly traverse of about 60km across the grain of the country. The shores of the lake showed good cross sections from the young molasse of the plain across the nose of the nappes of the High Calcareous Alps around the famous Rigi mountain. Along the Axenstrasse between Brunnen and Flüelen the rock folds are textbook quality. The road was narrow and had lots of short tunnels so we took a steamer trip between these two places to obtain a safe, standback view of the structures.

Our geologising was broad scale but assisted by the magnificent outcrops provided by glacial and post-glacial erosion. Donald took many photographs along the way and knew the best vantage points to observe geological structures. We were greatly assisted by the little handbooks published by the Swiss post office for all the routes taken by the Swiss post buses many of which we followed (the routes, that is). The booklets, as one came to expect, were very professional productions illustrated by lots of photographs and accompanied by beautiful accurate maps and coloured geological cross sections. The post buses had a distinctive melodious klaxon, probably based on an alpenhorn, whose notes would ring out at every bend or tunnel. The sound would echo through the valleys with a rather romantic ring and woe-betide anyone who did not give precedence to the post bus.

Near Wassen on the approach to the St. Gotthard Pass we observed the remarkable spiral rail tunnel system designed to gain ascent over to Andermatt and thence by the Gotthard tunnel to Ticino and Italy.

We saw the lead engine of a train emerging from the spiral on the mountainside some 50m above where the last carriage was entering the tunnel. It became clear as we travelled and observed that any infrastructure in Swiss terrain required the most thorough geological knowledge.

Wassen also marked a right angle change in direction as we swung towards the west to cross the Sustenpass (elevation 2258m) to Meiringen and back into the High Calcareous nappes along the lower ground through Interlaken and the lakes of Brienz and Thun. At Spiez we turned south into the Kiental towards Griesalp to observe a cross section through what is called the Diablerets nappe which rode over the top of the High Calcareous nappes.

By this stage one remarkable contrast for us, some eight years after the end of World War II, was that prosperous Switzerland had fortunately been spared untouched by that war, the effects of which were still closely felt and seen in Britain.

Returning to Spiez our route turned west along the Niedersimmental to Gstaad then southwards into French-speaking territory over the Col du Pillon (elevation 1550m) which is the watershed between Rhine-draining waters to the north and waters to the Rhone in the south, in other words a continental divide. On the way south to Aigle in the Rhone valley the views took in the impressive Dent du Midi (elevation 3257m) across the Rhone.

Here the Rhone lies in a rain shadow and the country was much drier and more Mediterranean than the alpine valleys. We now started a long leg to the ENE to the source of the Rhone from which many side excursions were made up tributary valleys. Having now been through several cantons we were aware of the pride the Swiss take not only in their national history and flag but also in their colourful cantonal flags and emblems as displayed, for instance, on every car number plate. Somewhere here we camped in a peach orchard and Donald Smith recalls breakfasting off the peaches, sheer luxury for any Scots lad.

The first Rhone side trip was up the Val d'Illiez above Monthey followed by sorties to the Col de la Forclaz, and then up the Grand St Bernard road as far as Orsières. In this area we were seated at lunch beside the road when a busload of teenagers on holiday passed with much waving, cheering and shouts of "bon appetit!" – a happy colloquial phrase which I had never heard before.

On the NW side of the Rhone above Sion we followed the road to Derborence and then climbed to Pas de Cheville (elevation 2038m) on very shaly steep slopes down which Donald Smith remembers the excitement of sliding out of control while leaning back on a sturdy wooden pole. Somewhere around here we were treated to a classic alpine summer thunderstorm which blew up out of nowhere, soaked everything, caused the local streams to rise rapidly and just as quickly dissipated.

From Sierre we sallied up to Crans-sur-Sierre and to Leukerbad to the north and into Val d'Anniviers to the south. In this area we experienced the diurnal variations in glacier-fed streams. Donald Smith remembers he left breakfast dishes to soak in the river at our camp only to find on return that the river level was up and no sign of dishes. Gone to the Mediterranean.

Our longest side diversion was 30km into Vispertal which forks at Stalden into the Saastal and Nikolaital. We drove up Nikolaital to St. Niklaus, then the road terminus, before taking the train, then the only access from Stalden to Zermatt. A one way ticket on the rack railway out of Zermatt saw us on the top of Gornergrat (elevation 3436m) with great views of Matterhorn (elevation 4478m) across the Gorner glacier and the Monte Rosa mass to the south (4634m). We ran down to Zermatt at 1616m 'out of control' according to Donald Smith 'to save the rail fare' and be in time to catch the regular train back to Stalden.

Our next turnoff was to the summit of the Simplon Pass (elevation 2005m). On up the Rhone we went, past Gletsch to begin the climb over the Furka Pass. Along the infant Rhone we could see successive terminal moraine deposits showing the extent of glacier retreat since the mid 19th century, measured in kilometres, a process even more rapidly in progress today. Ascending hairpin bends to the Furka (elevation 2423m) we had good views of the snout of the Rhonegletscher as we left the Rhone behind.

At Andermatt we began a long diversion to the south into the Italian-speaking canton of Ticino. Over the famous St Gotthard Pass (elevation 2108m) we went. The pass summit has gentle glacially smoothed surfaces and many lochans reminiscent of the Scottish Highlands. In fact, viewing extensive glaciers and their effects everywhere we looked, prompted Donald Smith to remark that he could visualise 'what Scotland was like 10,000 years ago'. After countless hairpin bends we reached Airolo where the famous rail tunnel emerges and so down the Ticino river to Bellinzona. South of the main watershed between the Rhone and Italy the mosquitoes became insufferable, especially at night. Quite often one or other of us posed for scale against an outcrop of rock and it was difficult to keep still while being bitten.

Through Lugano we continued south to the Italian border at Chiasso but did not cross as we did not have visas. This southern country, although mountainous, was much softer and less rugged than the main alpine chain. Social customs changed too. Donald Smith was impressed by youths scooting around on Vespas with girlfriends sitting side-saddle behind, dresses billowing. Geologically speaking we were now on the northern edge of the proto-African continent whose uplift assisted the huge Alpine nappes to slide and overfold to the north.

Returning northwards we crossed the Lukmanier Pass (elevation 1919m). We saw more cross sections of nappes before descending into the Rhine headwaters at Disentis. There the river flows ENE along the grain of the country and in the opposite direction to the Rhone which we saw so much of previously.

By this stage we had seen a wide range of the built infrastructure of Switzerland – houses, farms, roads, railways, bridges, tunnels, dams, cable cars, power stations and so forth. Having worked on a building site as a student, one lasting impression was the solid quality of built structures, whether in timber, stone, brick, concrete or metal, right down to the smallest of settlements. All this was coupled with Swiss orderliness.

At Chur the Rhine swings north and cross-sections of nappes were seen for about 30 km to Vaduz, capital of Liechtenstein, where we camped in an orchard under the Drei Schwestern peaks (elevation 2052 m) which form the border with Austria. At Vaduz we turned west across the Rhine into rugged Toggenburg where the spectacular limestone cliffs culminate in the mountain Santis. This mountain marks the northern front of the Alps proper which fall away to the rolling molasse terrain of green Appenzellerland. On to Nesslau and Wattwil where a sharp left turn southwards took us into the valleys around Glarus on the Linth. After Glarus we went westwards again along the grain of the country over Klausen Pass (elevation 1952 m) in Urnerboden. As much earlier at Susten Pass, the huge limestone cliffs marked the now familiar back end of nappes folded over to the north.

At Altdorf we came full circle to join our outward route and return to Luzern. Now we were truly headed for home, the geological tasks accomplished, across the Swiss Plain to pay respects again at Neuchâtel, maybe with some of that greenish wine. After all, Prof. Wegmann, his teacher Emile Argand and the geology department there had quite a role to play in making our trip come about. The connection was such that I recall Donald saying he was the geological grandchild of Argand who had founded the Neuchâtel geological institute. At Donald's suggestion we called in briefly at the tiny instrument factory of Meridian at Le Locle where I bought a Meridian compass and clinometer, one of the best, lightest and most robust instruments in the world at the time. I used it for many years afterwards in my geological work.

My main recollection of the return trip across northern France is our brief stop while passing through Paris. In the little blue van we circled the Place de la Concorde at least three times before being spat out of the maelstrom to cross the Seine to the Tour Eiffel. There our depleted funds only allowed us to buy a ticket to ascend to the 'premier étage'! My passport shows the exit from France at Calais on 14/9/53, five and a half weeks after entry and a continental road travel distance estimated at 3000 km.

For me, the Swiss excursion proved to be a geological inspiration and a cultural eye-opener, the benefits of which I have felt ever since. For that I am forever indebted to the generosity of Donald McIntyre, geologist extraordinaire, mentor and friend.

Canberra, Australia, July 2011.

Chapter 6
Pomona College
1954-1989

The Road Not Taken

Two roads diverged in a yellow wood,
And sorry I could not travel both
And be one traveler, long I stood
And looked down one as far as I could
To where it bent in the undergrowth;

Then took the other, as just as fair
And having perhaps the better claim,
Because it was grassy and wanted wear;
Though as for that, the passing there
Had worn them really about the same,

And both that morning equally lay
In leaves no step had trodden black
Oh, I kept the first for another day!
Yet knowing how way leads on to way,
I doubted if I should ever come back.

I shall be telling this with a sigh
Somewhere ages and ages hence:
Two roads diverged in a wood, and I -
I took the one less traveled by,
And that has made all the difference.

Robert Frost

★★★★★

Professor and students explore the desert geology.

Introduction

In 1954 other roads were open to Donald – a year at Massachusetts Institute of Technology among others – and though choice is always difficult and requires boldness, unimaginable adventure, advantages and opportunities will surely unfold. (We have both known elderly people who had never in their lives even crossed the border from Scotland into England.) But Donald's decision to move to a totally new environment in those distant times was a choice that far from ever provoking "a sigh" from either of us, led us both onto paths that have "made all the difference" – especially, undergirded as we were, by support from our loving families. Though our parents were far away in Scotland in those pre-jet and social media times, the power and the bonding resulting from putting pen to paper in letter-writing should never be discounted.

How can one begin to describe a place where, in great happiness, Donald and I both spent almost two-thirds of our married life? Pomona College is rooted in our very being – to people and to places that we have loved with passion and that have greatly shaped our lives. And although we left Claremont immediately on Donald's retirement a quarter of a century ago, thanks to e-mails and telephone contact, Ewen and I continue to cherish and be nourished by our ongoing relationship with Pomona College in both official and unofficial ways. We are greatly blessed.

Pomona College is one of a number of small undergraduate colleges known throughout the United States as "liberal arts colleges" – institutions which only offer undergraduate studies and, therefore, are not universities. However, the comparatively small number of students allows the faculty to develop close and rewarding relationships. Pomona graduates are often renowned for their well-founded scholarship and their ability to continue to shine in their chosen academic fields when they move on to study for specialised advanced degrees. (There were some 1,200 students at Pomona College throughout the 1960-70s.)

The term "liberal arts" describes succinctly how each student must enrol in a wide spectrum of courses, not concentrating uniquely on his or her chosen career subject. Over their four years at Pomona, students must succeed in courses in English as well as studying a language, religion or philosophy, economics and a science subject. By contrast, when Donald enrolled as a science major at Edinburgh University, all his courses were required to be in science.

The quality of Pomona College's education is favourably compared to that of undergraduate work at Harvard or Yale. And, as there is a cluster of five separate colleges in Claremont itself, the town has sometimes, in our day, perhaps just a little facetiously, been referred to as "The Oxford of the Orange Groves." In recent decades, the local orange groves have disappeared so perhaps that comparison is another demonstration of how Claremont has changed.

Pomona College was founded in 1887. To quote from the impressive publication *Pomona College: Reflections on a Campus, 2007'*:

"Nearly all of America's academic institutions were founded by religious denominations and offered classics-based curricula with a religious, though not necessarily sectarian, orientation; the college was generally understood to be a 'substitute for parental superintendence,' a responsibility not taken lightly. In these respects, Pomona fits the pattern." One hundred years on and in a very different world, it was a great honour for Donald to be invited to present the College's Centennial Convocation Address. (It appears in the Addresses section of this book.)

Over the years, the College administrators set out to create a campus of great beauty. The desert land upon which the first buildings were constructed – home to native sagebrush, cactus and tumbleweed – has gradually and thoughtfully been transformed into a unique and lovely academic haven. Today, amidst Southern California suburbia, these acres of fine architecture, magnificent landscaping and cloistered gardens, expansive lawns and mature trees, are both striking and beautiful. They are tended by modern water-saving devices and on ecological principles.

Under the presidency of Dr. E. Wilson Lyon, who appreciated the importance of Pomona keeping abreast of the expansion of modern scientific education, and thanks to the vision of alumnus Frank Seaver, the Robert A. Millikan Laboratory for Physics, Mathematics, and Astronomy, and Seaver Laboratory for Biology and Geology (Seaver South) were constructed in 1958. It was as result of this development that Donald, in gratitude and with pleasure, chose to remain at Pomona College throughout the three and a half decades of his career in America. Thanks to Mr Seaver's generosity, it became possible for Donald to ensure that, in the 1950s and 1970s, Pomona's Geology Department was recognised as one of the leading geology departments in the nation.

One injunction that Donald took seriously both for himself and for his students is inscribed on the College Gate at College Avenue and Sixth Street. Although some of the newer buildings now lie beyond this original boundary, the classically designed panels flanking the avenue continue to state a request:

Let only the eager, thoughtful and reverent enter here.
They only are loyal to this college who departing bear their
added riches in trust for mankind.

As time went on, apparently, President James A. Blaisdell, who had composed these lines when the gateway was built in 1914, himself came to ponder whether perhaps the first line of the inscription was a "trifle too prohibitive for entering students and that it might have been better to have omitted the word 'only." His reflection struck home to us. In 1956, when Gerhard Oertel had just arrived to join the geology faculty; his young children went out exploring their new neighbourhood. They soon returned home to tell their mother that they had read the inscription on the gateway and concluded that they were not eligible to walk through it!

And how did Donald come to be there?

Donald often recounted the tale, emphasising that it was because he was able to correctly identify a Swiss wine at the Turner's home in the summer of 1952 that an unheralded opportunity came his way. A year after a memorable interview in August 1953 with Dr. Lyon and his family in Oxford, England, Donald, an eligible bachelor, set out from windy, damp and chilly Scotland to be greeted by a Californian heat wave in Claremont. He found that Pomona College's Geology Department was only modestly equipped and predicted that he would probably just remain there for a three year experience. Fast-forward thirty-four years. Our family is always grateful that a glass of sparkling Swiss wine played such an crucial role in bringing all three of us such us a rich, full and interesting life in Claremont. (*See Chapter 11*)

Arrival at Pomona

Academic Procession

Unplucked, untended, late and soon,
Unornamental, June to June,
Professors, in their special way,
Are plants that bloom a single day.

Burst suddenly, in blazing flower,
They for a brief exciting hour
Enchant and awe the lookers on
Who, witness the phenomenon

And then, as suddenly, they shed
Their brilliant petals go quite dead,
And stay inexplicably sere
Until Commencement comes next year

Richard Armour
From The Claremont Quarterly, Vol. 4 No.
1, p. 22, Autumn 1956.

As Doctor of Science from Edinburgh University, Donald was always conspicuous and resplendent in the academic processions, donning his brilliant scarlet robe adorned with the green academic sash of the sciences. He never complained but the gown must have often felt extremely heavy and hot in the soaring autumnal temperatures. His large, floppy velvet John Knox cap added distinction to the splendour to these academic occasions.

Donald had an enduring recollection from September 1954 at his first

Opening Convocation of a new academic year. On this occasion a flickering torch was passed from hand to hand through the faculty. When the flame came to Donald, representing the new faculty members, the flame flickered and all but went out! What kind of omen was that?

I have not been able to trace Donald's earliest letters on his arrival at Pomona College, but he would recall that very shortly after settling in Claremont in late August 1954, there was a record heatwave, with temperatures in the high 90s to 100-plus Fahrenheit – quite a shock for a Scot used to cloudy skies and temperatures rarely exceeding 70F., though we always noted that high humidity makes Scottish "heatwaves" less tolerable than the "dry heat" of a typical California summer season – from late April to mid-October. Under extreme conditions, when trying to cool off in the tiny kitchen of his new home, Donald would resorted to dashing quickly in and out of the shower, perhaps dreaming a little nostalgically of the cool and refreshing showers of the Scottish Highlands.

Donald lived in a small College-owned apartment on East Seventh Street, which was demolished even before my arrival in Claremont in 1957. There were two small apartments, as I understand it, on either side of a short flight of stairs. The other was occupied by Donald Robertson, recently arrived from New Orleans to join the two-man faculty of Pomona's Art Department. No sooner had the academic year got underway than the head of that department left, so Donald Robertson, prematurely and inadvertently, became chair of his department!

Although they came from very different disciplines, Donald and Donald became firm friends, and Donald was always grateful to Donald R for opening eyes to a fuller appreciation of art and for introducing him to unusual books, especially *The Road to Xanadu: A Study in the Ways of the Imagination* by John Livingston Lowes. Lowes wrote: "The title of the volume is less cryptic than it seems. I propose to tell the story, so far as I have charted its course, of the genesis of two of the most remarkable poems in English, *The Rime of the Ancient Mariner* and *Kubla Khan*. This quest became, in the end, an absorbing adventure along the ways which the imagination follows in dealing with its multifarious materials, an adventure like a passage through the mazes of a labyrinth, to come out at last upon a wide and open sky. Those ways are the theme of the book. *The Road to Xanadu* is but a symbol of something which, when all is said, remains intangible."

Although Donald was expected to teach a heavy course load at Pomona, including at least one evening class, this was ever, in retrospect, a very happy time and an opportunity to learn of standard American ways. One evening, before class, Donald invited Alex Baird, a graduate student, to have a meal at his apartment. Donald cooked a simple Scottish dish of ground beef, using just a quarter of a pound of "mince" to share between the two of them. Donald got the message in no uncertain terms a week later when Alex staggered up the stairs to the apartment bearing an enormous casserole for their dinner. The Californian fashion of those days never became part of our approach to gastronomy – a steak large enough to cover most of a good-sized plate along with a massive chunk of unadorned iceberg lettuce and a baked potato! (Note the Dinner Party menu entry of January 1956!)

Pibroch at Pomona

It seems that Donald's fame as Scotsman and piper created a stir on his arrival at Pomona in September 1954. Shortly afterwards, Donald received a phone call from President E. Wilson Lyon asking if he would add to the festivity of the annual faculty dinner by playing the pipes that evening. As Dr. Lyon spoke to him on the phone, Donald misinterpreted the President's diffident manner and thought he detected a bit of a chuckle in Dr. Lyon's voice as he made this request. Donald took this as a challenge and decided, in his mischievous way, to hold his audience to ransom with a pibroch, not mere Scottish tunes or standard fare such as *Over the Sea to Skye*.

(Pibroch is a musical form played on the bagpipes comprising an extended theme with variations. It is, in short, the classical music for the pipes, complex and difficult.)

As I understand it, Donald did indeed play, and play, and play: around and around Frary Hall. Was he ever going to stop?! His choice of pibroch was, of course, deliberate – it was reputed to have been played at a time when some clan members had been hostage for a very long time in their ancestral castle.

Donald noted with amusement that he was never again formally invited to play the pipes at Pomona!

Students were also taking note of their resident piper:

Piping Professor

The eulogy (Pomona College Magazine, 2010), for Professor Donald B. McIntyre, was deservedly impressive but didn't mention his bagpipes. He would wear his kilt and play the pipes at dances and other grand occasions, saying a few words in his Scottish burr. As a history major, I took his geology class in 1956 as one of my "seven pillars." It was my first encounter with a scientist, and it shocked me with a first-quarter "C" grade. Apparently this thin, quiet and very young man assumed we were adults who would read the textbook without being given assignments. On exams, he wanted every single relevant fact – never mind writing a liberal-artsy essay! Second quarter, I caught up a few hundred pages and did much better. Meanwhile, some of us felt he needed a wife to feed him well and bring out his shy sense of humor. We were soon pleased to hear he'd brought one from Scotland, surely a rosy-cheeked and capable woman! I was not surprised that the eulogy described him as a loving husband and father. Certainly he was a fine person and professor – and a fine piper."

Lucy Dickinson Phillips, class of 1960, Dover, Mass.

Donald's letters to his family
Claremont, Christmas 1954

It doesn't seem like Christmas time approaching with the weather still beautiful and not a cloud in the sky. I have to admit however that it has been distinctly chillier of late and it is sometimes really quite cold at night. Last weekend Alex Baird and I went into Nevada to scout the country for a suitable place for our summer field class. We were up about 6-7000 feet and there was a little snow lying and it was really cold at night. If you have a map you will see our route going east from here to Las Vegas. We crossed the desert leaving here about 6 o'clock in the morning and of course Las Vegas is in Nevada. In Nevada there is no restriction on gambling; in fact it is encouraged for the state collects a tax and this is about the only tax you have to pay, or, I should say, need to pay in Nevada. For this reason hordes of people leave Los Angeles and go to Las Vegas as the nearest gambling place. You can imagine that it is a pretty expensive place and we didn't stop there. From Las Vegas we travelled on to Ely. To give you an idea of what this means I can see that the entire trip of 550 miles took us 10 hours, and yet there was little more strain than driving from Edinburgh to Inverness. The car was running well and the overdrive was wonderful. We cruised up the last few miles on a good, lonely, straight road at 90 mph and this is like doing 45 at home.

We were successful in our job and did it speedily with the help of the Shell geologists in Ely. On our way back we went west to Tonopah. This was the centre of gold and silver rushes in 1903. From there we struck south and east into Death Valley. The weather was glorious; in summer it would have been frightfully hot, but we found it at an ideal temperature. Much of this journey was across the Great Basin country. There are long north-south valleys separated by moderately high ridges, and we had to cross these on our way from east to west. To break the monotony we tried to guess the length of each valley as we came on to it. One was 25 miles: we could see the whole length of this from one end to the other, and the road is superb and no traffic at all, so you can no doubt understand how we were able to make good speed.

The other evening I took time off to go to the house of one of the executive men in order to hear a discussion of the football season which is now over. It is a very short season. The two coaches were there and about 20 people from the college turned up to discuss the strategy and tactics that had been employed. I may say that these had been very successful for the team won every game it played and this is the first time since 1904 or so since this has happened. It was exceedingly interesting. I told you before that the game was more like chess than anything else and of course it is the coaches who scan all their opponents very systematically and work out on paper suitable defences and attacks. They take films of all their own games and we saw many of the plays that evening. The projector can be stopped at any time and run backwards so that each man can be studied. After each game the team goes through all this information in detail with the coaches. The moves were worked out and discussed on the blackboard just as in a game of chess. Really a fascinating evening. Can you persuade the Scottish selectors to do something similar!

15 October 1955 *(note the difference: U.K. standard order – day, month, year).*

I am at a little café about five miles from Claremont. Don Robertson and I generally come here once a week to have a meal out and to visit the big supermarket next door. Tonight Don is out for dinner and I simply had to get to the store since I have a long committee meeting tomorrow evening and a class the following evening. I also had a class

(to)-night. So I am alone and take the chance of scribbling these lines –
with a ballpoint pen, which is not looking too well.

You may be interested in the system of shopping. You drive up to the
"store" (not shop of course) and there is a huge area for parking – all
laid out with lines to make most use of the space. The store is called the
Shopping Bag. Entering it you take a little trolley basket and wander
round the huge interior picking up whatever you want.

October 23 1955 *(note the difference: US standard order – month, day, year).*

Yesterday morning I had another talk with President Lyon. One of
the advantages of a small College is that you can go in and deal directly
with the people who count. I think he is going to meet my "demands"
to such an extent that I shall be morally obliged to turn down the offers
of Berkeley and UCLA, attractive though they may be. It now seems
very likely that I shall be able to get an associate professorship for
Gerhard Oertel *(who was then living and working in Goa with his wife and
three young children)*, and I believe that he would take this. Also I think I
shall be able to get a young palaeontologist as an assistant professor; he
is at present working with Shell in Nevada. Unfortunately Lionel
(Weiss) cannot be taken care of here on the ordinary staff because his
work and mine have been too similar....it might well be better for him
to take a more permanent teaching job in one of the bigger institutions
such as Berkeley, where he will be welcomed.

We have had mixed weather with rather a lot of fog and smog, but
today was just like a glorious summer day at home. The skies were blue
and the mountains clear, and the temperature was ideal. I had lunch
with the Crowells. John Crowell is a professor at UCLA and he joined
me for a trip in Switzerland when I was there with David Mackenzie
and Bill Brown. He was anxious to talk to me more about my joining
the UCLA staff. This semester he teaches one day a week as opposed to
my every day + 2 evenings. I walked up to the house (this is unusual in
this part of the world although the distance is quite short) and heard the
birds singing – this I haven't often heard here.

On Friday I go to Stanford University to give two lectures. I leave
after my morning class (at 11:30 a.m.) and John Shelton is going to fly
me up the San Andreas Fault zone in his plane—this should be a great
experience. As a matter of fact, I have never visited Stanford. The
University is only a little way south of San Francisco. We spend the
night with Professor and Mrs. Knopf. They used to be the two great

leaders of geology at Yale, but they retired to Stanford where they conduct seminars at the University. Mrs. Knopf (whom Lionel knows) has asked me to go up and I am looking forward to the trip very much. We fly back on Saturday morning.

I have just heard that it is almost certain that we shall be able to make a return visit to the San Benito Islands at the end of January. This is great news for it should mean that we shall be able to get a proper account of the geology of these interesting islands completed. However, I shall have to start stocking up with seasickness tablets right away.

Must leave this and get on with my dictation or I shall have nothing for Mrs. Bolton in the morning.

Claremont, December 22, 1955

I am scribbling out this note to tell you that I am leaving tomorrow to spend Christmas with the Turners in Berkeley. I return on Monday 26th. There have been terrible storms in the north and much fog here so I hope I shall not be held up by bad weather. ★★★

Yesterday I had a geological flight around the Salton Sea (Imperial Valley) with John Shelton. Very interesting to see that country from the air. I "had a go" at handling the plane and found it very hard to keep it from "bucking" – rather like managing the clutch of a car for the first time! I did not participate in the landing so we got down safely.

Gerhard Oertel's appointment is complete except for formal approval by the trustees on January 19. I have cabled the news and I think the prospect of leaving Goa for California has brightened his Christmas. I have not yet had word about the palaeontologist from the graduate school.

Two days ago I had a field trip on the ground to Imperial Valley with John Shelton and we hope to make another trip before the end of the vacation – Jan 3rd. This will put me badly behind in my desk work but it has been good to get out. Some of the evidence of recent faults in Imperial Valley is truly spectacular. Scarps of 200 ft. or so in the alluvium!! Last week they had considerable earthquakes at El Centro in the Valley.

★★★ *As it turned out – the density of the fog made driving very scary.*

Claremont, January 19 1956

We are once more in the midst of exams. The second semester is approaching and during the week's break between the semesters we return to "our islands." We leave on Monday Jan 30 and expect to return on February 8th. Thereafter my life will be a little easier, for Woody is going to take the evening seminar and another of my classes is for the first semester only; I am relieved of 2 classes. Woody is going to deal with the Geology of California and I look forward to sitting in – it will be a valuable summary for me.

The Air Force (after much diplomacy I believe) took a wonderful series of air photos of the Islands for us – the Mexicans are sensitive. The photos will be most useful; some of them are even in colour!

I received a letter from Bob Clark 2 days ago and he urged me to apply for the Edinburgh chair. At the same time I received the statement of conditions which Daddy had sent me. Last night I spoke to Frank Turner on the telephone for half an hour and I have given a lot of thought to the matter. I have concluded that it is best for my development to remain in this country for another 2-3 years and that at present I am not mature enough for such a position in my own University! If I were invited I think I would accept, but I do not feel sufficiently "ready" to justify me in applying. It is a pity the timing works out in this way, but there it is!

It is therefore virtually certain that I shall stay here for 2 years with Gerhard Oertel and then go to Berkeley. Since there I will be one of several (the staff is the finest group of geological researchers in the world), I will be able to continue to develop gradually.

I certainly could never regret coming here – although I could fill volumes if I wanted to criticise! My horizons in Art and Philosophy and History have been widened enormously. All this quite apart from the contacts I have made in my own and in other fields, and the geology I have learnt and seen. I feel that I have been un-dehydrated!

I have had word that I have received a National Science Foundation Grant of $13,500. The majority of this will be spent (over 2 years) on a helper in both research and teaching. I am hoping to get John Christie who is doing research in Assynt. You might like to get Lionel to bring him over to see you.

Since returning from Berkeley I have completely changed my way of eating and find that it is no more time consuming to have an elegant meal than to have a simple one. I am becoming quite an expert on sauces! Usually Donald Robertson joins me. To celebrate the change we gave a banquet for Prof and Mrs.Greene (Aesthetics and former Master of Sillliman College at Yale and Prof and Mrs. Leggewie (French). We even went the length of getting the menus printed and I am sending a copy to Sheila.

Dinner party 1956 – Bachelor style

Editorial note – Donald never did anything by halves! Although we entertained a great deal in the early days of our marriage, as his humble spouse/cook, I was never able to attain the dizzy heights of a dinner party of such elegance as that hosted by Donald and his neighbour, Donald Robertson of Pomona's Art Department and of New Orleans. They used recipes from the celebrated cookery book Le Guide Culinaire *by Auguste Escoffier (1846-1935) – nothing but the best! – and worked on the principle of Brillat-Savarin (1755-1806) who wrote "to receive guests is to take charge of their happiness during the entire time they are under your roof." He also gives perceptive tips to test guests' worthiness of the delicacies set before them! Note that on being offered grapes at the end of a fine dinner, Brillat-Savarin responded, "I do not take wine by way of pills!"*

The honoured guests included Robert Leggewie, Pomona's Professor of French, and his wife, Moreene. It was quite an occasion – as Robert never failed to remind me – that no matter what delicacy I were to roast, grill or simmer for them, nothing could begin to compare with that celebrated feast of Chefs Donald & Donald.

Donald remembered this evening with great merriment and would recount how Robert assumed that the printed menu of the evening had been taken and copied from a restaurant until it was pointed out that the guests' names and date of the occasion were also printed on the sheet!

Sherry maison	Sauterelles
	Antipasto
	Pasta Ravioli
Nina Duff Gordy	Tortue claire
Ch, Pontel Canet '50	Vol-au-vent Diamond-back rattlesnake
Ch. Laville-Baton '45	Pilaf de buffalo

Asperge hollandaise

Ch d'Yquem '46	Gateau
Eau de vie	Café

"May I be hanged if I like to see wine drunk as if it were against the law, with everyman in his own house pouring it down his gullet as down a drain, and not like a reasonable drinker; and all this without discussing its merits or its imperfections, or what might be done to make it better" 1835 Estebanez Calderon

The place: East Seventh Street, Claremont, California

The date: 11 January 1956

The hosts: *Donald B. McIntyre and Donald Robertson*

The guests: *Theodore M. Green; Mr. and Mrs. Robert Leggewie and Mr. John Wilkie.*

★★★★★

Shortly after this unique, gourmet occasion, Donald wrote to his sister, Sheila:

Perhaps an explanation is necessary! Don Robertson and I wanted to celebrate our first real live dinner-party so we printed the menus.

Sauterelles = grasshoppers, fried and dried (like salted nuts)

Antipasto = hors d'oeuvres. Arranged by us and served with our own dressing

Pasta = Ravioli cooked in our wine sauce

Sherry maison = our blending of Californian sherry

Tortue Claire = real turtle soup

The fish was served with our own tartare sauce and the peas with parsley sauce.

Vol-au-vent – these were baked for us and we filled them with rattlesnake meat in a delicious mushroom sauce.

Pilaf de buffalo – Buffalo (almost unobtainable since protected by law) stewed with saffron rice. We made the hollandaise sauce, which was acclaimed the piece de resistance.

The Yquem could not be spoiled so we served it with a slice of pound cake.

The Ponlet-Canel and the Leoville-Barton were served in the right order for the latter was much superior (as could have been expected from the source, age and vintage).

What a pity you were too far away to join me at my first attempt at a little home-made meal!

A ta santé! / Donald

★★★★★

Claremont, June 1 1956

How busy is it possible to be? Our fiscal year ends at the end of June as our Dept. budget evaporates i.e., any money left goes back into general funds. We are going to get several hundred dollars worth of equipment that we would otherwise not have had. This all takes time in planning, book-keeping, etc.

This is also the time for annual reports, arrangements for accommodation for Gerhard (Oertel) and John (Christie) next year, library inventories, plans for rearranging our space for next year's work, final exams, awarding fellowships, trying to get new stacks for our expanding library; interviews with prospective students, etc.

A week ago I played the pipes at a wedding in Pasadena – a cousin of Ian Campbell (Chairman of Geology Dept. at Caltech). This was good for I got them into fine condition once more and have played quite a bit since; the 1st year class asked me to play at the last lecture of the year.

On Monday night I lectured to the San Joaquin Valley Geology Club in Bakersfield. John Shelton flew me over the mountains for the evening (about 100 miles). The address was well received. On the way back (in the dark) we flew on radio beams. It is quite amazing how organized the facilities are. Once over Claremont, John called up to get the landing light switched on and down we came. He is a very good pilot.

Did I tell you that my neighbour, Donald Robertson (Art Dept.), is leaving for the University of Kansas? I have arranged for John Christie to get his apartment. So we will be able to have a joint ménage. I'll miss Don Robertson. He is a great character.

We are planning furiously for our trip to Baja. We sail on June 14 and return July 29. We'll get no mail and will be able to send none during that time. We'll be dropped by ship at a village where all the water comes by distilling seawater and then left until the ship returns. John Shelton will fly down and one party will come by jeep across the Vizcaino desert—if they can make it!

★★★★★

Claremont April 14 1957

Today is the end of our Easter "vacation." Although we operate, like most American colleges, on a semester (2 term) basis, we have a week's vacation at – or rather near – Easter. If one is going to stop for Christmas and Easter, I think one might as well stop for a little longer than we do and not have a break in between; in other words divide the year into 3 terms. At all events we are under way again tomorrow.

The break has enabled me to clear my desk. Gerhard has taken the field class to the desert for the whole week and John Christie arrived back from New Mexico, Arizona and the Grand Canyon last night. He thoroughly enjoyed it. During the week I had a phone call from Lionel; he is taking a field class out from Berkeley in 2 weeks time. I arranged to meet him in the desert (just one and a half hours from here.) I did this and took him up to the place where Gerhard and our students are camping. Olaf van West was with him, and Lionel had some people from Berkeley with him. Olaf and I had still a lot to do in Claremont so after lunch the following day we returned to town.

Next week will be a busy one. Tomorrow afternoon we are having a visit from John Hodgson, Director of the Dominion Seismological Station at Ottawa, and Mason Hill, one of our own alumni who is Director of Exploration of the Richfield Oil Corporation. They are coming to discuss the work John and I have been doing on the interpretation of earthquake data. This will take all afternoon and evening for we are all having dinner together. At the end of the week, the Geological Society of America and the Seismological Society are meeting in Los Angeles. I am too busy with classes to go except on the Saturday when the program interests me particularly.

I must find out from Ranald how much it would cost to hire a car. I expect to be on the continent during much of August, I don't know whether it would be worth driving out.

Donald didn't divulge that he had already arranged to join me for a week at Nature Conservation Youth Camp at King Victor Emmanuel's National Park in the Italian Alps where, as part of my job in Brussels (1955-57), I would be officially representing The International Union for the Conservation of Nature. In due course, we travelled by train from Brussels to Italy. Shortly after that extraordinary week in breathtakingly beautiful scenery and despite a Spartan diet of pasta – no sauce, just pasta! – it was on our return to Scotland that we became engaged at Nethy Bridge in the Highlands. All too soon thereafter, Donald had to return to Claremont but, in the deep mid-winter, he travelled back to Scotland where his father officiated at our marriage in Edinburgh on 23 December 1957, a joyful day though, as Donald would often comment, the sun barely rose above the horizon. (Because the date was so near the winter solstice.)

Wedding Day, Edinburgh, 23 December 1957

A Desert Trip – December 28 1958

Donald wrote to his aunt and uncle:

Whenever we get a chance, we go off on field trips and Ann finds great pleasure in exploring this fascinating country. To celebrate our wedding anniversary, we went down to a canyon in the mountains near the Salton Sea (a two-hour drive from Claremont) and spent the night in the back of our ranch wagon. During the night Ann awoke and thought that it had snowed. It turned out that the full moon, nearly directly overhead, was so bright through the clear desert air that the light-coloured rocks were bathed in light!

The following day we drove across the fertile floor of the Imperial Valley (which was totally desert until the waters of the Colorado River were brought in for irrigation) and sampled fresh dates and grapefruit at one of the large date groves below sea-level! We had never realized how delectable good dates were or how many varieties exist. It is a pity that all the finest ones are too soft to travel or we would send you a box. Perhaps you tasted similar fine dates in the old campaigning days?

After a delicious lunch in the gardens we set out westwards and crossed the Santa Rosa Mountains, which bound the Imperial Valley to that side. The road climbs very rapidly from below sea level to about 5,000 feet and is called, appropriately, the Palms to Pines highway! A wonderful botany lesson! Once over the mountains we descended to Hemet, one of the principal peach-growing districts in southern California and hence home.

This will give you some idea of the idyllic surroundings in which we live. A week ago we drove up a mountain road in the San Gabriel Mountains (immediately to the north of us) and in half an hour from the house were walking along a mountain path through the pines in the best Swiss tradition. And just yesterday we drove to the very center of Los Angeles also in half an hour. We were on our way to a Scottish Country Dance!

Normally, as I hope you will understand from the low frequency of my correspondence, I have no time for such "foolishness" as country dancing. I suppose my work as a teacher and scientist will always keep me busy, but there has been unusual activity in the past two years. We have succeeded in getting from the current income of one man $3.25 million. This money was given for a new maths-physics building (magnificently equipped) and for a new geology-biology building which will give us the finest facilities in the country. My budget for over $200,000 of geology equipment was approved and I have now the time-consuming job of placing orders, getting equipment through customs and then checking it to make sure it is right once it arrives. Quite a responsibility!

The maths-physics building is already completed and our building is nearing completion. We will move in about June 1st. Both buildings were dedicated in December, by Detlev Wulf Bronk, President of the National Academy of Sciences.

In addition to my teaching and administrative duties at the College, I often have to travel to give special lectures elsewhere. Just last week I flew to Berkeley one afternoon, I gave a lecture at the University of California that evening and drove back the following morning.

Last September I was honoured in being asked by Principal Sir Edward Appleton to represent the University of Edinburgh at the Inauguration of the new president of the University of California. There were ceremonies both at Los Angeles and Berkeley, and Ann came with me to San Francisco and enjoyed the functions. I am sending you a copy of the program. You will see in it that the delegates marched in the procession in the order of the founding of the University which they represented. Of the first five in the procession, Scotland had three! What a pity Aberdeen wasn't represented too!

Well, life is certainly full of interest and I cannot regret my decision to come to California. I feel that my education has continued in a way that would not have been possible otherwise. My horizons have been enormously broadened—both literally and metaphorically. How much pleasure would it give us if you decided to pay us a visit and share for a while our fascinating life in this friendly and sunny clime. Do consider this. Travel is now so easy and pleasant and we are sure you would be invigorated in your enjoyment of this happy place.

Donald and Ann

May 30 1965

I am sorry that so much time passes between my letters. Activity here has been even greater than usual. It is funny that when there is most to write about, when much has been happening, there is the least time to do anything about it!

In the last few months, and even in the last few weeks, Ewen has grown up a great deal. He is still anxious to "tell" anyone that Papa Wegmann left by helicopter, for example. He is able to use Sheila's "marble run" now and can put 2 marbles on at one time and then stop them with his hand before they come off. Also he is very anxious to share any nice and interesting thing so this gives considerable encouragement to his speech. He vocalizes several words now – but only the first syllable so there are often ambiguities. He uses his hands to help convey his meaning, and he nods and shakes his head for "yes" and "no. "

Doubtless you have heard of the rabbit! The dear little 10-year old son of our Mexican gardener, Manuel, is Ewen's best friend, by far. And of course it was he who brought the rabbit, on Easter day, naturally. Although sometimes the rabbit runs away too fast, it is amazing how far and how quickly Ewen will go after it. It is so nice to see him holding a carrot in his hand and feeding the rabbit. Ewen seems to have no fear of animals. At the zoo he fed the elephants without hesitation, and he often feeds horses here when other children are terrified to do so.

We had a wonderful visit from Professor Wegmann. Up to the MacColls (at Crestline) for a wonderful day in the mountains. And dinner at Mr. Dogweiler's Swiss restaurant in San Bernardino – just too many events to make it possible to write about. The weather was idyllic all the time he was here and he really enjoyed himself.

Unfortunately, this has been my busiest semester for a long time. Alex is on sabbatical leave (although he is here) this means extra work for me. Also I am chairman of a number of important committees which takes a lot of time—the library committee (the Ford Foundation has given us $1,260,000.for books) or, more strictly, several library committees; the computer committee (we have now hired a Director of the Computer Centre); and the Machine Shop Committee, amongst others.

Despite all this we have a good deal of entertaining and other social events, many of which are really obligatory. And I get a good deal of work done, mainly with the computer. I have been getting the computer to draft our maps and this has been a big task, now all but completed. I have been asked to be a consultant for Space Technology Laboratories (a very large organization which includes all the underwater work for the Navy as well as space work). This is because of my experience with computers. I hope this will finance Ann and Ewen's trip to Mrs. Bobath (world renowned physiotherapist in London), a considerable expense each year.

December 18 1966

What a heavenly day! Last night was clear and starry and, by our standards, cold; and this morning, the air is spectacularly clear and the sun is hot. The mountains are wonderful to see and the sky is as blue as can be.

Professor Wegmann, who arrived yesterday, walked with me to see the play that the Sunday School children performed. It was the manger scene, and Ewen was a shepherd. He sat in his new chair, and he wore a blue cloak and held a crook in his hand. On the side of his chair hung a sheep made from cotton wool balls stuck on a cardboard base. He was as happy as could be, and he beamed throughout the performance. Then we walked home together, enjoying the brilliant day and the sunshine. When we arrived back we found that a whole menagerie had been delivered in our absence. One of the neighbour children was going away for the holidays and had asked Ewen to look after her animals: a rabbit, two or three guinea pigs and a hamster. All these in addition to the guinea pig, rabbit, fish and turtles that we have already!

Yesterday we went to Wilmington to meet Professor Wegmann's ship, which had docked at midnight on Friday. We thought it would be fun for Manuel, Ewen's friend (a delightful young Mexican lad, son of our gardener) to come with us, and so it was. First of all we had a search to find the ship, because we didn't know which berth she was at and (as you know) the harbour is a big one. Fortunately, Ann spotted the name on the stern of the ship when we were a long way off, so we weren't too late. But Professor Wegmann was the only passenger on board and the customs officer was in no hurry to come to see him. This didn't matter, fortunately, because we were all invited to come on board for lunch, which was a good one. Ewen and Manuel got a chance to go all over the ship and to watch the unloading of the cargo from the vantage point of the Captain's bridge. It was a big ship, bigger than your one.

When, at last, the baggage was cleared, we drove round the coast to Marineland. It was a fine afternoon, although not so glorious as today, and the expedition was enjoyed by everyone. We saw the whale show and watched the fish being fed by the diver. But I think that the walruses were the attraction most appreciated. There are three walruses and they are amazingly playful under water. We watched them through underwater windows, and they rubbed their whiskered noses against Ewen's nose, to everyone's delight.

We were home in good time, just after dark. Professor Wegmann was ready to go to bed early, but Ann and I went to the Bairds for dinner. They have begun construction of a very large (and expensive) mountain "cabin" a few miles away from the MacColls. They hope that it will prove to be a good investment as the value of land rises and they hope to live there on weekends and have only a small apartment in Claremont for during the week.

The Zengers were there too, and they were very happy because Don Zenger has just been promoted to the rank of Associate Professor. Everyone was gay.

Professor Wegmann is in the back bedroom and Ewen is in our room on the rollaway bed. He never uses a cot any more. Last Thursday I went to visit his school and found his teacher enthusiastic about his progress; of course, we are enthusiastic about her!

We plan to have an early lunch and then to go for a walk up San Antonio Canyon in the early afternoon. We haven't been there since the recent heavy rain and we expect to see many changes. Don Zenger said that there had been 29 inches of rain in two days in the San Bernardino Mountains. We were glad that we had a new roof!

We are thinking very much about you and to think that you are so close to Ranald and his family, as well as to so many friends, at Christmas time.

Donald, Ann and Ewen

December 14 1967

Ho-ho! It's cold! Of course we shouldn't complain when you are probably blanketed by snow and all is thrown into chaos by real winter; but we just aren't used to it. Two nights ago it snowed in Claremont. That is to say Annette Haldenby called up at 11 p.m. (after we had gone to bed) to say it was snowing. Of course I looked out, but there was no snow at our house. You see, they live north of Foothill Boulevard and that might have made a difference. But although we have not seen the snow ourselves we have been cold. Last night the temperature dropped to 26 degrees F. This is the coldest recorded here in a long time. And we had quite a wind two days ago so the beautiful leaves of our liquidambar trees have all gone and autumn changed to winter in a few hours.

Ann has needed the car and I haven't fancied going on my bicycle (despite my old Scottish scarf and Grantown gloves, which I am most thankful for) so I have been walking to work these past two or three days.

Despite the change of weather it is not easy to picture Christmas so close. Ann has done well, but we are way behind in sending Christmas cards; no doubt you are in good shape for that. The house is bulging with toys; various ingenious ones that Ann has picked out for Ewen and for other children too. Tomorrow is Ewen's last day at school. Ann, as "room mother" will be there for the party. Did you hear about the successful bake-sale that Ann organised to raise money for the school last week? Always a lot going on.

Last week I went to the $100 a plate dinner with Mrs. Seaver. Ann couldn't come because of her organization of the bake sale. I guessed that the dinner party probably cost Mrs. Seaver $10,000 for we had the best seats there. This was an event to raise funds for the Republican Party. Next year is an election year so they are off to a good start.

I will be glad of the Christmas vacation, possibly a chance to catch up on things that have got out of hand. At the end of January I go on a long lecture tour and this I must prepare for during the vacation. The future of the Computer Center is still occupying a good amount of my time; some success, but some dangers are in sight.

Although busy I have managed to read Meredith's *Beauchamp's Career*; Fielding's *Amelia* and Hazlitt's *Spirit of the Age* in the past few weeks. I am now reading Fielding's *Jonathan Wild*, which is a powerful satire somewhat like Swift's; I am enjoying its irony, done in masterly fashion. The Fielding and Hazlitt were Daddy's and the Meredith I got at Grants. I also read Addison's *Spectator*; but, as I told you, it is best read one or two speculations at a time, for they were published daily.

Another book I read recently was the *Memoirs of Lord Chandos* (Oliver Lyttelton). You might like to dip into that, especially his three chapters that give his portrait of Winston Churchill in wartime. You could get it at the library I suspect.

I still want to tackle bookbinding, but have not been able to find a supplier of the necessary equipment. This is surprising and frustrating, but no doubt I will get the information sooner or later. (Editor's note: Donald did eventually find the equipment he wanted. Then he and Ewen together developed a little project. One of their products still exists. A finger-painting by Ewen, a mixture of magenta and black, was used and bound with a spine of green tape to become the cover of a little book listing the names of our dinner party guests and the menus that we served.)

Lake Sequoia, California, August 22 1973

The course is coming to an end. On Saturday night I will be back home. It has been remarkably successful. It is really remarkable how they accommodate pipers of so many different ages and abilities. I have been in a class with two others – one a doctor from Montana, who is here with his wife and son, and the other a teacher in the San Fernando Valley. We have an hour's instruction together each morning on the practice chanter; the first week with John MacCaskill and the second week with Hugh MacCallum, both great names in Scottish piping. Most mornings there is a lecture on some aspect of maintenance of the pipes, seasoning, the bag, selecting the reeds etc. Then from 2 to 3 we have a class of about 8 people in Advanced Pibroch, last week with Hugh MacCallum and this week with Seumas MacNeill.

Some of the classes have been so good that I have recorded them on tape so that I can listen and learn again later. But our schedule is such a busy one that there is little time here for listening to tapes. There never seems enough time to practice before the next class comes again and we have new tunes!

From 3 to 4, we all play the pipes. Nine or ten boys are learning to march in a band, and the sound is wonderful to hear across the lake. Dinner is at 5:30 and usually there is a recital thereafter. One of the instructors plays a recital, always including a pibroch. Also, Seumas MacNeill made a series of tapes for the BBC and I think we have heard three of these. I have recorded all of them.

There is no time to waste. Every minute is needed for practice. But on Saturday afternoon I took a boy from Scotland (he had won a scholarship to come to this camp) and two others to see the Big Trees at Grant Grove, 6 miles away.

February 2, 1976

I went back to the department this evening to use the computer to help me prepare the Department's budget for the coming year, and what a difference I found in the air. It reminded me of a November evening in Scotland, little gusts of wind with moisture in it under a grey sky that reflected the city lights. I turned on the car radio and heard that there was a 70% chance of rain tomorrow. There were drops of rain on the windshield. What is remarkable in this is that we had had no rain for over six months. Can you believe it? It is a record in the history of Californian weather of course.

March 21 1976

I wrote just yesterday but now I find this air-letter written long ago and unfinished. This is Sunday afternoon and I am sitting in the garden. Ann has taken Ewen and a blind girl, Jan, riding. A pigeon is coo-cooing, the sky is blue and the air warm and scented like the finest day of summer. All along the border against the Tibbals', our neighbours', wall are bluebells that mass to give that wonderful misty blue which I used to love in a Scottish wood, though I now can't remember where. The azaleas, red and white, under the kitchen window, are a treat to look at. How lucky we are to enjoy this.

Yesterday, which was another beautiful day; we had a visit from the MacColls who were in fine form. In the morning we walked through the Botanic Garden, which we always enjoy, and in the afternoon they were delighted to follow Ewen as he drove his new electric wheelchair round the block. Ann gave us a lovely meatloaf and fruit salad for lunch and the MacColls took off at 4 o'clock because they always like to be home before dark.

After they left, I finished the figures for our tax return. I have been so busy in the past three months that I had been unable to do these finishing touches, though I had done 95% of the job at Christmas. I must now make an appointment with our tax adviser.

This morning I was writing my Report on the meeting of the Geological Society of America Committee on Publications, for I am Chairman again. Meantime Ewen went to church for the first time in his electric wheelchair. He took it on the road (to avoid kerbs) in high gear—it has two gears—and Ann says she had to run to keep up. All his friends at Church were of course highly delighted.

Now I must turn to a great pile of examination papers, which are never any pleasure to correct. Tonight George Clark and his son, Marcus, come for dinner. His wife, Loredana, is visiting her family in Italy.

The Seaver Connection

In late 1957, shortly before our marriage in December, the planning began to bring Pomona College's science programme into the forefront of American college education. Two major new science buildings, Seaver North and Seaver South, were to become a reality – thanks to the vision and immense generosity of Frank Seaver (Pomona class of

1905), of Hydril USA, an oil firm that then made "bits" for oil drills. In all his philanthropic work, Mr. Seaver was always supported and encouraged by Blanche, his wife of positive and determined character!

The Seaver connection not only dramatically influenced Donald's career – because of these new developments at Pomona he determined not to pursue the offer to join the faculty of the Geology Department at Berkeley – but it also introduced us both to some unexpected and remarkable social opportunities. The Seavers were very gracious about inviting Pomona College faculty to some unique events, and for many years the faculty wives were invited on their own to elegant afternoon pre-Christmas tea-parties at the Seavers' home! Even driving to such events was fun – bringing together Pomona's scientists and their wives.

The first event that I recall, and possibly the first for us all, was in 1958, – a resplendent Republican dinner at $1,000 a table – an awesomely large sum in those days – in downtown Los Angeles. It turned out that on this occasion (the only one!) I was seated next to Mr. Seaver. I am not sure if he found it amusing, but in recollection and with hindsight, I do! At each place the table was set with our first course, a beautifully decorated half pineapple adorned with grapes and a small china elephant. "What a cute little elephant!" I exclaimed, making it painfully obvious that I was probably the only person of the hundreds of guests there who was totally unaware of the symbol of the Republican Party.

Republican Victory Dinner and Rally

HONORING

RICHARD M. NIXON, SPIRO T. AGNEW, DR. MAX RAFFERTY
and the 58 Los Angeles County Candidates for Congress and the State Legislature

FEATURED SPEAKERS
RONALD REAGAN — *Governor of California*
SPIRO T. AGNEW — *Governor of Maryland and Vice Presidental Candidate*

SPONSORED BY
NIXON-AGNEW COMMITTEE
UNITED REPUBLICAN FINANCE COMMITTEE OF LOS ANGELES COUNTY
REPUBLICAN STATE CENTRAL COMMITTEE OF CALIFORNIA

$125 a plate
Informal

Friday, November 1, 1968 — 7:00 p.m.
Los Angeles Sports Arena
3939 So. Figueroa St.

TABLE NUMBER

2

Dinner with Frank and Blanche Seaver

In the late 1960s, at another fine evening when U.S. Vice President, Spiro Agnew was honored guest, while Richard Nixon was President. On that occasion, we were seated directly beneath "The High Table" so that we were well placed to enjoy the corny jokes of the Master of Ceremonies of that occasion. As the evening unfolded, Nelson Smith, Pomona's Professor of Chemistry, decided to ask all the guests at that top table to sign his menu-card/programme but didn't go on to collect the signature of the "light-weight" Master of Ceremonies. Little did any of us know that, though Spiro Agnew was indeed Vice-President, the somewhat frivolous Master of Ceremonies was destined to become President – Ronald Reagan! And security was tight – when Donald rose to his feet intending to find the restroom, the Secret Service people mobilised instantly. Donald was a marked man, and equally instantly, he was back in his seat!

Donald recollected with pleasure the occasion when he was the dancing partner of Irene Dunne, five-time recipient of the Academy Award for best actress; my most celebrated partner was Buddy Roger (in a splendid red velvet jacket), actor and husband of Mary Pickford, the legend of silent film. (I should add that ballroom dancing was never a forte of either of us!) And there was an embarrassing occasion when Donald and others accompanied Mrs. Seaver to the opera. Arriving late, but led by their audacious hostess, they swept into the auditorium in regal fashion even as the performance was already well under way.

On one of these occasions- in fact, the ARTS Turf Club Ball honouring Dr Aries Jan Haagen-Smit of Caltech and Alfred G. Vanderbilt, man of racing – Donald wore his kilt and I donned my McIntyre silk tartan sash. To our surprise, next morning in a brief article about the evening's on-goings, The *Los Angeles Times* mentioned our appearance in attire that is not normally seen in Southern California. "Most charming, however, were the couple from Claremont – he in his kilt, she with the McIntyre tartan draped across the bodice of her white gown."

We attended another dinner when the speaker was Dixy Lee Ray, dynamic politician. She had recently become the only woman ever to chair the Atomic Energy Commission. At that time, when awareness about the use of gendered language was just coming into vogue, to everyone's delight, Dixy told us with her dry sense of humour: "I may technically be known as The Chairman of the Commission but, for my part, I prefer to term myself The Sofa Person!"

And there was the memorable occasion when we dined with Barry Goldwater, another presidential candidate and influential Republican at a vast football stadium where we witnessed thousands of Americans singing *The Star-Spangled Banner* with passion, hand on heart......unique events where we could greatly enjoy seeing history unfold but, at the same time, were able to be strangely detached since we weren't eligible to vote. We never became American citizens!

On a Friday afternoon, while Seaver South was under construction and the Chemistry and Geology departments were still housed in Mason Hall, Nelson Smith and Donald happened to be looking out of the window onto College Avenue when they spotted Mr. Seaver, who had Parkinson's Disease, struggling to cross the road below them. Wondering if perhaps he was unwell, they rushed down to ask if they could help him. Quick as a wink came the response "Get me to the bank! Get me to the bank!" Since Mr. Seaver was carrying a cheque for $10,000, he was determined to reach the bank before it closed to ensure that full interest could be accumulated over the weekend.

On another occasion, a group of librarians were invited to go to the Seavers' Los Angeles home to collect copies of old magazines that they had gifted to the College. While the workers parcelled up the copies in the attic, Mr. Seaver climbed the stairs to see for himself how they were getting on. He surveyed the scene for some minutes and then, with a wry smile, made the observation "If you cut the string closer to the knot, it would go further." Aspiring millionaires take note!

Shortly after Seaver North and South were opened, it was announced, with only short notice, that that the Seavers were coming to see the new buildings in action. There was a quick scurry around to have everything as spick and span as possible and, since Mrs. Seaver frowned upon some modern ways, making sure that there would be no sighting of a faculty member or student sporting a beard! And there was careful inspection to determine that bare floors would not reveal any tell-tale footprints of bare feet!

During that tour, Donald noted with interest how carefully Mr. Seaver would pose questions to all who showed him the superb modern equipment that the Geology Department, thanks to him, now possessed. It seemed, however, that Mr. Seaver was barely listening to the replies he was given; what he really wanted to ascertain was that the person using the equipment fully understood it.

The Seavers had no children of their own but were devoted to their nephew Richard who went on to carry forward the expansion of Hydril

Corporation; so the Pomona faculty became almost like family. Indeed, when Frank Seaver died in 1964, it was a honour for Donald and two of his Pomona colleagues to be part of the team of cord bearers who accompanied the coffin, both in the church and at the cemetery.

★★★★★

In the spring of 1959 we were delighted to have a visit from Donald's parents. They travelled by ship through the Panama Canal and, of course, we went to meet them as they arrived in the harbour in Los Angeles. They had both greatly enjoyed this experience. Donald's mother, ever active and energetic, had felt like part of the crew as she had helped to paint some of the fittings on the deck. They were both so interested and delighted with all the saw in The New World – except when a tea-bag in a cafe was served with a jug of lukewarm water!

Donald's father had long been a fan of Wild West stories and, to include me in this pleasure, he gave me a copy of *The Virginian,* by Owen Wister, first published in 1902 and which claims to be "the most famous Western novel ever written". In my now somewhat faded copy, Donald's father added a personal note to the printed phrase "A Much-Loved American Classic – and not least by Abu Donald who gives this copy to Ann with love. 17.2.60.' And so on Lincoln's Birthday holiday weekend, the four of us set out to visit the Nevada desert, to see the Joshua trees *and* the setting of the Gold Rush and the haunts of genuine cowboys.

On Saturday evening we dined at a tiny crowded cafe in Beatty, Nevada – our entry there was somewhat dramatic – the locals eyed the four of us with some astonishment for it wasn't everyday that they had a visit from an erect but elderly man in a long black overcoat, wearing a trilby hat and leaning on a walking stick. Meanwhile Donald's father stood at the door – absorbing the whole Western scene and summing up each of fellows in their bright checked shirts and leather "chaps". "Why, that's the baddie over there – and that's the Sheriff leaning against the counter at the bar!"

Next morning – to Donald and his father's dismay/disapproval(!) – his mother and I enjoyed trying our luck at the slot machine before, penniless, we all set off to drive into Death Valley by way of the spectacular desert scenery of the remote and starkly beautiful Titus Canyon. I still recall, while passing through a tiny area of open space between the canyon narrows to spot, on that 27 miles one-way drive, what must surely have been one of the world's most remote mail/post box! I wonder if it is still there!

Recollections of Distinguished Visitors

Pomona College receives many visitors of distinction. Donald and I were fortunate that when celebrated people came from the United Kingdom we were often invited to the President's House to meet them.

The visit of former British Prime Minister **Sir Edward Heath** was full of interest. As I recall, he and his assistant were on their way home after a visit to China in 1979. Sir Edward gave a lecture at Little Bridges Hall of Music and spoke about the United Kingdom's role within the European Union. At dinner I was seated beside Sir Edward but social chit-chat did not come easily to him! (Donald was more successful discussing political theories and found that conversation enlightening.)

After dinner we all gathered on the balcony of the President's House overlooking College Avenue. President Alexander, aware that Sir Edward was an accomplished organist, asked if he might like to play the organ recently installed in Pomona's music department. Sir Edward liked that idea and looking across the street to the building opposite, he caught sight of its name.

"Is that organ in the Thatcher building?" he asked.

President Alexander, somewhat embarrassed, admitted that was the case. "Yes.." But Sir Edward didn't lose a beat: "Then it will be rather shrill!!"

(The building had been named after a Pomona donor – rather than Heath's successor as leader of the Conservative Party in the UK – but, to his credit, Sir Edward did indeed grace the evening by playing the organ!)

Alfred M. Worden – Astronaut

In March 1975, Alfred Worden, pilot of Endeavour, the command-module for the Apollo 15 mission July 26-August 7, 1971 – the fourth lunar landing mission and the first truly scientific one – lectured at Pomona College. He came to dinner at our home and then the four of us went out into our garden to look up at the moon as we tried to comprehend that this lovely person standing right there beside us, had actually been there.

During Apollo 15 Colonel Worden had logged 295 hours in space, nearly 67 hours of them in complete solitude while his two companions were on the moon's surface. He gave Ewen a cherished copy of his poetry book *"Hello Earth, Greetings from Endeavour"*. The work here is reproduced with permission.

"Hello Earth,
> *I see you shining*
> *through the glaze of space*
> *Floating in the oil-slick void*
> *A quilt around your face.*

Hello Earth
> *It's clear you're hiding*
> *Worldly problems from my view*
> *Could it be you are forgetting*
> *I am worldly too?*

Hello Earth
> *Please stop pretending*
> *You are sinless, new and pure*
> *The scars that you are hiding*
> *Only heighten your allure.*

Hello Earth
> *I wish you'd answer*
> *And in answering take stock*
> *It's clear you are a spaceship*
> *And must do with what you've got.*

Hello Earth
> *Your life is finite*
> *Does the answer lie out here?*
> *If we don't resolve your problems*
> *Life on Earth may be too dear.*

Hello Earth
> *Greetings from Endeavour!!"*

(With permission from Colonel Worden)

Special Friends at Pomona

Throughout his life Donald had a remarkable capacity for deep and enduring friendship, enhanced perhaps by the fact that he never stooped to the petty – gossip and trivia were of no interest to him. Indeed, Pomona was a perfect environment for Donald. He eagerly grasped the opportunities of a small liberal arts college (with approximately 1,200 students in our time) and the stimulation of intermingling with faculty members of many different of disciplines.

In early days, while **Alex Baird** (1932-85) was still a student, Donald and he worked closely together. In August 1955 they completed a mammoth tour of the geology of the Northwest, travelling through Oregon, Washington, Idaho, Montana, Wyoming, Colorado, Utah, Arizona and home to California. Donald's detailed notes in preparation for this trip still exist, complete with drawings and numerous literary references. For Donald, newcomer to the United States of America, this was an essential experience to teach geology more adequately in that country. In due course, Alex and Donald's pleasure in each other's work and interests continued through Alex's joining the faculty. As computer skills and technology developed, they shared in pioneer work of national interest through the analysis of rocks from Mars. Sadly, Alex died prematurely from a heart attack.

Among geologists/friends who joined the Geology Department, albeit somewhat briefly, were **Gerhard Oertel** and **John Christie**. Donald had worked with both of these men in Edinburgh days and, as the Pomona department expanded, was delighted to invite them to join the faculty. Gerhard, who came by way of Goa, and John from Scotland, both moved on to distinguished careers at UCLA.

Nelson Smith, much loved and honoured Professor of Chemistry, worked closely with Donald throughout the building of the Seaver labs. There are many delightful and humorous stories about Nelson and the jokes he and the students played upon each other – I recall tales of an automobile that miraculously appeared in the lab at a chemistry class; and of the toilet that, one evening, enterprising students welded in place of the desk in Nelson's office and yet, of which there was absolutely no trace next morning!

And there was the prank that John Christie, of the Geology faculty, played upon Nelson while accompanying Donald and the newly arrived Gerhard and Irmgard Oertel on a tour of Mason Hall, which the chemistry department shared with geology. As the party arrived in the attic, Nelson was in the throes of the messy task of cleaning the chemistry still. From his stance inside the still, Nelson greeted the party cordially. His pants/trousers were carefully folded over the rim of the still but, leaving no time for protest, John whisked them away commenting that Nelson would find them flying from the flagpole! Needless to say, in due course Nelson ensured that he got his revenge! It was a sad day indeed when Nelson lost his life while he and his son, Roger, were hiking in snow on his beloved Mount Baldy. Indeed, in the 1960s, while working in tandem with Frank R. Seaver, benefactor, it would be impossible to estimate the immeasurable role that Donald and Nelson, together with Corwin Hansch, Professor of Chemistry and with Charles Fowler, Professor of Physics, played in enhancing the science programmes of Pomona College.

For many happy years Donald looked forward to lunch most weekdays at The Claremont Colleges Faculty House. It was a considerable honour to be invited as a regular at "Vincent's Table" hosted by Vincent Learnihan, Professor of Medieval History. There, where intellectual conversation and laughter mingled abundantly, Donald was in his element, stimulated and cheered by this lively mid-day break in the company of other warm and witty campus personalities – President David Alexander; Harry Carroll, Professor of Greek; Wayne Steinmetz, of Chemistry and Rosemary Choate, Pomona alumna, to name but a few.

Donald's contacts on the campus were wide and varied. He had much pleasure in running two summer programs with **Martha Andresen,** Professor of English and renowned Shakespearean scholar. On one occasion Donald invited **Robert Mezey,** then poet in the English Department, to discuss Robert Frost's poem *Sitting by a Bush in Broad Sunlight* with his beginning geology class. To this day, Bob recalls his pleasure in this unusual experience. He claims that scientists who appreciate poetry are few and far between. Donald enjoyed his friendship with **Bob Woods** of the History department; **David Davis,** Director of the Honnold Library; and many many others.

Throughout most of Donald's years at Pomona, the Geology Department Library was housed within the Department, later to be integrated into Honnold Library In those early days, librarian **Brian Ebersole** was frequently to be found at Seaver South, ever a much admired friend and member of the departmental team. Donald and Brian shared great respect and friendship. Another firm friend and supporter was **Gerhard Ott,** technician in the Zoology Department – which shared the Seaver South building with the Geology department. Gerhard helped Donald in so many ways – especially with photographic work. Gerhard and his lovely wife Uschi have been wonderful family friends all through the decades.

The Geology Department has always been blessed by its secretary/administrators. **Shirley Bolton** and **Jean Mackay** were both exceptionally efficient and much appreciated as trusted colleagues and friends by Donald and Don Zenger as well as being "surrogate parental" friends and advisers to generations of students. Many, many others – both as faculty members and as students – came and moved on in our time. I think especially of **George Clark** who returned to the department as a mature student. Through friendship with Donald, George entered into the burgeoning world of computing which in due course, led him to master and enjoy a complete change of career. **Don Doehring** and **Ed Welday,** also enrolled as mature students to find that their lives took off in new and unexpected directions as a result of their work with Donald at Pomona's Geology Department .

And throughout those many years from 1964, Donald and **Don Zenger** continuously complemented and supported each other in a beautiful way. Indeed, it speaks volumes that their teachings and happy team-work together have significantly contributed to the education of some of America's finest geologists of our times.

Of course there were many, many other friends whose relationship with Donald intermingled with the life of the College. One of these was the San Francisco publisher, **W. H. Freeman,** who would have eagerly included a work by Donald on his book list had Donald found the time to write it! Bill wrote: "You, Donald, continue to amaze me! I have never known one who so combines breadth with depth, lucidity with precision, and conviction with modesty about it." Bill often visited our home and I carry a picture of him still – he would be with us in vivacious conversation and then, when it was time to leave, he would walk away briskly and determinedly down our garden pathway, with never a backward glance.

As I reflect upon the influence Donald has had upon so many (not least myself!) – I marvel in deep and humble gratitude.

The McColls of Crestline

Here is a tale, albeit inadequate, of one of our most significant and precious family friendships. Alas, it came to us through tragedy.

Donald took great care, and found much pleasure, in teaching **Robert McColl (1938-1961)**. Bob had grown up amidst the big trees of the San Bernardino Mountains, deeply in touch with his environment, exploring all the rugged mountain creeks, the forests and desert beyond, questioning and probing the secrets of nature. He wanted to know more and came to realise that this could be achieved by studying geology. Somehow, I know not how, Bob came to Pomona College. Studying there was certainly a challenge, for Bob did not have the advantage of the academic background of many of the Claremont Colleges' students, but determination won out and he graduated from Pomona in 1961, with a major in the Department of Geology that Donald led.

The summer of Bob's graduation ("Bobby" to his family), Donald helped him arrange the adventure of a lifetime, a month's geological research in the wilds of Alaska under the auspices of The Geological Survey. Bob sent glowing reports of his experience to his parents. And then, on August 6, came the terrible news that he and his companion, Don Miller, had been rafting down the Kiagna River when they were swept away in a flash flood without hope of survival. Their bodies were discovered by pilot Howard Knutson who, checking on them from his plane, had seen them alive just the day before.

On hearing of this tragedy, Donald and his mother, both quicksilver of character, jumped into our car and sped up the mountain to visit Bob's parents in the log cabin home they had built themselves. Donald had never met them before. (Donald's mother, I should add, just three months widowed, had come to be with us for the summer. Ewen was one month old.)

Over the next twenty-eight years, it was at Crestline, perhaps more than anywhere else, that Donald would totally relax. And his role as their son's professor continued in a sense, as Donald shared informally his passion and knowledge of geology and astronomy with Bob's parents. Indeed we venture to surmise that Bob's grieving father may have found his greatest consolation in having Donald augment his profound understanding and insights about the mountains that he knew and loved so much. And they supported us as new parents, Ewen's beloved "Auntie Della and Uncle Bob."

Della was extraordinarily gifted as a cook and loved to experiment with new recipes; the family cookie jar was always filled with delectable goodies. She was talented too with her hands and shared her gifts generously, making beautiful covers to keep Ewen cosy on his mountain visits and creating for us many exquisite, fragile artistic ornaments that have stood the test of time. Bob, eminently practical too, ran his own upholstery business. He restored several of our living room chairs and, some 50 years on, they continue to grace our home.

Along with Ewen, we all hiked together, camped together, and laughed together. A memorable trip to the Mojave Desert included camping close to a noisy pack of wild donkeys and visiting the Ubehebe Crater to the north of Death Valley. And occasionally, in the summer, when Ewen and I were in London for Ewen's intensive therapy sessions with Mrs Bobath, Donald would enjoy peace and therapy too, at Crestline.

One summer Della collected a cocoon of a Monarch Butterfly. She carefully brought this to Ewen so that we three could enjoy the remarkable experience of seeing the beautiful butterfly emerge to hang gracefully from the branch of a tree in our garden before it took off on its own life adventure.

In the spring of 1970, Bob and Della visited us in Scotland during Donald's sabbatical leave year in Edinburgh. Della researched many details of our pre-planned itinerary before arriving in Scotland, no mean feat in pre-Internet access days. We visited Linlithgow Palace, the Romans in Falkirk; the history of the Picts and of the Highlands and Islands. In northwest Scotland, we even tracked down other members of the McColl clan and went on to enjoy the majestic scenery of the Great Glen so intimately known to Donald. And then, finally with Ewen, we all visited my parents on their sheep farm by the Devil's Beef Tub in the Scottish Borders. It was a wonderful, memorable and bonding time.

In 1990, Della, still vibrant with her great sense of fun and adventure, visited us with her daughter Barbara at our country home at Kinfauns. We all enjoyed two happy and full weeks exploring and relishing the great beauty of Perthshire and Fife.

It seemed almost incomprehensible when we heard that, on arriving back home in California, the very next morning our beloved Della drove to the post office high in the San Bernardino Mountains. While parking the car, she mistakenly put it into reverse gear and backed over the edge of the road. She died in the car.

While composing this vignette, Barbara and I have corresponded. What she has told is a revealing tale of great courage. I just wish Donald had known of it.

Barbara writes: "About six months before Della and I visited you in Scotland, she spent a couple of days preparing for her death. She made sure I knew everything I needed to know and where I could find all the important papers to deal with family affairs as my father was already suffering from dementia by that time.

"Della had had heart trouble; she knew that her time was near and that the trip to Scotland would be her last grand adventure. She lived long enough to spend her last days with you. You and Donald made her last days glorious. After her death her doctor asked me if she had planned her death and I then realised that, yes, she had planned her death. The trip would kill her and she knew it. That is the way she wanted to die. It just so happened that it came when she was in the car."

For several years, Bob continued to live in their home in the woods, ever fiercely independent and even defying authorities when a forest fire order decreed that all residents evacuate their homes!

Our family has been greatly privileged to have shared in the life of such a remarkable and courageous family. Barbara, who once raised a prairie wolf (coyote) as a family pet, writes, "It is fun to live in my childhood home. My children, grandchildren and great-grandchildren are all enjoying the family home as Della would have wanted.

A Salute to Donald McIntyre – March 1989

Mason L. Hill, Chief Geologist of Richfield Oil Corporation, Class of 1926 – and, in 1991, recipient of the first Alumni Distinguished Service Award from Pomona College.

Donald McIntyre came directly to Pomona College from his teaching position at the University of Edinburgh to replace A. O. Woodford (Chairman of the Geology Department since established by him in 1920). Consequently, he faced comparisons, especially by Woodford's loyal geology graduates.

However, I quickly discovered Donald's competence by checking on how my son Jim (history major, class of '57) had gotten an A in Donald's first class at Pomona. Knowing that Jim had no bent for science, I wondered if Donald had been too easy on him. After seeing Jim's class notes, it became clear to me that Donald gave a solid comprehensive and comprehensible beginning geology course (and that Jim took good notes).

Geology Professors – Dr A.O. Woodford
(Woody) and Donald.

I had no opportunity to become well acquainted with Donald until after my 1969 retirement from ARCO, but by 1974 I was given a second home in the geology department by Donald, which I continue to cherish and enjoy through the courtesy of Don Zenger and his staff. As I have become better and better acquainted with Donald, my appreciation of him and his talents has become greater and greater.

I see some of his talents to be: 1) his intellectual ability to keep up on new concepts in geology, and other sciences while placing them in a context of the history of science; 2) his outstanding ability to present these concepts and their histories by speaking with enthusiasm to excite his listeners, from one person to large audiences, and 3) he obviously prepares well for each lecture, although he may have to present the subject a multitude of times in the classroom. However, his resourcefulness is illustrated by a lecture at CalTech a few years ago.

In this case, no projector for his slides was available, so Donald proceeded to present his subject in a most interesting manner by reading in his inimitable way from some of the literature he had available. His lectures are all so interesting that my wife, Marie, and I go far to hear him – and the same general subjects are so freshly presented that they are new (recently, March 13, 1989, we heard Donald speak on the history of geology to a Pitzer College class on the history of science).

Donald is in demand as a speaker for special occasions in near and far-away places (e.g. in China a few years ago). Most of these talks have been carefully researched and written in preparation for the presentation, but rarely are his manuscripts available to potential readers. Most of them would be enjoyed by a large readership but Donald is, mistakenly in my opinion, not interested in publication. Some of these that I know about are: l) John Clerk of Eldin: His Life and Times, and Contributions to Geology, 134-page manuscript written in connection with the recent publication of the Lost Illustrations (lost for 200 years and discovered by Donald McIntyre in the inherited archives of the current John Clerk).

These geologic field drawings by John Clerk were to have been in Hutton's 3rd volume of the Theory of the Earth (first volume published in 1788, the second in 1825, and the third never published because the illustrations were not available). Donald's beautifully written and wonderfully informative text (used by him in Edinburgh for the bicentennial celebration in Edinburgh of Hutton's Theory of the Earth) was typed by Jean MacKay and read by me (and no one else, probably not excepting Donald himself). It should be available in print for a readership such as that of the *New Yorker* magazine; 2) his 1985, 23-page manuscript on James Hutton (1726-1797) and the Abyss of Time; 3) The Dark Backward and Abysm of Time: A case study of creativity (10 p.) presented at the University of Idaho in 1986; 4) Explorations in Science (23 p.), John Wesley Powell Lecture for the AAAS in Wichita, Kansas in 1988, and 5) other unpublished manuscripts such as the one presented by Donald at the 1988 Convocation of Pomona College.

In addition, Donald leads a double career by becoming an authority on the APL computer language which has made him in demand as a speaker for computer scientists worldwide (others will attest to Donald's role in this field).

Pomona College, its students and many of his associates are now to be left in a sort of vacuum without Donald. I, for one (as an 85-year-old student of Donald's), will greatly miss his intellect and day-to-year friendship. My last line can only be a wish for many happy and productive years for Donald, Ann and Ewen, in Scotland.

★★★★★

On Donald's Retirement in July 1989 he received a large volume filled with beautiful letters from former students at Pomona College.

Though Donald might not have chosen to have these quotations published, they paint such a fine picture of Donald – the teacher – that they deserve to be shared.

They are here with gratitude to the students who have given their permission for publication.

Here are some excerpts.

Neville L Carter, Director and Professor, Texas A & M University, Class of 1956

When you arrived at the beginning of my junior year at Pomona, it was like a fresh breeze (or gale) which, in fact, carried with it a great deal of inspiration concerning new concepts in structural geology.

Because of your rare and engaging personality, and because you are a true scholar, the history of earth sciences became alive and exciting at your many invited keynote lectures. For all these reasons, you live in the hearts of many.

But that academic stuff is much less interesting than the spirit of the man himself – he was so bright, witty and fun. Some of my fondest memories come from extended field trips, both at spring break my junior year (1955) and at summer field camp (6 weeks) that same year. Spring break took place in some freezing cold marble mountains and at the end of each day, Donald and about six students shared a gallon of cheap wine after which he broke out the bagpipes and walked away up a ravine, the pipes wailing a slowly fading mournful tune – majestic! Bagpipes were also involved in the hot, dry Nevada desert during the summer. Across the street from our trailer quarters was a cowboy bar in nowhere Nevada, a bar that provided a beer or two for the students after a sweltering field day. On July 4th, the place was packed and somehow we persuaded Donald to break out the pipes and give a concert to the crude cowboys there, none of whom, I'm sure, had ever heard bagpipes, or seen a Scotsman, before! Reluctantly, Donald did so in this ultra-strange venue and, surprisingly, the performance was politely received by the lubricated audience, though we were on edge the whole time and would not have pulled such a stunt had we any sense or maturity at all!

And in November 2009, Neville wrote to Ann ... I was truly impressed by Donald's scholarship far afield from his science. I had the pleasure of attending several banquets at which he was MC or guest speaker, and was blown away by the diverse and fascinating topic delivered, always with incredible enthusiasm and wit. I've been to many such in my career and have never been captivated or entertained so well!

Donald McIntyre was truly a remarkable human being – a giant on whose shoulders we have all become better people and a man loved by all of merit – he's truly missed and anything you can do to keep him alive in our minds will be most appreciated.

L. J. Patrick Muffler, United States Department of the Interior, Geological Survey, California, Class of 1958

Surprisingly, one of my keenest memories of your classes at Pomona is of invertebrate palaeontology, a required course hardly fitting your primary specialities. The easiest thing for you would have been to have marched pedantically through the textbook, simply preparing us with a mass of trivia to spew forth on the graduate record exam, but equally likely to turn us off from that branch of earth science. Instead, as I remember, we spent about 98% of our time on the details of brachiopod morphology. I suspect that at the beginning of the course you knew precious little about brachiopod morphology, but your insatiable curiosity found all sorts of interesting aspects: the mathematics of the shell patterns, the ecology of their environment, and the principles by which palaeontologists discriminated the different species. Those of us fortunate enough to have taken that course learned about paleontological principles and scientific excitement, far more important and long-lasting than a memorized list of Latin names keyed to sketches that we might see on some required (and soon to be forgotten) examination.

Since you and I arrived at Pomona the same month, if not the same day, and since I was present at your first lecture in Geology 1, I guess I can claim to be one of your first Pomona students. I'm proud to make that claim. Your enthusiasm, dedication, and brilliance had a profound impact on me and my career. Simply, I can't imagine a better teacher.

Barry Raleigh, Lamont-Doherty Geological Observatory, Palisades, N,Y. Class of 1956.

On the occasion of this move from Pomona, you should know that for your students an inexplicable phenomenon called the McIntyre Effect was profound. There is almost always in the early stages of any scientist's career a collision; with a senior colleague where, in transferring part of the teacher's momentum to the student, who then accelerates with no less of momentum by his mentor, Newton's laws are defied. You certainly accomplished that feat repeatedly but I can tell you that, in my case, despite large inertial forces, the acceleration was dramatic. I found at Pomona an absorption and life-long love for our subject that has truly illuminated my entire life.

Robert Tilling ,United States Department of the Interior, Geological Survey, Menlo Park; California, Class of 1958

The passing years have clouded my memory some, but I still remember vividly how I decided to become a geology major. Toward the end of my freshman; year, I was beginning to have some serious doubts about sticking with my declared major (mechanical engineering). Knowing my interest in science and keen appreciation of the outdoors, Neville Carter ('56) suggested that I take a geology class "for kicks." Neville also said "this new guy McIntyre is *really neat*" and so I took your Geology 1 course. If I remember correctly, you (dressed in kilts) introduced the first lecture with a brief piece on your bagpipes, followed by a fascinating, animated lecture on the early development of geology. To say that I was impressed would be an understatement. As the course progressed and the novelty of your Scottish accent became routine (well, almost), I became thoroughly absorbed in the exciting new world of geology you unfolded with each lecture or assignment.

Arthur G. Sylvester, Editor of The Geological Society of America Bulletin and Chair of the Geology Department at the University of California, Santa Barbara, class of 1959

You have heard me relate two stories of how you inspired me when I was a wayward geology major. The most vivid incident was on a senior field studies trip to Mountain Pass where Barry Watson and I had studied the petrology of the alkaline rocks and rare earth deposits there......we went there one weekend with you and the rest of the class and you dutifully followed us around listening with half an ear to what we were parroting from the published literature. After a couple of hours, you asked us if we knew what was the sharp, colourful contact a few hundred meters up the hill where, incidentally, neither Barry or I had visited, nor where there was a trail. Barry and I fumbled and mumbled in our ignorance and embarrassment, but when we consulted a map, we realized it was a thrust fault. You, being a proper thrust-oriented Scottish structural geologist and less interested in the petrology of strange rocks, asked if we had been there and what did it look like. We said sheepishly that we did not know, whereupon; your eyes sparkled as you said "Well, let's go and see!" and you proceeded at a trot straight up the hill without benefit of so much as a trail. That was the first time I had ever seen someone evince genuine intellectual curiosity and excitement. Now, nearly two score years later, I realize it is something that must be experienced. One cannot learn it from a book.

Another incident ...I went to see you in your office for advice in my junior *(3rd)* year about where I was heading. My recollection is that the meeting was quite brief. You looked at my grade record and simply remarked "You can't play football all your life". These may have been the only words you spoke, but they were more than sufficient......

Bob Dickey, Geotechnical Incorporated, California, Class of 1964

The most outstanding of your abilities to me were your energy and your ability to explain everything in an infinite variety of ways. I was young and considered myself an athlete, but I felt like a steer next to a racehorse in your presence. And if brains had tachometers, mine registered 600 rpm to your 6000. The most amazing physical feat was during the spring '64 field trip. Dear Bob decided to pass along to all his mountain climbing tips, being unaware of your childhood romps with Hillary (i.e. W.H. Murray) et al.. Having heard enough of Bob's advice you challenged the class to a race from the Mountain Pass thrust fault down to the Travelall, and whipped us all! Explanations made to me through my years in your classes were clear and concise. Of course, every student didn't understand each point immediately, so you would read their faces and explain again differently until you knew they understood.

Eugene Pearson, Professor and Chair, Department of Geology and Geography, College of the Pacific, California, Class of 1967

Your passion for learning and your joy at discovering continue to inspire me twenty-two years after my departure from your geology department. By your example, you taught me to value knowledge and to never stop learning and inquiring.

One of my fondest Pomona College memories is crossing an alluvial fan riding in the Pomona College field vehicle with Donald McIntyre at the controls. The jeep-trail, if it existed, was in terrible condition. While you fought to control the vehicle as it bounded across the fan, you continued to explain the structural features of the mountain range to the west in the perfectly organized and controlled manner of an instructor in a quiet classroom.

Allen F. Glazner, Professor, The University of North Carolina, at Chapel Hill, Department of Geology, Class of 1976 – Allen struggled with his early experiences of computing using Fortran and wrote to Donald.

…… *so* I concluded that computers weren't much good for anything. Then came mineralogy, and a much simpler way of doing computing. I remember asking you how hard it would be to do linear regression in APL; and you smiled and said "Not hard at all!" You then took me down the hall, called up the computer (this was in the days of the Selectric/acoustic coupler setup) and solved the problem in a few seconds. l was convinced on the spot that FORTRAN was dead.

I am grateful that you taught us that there is nothing wrong with delving into subjects that one isn't supposed to understand, as long as you do it with an open mind. Your greatest skill as a teacher was in showing students how to think about problems, rather than in filling their heads with facts.

Ray Weldon, Professor of Geology, University of Oregon, Class of 1977

One of my fondest memories of Pomona recently shared with other students of our era was a field trip you led with us to look at low angle structures and megabreccias in eastern California. We remembered drinking Irish coffees, and you requesting an Irish coffee without the coffee; we remembered our rousting us out of the gully we were sleeping in as it started raining (Ed. note: *it was a flash flood in which the McIntyre red plastic kitchen basin was swept away forever*) and eating breakfast at some ungodly hour in Las Vegas (*where obsessed gamblers were unceasingly busy at the slot machines).* We remember cycling people to the front of the van so that there were fresh people to keep up with your enthusiastic monologue at all times. I feel that at the end of my career, if my students had similar remembrances of me, I would be very proud and would consider my efforts a success.

Sorena Sorensen, Curator in charge, Rock and Ore Collections, Smithsonian Institute, Washington .D.C. Class of 1978

I was bright, diligent, and yes, even "eager, thoughtful and reverent," when I entered the little world of the Pomona Geology Department, but I was also nervous, insecure, awkward, and frankly terrified of persons in authority. Mercifully I am less of all these things now, and my transformation began in part by your efforts. You encouraged me to enter the larger world of the scholar, to enjoy, in that liberal arts cliché "learning for its own sake" and to try to understand the language of the history written by rocks, as well as to interpret the past attempts of others to comprehend the Earth.

Eleanour Snow, the University of Arizona, Department of Geosciences, Class of 1982.

Donald McIntyre was an exciting lecturer. From the first day of class he had me hooked. His lectures were so well timed, we used to say that he went from zero to sixty in three-point-nine seconds, and he cruised along until the final bell, when he stopped on a dime. Those precious 90 minutes in between were filled with energy, excitement and discovery. They left me thrilled and exhausted, as they must surely have left him . . . He lit a fire in my curiosity which burns stronger every day. I will be thrilled if some day I am able to inspire someone else, as Donald McIntyre did me.

John-Mark Staude, Harvard University, Department of Earth and Planetary Sciences, Class of 1987.

While at Pomona I enjoyed your classes and was the first to go hear your campus-wide lectures. The crowds did flock, no one ever knew what Donald McIntyre might pull out of his hat, but without a doubt and without fail, it was original, memorable, and even worth missing lunch. Of all my meetings and classes with Dr McIntyre, the time that stands out most clearly in my mind, is the time I asked him about finding references on garnet. ...he took me to his computer and we spent all Sunday afternoon on his computer working with GeoRef and I didn't realise until well after 8 p.m. that we had missed dinner. I guess I still have one meal left but I'd give that up at the drop of a stone to go to the library or just exploring with Dr. McIntyre. Here at Harvard I *run* from library to library and think maybe someday I'll be like Dr McIntyre.

Cara Davis, Class of 1988.

I remember a day not long ago when I shivered with cold and awe as the glorious majesty of the Swiss Alps was unfurled before me. The mountains pierced the snow-laden pines, soaring high above to a jagged grey and white horizon cutting a steel-blue sky. I gazed at the wildly twisting layers of rock, pulled and folded like taffy at the fury of the ancient gods. But my trip to the Alps was somewhat unconventional; it took place inside a small classroom on the second floor of a California university science building. In that dark room, with the slide projector humming and the air conditioning circulating arctic air, a certain Scottish professor wove a special Alpine magic.

We not only ranged the continents in that tiny classroom, we travelled in time as well. The magic carried us to another century where we watched scientists who raved of jams and frothy soups, and of rocks squished like toothpaste between colliding continents. We saw their original sketches and maps, we read their books, and we were granted glimpses of their oft-tormented souls. We travelled through the changing centuries and decades, and watched science and society mature towards one another. And there were yet other journeys; we were swept by seismic wave to the steaming bowels of the earth, and by bolt of light to the far reaches of the solar system. In a nearby classroom, the same magic led us to the inner world of many an innocent crystal where we watched atoms arranged in a multitude of symmetries and patterns. There were many journeys, and many kinds of magic.

Who would ever guess that this small slim professor in the grey cardigan is such a sorcerer? Who would imagine that this modest man who drinks plain hot water and serves the best scotch shortbread could be a world-renowned computer program expert who dusts a pack of 20-year-olds on a rugged eight-mile hike and recommends "new age" books on Gaia and extraterrestrials? Despite his maturity and wealth of knowledge and experience, he retains a young child's curiosity and fascination with the world. This is his magic. And he weaves his spells so that we may discover for ourselves – once again as children – the labyrinth interconnectedness of everything.

I may forget some of the names and places and times through which we travelled. But the thrill of the great mysteries unfolding and connecting, yet forever expanding, I can never forget.

Torchbearers

Southland slopes in their sunlit repose
Lie around Pomona, around Pomona.
Soft winds breathing of poppy and rose
Sigh around Pomona, around Pomona.
Stern was the promise our fathers knew,
Pine-clad ranges soft misted blue,
Scent of the sagebrush and yucca that grew
High around Pomona, around Pomona.
Ours be the faith of the builders whose dreams
Rais'd our fair Pomona, our fair Pomona.
Bear we the torch of their honor whose gleam
Blaz'd o'er fair Pomona, o'er fair Pomona.
Where bleak and barren the sagebrush roll'd
Rise green orchards of fruited gold,
Glory to those who, with vision of old
Gaz'd o'er fair Pomona, o'er fair Pomona.

Pomona College song

Donald's Centennial Address at Pomona College in 1987, along his tributes to Frank R.Seaver, Trustee of Pomona College; to Dr E.Wilson Lyon, President of Pomona College, to Dr. Nelson Smith, Professor of Chemistry and to Dr. Harry J Carroll, Professor of Greek, appear together at the end of this volume.

Chapter 7
Travels

"The world is charged with the Grandeur of God"

Gerard Manley Hopkins

Both as a geologist and later through his involvement with the computer languages of APL and J, Donald had many opportunities to travel and to give lectures both in the United States and in Scotland.

In the summer of 1955, Donald, with Alex Baird, a young faculty member, made a Grand Geological Tour of the western United States. Unfortunately, no record has been found of this six-week tour but it certainly played a very important role in Donald's understanding of the European approach to geology to that of the New World – land of tornadoes, earthquakes and active volcanoes.

In 1956, his second summer at Pomona College, Donald organized an ambitious trip along with his faculty colleague, John Shelton, and the Geology major students of that era. At my request some fifty years on, Stan Madsen, with editorial input from Peter Newman (also on the trip), has kindly written his recollections of that adventure.

Pomona College Summer Field Trip, 1956
by Stan Madsen
edited by Peter Newman,

In the summer of 1956 all of the geology majors at Pomona College who were going into their senior year, attended a six-week field program near Bahia Tortugas (Bay of Turtles) in Baja, Mexico. It is located on the Pacific Ocean side of Baja about 330 miles south of the U.S. border. The students attending the field trip were: Tom Jeter, John Killen, George Lloyd, Stan Madsen, Grant Meyer, Pete Newman, Bill Recht, Bob Ward and Tom Wright. The professors in charge of the field trip were Dr. John Shelton and Dr. Donald McIntyre.

The area selected for the field program was based on geologic studies that Don was doing for Scripps Institute of Oceanography on Cedros Island, off the coast of Baja. The rocks on the island were highly deformed and Don postulated that there must be a major fault system causing the deformation. Based on the orientation of the stresses, he further postulated that the fault system extended into the mainland of Baja near Bahia Tortugas.

Pomona College Baja California
Summer Field Trip, 1956

Because Bahia Tortugas was a small fishing village in a remote area with no roads to the town, it was necessary to establish a self-contained camp. There were two-man tents for the geologists and one larger tent for cooking and eating. There was no fresh water supply and the only water available was the seawater processed from the village's fishing cannery. We were allowed to get several cans of water per day. Because of the limited supply, we recycled it several times before throwing it out.

John Shelton was responsible for ordering the food for the trip. We had to live on canned products and powdered eggs and milk. John decided we needed only one meat product—Vienna sausages. We would put sausages in the powdered eggs, take a can of sausages into the field for lunch, and then add sausages to the spaghetti for dinner. After one week I was sick of Vienna sausages and have not eaten any since. The only ones who liked the sausages were Julio and Manuel, our two little camp followers from the village. For them this was new and exciting Gringo food (i.e., it wasn't fish). Peanut butter and jelly sandwiches were provided for our lunches. Since I do not like peanut butter, I lived on jelly sandwiches for six weeks. When we ran out of bread, we made pancakes and used them as bread.

Transportation to the site was a challenge as there were no roads. Most of us traveled to the site on a Scripps Institute of Oceanography research vessel which was harbored at their complex in La Jolla. We slept on cots on deck and encountered some heavy swells on our trip south. Pete Newman and Grant Meyer drove to the site in a 4-wheel drive Jeep pickup. This required them to drive cross-country for about 90 miles. John Shelton flew his Cessna plane and was able to land near our camping site.

Before we could do any field mapping, we had to get permission from the Mexican government. The document we received stated that we could do geologic mapping along the coast. We showed this document to a lieutenant stationed in Bahía Tortugas. He was in charge of a local Army unit consisting of five men. He interpreted the document to mean that we could only do geologic studies along the coast. We immediately made contact with the Mexican government to revise the document so we could go inland.

After a week we still did not have a revised document, so we decided to cheat a little. Tom Jeter and I got in our boat and rowed around the point where we were quite sure that no one would see us. We did go inland to do some mapping. We got back in the boat just before dusk to row back to the camp, but did not realize that a strong wind had come up and we were rowing against it. We made slow progress and, as it got dark, it was hard to see where we were going. Finally we saw the lanterns at our campsite and headed for the light. As we neared camp, we realized there were three-foot-high waves. Fortunately, we caught one of these waves and rode right up on the beach as though we had planned it that way. The rest of the geologists were just forming a team to go search for us.

We finally got permission to go inland so we could start mapping the area of interest. Because there were no topographic maps of the area, we had to make our own. This involved building two primary survey monuments, a number of secondary monuments and locating them on our map. Then we used plane tables and alidades to locate our position on the map by triangulation. This whole process taught us mapping skills that most geologists, even back in those days, never learned.

After a long day in the field, we would return to our camp and go for a swim as a substitute for a shower. On some evenings we would get together after dinner to discuss what we had seen in the field. These discussions were very interesting because Don would share his thoughts. He observed a lot more than we did. He also shared some great stories about his past experiences which were always interesting and amusing.

Each day two of us would stay in camp and be in charge of KP duty. We would prepare the breakfast and the dinner, clean up around the camp, and walk over to the fish cannery and get our quota of water. We waited in line with the local people who came to get their one bucket of water each day. One time they let us go to the front of the line and we did not know why. Apparently, they had just cleaned out their equipment and the water had a very strong odor.

When we were on KP duty we had some free time in the afternoon. Most of us would hike to an area where we had been told there were sharks teeth in a sedimentary unit. After digging with our geology picks, most of us did find some. I found about seven sharks teeth and I still have them. On the day Tom Jeter and I did our sharks teeth exploration, we decided to go for a swim at a nearby isolated beach. I was the first one in the water and was standing in water up to my knees. Suddenly, I felt all the sand below my feet begin to move. I headed for shore as fast as I could. I think I was standing on top of a nest of stingrays bedded in the sand! I did not go back to investigate further.

During one of the days when most of us were in camp, we noticed a small motorboat entering the bay. It circled around for a while, apparently checking out what was happening on shore. We could see that there was a man, a woman, several children and a large dog. They anchored off shore and the man came ashore by himself into our camp. He asked what we were doing there and we told him we were on a geologic field trip from Pomona College in California. He said "Oh, geologists; I hire and fire them all the time. You probably know me, my name is Steen." We students did not recognize the name, but Professor Shelton did and said; "You are the man who discovered the uranium mine, Mi Vida, in Utah." Charles Steen then told us about how he discovered the mine. He had been exploring the mine for several years, but did not realize that he had found uranium until he felt ill, went to a doctor and was diagnosed with uranium poisoning. He then went back to the places he had slept in his explorations and found his lode which he eventually sold to the U.S. Government for something over 50 million dollars. Mr. Steen was very full of himself while his wife was busy cooking and taking care of their children and the dog on a yacht that had a broken propeller. He had radioed for help and was waiting for his plane to bring a new one. After the new propeller had been installed, we saw them leaving the harbor as we were heading out into the field. When we returned that evening we noticed that the yacht was being towed back into the harbor. I guess owning a plane and a yacht has its own set of problems.

The native Mexicans at Bahía Tortugas were basically very friendly, but the military authorities there did not allow them to visit our camp. We did shop for bread at the local market while filling our cans with water. We were also invited to a celebration they had where they elected "Miss Bahía Tortugas" from the local "belles." As the population was very small, it was a limited selection, but they did have a baseball game, and lots of *cerveza* imbibed by the spectators. It was an enjoyable afternoon and a nice change of pace from our geologic mapping. One afternoon we had several drops of rain—the first rain in 106 years, according to the locals.

One evening after mapping along the coast, John Killen and one of the other geologists decided to camp in a little inlet near where two fishermen were living. As the geologists were preparing their Vienna sausage dinner, the fishermen asked if they would like lobster instead. The obvious answer was si, si! Since they had no cooking utensils, the fishermen loaned them a big cast-iron frying pan. They did have some margarine with them, so they pan-fried the lobsters and had the best meal of all while in Baja. After dinner, John started to clean the pan using the sand from the beach. The two fishermen came running out of their beach shack screaming "no, no, no!" They explained that it took years to build up the dark color and old grease deposits in the pan, and cleaning it would remove the wonderful flavor from their cooking. John gave them some bread and Vienna sausages when they left next morning.

We completed our mapping in the six-week period and returned home in the same manner we had arrived. Don's postulation of a major fault system was correct and we were the first ones to map it. When we returned home, each of us had to write a geologic report.

Since there were no roads and the terrain was very rough, our all-important Jeep took a real beating and at one point, the body became partially detached from the frame. This presented a major problem.

The fix could not be a regular nuts-and-bolts repair job, so we took it to the fish cannery where they had an arc welder. We could not get the Jeep very close to the welding unit, which meant that the ground cable – an electric connection – was too short. People living in remote, isolated areas have to be creative, so the clever Mexicans simply extended the cable by screwing lengths of old water pipe together and laying it down the drive. ("No touch the pipe, Señor!") The weld was perfect and the work continued without further problems.

About 15 years after the trip, I was at a Nu Alpha Phi fraternity reunion breakfast and John Shelton was there. We were all sharing Pomona College stories so I told about our field trip to Baja. I told how John Shelton had ordered Vienna sausages as our only meat source and I got sick of them after a week. John immediately got up and said he did not like them either!

"To Dr. Donald McIntyre – A little something to alleviate the hardships of the trip, given with thanks for many pleasant evenings in Bahia Tortuga"

> *When on a trip to Southern Isles,*
> *There's time for work and time for smiles.*
> *Dawn brings hours of work and test,*
> *But with the eve, it's time for rest,*
> *For then the world seems mighty dandy*
> *And to increase your pleasure, drink the -------*
> *But if, next morn, the world seems dismal,*
> *There's only one cure, the ---------*
> *For this is the time, when memories you are ruing,*
> *That someone will say, "I know what you've been doing.*

John Killen (class of 1956)

Six months later, Donald returned to Baja California. He wrote to his parents from Claremont

January 29 1957

The trip to Cedros Island was a considerable success – and very pleasant indeed. By taking the Dramamine the night before we sailed each time, I was perfectly all right at sea. The weather was – and still is – bad here, but we had glorious warm days all the time we were on the island. The broken weather has lasted an exceptionally long time, and it has rained almost every day for the past two weeks or more. Yesterday it snowed here in Claremont and Alex and Lionel needed chains to drive north to Berkeley. It is rather unusual and strangely odd to see snow lying on the orange trees, especially as there is fruit on the trees, but of course the snow didn't last very long down here.

Our ship was a converted ocean tug, about 150 ft. long and displacing about 600 tons. The journey itself was rather dull for we are out of sight of land most of the way and it was rather too cold most of the time for sitting on deck. We saw the usual occasional whales, schools of porpoises, flying fish (some even came on board by mistake) and the albatross and the journey took about 30 hours each way.

One night we were given a "lift" along the coast by some Mexican fishermen who know the rocks and coves very well and who can safely take their boats out on a dark night. The water was quite phosphorescent in the wake. This and the mention of the albatross remind me of *The Ancient Mariner*. I discovered that The *Road to Xanadu* is available in a reprint edition. I got a copy the other day. I have had time only to read the first part but I have enjoyed it very much indeed. I am to lecture in March to the History of Science Club in Berkeley, on James Hutton, and I have been much interested in the origins of his ideas; this is what put me in mind of Lowes's book.

John Christie has started to coach a rugger team here. Yesterday, in the field, he twisted his ankle and it swelled badly; fortunately it's down now. We are just completing a joint paper on recent earthquakes, and I have a manuscript to work over for Lionel for a joint paper with him on Loch Leven. This is all grist to the mill for the book which Lionel, Gerhard and I are going to do together.

Editor's note: *When sailing to Baja California, long before the days of high technology, Donald noted how readily the ship's captain could determine their ship's sailing speed. The captain explained that this was easy. All he had to do was to spit into the ocean and observe how rapidly the spittle moved through the sea!*

Hudson Bay Gravimeter Expedition – Summer 1958

The abstract of Donald's paper

'Impact Metamorphism at Clearwater Lake, Quebec'

In 1958, the Dominion Observatory of Canada made an extensive gravity survey east of Hudson Bay. Unusual metamorphic rocks were collected at stations on islands in Clearwater Lake. The lake consists of two circular bodies of water, 30km and 20km in diameter. The smaller is over 450 feet deep and is probably floored by arkose and Paleozoic limestone. The larger contains a ring of islands with topographic indication of gentle dip towards the center where re-crystallized diorite is exposed. The crudely layered rocks are probably mega-breccias and are interpreted as resulting from a meteorite impact. Locally there are abundant boulders of fossiliferous Paleozoic limestone (submitted to the Geological Survey of Canada). No evidence of volcanic activity was observed.

The predominant rock is hematite-stained breccia, with a glassy vesicular matrix, containing fragments of altered granites. Feldspars are recrystallized in sheaf-like aggregates, amphibole and biotite are converted to pyroxene, and quartz is granular. Quartz paramorphs after tridymite are conspicuous. Shattered granite passes into micro-breccias with numerous deformation lamellae in the quartz. Veins of vesicular glass, with feathery feldspars, traverse the breccia. Recrystallization of feldspar separating the quartz crystals may have prevented the formation of coesite.

Later on, Donald wrote an article entitled "Shock Metamorphism of Natural Materials and ended it with this statement acknowledging some differences of opinion about the Clearwater Lake geology:

"In 1961 I learned that field parties of the Geological Survey of Canada had studied the Clearwater Lake areas and had concluded the origin of the feature to be volcanic. Many geologists have now visited Clearwater Lake for much longer periods of time than I did in 1958, and there exist collections that doubtless are more extensive and representative than mine. But I welcome this invitation to publish some of the photo-micrographs that show the evidence which impressed me with the case for impact metamorphism of Clearwater Lake".

Donald wrote to his parents on July 24 1958

The last letter I wrote is still sitting here because the wretched plane landed the gas drums at another beach and took off again without either dropping or picking up mails. Last night the Dominion Astronomer, Dr Beals, arrived for a night or two, and I hope to get this letter out with him. I don't know when you will get it.

Things are going well. A lot of work has been done and we should be out of here early if we have any luck with the weather. We work long

hours. Breakfast at 6 a.m. and sometimes not back till 7:30 p.m. And the maps to be inked, specimens packed and soon. The result is we can write only when the weather is bad and then everyone is so depressed that's it isn't funny. We have now completed work at our first 3 base camps and are waiting for the clouds to lift so that we can pack and fly on to Camp 4. Our last camp will be number 5.

We are covering a fantastic area and of course it is very interesting. We land on a lake – this is a country of lakes – and taxi to the shore and land with waders. There are 2 planes flying with 2 gravimeters (weight 10 lbs or so) and I go along with one of them. Then it's on to the next lake maybe 10 miles away – and so fortunately, I am completely used to the plane and quite enjoy the whole thing on the way from lake to lake when I try to see as much geology as I can. One of the planes has just come to say to get ready for moving. We moved camp yesterday and spent the night at Clearwater Lake. Dr Beals is taking this to Great Whale, so he will be postman!

Donald often chuckled about what the local Inuit might have thought when the plane "landed" on a lake. They would see two men emerge from the plane and walk through the water. Then one of them would place a small object on the ground – was it a shrine? Why was the man on his knees before it? Why was he bowing to it? And why was it such a brief ceremony? – for in no time at all, the men returned to the plane and flew off – and they knew not whither.

It was just six months after our marriage that Donald went to Hudson Bay, Canada on a six week expedition. Although I was devastated about this long absence – in retrospect, it was not only a great experience for Donald, but A Good Thing for me too. Finding my feet in Claremont alone helped me establish my own friendships – in the general store on Yale Avenue, the butcher told me that "my sister had just been in!" This was Helen Christie – from Invergowrie, Scotland, also a 1957 bride. From that day on and ever since, Helen has been my "near sister" and cherished friend. Inevitably Donald's letters were few and far between but, joy of joy, he came home a week earlier than anticipated – they had run out of supplies and were going to have to have a diet exclusively of fish for another week. Fortunately Donald was able to "escape" this terrible fate – he always hated eating fish – and was air-lifted out by a visiting plane. He brought home our greatly treasured Inuit soap-stone carvings.

For my part, I enjoyed some lovely experiences, learning to stand on my own two feet. I particularly remember a beautiful trip to Santa Barbara with Mr and Mrs Bunnell, owners of our first home on Alexander Avenue, Claremont – this was quite a coincidence as my maiden name was Alexander! On this occasion we drove exclusively on minor back roads – though, even then in 1958, we could have travelled on the freeways. I still recall with delight the beauty of the flower bespangled country hedgerows.

Professional Trips

Both as a geologist and later through his involvement with computer languages

(APL and J), Donald had many opportunities to travel and to lecture in the USA. For several years in the 1970s, he appreciated being a member and attending many meetings of the American Geological Society's Publications Committee and travelling extensively to APL and J conferences. In the early 1980s, h e spent a memorable summer working day and most of the night in Philadelphia with Ken Iverson. Donald would often comment on what a very special summer that had been and though sleep was minimal he never felt tired. In August Donald travelled on to join Ewen and me in London – I can testify that he *was* indeed tired by that time.

In 1977-78 Donald enjoyed a long and busy lecture tour across the United States which was organised by American Association of Petroleum Geologists (AAPG) – it was an experience which was an education in itself. He made many new friendships including Daniel F. Merriam of the University of Kansas. Dan visited us in Scotland and always shared Donald's enthusiasm for the role of computers in geology.

Adventure in Hawaii

In 1986 Donald had the opportunity to visit Hawaii and meet with former students and friends – Jim Kauahikaua, now Scientist-in-Charge at the US Geological Survey's Hawaiian Volcano Observatory, Paul T. Delaney and others. Together they visited Kilauea's active volcanic vent, Kupaianaha. After this thrilling opportunity walking on the molten lava, Donald would often proclaim that this occasion topped his list of exciting – for which read "dangerous" – experiences of his life!

*Lava from Kilauea Volcano's fiery eruption,
Hawaii, 1983*

A dash to Australia

In 1988 Donald was invited to give a keynote address at the APL conference in Australia. This was an even briefer visit than planned – when Donald arrived at Los Angeles airport, he was asked to show his visa for entry to Australia. As a British citizen, Donald assumed that it was not necessary to apply for a visa to travel there. Alas, this was not the case. Donald rushed off to the Australian embassy, but had to return home. Finally, two days later, he did leave – visa in hand – arriving in Australia just in the nick of time to give his lecture. In spite of its brevity, that trip turned out to be a splendid occasion including a trip around Sydney harbour to admire their world-famous Opera House shining brightly in the light of an "upside-down" moon!

China – A Friend – by Dennis Rodkin – (from "Pomona Today" 1985)

The gaps that separate old friends hang open in our memories. Years after a friend disappears on the far side of a chasm of time or geography, we catch ourselves wondering about loose threads in the person's life

Donald McIntyre had often wanted to track down Ma Xingyuan, an intimate pal from his grad school days at the University of Edinburgh in his native Scotland, but was afraid even to try to bridge the gap that had opened abruptly nearly thirty-six years earlier.

"I got a card from him from Hong Kong in 1949, a week before Mao took over the government of China," geology professor McIntyre recalled recently, "and I never heard from my friend again. We were told we couldn't risk getting in touch with him, because it would have been very bad to emphasize his western connection at that time."

The two friends had last seen each other in 1947 in Switzerland, where McIntyre was doing postdoctoral research on the structure of the Alps. At Edinburgh, Ma and McIntyre had been constant companions, Ma spending much of his time with McIntyre's mother and sister.

"We did rock climbing and ice climbing together in Scotland," McIntyre said, "so we were literally tied together with a rope many times." When McIntyre left for Switzerland, Ma joined him briefly before returning to Edinburgh to finish his own doctorate. They corresponded for the next two years, until Ma left Scotland in 1949. "All I knew was that he had gone back to China and after that we couldn't communicate with him," McIntyre said. "I didn't know if he was alive or dead, which side he was on, or anything."

A surprise phone call early in 1985 cleared up thirty-six years of questions. Doctor Ma, it turns out, had risen to the top of his field and, as director of the national Seismological Bureau in Beijing, was in Washington, D.C., for a meeting with American scientists. He invited McIntyre to come to China as his guest to lecture on geology and computer science. McIntyre accepted, hoping to answer his own questions about China while catching up with a friend he had thought was lost.

"The last big earthquake in China was in 1976, and half a million people were killed," McIntyre said, "so in terms of seismography they do things in a big way." However, all he really knew about the sciences in China was that all work "is very practically oriented." From the start of the Cultural Revolution until China's recent reopening to outsiders, Westerners had only the barest hints about research and advances there.

So McIntyre and his wife, Ann, began planning a two week trip to Beijing and Nanjing, home of a university with a five-year-old exchange program with Pomona. In the meantime, McIntyre flew to San Francisco for a brief reunion before Ma returned to China. He came back reassured that Ma "hadn't changed one little bit," Ann McIntyre said. The McIntyres left for China as neither diplomats nor

tourists, but with a little of both roles in mind. They took a banner proclaiming the Christian Pentecost as a gift from the congregation of the Claremont Presbyterian Church to members of a Beijing Christian Church, and they took a camera.

"We went there with a lot of questions, some of which could probably have been answered in Claremont," McIntyre said after returning home, "but we came away with even more questions than we went with." The biggest question had less to do with China itself than with the wide split between Eastern and Western cultural values they detected. He was taken to visit rock mechanics labs and several Beijing scientific institutes, and was often surprised by what he found.

"You would see some evidence of high technology in a facility with outside toilets," he said. "Well, if I showed you some geological institute in the United States and on the way in I pointed out to you that the toilet was outside and a few a blocks away, you would wonder what kind of scientific institute you were going to see."

"In the West we perceive a very high correlation between the cleanliness of the toilet and the prestige," he said, "not just of a rock mechanics lab, but of an English department as well."

"But if you think of it, is it really necessary to have an inside toilet in order to do scientific work?" He did not say whether he will be setting up outhouses behind Seaver South soon, but from his comments it was clear that this career scientist is rethinking some of his priorities since his tour of China.

"We thought we had the absolutes before we left on our trip," he said, confessing naiveté about the realities of modern China. "But it's like having a magnet that points north and going to a place where all the rocks are magnetic." One incident that set his compass spinning came during a lecture, when he mentioned that the Italian mathematician Fibonacci brought the concept of zero to the West in the year 1202. Members of McIntyre's Chinese audience asked, "Are you talking about B.C. or A.D.!" and noted that their culture had grasped the concept a few thousand years earlier.

"Yet we too often say that China is a primitive place," he said.

The comfortable mix of new technology and what Westerners might call out-dated method was pervasive, McIntyre said, telling of his chance stop at a Beijing computer store. Riding through the city in the hired taxi that was their limousine in Beijing, he noted a sign, in English, advertising IBM PC computers and other American-made models. He asked the driver to stop, and, rushing inside, found a store full of sparkling new computer equipment.

"And on top of the counter they had an abacus for adding up your purchase" as efficiently as a Western cashier using an electronic cash register with all the bells and whistles, he said.

Once, driving along a main Beijing highway, the McIntyres noticed that an entire lane appeared to be covered with an even bed of sand. They discovered that local farmers had spread their grain along the smooth roadbed, and were using it as a makeshift threshing floor.

"There was a feeling throughout our trip that our own sense of what was important and what we could expect was no longer valid," McIntyre said. "it was like weightlessness in space. You could really lose your sense of balance if unwilling to question preconceptions with each new revelation about modern Chinese life."

A dragon of the Forbidden City, Beijing

McIntyre spent most of his stay in Beijing giving lectures to Chinese scientists and graduate students on geology and computer science, and visiting faults and other points of scientific interest. Ann McIntyre filled her time with day trips throughout the city. Whether escorted by Ma's grad students, riding with the driver who became their friend, or one occasion persuaded her hosts to let her visit a post office and a park by herself. She always tried to go, "where I could meet people and see how they really are."

"I could walk anywhere and feel completely safe," she said, "and none of the problems that would spring to your mind in the West even mattered." She visited shops and open markets, parks and historical sites, and reported afterwards that "the impression of warm and caring people came through at every turn."

"You feel their warmth everywhere you go," she said "and they're always smiling genuine smiles that are really from inside them." She compared the affable ease in China with the mood in Europe in the late 1940s, when the towns and villages had not been overrun yet with abrasive tourists and the people were delighted to meet any new visitor. The happiest of all the people she saw in Beijing were the children. After several days of observing gleeful youngsters, Ann McIntyre decided they were content because their parents do not push their kids around in Western down-sized shopping carts.

"They simply do not have strollers," she said. "They carry their children everywhere until the age of three or four. So the child, instead of being a little insignificant little thing somewhere near the ground, is right up on either the mother's or father's arm, and is the king of all he surveys."

On a break from touring the city, she learned that governmental programs designed to help the disabled are sometimes rebuffed by families who cling to the Chinese tradition of the self-sufficient family. Ewen, the McIntyres' 23-year-old son, is a quadriplegic with cerebral palsy. In working with him they have developed a deep concern for the rights and care of the disabled. So it was natural for Ann McIntyre, on vacation in the Far East, to locate and meet with a Chinese professor of special education.

In China, she learnt, parents might be defensive and say there's nothing wrong with the child. They haven't had the awareness that has grown in this country that authorities may come in and seem to be interfering even though they are really helping."

When McIntyre's lectures and long-overdue reunion with Ma were over, the couple set out by train for Nanjing, where they would spend a few days with Zhao Shuming, Wang Jia-song, and others from the university there who earlier spent time at Pomona. During the overnight ride, they had a memorable lesson in an important difference between the congenial Chinese and sometimes arrogant Americans.

A Chinese banquet with Ma Xingyuan,
Beijing, May 1985

Arriving in their travelling compartment, the McIntyres found one of the two men who were to share the space during the 20-hour train ride. He was smoking a cigarette. The student helping them get settled for the trip asked them to quit, saying the smoke would annoy Mrs. McIntyre. Without a moment's hesitation or the begrudging glare an American might have given the couple, the man put out his cigarette.

Soon a second man arrived. He, too, was smoking. "We could tell that the []rst told him", McIntyre said, "because he put out his cigarette and beamed at us". Neither appeared strained by the politeness, both McIntyre and his wife reported, but seemed to think what they had done was the only fair way to behave."

"That kind of courtesy is amazing," Ann McIntyre said, "and not often encountered in the West."

While in Nanjing, Dr. McIntyre delivered more guest lectures, and the couple enjoyed time with friends they had made through the Pomona-Nanjing exchange. In Nanjing the 'Claremont connection' was very strong, and we got the impression that they had more Western visitors there than in the part of Beijing we were in," Ann McIntyre said, "so we were less of a novelty. " Less time was spent answering questions about the U.S., she said, more in discussing the relative differences between the people of the two nations.

The McIntyres returned to this country on June 29 full of answers and new questions. Their whirlwind tour had left them little time to write down the names of people and Chinese places, and McIntyre came away with one very important question unanswered. He still did not know how to use the little strips of wood that confound many Westerners.

"I thought, 'Why should I bother to find out how to use chopsticks when I'm going to be with people who will certainly be able to show me very quickly?" he said. Except for a few banquets, though, the McIntyres ate most of their meals alone. Friends gave him pointers at the banquets, but "I would have starved to death had I not figured it out".

Ann's Memories of China, May 1985

We were fortunate that we could visit China together in May 1985, when that country's life-style was still simple – restricted and unpretentious. Visiting foreigners were still a novelty there and some Ma's students were delighted at the opportunity to accompany us in a hired car with a woman driver whisking us hither and yonder on quiet main roads. On our memorable trip to walk on The Great Wall we drove past oxen drawing battered carts, sheets of grain being raked and spread out to dry on a paved surface near the main highway; smiling children selling watermelons by the roadside and little girls walking in the rain sheltering under their bright umbrellas..

In Beijing we visited The Forbidden City, the Summer Palace and many other historic and fascinating places. Simple features of daily life were striking – a vast vegetable market filled to the brim with a mountain of cabbages; the pathways lined with tiny cabin-style bunk-beds homes and, at break of day, we were puzzled to see long queues – people waiting their turn for access to the primitive community toilets. We noted how Tiananmen Square (Gate of Heavenly peace) was marked off in small numbered squares – each little space allocated to individuals for public gatherings. And there were cyclists everywhere – some transporting live and squawking ducks in pannier bags hanging over the bicycle's rear wheel.

On an early city morning walk – one of the few times when we were out and about on our own! – we enjoyed a tranquil scene where an elderly man was practicing Tai-chi in the public gardens with a caged bird at his side – perhaps both its owner and his bird alike were escaping briefly into the fresh air away from their cramped bunk-bed living quarters and primitive toilets. We were shown where Ma lived – in a complex of flats within a modest courtyard beside a bicycle repair workshop. We were never invited into anyone's home.

It was quite difficult – and perhaps, in fairness to our hosts, we shouldn't have attempted to deliver the banner from our church in Claremont to the Christian Church in the city of Beijing. When I told Ma that I was hoping to deliver the banner, he exclaimed "churches, I had forgotten such places exist!"" and later, "it's a very long street; you will never find it" – but we did. I can only hope that nobody suffered repercussions from what I now see as my foolish determination to complete my mission. On ringing the doorbell of a magnificent magenta coloured doorway, a hand shot out, grasped the banner and quickly closed the door agan.

I asked if I might visit a school in Beijing but was taken instead to a children's playground; but – wherever we went, we were greeted by smiling, welcoming people. In Nanjing, however. I was taken to visit a children's crèche but the youngest children, two year-olds, cried when they saw me. "Could this be some sort of monster with such strange colouring and features!?"

On our return home – still a little shell-shocked – it took some time to clarify our impressions. To that end, we really appreciated the opportunity to talk of our experience with Dennis Rodkin.

Ann's doggerel – Our Visit to China – May 1985

McIntyres the praises sing
Of the land of Quin and Ming
With Ma, Ma Li, Yang and Su.
We have learnt so much that's new:

Climbing high on the Great Wall
Learning where the arrows fall,
Visiting the Tombs of Ming
And the secrets hid within.

Eating duck and luscious cake,
Learning how the Chinese bake.
Seeing how the people bike,
And lick the ice-cream that they like.

Watching how the Opera goes
For Su the symbols really knows,
Walking Summer Palace Ways
And finding them a wondrous maze.

Talking much of APL
And how Sharp a "rom" must sell.
Seeing babies carried close
With love that is the most.

Learning what is good and bad,
And of the things that make them sad.
Of Professor Holmes we think
Who for us has made this link.

May our friendship always grow
And let our understanding flow.
Thank you, thank you for our stay
And helping us in such a way!
Till we meet again one day!

.....and that did indeed did happen – Ma's daughter, Ma Li, came to visit us both in Claremont and in Perth, Scotland. She was surprised and even felt uncomfortable in the spaciousness of Western homes. ("Why are only three people living here?). And when helping me in the kitchen, she would stand very close to me – shoulder to shoulder – in what I tend to consider as "my space."

Chapter 8
Pioneering with Computers

With much gratitude to Donald's friend Professor Emeritus Keith Smillie of the

University of Alberta, Edmonton, Canada who has edited this text with unique expertise and care.

"The relationship of master and pupil is acknowledged as a spiritual and lifelong tie, connecting successive generations of great thinkers with each other in an unbroken chain." J.J. Sylvester, mathematician (1814-1897).

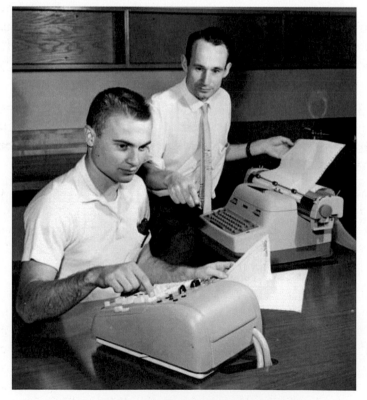

*James Williams (class of 1964) experiments
with computing under Donald's watchful eye.*

My Involvement in the Use of Computers

This is Donald's own description of the introduction and early use of computers at Pomona College, of his work with Ken Iverson and the development of the computer languages APL and J. This is a slightly edited version of a draft dated January 2, 2001

My former colleague, Corwin Hansch, Emeritus Professor of Chemistry at Pomona College, has sent me his personal essay entitled "The Advent and Evolution of QSAR at Pomona College". Stimulated by Corwin's essay, I have spent a few hours writing an account of my involvement in the development of computer usage at Pomona College. There are undoubtedly errors in this hastily written account, and I will try to make corrections later. My excuse for sending this imperfect account is twofold, pressure of other commitments on the one hand, and on the other hand my desire to give Corwin a speedy response as a basis for making a few minor corrections to his essay.

I arrived in Claremont in September 1954 to succeed A.O. Woodford as Chairman of the Geology Department. The Department was in the basement of Mason Hall. As the other floors were occupied by the Chemistry Department, Nelson Smith, Professor of Chemistry, soon became a close friend and colleague.

In 1956 Frank Seaver, a Pomona alumnus, undertook to provide the entire cost of a new physics building and its equipment, and in September 1958 the Millikan Laboratory for Physics and Mathematics was completed. In 1957 the USSR launched Sputnik.

While the Millikan building was nearing completion, Mr Seaver decided to contribute a second building to house Zoology and Geology. There was no mention, however, of new equipment until construction was well under way. This posed a problem for me, because, as I recall, I had little more than a long weekend to draw up a list of desired equipment.

Being in a small college, I was able to consult with colleagues in different disciplines, and it was Burt Henke, a gifted experimentalist in the Physics Department, who opened my eyes to the possibility of using X-ray fluorescence (XRF) to make chemical analyses of silicate rocks. The minerals that make common rocks are compounds of light elements, and Henke had designed a novel X-ray tube (later marketed commercially by Philips Electronics as the "Henke Tube") capable of making these elements emit their characteristic X-rays.

President Lyon got a shock when I gave him my recommended list of equipment. As the total was more like the College budget, he said he would need an independent advisor. I suggested the name of Professor Frank Turner, then distinguished Chairman of the Geology Department at UC Berkeley, and the man who had been responsible for bringing me to California as a Fulbright Fellow in the summer of 1951. Turner approved of all items on the list with the exception of the XRF equipment – because they didn't have it at Berkeley he thought I could get on very well without it! So I had to take it off the list.

I had a meeting with Mr Wig, then the Chairman of the Board of Trustees. He was angry, saying there was something wrong with my bottom-line figure. Drops of blood oozed from my forehead, until I realised what the problem was. I explained that there had been two lists – my original list (with XRF) and an edited list with XRF removed on the advice of the Chairman of the UC Berkeley Department. I mistakenly thought that this information would solve the problem. But no! Mr Wig asked why XRF had been taken off the list. I explained that Turner didn't think we needed it. That information made matters worse! Mr Wig rounded on me and asked, if it wasn't necessary why had I put it on the list in the first place. I replied that I understood that Mr Seaver wanted the Department to be the best in the country. Mr Wig then ended the conversation by announcing that XRF was to be returned to the list without further delay!

As the XRF equipment and the cooperation with Burt Henke made it possible for Pomona College to participate in the Viking Landers on Mars, we were later to be able to claim that we were the only Geology Department with two field stations on another planet. This episode says a great deal about the attitude of Rudolph J. Wig and Frank R. Seaver! It was a great privilege to work with them.

Geology had been a subject where the principal tools were field boots, a hammer, a microscope and a feather duster. But I saw that this situation was about to change drastically. We were setting up equipment that could make quantitative measurements. In the past chemical analyses of rocks like granite were made at great expense by specialized laboratories. As a result no one ever made a second analysis of the same rock, and consequently no one knew the precision and accuracy of an analysis.

Dr Woodford one day asked me in the corridor if one rock was dated as 10 million years old and another as 11 million years, which was the older. This stimulated me to write an article entitled "Precision and Resolution of Geochronometry" in which I explained the basic principles of statistical analysis. The article appeared in *Fabric of Geology* which was published to commemorate the 75th Anniversary of the Geological Society of America. Today these principles are known to every student of elementary chemistry, but in 1963 this was revolutionary stuff. Alan Cox, later Dean of Earth Sciences at Stanford, used the paper as the topic of a seminar at UC Berkeley, and came to Pomona to do the calculations which enabled him to document the reversal chronology of the Earth's magnetic field.

While the Seaver Laboratory was under construction, Mr Seaver enabled me to purchase two electrical-mechanical calculators: a Marchant and a Friden. These marvellous machines allowed us to compute the sums of numbers and the sums of their products – the first steps in the calculation of arithmetic means and standard deviations. They were essential tools to use while I taught myself statistics and quality control, and passed on the knowledge to my colleagues and students.

The XRF equipment was delivered once we moved into the Seaver Laboratory in the summer and autumn of 1959. I was joined by a new colleague, Alex Baird '54, who became my assistant when I arrived on campus, and who in 1959 was completing the work for his Ph.D. at Berkeley. I encouraged Baird to seize this unique opportunity and become a pioneer in the application of XRF to petrology. He attended one of the first workshops in XRF technology offered by Philips Electronics, and later was in demand as the instructor.

One day Mr Seaver paid a visit to inspect the new building. While conducting him on a tour, I took him into the room where Baird was installing the new equipment. Baird dutifully explained to Mr Seaver how XRF worked and the use we intended to make of it. Mr Seaver had Parkinson's disease. He spoke tersely and shuffled as he walked. Before Baird had finished, Mr Seaver turned aside and walked out of the room. Naturally I went with him, leaving Baird in consternation. What had he done wrong? After Mr Seaver finished his tour and left, I explained to Baird that Mr Seaver had no great desire to learn how the equipment worked. What he wanted to know was whether Baird knew what he was talking about. Mr Seaver left once he was persuaded by Baird's enthusiastic demonstration. Mr Seaver judged men rather than apparatus.

Baird and Henke collaborated on the X-ray technology, giving joint papers at the Conferences on "Advances in X-ray Analysis". The Proceedings were published annually, starting in 1960. Meantime I contributed the statistical methods that provided efficient quality control both in the field and the laboratory. The Seaver Lab soon became known for its pioneering efforts in this field, and as a result Baird was chosen as a Principal Investigator for NASA when the Viking Landers went to Mars.

Mr Seaver had provided a Bendix G-15 computer for the Millikan Laboratory. This early computer had a drum memory and was programmed in machine language. The interests of the Mathematics Department were traditional and theoretical and the faculty had no interest in the Bendix G-15. The Physics Department used the computer, but it wasn't available for other users. As our computational needs in the Geology Department grew, I was on the lookout for a way of acquiring some kind of a computer. It was necessary that we should be able to make use of it unaided, and yet that it would not be so powerful that it would compete with the Bendix G-15 in Physics. In short it had to be part of the Geology Department with all the rights and duties this implied.

In 1960 I learned that the Clary Corporation in Pasadena, the manufacturer of well-known calculators, had produced a small computer called the Clary DE60. Studying the literature, I felt that the Clary would meet all our requirements, and above all I felt confident that I would be able to master its use within the Geology Department. The Clary cost $20,000. It had a memory of two 16-word channels. Today the cheapest laptop will come with many gigabytes of memory, but the Clary could store a maximum of 32 numbers – not kilobytes or gigabytes, but just 32 numbers! Programs consisted of wired boards and there was a slot for plugging in a single cartridge that was pre-wired to compute a square root. Later I designed a trigonometrical cartridge which the Clary Corporation marketed.

Mr Wig – not President Lyon – controlled our access to Mr Seaver, and I knew Mr Wig well enough to ask him for permission to ask Mr Seaver for this extra item of equipment, which I would certainly have had on the original list had the Clary been available a year earlier. I duly went to meet Mr Seaver in his Los Angeles office. He took me by surprise when he asked me two questions: (1) Would President Lyon give priority to a new Women's Gymnasium or to a Clary DE-60 computer for the Geology Department? To which I answered that President Lyon would undoubtedly have preferred the Gymnasium, but that my task was to make sure that the Seaver Lab was properly equipped as the most outstanding in the country. And (2) For what price had Mr Clary sold his Calculator business? To which I said that I did not know but would find out. It was like the fairy story in which the hero is given a task that must be completed before yet another task is assigned.

The name Clary was well known to me because I knew Will Clary [William W. Clary], an alumnus and Member of the Board of Trustees of Pomona, the donor of the Oxford Room in the Honnold Library, a Member of the Board of Fellows of what became the Claremont University Center, its Chairman for ten years, and Acting President during 1963. I did not know Will Clary's brother, Hugh L. Clary, also a Pomona alumnus, who founded the Clary Corporation in 1939. The Clary Corporation was well known for its adding machines, cash registers, and related equipment.

It fell to me, therefore, to make an appointment with Mr Hugh Clary, and I visited him in his office in Pasadena. When he asked me what it was that I wanted, I replied that I was eager to acquire a Clary DE-60 for Pomona's Geology Department and that Mr Seaver – whom of course he knew – was interested in purchasing it for us. I told him that I hoped to be able to answer Mr Seaver's question; namely the amount that had been paid for the Clary calculator business. I think Mr Clary smiled a little, as he drew a folder from his desk drawer, and answered the question. I think the sum was $1,000,000. I can't now be sure, but at the time it seemed a lot of money. I can't remember the name of the firm that acquired the Clary calculators, but it was well known to me then. At my next meeting with Mr Seaver I duly reported what Mr Clary had told me, and Mr Seaver gave us the Clary DE-60.

Because of what now seems the infinitesimal memory of the DE-60, each program step had to be crafted with great care. There was no floating-point hardware – after all, only 6 years earlier, IBM's 704 computer had floating-point hardware only because of John Backus' personal insistence! Consequently, on the Clary, we had to decide every decimal-shift required in order to maintain significant figures throughout the calculations.

A great advantage with the Clary DE-60 was our subsequent contact with Clary's Systems Engineer – whose name I have most regrettably forgotten. I learned an immense amount about practical mathematics and computing methods, e.g., he introduced me to Cecil Hastings' *Approximations for Digital Computers* (1955) which for a time became my bible. Some of the books that greatly helped me when I was learning statistics on my own were Edwin L. Crowe, F.A. Davis, and M.W. Maxfield's *Statistics Manual, with Examples taken from Ordnance Development* reprinted by Dover (1960), Carl A. Bennett's *Statistical Analysis in Chemistry and the Chemical Industry* (1954); and Sir Ronald A. Fisher's *The Design of Experiments* (1949; 9th Edition 1971).

In 1961, encouraged by Clary's systems engineer, I gave a paper on "A General Program for Analysis of Variance Suitable for a Small Computer" at the Fourth Annual Technical Symposium, Association for Computing Machinery, Santa Monica, California.

I don't remember when it was that with missionary zeal I suggested to Nelson Smith and Corwin Hansch (my chemistry colleagues in Seaver North) that they should use the Clary to simplify the task of curve fitting and general statistics. But under my tutelage, Corwin's assistant, Dr Edna Deutsch, became a regular user of the Geology Department's Clary. One Alumni Day, I was working on the Clary with a couple of students, when the door opened. In came Hugh Clary with three or four of his alumni friends. He was delighted to be able to demonstrate so convincingly that the Clary DE-60 was a tool of real practical use! I explained that the Chemistry Department used the Clary also, and soon after that Hugh Clary gave the Chemistry Department its own Clary! I wish I knew the date.

Late in 1962 Harvey Mudd College, which was founded in 1961 as one of the cluster of five colleges in Claremont, installed an IBM 1620 and I attended a short course on FORTRAN taught by an IBM systems engineer. The 1620 was IBM's smallest computer. It was a true decimal machine with a memory of 20K decimal (which could be increased to 60K). IBMers called it CADET – because (as they said) it "Can't Add Doesn't Even Try". Addition was performed by reference to an Add Table. I never used HMC's 1620, but when Claremont Men's College installed a 1620, John Ferling (CMC Mathematics) let me make a good deal of use of it.

For me the important thing about the 1620 was that I was able to get hands-on FORTRAN experience without leaving the campus. About the same time IBM and UCLA combined to create Western Data Processing Center (WDPC). IBM provided the computer and the staff to run it and got the use of the system at night; UCLA provided the building and the necessary staff to run the Center. This excellent arrangement made IBM's largest scientific computer – the IBM 7090 (later 7094) -- available free of charge to all colleges west of the Mississippi.

My introduction to WDPC was through a visit from its Director. He gave a talk – perhaps even two or three talks – in the auditorium in Millikan, though I believe I was the only person who actually took action after hearing him.

For years WDPC had only two geological users: Frank Press and myself. Press had succeeded Beno Gutenberg as Director of CalTech's Seismology Lab; he later became a Professor at Harvard, President of the National Academy of Science, and Science Advisor to President Carter. I owe a debt also to the staff of WDPC for advice and education on all matters relating to computing: machine architecture and design; and computer language from machine language and assembly language to FORTRAN. I learned to read, write and do simple arithmetic in binary and octal – a necessary skill for debugging a computer dump. I also learned the concentration to detail and the perseverance and patience required in finding and correcting errors. I recall that one day a systems engineer at WDPC told me he had noticed the odometer on his car was a string of 1s – he nearly had an accident as he watched to see what the next number was going to be! He was thinking in binary or octal!

Incidentally the word FORTRAN was always written in upper-case letters because in those days printers were incapable of printing both upper- and lower-case.

Access to the IBM 7090 required IBM punch cards, and in the early days I made regular trips from Claremont to WDPC in order to use an IBM 026 card punch! Eventually we got our own card punch and also a typewriter machine that could read cards or punch paper and type the information (no IBM typeball!). By this time we had gone a long way to automate the XRF equipment. The reading of X-ray flux (counts per second) was a measure of the quantity of a particular element in the sample we were testing. These readings were recorded on paper-tape and our new IBM equipment could read the paper-tape and punch the information on to IBM cards. We then posted the card deck to WDPC; the program was run as a batch job – no interactive online computing then! – and the results returned to us by post for further debugging and re-submission. The turn-around time was about five days.

I needed to plot contour maps showing the distribution of each chemical element over the areas we had sampled in the field. The contouring program I wrote for this purpose was made generally available by the Kansas Geological Survey, and I saw it in use by an electronics company in Edinburgh, Scotland. Through Dinny McIsaac '59, then studying for a Ph.D. in Education at the Claremont Graduate School, I got access to large flat-bed plotters at TRW Systems (where McIsaac Sr. was a Director) in Los Angeles. (Dinny McIsaac later became Professor, Dean, and Director of the Computer Center at Wisconsin). Once the necessary programs and procedures were debugged, I was able to plot the geochemical maps. The procedure was to post the card-deck to UCLA, where the program was run and the output captured on computer tape (there were no disks then!). I then had to collect the tape at WDPC and take it with me to TRW – all these steps took time!. Later on we acquired an IBM device that transmitted card images by telephone to magnetic tape at WDPC. This device was housed at Harper Hall, and one of my daily tasks was to go there to transmit the card-decks. Incidentally, the IBM 7090 and its 7094 successor were in large computer rooms round which perhaps twenty tape drives stood like telephone kiosks.

The year 1963 was significant because it was the year when ASCII (American Standard Code for Information Interchange) was published. The year was also an active one for me: I taught a class in computer programming (FORTRAN and Assembler) attended by faculty and administration, including staff of the Library and the Business Office; I was an invited participant at the first conference on "Computer Utilization in Geology", sponsored by the National Academy of Science and the National Research Council (Pomona College and Stanford University were the only academic institutions west of the Mississippi represented); and I presented a paper on "The use of a high-speed computer in light-element analysis by X-ray fluorescence" at the 2nd National Meeting of the Society of Applied Spectroscopy.

After the Chemistry Department had its own Clary computer, Corwin Hansch's assistant still used the Clary in Seaver South from time to time. Perhaps something was wrong with Chemistry's Clary or it was in heavy use.

One day Edna Deutch came to Seaver South carrying an armful of program boards. She asked me if she could use the Geology Department's computer. Although no one else was using it at that time, I said "No". Edna was astonished; she said that on every other occasion I had always readily said "Yes". My reply was that if her program had grown to the size indicated by the number of program boards she was carrying, then she had outgrown the Clary. I said to her that she ought now to use FORTRAN and run her programs at WDPC. Edna had heard of FORTRAN but was terrified at the thought of switching from the known and familiar to the unknown. As I knew quite a lot about Corwin's work and had, indeed, helped to write some of the programs used, I took Edna into our computer room and with pencil and paper I wrote out the necessary FORTRAN program. We had our own IBM 026 card punch, so I punched the necessary cards. We sent the deck to WDPC and in a few days the results came back. All was well, but Edna was distressed. She said the computer had done her out of a job! It had done the job so much faster than she could have done it in the old way! I said: "You know that, and I know that, but Corwin doesn't know that!" In this way much of Corwin's computational work was transferred to WDPC. There was also a happy ending for Edna Deutch; she became Director of the Computer Centre at the New York State University at Albany!

By late 1963 I had recognised that we needed a computer capable of running FORTRAN, and I looked into the possibility of getting the latest model of the IBM 1620. But my contacts within IBM advised me to be patient, that it was worth waiting for a revolutionary new computer then in design stage. Mr Wig and Mr Seaver agreed, and accordingly on April 7, 1964 I went to IBM's Riverside Office for what was the announcement of IBM System/360, and Pomona placed an order to purchase a Model 40 that day. The Model 40 happened to be not only the appropriate one for Pomona but also the first model on the production line.

I believe Pomona was the first general customer site at which a System/360 was installed. We had to wait for delivery until October 1965, but the time was used to advantage. For part of the time I had access to a System/360 at IBM's Data Center in Los Angeles, and had informal tuition from IBM system engineers. This let me understand the machine architecture and master System/360 Assembler Language.

System/360 was remarkable for several reasons: it was a family of computers from small to large with a common architecture; it was IBM's first widely distributed transistorised machine; it was the first IBM machine designed to run under control of an operating system; its unit of addressable memory was an 8-bit byte; and it was designed to be equally suitable for commercial and scientific computing. The IBM 7030 Stretch computer (1960) incorporated some of these features, including the 8-bit byte, but only a small number of these big machines were constructed – notably one at Los Alamos.

Today everyone knows that even a laptop PC runs under an operating system, but in the days when we were using WDPC the machine room was staffed by operators who were like traffic controllers in an airport control room. The human operators decided the order in which batch jobs were to be run and how the machine resources were to be allocated between competing users. When our order was placed, neither we nor the local IBMers thought that as we were to have a card reader and a 200-line/minute printer we would have no need of a typewriter for input and output. Only later did we discover that a console typewriter was required for an operator to communicate with the Operating System. Our original programming was in Basic Assembler which was only one remove from machine language. The Operating System prevented ordinary users from accessing various parts of the machine; e.g., the System itself and areas of memory which had been allocated to other users. The Program Status Word (PSW) was the key to the Operating System, but for some time after our Model 40 was installed we ran jobs that took control over the entire machine. Our early programs all used the instruction LPSW – Load Program Status Word! I was firmly convinced that all this exploration of the rapidly expanding world of computers was vital and I took every opportunity to spread the word to students and colleagues, and to the administration.

Prior to System/360, IBM supported two different kinds of computers starting in 1954: the IBM 704 for scientific work and the IBM 705 for commercial applications. Commercial work requires storage of alphabetic information and numeric information to two decimal places. The ten decimal digits (0-9) can be encoded in a group of 4 bits (each 0 or 1); this code being called Binary Coded Decimal (BCD). The English alphabet has 26 letters, which with the 10 decimal digits gives a total of 36 characters. With 5 bits (each 0 or 1) we can encode only 32 distinct characters; consequently each unit of memory must have at least 6 bits (which gives 64 unique codes). With 6 bits there is room for a limited number of punctuation symbols, characters representing plus, minus, multiply and divide, printer codes, and so on. The IBM 705 was therefore based on groups of 6 bits: "the 705 character code". There wasn't room, however for lower case letters, and this is why early computers using FORTRAN and COBOL printed in uppercase only. Had our language used a larger alphabet, or had we used a larger non-decimal number base, the unit of computer memory would have had more than 6 bits.

The unit of memory in System/360 – and also in essentially all later computers, big or small – is an 8-bit byte, which allows us to encode 256 distinct combinations. IBM called the code "EBCDIC" (Extended Binary-Coded-Decimal Interchange Code). Although the code now commonly used is ASCII extended to 8 bits, there is general agreement on the coding of the first 7 bits, i.e., 128 characters.

Scientific computing, on the other hand, requires dealing with numbers ranging from very small to very large, each represented to a certain number of significant figures. This requirement is met by the use of the so-called "scientific notation" in which separate space is allocated for coding the sign, the exponent, and the fraction. This is achieved by giving the central processing unit power to work on a sequence of bytes (normally four or eight) representing a single number.

The 360 was named to emphasize that it was an "all-round" machine, capable of working equally on both character and numeric data. As a result IBM unified its operation, which before had required two groups in manufacturing, in software development, in sales, and in customer support.

In 1964 most members of the Pomona faculty thought of computers, at best, only as machines for numerical calculation. I felt it was imperative to spread the word that computers could also serve the arts and humanities. This was not always an easy task. For example, Fred Mulhauser, Chairman of the English Department, wrote me a short memo stating that "the English Department would NEVER use a computer". This attitude was evidence of a profound misunderstanding about the function and potential of computer technology. A course in computing was thought the equivalent of a course in changing the oil in an automobile.

I addressed the problem by demonstrating practical applications of computers to non-numerical tasks. David Davies, Director of the Honnold Library, was an ally. I knew him well both socially and because I was Chairman of the Library Committee. I recall a seminar at his home – W.T. Jones, Professor of Philosophy, was one of those present – when I explained the possible application of computers to tasks relevant to the Humanities. With this in mind I made sure that the first two programs written for our 360 were (1) a program to make a concordance of the works of Gerard Manley Hopkins, and (2) a program to invert a matrix. I gave seminars and for the first of these Dave Davies supported me by arranged to have Hopkins' text punched on IBM cards. For the second, I had the help of Roger Smith in converting a program written for the IBM 7090 at WDPC. (Roger, the son of Chemistry Professor R. Nelson Smith, spent a summer working with me on System/360 Assembly Language.)

I demonstrated how the Honnold Library catalog could be efficiently managed and used with the computer. This project was adopted enthusiastically by Dave Davies and by Bob Teare, the senior librarian. Funds from the Ford Foundation enabled the Library to upgrade the 360, adding the hardware for decimal arithmetic, increasing the memory, adding tape drives and a faster printer. There was wonderful co-operation between these diverse parts of the College community. Although we installed COBOL (Common Business Oriented Language) for the Library and the Business Office, for a long time Bob Teare chose to continue to maintain and develop his programs for the Library in Assembler Language – a tribute to his enthusiastic embrace of the new technology. It was an exciting time for all of us!

In the summer of 1966, Pomona College initiated a course, funded by NSF, for advanced prospective students. I had no part in the course, but at the Computer Centre I met Winifred (Tim) Asprey, Professor of Mathematics at Vassar, whose services had been obtained to teach the students FORTRAN. Tim was available because her elderly parents lived in Anaheim and she was spending the summer in Southern California. We shared common interests and immediately became great friends. Vassar had placed an order for an IBM 360 Model 30, and was eager to learn all I could teach her at the console of our Model 40, using machine language, Basic Assembler, and FORTRAN. It was with particular satisfaction that in those early days we were able to teach students pure machine language. Sitting at the console and setting the individual bits in two registers, then setting the instruction to ADD, and finally executing that instruction. Today what happens at that low level within the computer is not so easily made visible.

In later years I paid several visits to Vassar, notably in 1969 when I gave the Matthew Vassar Lecture, "Hooked on APL" and met Steve Dunwell, an IBM Fellow, who had been instrumental in establishing APL at Vassar. Dunwell was the architect of the IBM's Stretch computer, prototype of the 360 and the first computer to use byte architecture.

Vassar's Model 30 was installed in January 1967. The Trustees assembled for a demonstration of this new computer of which they were naturally very proud. Tim (being a mathematician rather than a social or natural scientist) chose an example from pure mathematics: she wrote a FORTRAN program to compute pi by Archimedes' method of inscribed and superscribed polygons. Tim phoned for advice: the computer found the value of pi to be exactly 3 to as many significant figures as could be displayed. What was wrong? The IBM Engineers were taking the computer apart to find out!

In the leisure of retirement I published the complete explanation in a paper entitled: "The perils of subtraction: A new language for an old algorithm" (*Vector*, 1995, vol. 11, no. 4, p.93-103"). The acknowledgement reads: "I dedicate this study to Professor Winifred Asprey, Emeritus Professor of Mathematics, Vassar College, in whose honour the Computer Centre at Vassar is named. In 1967, when Vassar received the first IBM [System/360] Model 30 installed at a customer site, Dr Asprey told me that this algorithm had been run (in Fortran) as a demonstration for the Trustees of the College. To everyone's embarrassment, the computer reported the value of pi to be 3. I suggested running the program in double precision. This was duly done, only to find that the value was still 3 – to a greater number of decimal places." Professor Asprey had 60 students in her APL class at Vassar in 1982 before she retired that year.

I am grateful to many systems engineers and other technical staff, particularly in the Clary Corporation, WDPC, TRW, and IBM who gave me and my colleagues education and guidance notably in the 1960s. Their names, so well known to me once, sadly too often now escape me. I don't recall the name of the IBM Account Representative who, in early 1964, alerted me about the announcement of System/360. (It is interesting to remember that this was the year in which IBM created the term "Word Processing"!) Our IBM Representative came to my office when I was in class and left on my desk a copy of the IBM Systems Journal, April 1964, vol.3, nos. 2 & 3, in which the designers explained the structure of System/360. This copy of the Journal – which I have on my desk as I write 37 years later -- is decorated by a sample of a dozen lines of what appears frighteningly complex mathematics. But, of course, nothing is more complex than a notation to which you don't possess the key. I suspect that when he delivered the Journal, our IBM representative was glad that I wasn't there to question him!

The notation on the cover was a sample from the "Formal Description of System/360" by A. D. Falkoff, K. E. Iverson and E. H. Sussenguth which makes up almost half of the April issue of the *Journal*. Just as, if a stone is thrown in the air, you can determine its position at any moment of time provided you know its mass and initial velocity, so the formal description, like a mathematical equation, answers every question regarding System/360s behavior. The idea that a system of such complexity could be described in this way enormously excited me. Its recognition was one of the turning points in my life.

The references informed me that the notation had already been used by Iverson in his book *A Programming Language* (1962), a copy of which I discovered in Pomona's mathematics library. A preliminary chapter of the book describes the language. It is followed by a chapter entitled "Microprogramming", in which the notation is used to describe the IBM 7090 "at a level approximately suited to the programmer and the system designer". Because of my experience with the IBM 7090 at WDPC, I was able to follow Iverson's description with comparative ease, and started to teach "Iverson Notation" to anyone who would listen.

Soon after graduating from Pomona in 1967, Don Stanger became our IBM account representative. Sometime late in 1968 he came into my office, and noticing Iverson's *A Programming Language* on my desk, he told me that IBM had implemented Iverson Notation as a computer language with the name APL, obviously taken from the title of Iverson's 1962 book. I could hardly believe what he was telling me. This soon led to my meeting Dr William J. [Bill] Bergquist, who was IBM's only "salesman" for APL. Bill was a mathematician, and though he covered the whole of the U.S., he was based at Cal Tech. We quickly became close friends and he paid many visits to Pomona before his untimely death in the 1980s from a brain tumour.

Bill's attempt to demonstrate APL to us in Claremont was a failure because the connection (with an acoustic coupler) through the College telephone system was inadequate. In those days connections were not only very slow by today's standards, but were often too weak and noisy. It is interesting to reflect that for a time the telephone operators wanted to prohibit machine transmission, and the Post Office attempted to prohibit mail containing computer tapes – because it was considered "cheating" to send so much text with so little weight and hence at relatively so little cost.

In 1968 Bill gave me a demonstration of APL at IBM's Scientific Center in Los Angeles. My enthusiasm never diminished. On February 15, 1969 I started teaching Iverson notation, APL, FORTRAN, and PL/1 to students in my class, Computer Science 51. The class included the study of the internal architecture of various computers including the IBM 1620, IBM 360, IBM 1130 , IBM 7090, 7030. Two students completed a project that involved designing a small computer, using Iverson Notation to write a formal description of their model. The next step was to rewrite the description in executable APL. Through Don Stanger's cooperation we were able to visit the Riverside IBM Office after hours and connect to Iverson's computer at the Thomas J. Watson Research Center in Yorktown Heights. The result was the creation of a working model of the students' computer!

I sent a copy of this project to Dr Iverson. He was delighted and invited me to visit him at Yorktown Heights. As it happened in the summer of 1969 I was traveling to Scotland for a sabbatical. Iverson suggested that I time my trip so that I could attend the first APL Users Conference, "The March on Armonk" at Binghamton. I did this, visiting Tim Asprey in Vassar and Iverson and Falkoff in Yorktown Heights at the same time.

In 1969 IBM made APL available for IBM's new small 1130 computer. By carrying a deck of cards with me, I made APL available at the University of Neuchâtel in Switzerland. As Swiney Lecturer (British Museum) I gave a course of lectures on "APL Applications in Geology" at Edinburgh University, and spoke at the Universities of St. Andrews, Aberdeen, and Liverpool.

In 1969-70 I was a John Simon Guggenheim Fellow in Edinburgh, but I returned to attend the Geological Society of America's Annual Meeting in Philadelphia and was an invited speaker at the Course on Models of Geologic Processes – An Introduction to Mathematical Geology, organised by the American Geological Institute. I presented the course using direct telephone access to APL on the computer at the Thomas J. Watson Research Centre in Yorktown Heights. While in Edinburgh, however, I had no computer access and typed my paper, "Introduction to the Study of Data Matrices", with an APL ball on an IBM Selectric typewriter. In 1999 I was also an invited speaker at the International Symposium on Computer Applications in the Earth Sciences, at the University of Kansas.

In 1971, after being appointed an IBM Fellow, Ken Iverson invited me to join him for a year at the IBM Scientific Center in Philadelphia. This was not possible, but I did join him for several weeks as a Research Associate.

In 1975 IBM produced its first desktop computer, the IBM 5100. The Geology Department obtained the second 5100 at a customer site, and this machine greatly facilitated the use of APL not only in the Geology Department, but in other departments in the College. e.g.. Botany, Mathematics, Economics, and Chemistry.

In 1976 Iverson announced a new direct way to define APL functions. At his invitation I reviewed his paper before publication. I then did much by teaching and publication to promote the use of Direct Definition. The following year, Iverson arranged with Dean Vockel that Don Orth, an IBM colleague with extensive knowledge of APL, to teach the use of APL to both Faculty and students under the sponsorship of the Mellon Foundation.

I was the only person invited to speak at all three of the APL Users Conferences in Toronto 1978, 1980, 1982. I spoke on Experience with Direct Definition One-Liners in Writing APL Applications; The Architectural Elegance of Crystals Made Clear by APL.

In 1981 IBM produced its first PC, the first personal computer with the potential of running APL. I bought my own PC in October 1981 and persuaded Pomona College to buy one for the Computer Center a few months later. I got an early version of APL for the PC from the University of Waterloo in 1982 and got STSC's APL for the PC in 1983. This enormously increased the availability and use of APL.

In 1983 I was Keynote speaker at the first Tool of Thought Conference, organised by the Association for Computing Machinery, New York, and I gave the Banquet Address at the International APL83 Conference, Washington, DC.

From 1985 I served as a National Lecturer for ACM each year until I retired and left for Scotland in 1989, speaking and running APL workshops from Toronto and New York to Sydney, Australia.

In 1985 I conducted workshops on APL at the State Seismological Institute in Beijing, China. In 1986 I was an invited speaker (two lectures) at the Conference celebrating the 20th Anniversary of the APL language, Thomas J. Watson Research Center, IBM, Yorktown Heights, New York. I was the only person present who had not been an IBM employee.

In 1990 Iverson announced his revolutionary new successor to APL called J. Before the public announcement he visited me in Scotland to encourage me to make use of J. At his request I gave an address entitled Mastering J at the APL91 Conference in Stanford.

My invited paper "Language as an Intellectual Tool: From Hieroglyphics to APL" was published in the *IBM Systems Journal* (vol. 30, no.4, p.554-581) in 1991. This was a special issue celebrating the 25th anniversary of the APL language, and I believe I was the only contributor who had not been an IBM employee.

In 1991 I spoke on APL and J at the Universities of Edinburgh and St Andrews.

In 1992 I conducted a Tutorial Day – J Workshop for the British APL Association, London, 1992. As a result of the success of this workshop, Iverson proposed that I go on tour in North America. Starting in Toronto I ran workshops in Toronto, The University of Waterloo, Lawrence, Dallas, Phoenix, Claremont, Palo Alto, Washington DC, and the College of Wooster OH. I gave workshops again in Toronto in 1993.

In 1993 my invited paper entitled "An Executable Notation, with illustrations from elementary crystallography", was published In *Computers in Geology: 25 years of progress*, Oxford University Press, pp.231-240.

In 1994 I received the Kenneth E. Iverson Award from the Association for Computing Machinery (ACM) in Antwerp.

In 1995 I spoke on The Composition of Functions at the APL95 International Conference in San Antonio, Texas

From 1996 onwards I was very much involved in the Bicentenary of the death of James Hutton, the founder of modern geology, and was less active in the computing field.

In 2000 I gave an invited address on "The History of APL & J" at the Conference on J in Toronto.

In reflecting on this history I am struck with the number of chance occurrences that have played so great a role in determining my professional life. Frequently these occurrences related to meeting someone who gave me help at some critical point and opened an unexpected door. I keep thinking of Robert Frost's *The Road Not Taken*

> *Two roads diverged in a wood, and I ---*
> *I took the one less travelled by,*
> *And that has made all the difference.*

I became involved in computing because I needed to have efficient quality control in our work in X-ray Fluorescence.

As a student in Edinburgh I took an elementary class in physics. It was taught by Professor Barkla. Charles Glover Barkla was born on June 7, 1877. From 1913 until his death on October 23, 1944 he was Professor of Natural Philosophy at Edinburgh University. In 1917 Barkla received the Nobel Prize. The following is an extract from the citation:

"Barkla has made a long series of very careful investigations into the nature of the latter of the two types of radiation. In the first place he discovered that there are two different kinds of X-rays in the secondary radiation. The absorption coefficients of one of these two varieties are the same as those of the incident X-rays. Thus the rays have the same penetrability as the primary rays, and, as they prove in other respects to have the same qualities as the primary rays, they must be regarded as a diffused primary radiation."

The intensity of this diffuse radiation varies in different directions in relation to that of the incident primary radiation. By measuring the distribution of intensity of the diffuse radiation, Barkla was able to determine the total emission of a series of substances under varying conditions. One very important result among others that his investigations led to, enabled Barkla at an early stage to estimate approximately the number of electrons contained in an atom.

The other variety of X-rays is wholly independent of the character of the incident radiation. Barkla showed that this radiation is homogeneous, that its absorption coefficient is not dependent on the incident radiation, but is determined by the irradiated substance. Further, he made the important discovery that the character of the rays is solely dependent on the qualities of the atoms constituting the substance, irrespective of their grouping and influence upon each other, that is to say, independent of the chemical composition of the substance. Every chemical element yields a secondary radiation that is characteristic of that element. Hence Barkla named this variety of radiation the characteristic X-radiation.

This variety of radiation may be most conveniently studied in elements of relatively high atomic weight, for in them it is stronger than the diffuse radiation. The characteristic radiation, however, being, in contrast to the diffuse radiation, perfectly homogeneous, can be distinguished from the latter, and thus Barkla could trace the characteristic radiation down to elements of the atomic weight of 27.

Barkla was responsible for discovering and naming the K, L, and M shells of electrons in the structure of atoms – he originally named them A, B, and C. Yet his name is hardly known to Physics students today. Barkla never mentioned characteristic radiation in his lectures to the elementary class in which I was enrolled. Yet it was Barkla's work – extended to the light elements that constitute common rocks – that was the unknown basis for the work that necessitated my involvement with computers. In 1968 I was appointed a Sigma-Xi National Lecturer. Although my topic was X-ray Fluorescence – a new tool for the petrologist, but my lectures were given as a tribute to Barkla's brilliant researches so long before.

Had it not been for the discoveries made by Barkla, I would not have been involved with XRF and I would have then lacked the strong motivation to use computers. Corwin's generous tribute says that I helped him to "get through the early years". Perhaps without Barkla he would have found life harder. We all owe so much to others!

The 1978 History of Programming Languages Conference

The following article first appeared as one of Donald's contributions to "Computer Corner" in Computers & GeoSciences, vol. 4, no. 4, 1978, pp. 351 – 352.

No one who was fortunate enough to attend it is likely to forget the Los Angeles Conference on the History of Programming Languages, held in June under the auspices of the Association for Computing Machinery (ACM). After Grace Murray Hopper's fascinating keynote address on early history, the program took two and a half days to pass through the spectrum from FORTRAN to APL. The languages represented at the Conference were all created and in use by 1967. They remain in use 10 years later, and each has had considerable influence on the field of computing. The speakers (each of whom was one of the designers) attempted to tell why they created the languages in the ways they did, what purposes they intended, and what constraints were imposed by machine implementation.

The historic nature of the conference became evident at the very first session, when John Backus introduced Cuthbert Hurd. In 1953 Hurd had approved Backus' proposal to develop a practical automatic programming system for the IBM 704. That, of course, was the birth of FORTRAN. The last session of the Conference was remarkable for the discussion by Fred Brooks, a principal architect of IBM System/360, of the paper by A D Falkoff and K. E Iverson on "The Evolution of APL". The influence of machine structure on language design should interest a geologist, because his business is with evolution and its controlling factors. For example, because the 36-bit word of a 704 can encode six characters, each occupying six bits, FORTRAN restricted the length of names to six characters, and continued to do so even when implemented on later machines of different structure. On the other hand, according to Backus, the fact that the 704 had only three index registers was a coincidence and not a factor when the designers imposed a limit of three subscripts on arrays.

APL, in contrast, began in the late 1950s as a means of communication with people, not at first with machines. Iverson used it in his classes at Harvard when describing topics such as linear programming, sorting, and the structure and operation of machines. Although already published in book form in 1962 (K. E. Iverson, *A Programming Language*, John Wiley & Sons), APL attracted a new audience when used to describe the detailed behavior of the newly announced System/360 m Apnl 1964 (A D Falkoff, K E Iverson. and E H Sussenguth, 1964, "A Formal Description of System/360". *IBM Systems Journal*, v. 3, pp. 198-263.)

Because APL uses a rich set of symbols not available on card punches, it probably seemed difficult at first to implement. Indeed, amongst programming languages it has the distinction of being used at the desk and on the blackboard independently of the existence of any computer implementation. At just the right time, however, IBM developed the 1050 terminal and the Selectric typeball. It was therefore possible to provide a font and to communicate interactively in APL with a computer .This was accomplished on the IBM 7090 in 1965. Falkoff and Iverson have discussed the influence of the terminal keyboard and typeball on the development of the language, and what is especially interesting is their recognition that unwelcome physical constraints frequently resulted in significant improve-ments and generalizations in the language.

Early computers had memories so small that great skill and ingenuity was required to use them at all. For example, the first computer in Pomona College's Geology Department had only 32 words of memory, the programs being on wired boards. Yet, minute though this is by today's standards, we accomplished useful work with it. But so much attention had to be given to the efficient use of early machines that we became myopic, concentrating on hardware and losing sight of the evolution of mathematical notation that preceded the computer age and still continues.

At the Los Angeles Conference, John Backus, who was manager of the original Programming Research Group responsible for creating the FORTRAN language, said that all conventional languages, such as FORTRAN and ALGOL, "create enormous, unnecessary intellectual roadblocks in thinking about programs. These 'Von Neumann' languages constantly keep our noses pressed in the dirt of address computation and the separate computation of single words, whereas we should be focussing on the form and content of the overall result we are trying to produce. The fact that such languages have dominated our thinking for twenty years is unfortunate because their long-standing familiarity will make it hard for us to understand and adopt new programming styles which one day will offer far greater intellectual and computational power."

Although Backus did not mention APL in his talk, it answers his description of a programming style rising above "the separate computation of single words" and possessing far greater intellectual power than do the conventional languages. It can be truly said that its symbols "make reasoning easier", it is a language to think in. If one objects, as some do, that the notation is unfamiliar and too complex for non-specialists, we should remember the words of William Oughtred, pioneer in mathematical symbolism. Writing in 1647, he said "Which Treatise being not written in the usual synthetical manner, nor with verbous expressions, but in the inventive way of Analitice, and with symboles or notes of things instead of words, seemed unto many very hard, though indeed it was but their owne diffidence, being scared by the newness of the delivery, and not any difficulty in the thing it selfe. For this specious and symbolicall manner, neither racketh the memory with multiplicity of words, nor chargeth the phantaste with comparing and laying things together, but plainly presenteth to the eye the whole course and processe of every operation and argumentation." And also in 1632 "This manner of setting downe Theoremes, whether they be Proportions, or Equations, by Symboles or notes of words, is most excellent, arttficiall, and doctrinall. Wherefore I earnestly exhort every one, that desireth though but to looke into these noble Sciences Mathematicall, to accustome themselves unto it. And indeede it is easie, being most agreeable to reason, yea even to sence. And out of this working may many singular consectaries be drawne, which without this would, it may be, for ever lye hid". In these passages Oughtred was encouraging his readers not to be afraid of his new symbols, which included the St Andrews cross, x, introduced for multiplication in 1631.

Developments in computer technology, such as the availability of megabyte memories and virtual storage on what we used to call mini-computers only a year or two ago, both require and make possible the style of programming that is characteristic of APL. Its symbolism helps us grasp the intellectual content of an algorithm without extraneous and irrelevant matters prescribed by a machine. Bertrand Russell said "A good notation has a subtlety and suggestiveness which at times make it seem almost like a live teacher." Slowly, like acceptance of Oughtred's symbol for multiplication, people in many fields are recognizing that APL provides the good notation we need.

*****

Among Donald's papers there is a draft of an account of Ken Iverson's career, dated September 29, 2004. Over the years, Donald urged Ken to record his unique contribution to the history of computing and Ken, a man of great modesty, would respond "But It is not important...." Donald dared to disagree and kept urging Ken on, until he himself began to realise that there might indeed be some value in recording the history of computing from his perspective and that possibly his account might be published. Ken and Donald were in contact daily, both by e-mail and phone conversations. When Ken died very suddenly Donald's sense of loss and grief made it impossible for him to continue working on this material. However, these notes, edited by Roger Hui, have been named "The Story of APL and J" and can be found on the Jsoftware website as http://www.jsoftware.com/papers/autobio.htm and were published in APL/J magazine Vector http://archive.vector.org.uk/art10012020 Volume 23, number 4, September 2008.

Ken Iverson's preamble speaks for itself:

My friend Dr. Donald McIntyre has a penchant for well-documented historical treatments of topics that interest him. His more important works concern his chosen discipline of geology; notably his discovery and discussion of the lost drawings of James Hutton, and his commemorative works on the occasion of Hutton's bicentennial.

Because of his fruitful use of my APL programming language, and its derivative language J, Donald has asked me many questions concerning their development. I finally suggested (or perhaps agreed to) he writing of a few thoughts on these and related matters.

Because of my other interests in developing and applying J, I have deferred work on these essays, but now realize that the further application of J has already fallen into younger and better hands, such as those of Professor Clifford Reiter in his *Fractals, Visualization in Mathematics, and J*.

Likewise, the further development and implementation of J is now in better hands, such as those of Roger Hui, my son Eric and nephew Kirk, and, last but not least, Chris Burke.

Because of my negligence in the keeping of records, I am relieved to realize that I can now in good conscience ignore the provision of carefully documented references, leaving such matters to McIntyre's expertise. I will also exercise the freedom to explore ideas as they arise, and not restrict myself to fulfilling Donald's expressed desires…..

Donald's Memorial Tribute to Ken Iverson *was first published in Vector, Journal of the British APL Association, vol. 22., no. 3, 2005, pp. 109 – 114, and also appears as part of Donald's material to be found on Donald's own website at*

www.mcintyre.me.uk/index_f/menu_f/j_f/kei_tribute.pdf

Donald's Salute to Roger Hui when he received the Kenneth E. Iverson Award, 1996 This article gives an account of Roger Hui's work in the application of APL and his pivotal role in the design and implementation of J. It also is a testimony to the high esteem that Donald had for him. It can be found on

www.mcintyre.me.uk/index_f/menu_f/j_f/hui_tribute.htm

Chapter 9
James Hutton – Donald's friend

Theory of the Earth

James Hutton that true son of fire who said
to Burns 'Aye man, the rocks melt wi the sun'
was sure the age of reason's time was done:
what but imagination could have read
granite boulders back to their molten roots?
And how far back was back, and how far on
would basalt still be basalt, iron iron?
Would second seas re-drown the fossil brutes?
'We find no vestige of a beginning,
no prospect of an end.' They died almost
together, poet and geologist,
And lie in wait for hilltop buoys to ring,
or aw the seas gang dry and Scotland's coast
dissolve in crinkled sand and pungent mist.

From Edwin Morgan's *Sonnets from Scotland* [1984]
and published with permission from Carcanet Press

James Hutton (1726-97), one of the principal figures of the Scottish Enlightenment, and the acknowledged founder of modern geology, was born and died in Edinburgh. His close friends included Adam Smith, Joseph Black, William Robertson, John Playfair, John Clerk of Eldin and his son John Clerk, Lord Eldin – all, except Adam Smith, subjects of Raeburn's portraits. From perceptive field observations over many years, Hutton concluded that the present land was formed from the debris of former lands, and that consequently the Earth must be vastly older than was commonly believed. Hutton's discovery of 'Deep Time' made it possible for us to perceive that, in the words of Nobel laureate George Wald: 'We live in a historical universe, one in which not only living organisms but stars and galaxies are born, mature, grow old and die'.

Donald's comments on Sir Henry Raeburn's portrait of James Hutton

Hutton presented his 'Theory of the Earth' to the Royal Society of Edinburgh in 1785, and published a longer though unfinished account in 1795. Despite a painful urological illness during his last years, Hutton left over 4,500 printed pages and over 1,000 pages of manuscript on a wide range of subjects from agriculture to philosophy. Raeburn's portrait features a quill pen and a great pile of manuscript pages as well as geological specimens which provided evidence for his Theory.

The portrait was commissioned (date unknown) by John Davidson of Stewart␣eld, Deputy Keeper of the Signet in Edinburgh (John Playfair, 1805, p.95). At the beginning of the twentieth century scholars dated the portrait to the second half of the 1770s. They believed that Raeburn (1756-1823) was a prodigy, painting life-size, full-length portraits in his early twenties. When the portrait was purchased by the Gallery it was thought to date from 1778. In his complete catalogue of Raeburn portraits (1994) David Mackie, art historian, has, however, shown that Raeburn painted the portrait shortly before 1790. This date, which is after the artist's visit to Rome in 1784-1786, is more in accord with what we know of the sitter's life and work.

John Playfair, James Hutton's biographer, wrote this word-portrait of Hutton and it could be, to some extent, a description of Donald McIntyre!

His figure was slender, but indicated activity, while a thin countenance, high forehead, and a nose somewhat aquiline, bespoke extraordinary acuteness and vigour of mind. His eye was penetrating and keen, but full of gentleness and benignity.

His conversation was inestimable; as great talents, the most perfect candour, and the utmost simplicity of character and manners, all united to stamp a value upon it. He had, indeed, that genuine simplicity, originating in the absence of all selfishness and vanity, by which a man loses sight of himself altogether, and neither conceals what is, nor affects what is not. His conversation was extremely animated and forcible, and, whether serious or gay, full of ingenious and original observation. Great information, and an excellent memory, supplied an inexhaustible fund of illustration, always happily introduced, and in which, when the subject admitted of it, the witty and the ludicrous never failed to occupy a considerable place.

With this relish for whatever is beautiful and sublime in science, we may easily conceive what pleasure he derived from his own geological speculations.

.......He was, perhaps in the most enviable situation in which a man of science can be placed. He was in the midst of a literary society of men of the first abilities, to all of whom he was peculiarly acceptable.

Playfair goes on to state that among the original members of the Oyster Club were Adam Smith, economist, and Joseph Black, chemist. Donald often enjoyed recounting of how Joseph Black died seated in his chair, holding a cup of milk – and not a drop was spilled. When Donald's time came, he too was seated and at peace – quitting this sphere in remarkably similar circumstances!

Donald was part of a mini-version of The Oyster Club. At the Claremont Colleges Faculty House, it was a honour for a few colleagues from diverse academic disciplines to enjoy lunch on a daily basis with Vincent Learnihan, Pomona College's erudite and lively Professor of Medieval History. Discussions at "Vincent's table" were always wide-ranging, scholarly and filled with wit and laughter.

Two Portraits, Probably More.

David Mackie, art historian, St Catharine's College, Cambridge, describes his first meeting with Donald.

A noticeable man is what I'd now say, thirteen years down the road, even if he hadn't done what he did next. The lecture ended and he shot to his feet. He welcomed with some excitement "this extraordinary new information". Some minutes later, at the end of questions, he was at the lectern shaking hands, introducing himself, saying he would have to leave immediately, that he would like to meet again, soon, that he was leaving the country on a trip. The voice? Voices say so much. His had the modified tones of someone who had fitted in. Where? Only Canada or the US were possibilities. An unusual briefcase and clothing; the tweed jacket wasn't Scottish; they too were North American. But the voice had been fully Scottish in the past. Now it was mid-Atlantic. Who was he? He had speed, quiet authority and command with no hint of aggression. A dying breed that was never numerous. The erudition was rare beyond imagining. How did this man understand so quickly and so well something so out of the way? After all, what had been proposed may have been a major change, but it was part of a very small seam of research mined by few. To business: Would it be possible for him to include with acknowledgement my work in his book, which was already at the publisher, but because of this lecture it must instantly be changed? Superb high-speed courtesy. That's very rare indeed; never seen before by me and never seen since. Of course it would be possible, an honour, thank you, etc.

My mind instantly casts all names into its own outer darkness and they are never retrieved, but the character and form are indelible. Who was this? The glance, all seeing, suggested uncritical acceptance with no tricks missed; it seemed used to people erring, yet was kindly and displayed the constant activity of a very sharp mind. Yes, a noticeable man. Your response to him, those of you who did not know him? You would, I feel sure, have been aware of him as he shot past you. He would have registered on you. Any encounter would have been quietly formal, extremely polite, gentle, not stiff, significant for you in some way, and it would not have been forgotten by you for some reason of your own. The answer should have been obvious to me. He was a senior scholar in a fine teaching college. We did indeed meet later and the friendship quickly expanded to include Ann and Ewen, their family, their friends, my family and friends. Doors opened, circles overlapped and life was shared.

As well as many other things, Donald McIntyre was the distinguished authority on the life and work of the geologist James Hutton. He had been perplexed throughout his career by the writings of the art historians on Hutton's portrait by Sir Henry Raeburn, which was the subject of my lecture that day in the Scottish National Portrait Gallery. And he should have been perplexed, for the writings were wrong. Donald knew this but feared to believe it without supporting evidence from an art historian. Now, suddenly, after decades, he had it. The complete catalogue of Raeburn had been finished by me before our meeting and a new history of Raeburn had been offered with important portraits bearing new dates. Stylistic features, obvious when pointed out, showed that the portrait of Hutton had been misdated. The portrait's style indicated to me a date c. 1787-91. Not some date in or before 1784, as the books said.

The distinction is far more significant than the arithmetic suggests, but that would lead us into technicalities, which are always dull, and they do not concern Donald's work. But with this new date the entire history of Raeburn fell apart in my hands. My views were pooh-poohed by the few insiders who knew of them. Donald knew the elders were wrong. Later I discovered his reasoning, and it is brilliantly simple. There was no cause for Hutton to be painted as early as c.1783 for there was nothing to celebrate. That's it; end of story. The experts' date must be wrong. Donald knew the portrait had to be later. What Donald didn't know was how much later. No one does. Raeburn returned from his studies in Rome in c.1787. By then, Hutton had completed major scientific work and there was good reason for a friend to commission his portrait. On stylistic grounds, as I said, Raeburn's portrait of Hutton was painted somewhere in the years between 1787 and 1791, perhaps in 1788. The new date of the Hutton portrait did much to disprove the history of Raeburn published when Victoria was on the throne.

That history had been dutifully followed by everyone except Donald and me. He couldn't get the experts to listen and, sensibly, he deferred – until the day of the lecture. Donald was probably the only person in the room who understood the significance of what was said. A historian of science and a historian of art, separated by thousands of miles, by decades in age and by decades in departure date, had travelled independently from different starting points and arrived at the same conclusion, both of us using the simplest techniques in our disciplines' armouries. With Donald's help, my work on Raeburn became known, and so it was that those writings took the old route: heresy to orthodoxy. Thanks Donald, thanks for everything!

Donald was always impressed by American geologists' depth of interest and warm appreciation of James Hutton's work. His early talks about Hutton were presented in California.

James Hutton and the Philosophy of Geology

Address at the banquet of the Geological Society of America (Cordilleran Section), the Seismological Society of America, and the Paleontological Society (Pacific Coast Section), San Diego, California, March 23 1961

(Some of the substance of the following address was previously presented at the History of Science Club, Berkeley, CA in 1957.)

When 'Omer smote 'is bloomin lyre
He'd 'eard men sing by land an' sea,
And what 'e thought 'e might require
'E went an' took – the same as me!

The market-girls an' fishermen,
The shepherds an' the sailors too,
They 'eard old songs turn up again,
But kep' it quiet – same as you!

They knew 'e stole; 'e knew they knowed;
They didn't tell, nor make a fuss,
But winked at 'Omer down the road,
An' 'e winked back – the same as us!

Rudyard Kipling

This evening I have the privilege of tracing with you the parentage of the most important and possibly the most original single concept in geology: namely James Hutton's theory of the circulation of matter by erosion, sedimentation, metamorphism and uplift – the so-called geostrophic cycle.

On the 150th anniversary of Hutton's death it was my good fortune to attend, in Edinburgh, a memorable lecture by S.I.Tomkieff. The effect it had on me was profound and, because my present talk is on the borrowing of ideas, I haven't hesitated to adopt Tomkieff's title – and perhaps a little more besides. (The extent of my indebtedness may be gauged by reference to Tomkieff's *Trans. Edin. Geol. Soc. vol 14, Part 2, 1948.*)

Now, prior to Hutton, geology didn't exist; and I think it is generally agreed that the science was created in the fifty years between 1775 and 1825. In 1775, Hutton's close friend, James Watt, constructed his first working steam engine; and Werner, who was to become the leader of the Neptunists, began teaching at the Mining Academy of Freiberg. By 1825, the first passenger train was in operation; and Lyell, who was born the year Hutton died, was at work on his *Principles of Geology* – "the coping stone" of the new science. The same years saw the American War of Independence, the Industrial Revolution, the French Revolution and the Napoleonic wars. It was the age of Wordsworth and Coleridge; Byron and Shelley; Goethe and Schiller; Scott and Burns.

During this period, the necessary foundations for petrology, and the study of the materials of the crust, were laid by the work of Hauy on crystallography, Werner on the physical properties of minerals, and Joseph Black on their chemical composition. Stratigraphical palaeontology and the technique of field mapping were initiated by William Smith; but it was Hutton – and Hutton alone – who provided geology with a dynamic scheme – a theory, in the original sense of "something seen in the mind". Thus Hutton plays the same role in Geology as Newton in Astronomy, or Darwin in Biology. Comprehension is the power of the mind to understand; and these intellectual giants have given us comprehension of the great processes which go on around us. For this reason, Hutton truly deserves the title: "Founder of Modern Geology".

Fortunately for posterity, Hutton had a most eloquent biographer in John Playfair, Professor of Physics and of Mathematics at the University of Edinburgh, and one of the finest writers of scientific prose the English language has known. If the history of science is to be the study of the origin and development of ideas, then the history of geology needs to give attention to Playfair's remark: "It would be desirable to trace the progress of Dr. Hutton's mind in the formation of a system where so many new and enlarged views of nature occur, and where so much originality is displayed."

But how can anyone, other than the author himself, possibly hope to follow the sequence of ideas in a creative mind? The classic answer to this question has been given by John Livingston Lowes in his study of the process of creation in the mind of Coleridge entitled *The Road to Xanadu* – one of the most remarkable works of detection ever written. Coleridge kept a notebook, in which he recorded facts and phrases which had attention; and Lowes was able to use this book, along with library records, to follow Coleridge through his reading and hence "to retrace", as he said, "the obliterated vestiges of creation." The result is astonishing; The origin of almost every phrase and analogy in *The Rhyme of the Ancient Mariner* is known; and quite an assortment these sources are, including as they do such unlikely works as Burnett's *Sacred Theory of the Earth*, Maupertuis' geodetic study on *The Figure of the Earth*, Father Bourges' *Luminous Appearances in the Wakes of Ships*, and the Astronomer Royal's paper in the Philosophical Transactions of the Royal Society entitled *An account of an appearance, like a star, seen in the dark part of the moon*.

Hutton, we are told, "was in the habit of using his pen continually as an instrument of thought", and he left behind him what is described as "an incredible quantity of manuscript"; unhappily almost none has survived, so we are deprived of the clues his notebooks would have afforded.

Coleridge himself wrote that "the imagination, the true inward creatix", constantly working on "the shattered fragments of memory, dissolves, diffuses, dissipates, in order to recreate". And elsewhere he wrote that the "hooks-and-eyes of memory permit a confluence of our recollections". The analogy is reminiscent of Poincaré's image of mathematical discovery, in which he pictures ideas as hooked atoms ploughing through space like the molecules in the kinetic theory of gases. The number of possible combinations is so vast that even in a lifetime they couldn't all be examined; and Poincaré concluded that aesthetic sensibility, the appreciation of the beauty of an elegant solution, acts in the subconscious like a delicate sieve to catch combinations worthy of the attention of the conscious mind. Thus, the creation of a poem and the discovery of a mathematical law may have much in common. Perhaps a geological theory is born in the same manner.

A long time ago that giant of American geology, Grove Karl Gilbert, elaborated this theme in two masterly presidential addresses★: one was entitled *The inculcation of scientific method by example* and the other *The origin of hypotheses*. Gilbert, himself no mean divisor of brilliant and ingenious ideas, made a practice of trying to analyse the methods he and his associates used in geologic research.

He wrote: "Just as in the domain of matter, nothing is created from nothing, just as in the domain of life, there is no spontaneous generation, so in the domain of mind there are no ideas which do not owe their existence to antecedent Ideas which stand in the relation of parent to child. It is only because our mental processes are largely conducted outside of consciousness that the lineage of ideas is difficult to trace....To explain the origin of hypotheses," wrote Gilbert, "I have a hypothesis to present. It is, that hypotheses are always suggested through analogy. Consequential relations of nature are infinite in variety, and he who is acquainted with the largest number has the broadest base for the analogic suggestion of hypotheses." I believe that it was H. H. Read who, returning to London after touring North America and South Africa, affirmed that "the best geologist is he who has seen the most geology". At any rate, there is undoubtedly some truth in the remark.

★*Grove Karl Gilbert was President of the Geological Society of America in 1892 and in 1909.*

The conclusion we reach seems to be that the equipment necessary to devise hypotheses include:

First, an excellent memory and an extensive knowledge of the relevant material:

Second, the ability to form associations of ideas, and to reason by the analogy; and

Third, the possession of an unusually high degree of aesthetic feeling for an elegant solution, and a burning enthusiasm for the subject.

Now Playfair informs us that: Dr Hutton "had acquired great information; and an excellent memory supplied by an inexhaustible fund of illustration, always happily introduced. He used regularly to unbend himself (delightful phrase) with a few friends in a little society known by the name of the Oyster Club. The original members were: Mr Adam Smith (the author of The Wealth of Nations), Dr Joseph Black (the discoverer of latent heat and of carbon dioxide, and who introduced quantitative methods in chemistry), and Dr Hutton: and round them soon formed a knot of those who knew how to value the familiar and social converse of these illustrious men. As all three possessed great talents, enlarged views and extensive information, without any of the staleness and formality which men of letters think it sometimes necessary to affect; as they were all three easily amused – and were equally prepared to speak and to listen, and, as the sincerity of their friendship had never been darkened by the least shade of envy; it would be hard to find an example where everything favourable to good society was more perfectly united, and everything adverse more entirely excluded. The conversion was always free, often scientific, but never didactic or disputatious, and as this club was much the resort of the strangers who visited Edinburgh, from any object connected with art or with science, it derived from thence and extraordinary degree of variety and interest."

Hutton, then, was peculiarly well placed for the accumulation of diverse information and ideas, and he had an excellent memory. What of his ability to reason by analogy? Playfair records that Hutton possessed "the experienced eye, the power of perceiving the minute differences and fine analogies which discriminate or unite the objects of science; and the readiness of comparing new phenomena with others already treasured up in the mind."

What then of his appreciation of the beauty of an elegant solution, and what of his enthusiasm?

"A circumstance which greatly distinguished the intellectual character of the philosopher of whom we now speak," says Playfair, " was an uncommon activity and ardour of mind upheld by the greatest admiration of whatever in science was new, beautiful, or sublime. The acquisition of fortune and the enjoyments which most directly address the senses, do not call up more lively expressions of joy in other men, than hearing of a new invention, or being made aware of a new truth, would at any time do in Dr Hutton. This sensibility to intellectual pleasure was not confined to a few objects, or to the sciences which he particularly cultivated: he would rejoice over Watt's improvements on the steam engine, or Cook's discoveries in the South Sea, with all the warmth of a man who was to share in the honour, or the profit about to accrue from them. The fire of his expression on such occasions, and the animation of his countenance, are not to be described; they were always seen with great delight by those who could enter into his sentiments, and often with great astonishment by those who could not. With this exquisite relish for whatever is beautiful and sublime in science, we may easily conceive what pleasure he derived from his own geological speculations. The novelty and grandeur of the objects offered by them to the imagination, the simple and uniform order given to the whole natural history of the earth, are things to which hardly any man could be insensible; but to him they were matters, not of transient delight, but of solid and permanent happiness."

Elsewhere Playfair remarks that both Hutton and Black were "formed with a taste for what is beautiful and great in science, with minds inventive and fertile in new combinations." Clearly Hutton had all the qualities we have suggested as necessary in a great scientific synthesiser – and he possessed them to a remarkable degree. We must now look at the most likely sources of his ideas; his immediate background and the achievements of his friends.

Hutton's first serious studies were in chemistry and medicine; first in Edinburgh, then in Paris and finally in Leyden where he took his M.D. degree at the age of 23. However, he never practised medicine, for, on his return to Scotland he took charge of a small farm which he had inherited from his father. Hutton, who never did things by halves, immediately applied his scientific training to agriculture. He introduced new methods to Scottish farming and he travelled to Norfolk and the Low Countries in search of the best techniques and practices. While on these journeys he became increasingly interested in the origin of soil and in the processes of geology.

After 13 years of successful farming, he moved to Edinburgh where his principal income was from his ammonium chloride plant – the first in Britain. His time was spent in reading; in chemical experiments, often together with Black; and in the company of his illustrious and stimulating friends. He was a member of the Council of the newly organised Royal Society of Edinburgh. For the first volume of the Society's Transactions he prepared his paper on the *Theory of the Earth, or an investigation of the laws observable in the composition, dissolution and restoration of land upon the globe*. The paper was read at two successive meetings and the first part of his paper was read by his friend Joseph Black.

In addition to his studies of medicine, agriculture, chemistry, meteorology and geology, he published a 3-volume work on philosophy and a dissertation on Chinese language.

The accomplishments of his friends are so extensive that we can afford only a catalogue. His intimate acquaintances were responsible for the discovery of carbon dioxide, nitrogen, oxygen and strontium, and he himself was the first to extract sodium from silicate. The list includes the discovery that water has a point of maximum and that latent heat is needed to change its state. His friends included men responsible for the development of the steam engine; for the founding of iron works, and a sulphuric acid plant for the use of chlorine in bleaching; the author of the first book on agricultural chemistry; the author of the *Wealth of Nations*; the man to whom Sir Walter Scott dedicated *Waverley*; and that remarkable man who, never having been to sea, devised a system of naval tactics which won the British fleet several victories and which was quoted in Nelson's battle orders at Trafalgar.

With this background we are now equipped to examine Hutton's Theory and we will also draw somewhat on the unpublished manuscript of his *Elements of Agriculture* on which he was working at the time of his death. In so far as is practicable, I will give you Hutton's own words.

First of all we need to know that for Hutton, "A theory is nothing but the generalisation of particular facts; and, in the theory of the earth, those facts must be taken from the observations of natural history." For Hutton, a phenomenon (what he termed an "appearance") was "explained" when it had been "comprehended" by a theory, that is to say incorporated into the structure of the theory.

Second, Hutton remarked that "It is with pleasure that man observes regularity in the works of nature, instead of becoming disgusted with disorder and confusion. If the stone which fell today," he wrote, "were to rise tomorrow, there would be an end of natural philosophy, our principles would fail, and we would no longer investigate the rules of nature from our observations."

This, of course, is the doctrine of uniformitarianism, but it wasn't original with Hutton. Before Hutton went to Leyden, the Professor of Astronomy there wrote; "When, as a result of certain observations, we anticipate other cases which we have not directly observed, our prediction is based on the axiom of uniformity of nature. All action would be impossible if we could not assume that the lessons of former experience would be valid in the future.

For Hutton it was therefore clear that, in his own words, "We must read the transactions of the past in the present state of natural bodies, and, for the reading of this character, we have nothing but the laws of nature, established in the laws of science of man by his inductive reasoning. For man is not satisfied in seeing things which are; he seeks to know how things have been, and what they are to be". However, it was Sir Archibald Geikie and not James Hutton who crystallised this concept in the memorable dictum: "the present is the key to the past".

In Hutton's own opinion, it was agriculture that had been the study of his life; geology had been incidental. Accordingly he looked on the world as a well-run ranch, designed to sustain plants and animals, and with rotation, necessary to maintain fertility. Indeed, the secret of Hutton is that he thought of the world as a sort of superorganism. His was not the mind of a narrow specialist. For him the biological sciences were completely integrated with the physical. "Here," he said, "is a compound system of things, forming one whole living world."

"The most solid rocks," he wrote, "moulder and decay upon the surface of the earth, and thus produce a soil, either immediately upon the place which, thus, had given it birth, or remotely upon some other place where it may be transported by water or the wind. For this great purpose of the world, the solid structure of the earth must be sacrificed; for the fertility of the soil depends upon the loose and incoherent state of its materials; and this state of the fertile soil necessarily exposes it to the ravages of the rain upon the inclined surface of the earth."

"From the tops of the mountains to the shores of the sea, all the soils are subject to be moved from their places, and to be deposited in a lower situation; thus gradually proceeding from the mountain to the river; and from the river, step by step, into the sea. If the vegetable soil is thus constantly removed from the surface of the land, and if its place is thus to be supplied from the dissolution of the solid earth, we may perceive an end to this beautiful machine; an end arising from that destructibility of its land which is so necessary in the system of the globe, in the economy of life and vegetation. It may be concluded that the apparent permanency of this earth is not real or absolute, and that the fertility of its surface, like the healthy state of animal bodies, must have its period and be succeeded by another."

"We have now considered the globe of this earth as a machine constructed upon chemical as well as mechanical principles. But is this world," he asks, "to be considered thus merely as a machine, to last no longer than its parts retain their present position, their proper forms and qualities? Or may it not also be considered as an organised body such as has a constitution in which the necessary decay of the machine is naturally repaired? Is there in the constitution of the world a reproductive operation by which a ruined constitution may be again repaired?" And here we see the physician and the farmer.

"From the constitution of these materials which compose the present land, we have reason to conclude that, during the time this land was forming, by the collection of its materials at the bottom of the sea, there had been a former land containing minerals similar to those we find at present in examining the earth......A habitable earth is made to rise out of the wreck of a former world." And this is Hutton the geologist.

The whole spirit of Hutton's geology is contained in a statement that "The matter of this active world is perpetually moved, in that salutary circulation (a good medical expression!) by which provision is so wisely made for the growth and prosperity of plants, and for the life and comfort of the various animals."

Now it is a most remarkable fact that, immediately prior to the publication of Hutton's Theory in 1788, there was a man, today almost completely forgotten, who viewed the earth just as Hutton did. His name was George Hoggart Toulmin. In the library of the Geology Department at Pomona College there is a copy of his very rare book *The Antiquity and Duration of the World*, it is in the second edition, published 1783. No one familiar with Hutton's writings can read this book without being impressed by an astonishing similarity. For my own part, I find it impossible to avoid the conclusion that Hutton had read it prior to writing his own paper.

Like Hutton, Toulmin took a remarkably comprehensive view of the earth, referring to "the beautiful order and disposition of the several parts that compose the stupendous whole." Like Hutton, he adopted a fundamental uniformitarianism: "Nature is always the same, her laws are eternal and immutable." Like Hutton, he believed that slow changes, long continued, can produce far-reaching results: "These immutable truths should never be forgot," he writes, "that animals and vegetables flourish and decay; that earths are formed by slow degrees; that they too change by time; that stone is formed, is decomposed or altered in its composition; that mountains now are elevated; now depressed; that nature lives in motion."

Like Hutton he recognised the significance of sedimentary rocks as proof of the circulation of matter. But to me it was of particular interest that Toulmin's very words and phrases echoed what I knew in Hutton: "The continual formation and decay of every existing substance, the unceasing circulation of matter, produces no disorder. A continual waste in every part is necessary to the incessant repairs of the whole. The closest sympathy and connection is preserved throughout the entire system of things."

Keep in mind these words and listen to Hutton. We are "led to acknowledge an order in a subject which, in another view, has appeared as absolute disorder and confusion.....There is a certain order established for the progress of nature, for the succession of things, and for the circulation of matter upon the surface of the globe....We must see how this machine is so contained as to have these parts which are wasting and decaying, again improved...the necessary decay is naturally repaired."

"We are," says Hutton, "thus led to see a circulation in the matter of the globe, and a system of beautiful economy in the works of nature. This earth, like the body of an animal, is wasted at the same time that it is repaired. It has a state of growth and augmentation; it has another state which is that of diminution and decay. This world is thus destroyed in one part, but it is renewed in another."

The last sentence of Toulmin's book ends: "We have by no means been led to contravent....the existence of infinite intelligence and wisdom." And elsewhere he refers to "nature, whose every operation is stamped with wisdom and consistency." The last paragraph of Hutton's paper begins, "We have now got to the end of our reasoning; we have the satisfaction to find that in nature there is wisdom, system and consistency."

Toulmin wrote: "there has never been a succession of events, something similar to what is continually observed....a vast succession of ages....We have been induced to conclude that the whole system of things," and so on. Hutton put it thus: "having seen a succession of worlds, we may from this conclude that there is a system in nature."

Toulmin said: "In the circle of existence, in vain do we seek the beginning of things." And Hutton, intimating that he had reached the limit of his vision into the past, wrote: "It is in vain to look for anything higher in the origin of the earth."

Toulmin's main point is that "through the whole of this enquiry we have endeavoured to demonstrate.....that, as there never was any beginning, so will there never be any conclusion...." And he repeats, "the whole system of things never had any beginning, nor will have any termination." And the final sentence of Hutton's paper is: "The result, therefore, of our present enquiry is that we find no vestige of a beginning, no prospect of an end." Are we not, like John Livingston Lowes, "retracing the obliterated vestiges of creation"?

In 1749 Hutton was granted the M.D. at Leyden for his thesis on 'the blood and circulation in the microcosm." The title reminds us that, from the beginning of speculative thought, philosophers have pondered the concept that man, the microcosm, is the epitome of the macrocosm or the world in which he lives. Attempts were constantly being made to find to find analogies or correspondences between aspects of the anatomy and physiology of man, and the structure and workings of the universe. One of the oldest was the analogy between the sun, as the ruling power of the microcosm, and the heart, the governing power of the microcosm. Now, at a medical school with the reputation of that at Leyden, Hutton could not have taken the circulation of blood as his subject without becoming very familiar with Harvey's classic book *On the movement of the heart and blood*, published in 1628.

Harvey began his dedication, to King Charles I, thus: "The animal's heart is the basis of its life, its chief member, the sun of its microcosm; on the heart all activity depends, from the heart all its liveliness and strength depends. Equally is the king the basis of his kingdoms, the sun of his microcosm, the heart of the state." And in his text Harvey wrote: "I began to think whether there might not be a notion, as it were in a circle, in the same sense that Aristotle uses when he says that air and rain emulate the circular movement of the heavenly bodies; for the moist earth warmed by the sun evaporates; the vapours drawn upwards are condensed and fall as rain to moisten the earth again, so producing succession of fresh life. In similar fashion the circular movement of the sun gives rise to storms and atmospheric phenomena. And so, in all likelihood is it in the body, through the motion of the blood....The heart deserves to be styled the starting point of life and the sun of our microcosm just as much as the sun deserves to be styled the heart of the world." So wrote Harvey.

That the suggestion I am hinting at is not far fetched is made clear by the following quotation from Hutton: "The circulation of the blood is that efficient cause of life; but life is the final cause, not only for the circulation of blood, but for the revolution of the globe: without a central luminary and a revolution of the planetary body, there would not have been a living creature upon the face of the earth." Now this quotation is not from his medical thesis, but from the *Theory of the Earth*, written 46 years after he left Leyden! And twice, in that geologic classic, does Hutton refer to the "physiology" of the earth – a most significant phrase, and one reminiscent, incidentally, of Thomas Robinson's book, *The Anatomy of the Earth*, published in 1694, which proclaimed that the earth was a superorganism with "a constant circulation of water, as in other animals of blood."

Analogy of microcosm and macrocosm
Analogy of celestial spheres and atmosphere
Analogy of heart and sun
Analogy of blood and rain

This is the heredity of Hutton's Theory – of our Theory. And the heart of the theory (if I may use the analogy) is the concept of circulation of matter in the macrocosm. One of the famous teachers at Leyden, just before Hutton's time there, wrote that "the author of nature has made it necessary for us to reason by analogy". I know that Grove Karl Gilbert would have approved of this. The moral seems to be that analogies are so important in the genesis of scientific hypotheses that sometimes even false analogies are sometimes extremely fertile.

In closing I should like to report to you on the Circulation Club which was founded in Edinburgh three years before Hutton's paper was read to the Royal Society. To the strains of Gounod's *March of a Marionette*, initiates had to consume an ox heart before scrutineers who reported on mastication, deglutition, and probable assimilation – for in those days there were no anti-hazing laws!

The object of the club was, and here I quote from the Constitution: "to commemorate the discovery of the circulation of the blood by the circulation of the glass." Ladies and gentlemen: let us adopt and adapt that old tradition; let our hearts beat faster and our blood thrill as we commemorate the discovery of circulation in the macrocosm, and drink to the immortal name of the founder of geology, James Hutton, M.D.

(Note – This paper was prepared for oral presentation and ellipsis is not everywhere indicated.)

In July 1970 Donald gave an address to the Royal Society of Edinburgh.

The Significance of the Rare Event in Geology

There is no written text of this lecture but hand-written notes show that quoting liberally from Hutton, Playfair, Lyell and Holmes, Donald demonstrated that the European historical approach to geology differed from what he himself had seen in America.

Donald referred to James Geikie, President of the Royal Society 1913-15, as his "spiritual grand-father" and quoted from his revolutionary book *Earth Sculpture* (1898): "It was eventually recognised that no hard-and-fast-line separates past and present. The belief in worldwide catastrophes disappeared" and also from his own teacher, Professor Arthur Holmes: "The effects of slow processes acting for long periods have been fully adequate to account for all the successive transformations of landscape that the earth has witnessed" and from Louis Agassiz (1807-73) who remarked that "It was in Scotland where I acquired precision in my ideas regarding ancient glaciers."

(Agassiz found evidence to affirm his theories at Blackford Hill quarry, Edinburgh. In the early 1950s, Donald used this historical fact to help win a court case that saved the quarry from destruction.)

In 2013 – some forty-three years on – our friend, Dr Charles Waterston, still recalls attending that lecture and drew attention to The Royal Society of Edinburgh's note in their *"Proceedings of the Tenth and last Ordinary meeting of the Society on Monday, July 6 1970"*. This is reprinted here with the Society's kind permission.

"The President introduced Professor D.B. McIntyre, Department of Geology, Pomona College California and invited him to address the Society on "The Significance of the Rare Event in Geology". Professor McIntyre delivered a most stimulating lecture on the geological changes produced by infrequent events such as earthquakes, flash floods, ice barriers and the like, and in a brief statistical treatment showed that rarity was a function of time, and that given long enough, events which were extremely rare in human experience became near-certainties on a geological time-scale. His lecture was illustrated with admirable colour slides."

These slides, taken on Donald's travels in America, illustrated the effects of catastrophes. To emphasise his point, he quoted from 20th-century rainfall records showing that a mean 26" to 150" rain fell annually in Scotland, while, in 1921, 40" of rain fell in Texas within 24 hours and, in 1914, 72" of rain within 30 minutes in Cambridge, Ohio!

Discoveries in Geoscience in the 21st- century continue to affirm the importance of the "Rare Event" in the history of our planet and the importance of Donald's American illustrations in 1970 to the geological understanding of his Edinburgh audience.

A Remarkable Gift

In the early summer of 1988 Sir John Clerk of Penicuik spent a few days at our home in Claremont, California en route to the opening ceremony for The James Clerk Maxwell sub-millimetre and wavelength astronomical telescope at Mauna Kea Observatory in Hawaii. Sir John brought generous gifts to all three of us, which we opened in the cool of the evening on our patio.

Sir John's present to Donald was an unframed John Clerk of Eldin painting. Donald was greatly delighted to have this and, while handling it gently, he turned the painting over – and there, to his astonishment and rapture, he found John Clerk of Eldin's 200 years old faint pencil sketch of a boulder from the River Tarf – a tributary of the River Tilt, Blair Atholl, Perthshire. The sketch, inaccurately labelled by Clerk as coming from Glen Tilt, shows layered schist that has been cut by granite, both being cut by a still younger vein of "red porphyry".

Donald wrote: "The original of the Clerk field-sketch of the Glen Tarf boulder is very faint. Modern published copies of the sketch result from computer enhancement from the original and were made by the United States Geological Survey. This work is thanks to Roy R. Mullen, Associate Chief, National Mapping Division, USGS; Lee C. Gerhard, Director, Kansas Geological Survey; and Jim Allan Photographic Unit, University of St Andrews, Scotland. The maximum diameter of the boulder as depicted in the original drawing is 1.5 inches. The photocopies are therefore magnified 2.9 times and 3.7 times."

Donald points to the granite veins in Glen Tilt

"I consider that this drawing is one of the most important of all the Clerk drawings because it illustrates that in 1785 Hutton was applying superposition to the determination of chronological sequence. To emphasise the drawing's significance, I enclose an enlarged photocopy of a portion of Clerk's drawing of the Moon, apparently made on 14 May 1785, i.e. probably about six months before Hutton and Clerk went to Glen Tilt. Fracastorius is a young crater superimposed on part of the old crater of Cyrillus. I contend that men, who could recognise evidence of a sequence of events in the boulder, could not have failed to recognise in the lunar drawing evidence for a sequence of events on the Moon."

"The Moon drawing should acknowledge the work of Jim Allan, Photographic Unit, University of St Andrews as well, of course, to Sir John D. Clerk, Bart."

A handsome volume "The Etchings of John Clerk of Eldin" was published by Geoffrey Bertram, Enterprise Editions, 2012.

Hutton/McIntyre Geological Tours

On retirement Donald led many successful geological trips throughout Scotland with emphasis on visiting Huttonian sites – to the island of Arran; the Scottish Borders, Portsoy on the Moray Firth, Glen Tilt and other Perthshire locations. A group of members of the Southern California Geological Society visited Scotland to enjoy an intensive week long excursion with the pleasurable finale in Perth.

Among others, Dr A.M. Sengör, Professor of Geology in Istanbul, Turkey with his wife and son, also appreciated a Hutton tour – McIntyre style. Dr Sengör is the author of *Is the Present the Key to the Past or the Past the Key to the Present? James Hutton and Adam Smith Versus Abraham Gottlob Werner and Karl Marx in Interpreting History* where he states that "both Adam Smith and James Hutton realised that history can only be interpreted by models and that the only models that we could have with any confidence were those constructed on most complete evidence, i.e. models of present-day objects and events. Smith studied the present markets to develop models for economic history; Hutton the present landscape to develop models for geologic history…..Hutton and Smith were out to find out what indeed had happened in history and why. This has been misunderstood in that the attitude of Smith and Hutton has been considered 'ahistorical' as opposed to the 'historical' sense of Marx and Werner."

Professor James Secord of Christ's College, Cambridge, wrote to Donald in March 1989:

Hutton, whose letters (now in the Scottish Record Office) are as remarkable as they are few in number, could have said all this much better than I can. In looking back I remember your help and enthusiasm from the day I came in to see you at the start of my Pomona College freshman year, to the time (just before my Watson scholarship year) that you gave me some desperately needed lessons on the pronunciation of Scottish names. Especially I remember our travels in Scotland, on Arran, at Glen Tilt, the Southern Uplands, and in Edinburgh, all in search of Clerk and Hutton. That time is still very vivid for me, not least because of the chances we have had to meet in Scotland since then, the last time including the Edinburgh Festival, and Macbeth in the most remarkable performance I have ever soon. Certainly "retiring" is about the last word that will ever be applied to you!

The more you owe to someone, the harder it is to say thank you in any way that seems at all appropriate.

Dennis Dean. Emeritus Professor of English and Humanities at the University of Wisconsin wrote to Ann in May 2012 – a sample of their trip together.

"I found my trip diary including my first meeting Donald. In accord with previously made arrangements, we met for the first time at Glasgow Airport on 14th August 1991 and were close companions until 27 August, when I left Edinburgh for Aberdeen, from where I flew to Norway. My record for these days is quite detailed, but the details are interesting. Here is the relevant part of my account of 14th August.

Arrival: Touchdown, 4am. Chicago time (10am local time). Walk in 58° F weather to nearby Arrival: One line for 'EC Nationals', the other for 'Other'. Reclaim suitcase and walk through Customs unchallenged. At exit from Customs (indoors) find myself greeted by Donald McIntyre in sport coat, shirt and tie (silver, balding hair, delightful smile), who recognises me from passport photo I sent him and from the DRD initials in my flight bag. We go outside; my stuff still on a luggage cart, then re-enter the terminal so that I can cash $100 in traveler's checks, the amount Donald recommended. Then I wait outside in the pickup area until he comes by in his red Subaru station wagon. Once I'm inside the car he immediately presents me with the folio-sized Philips Road Atlas to Scotland and Borders, and a geological map of

Scotland. I express my gratitude to him for the trip that has now begun and my enthusiasm for it.

With me helping on navigation – a nice day, no rain – we head west on M8 getting good views of the Clyde and across it to Dumbarton Castle. After Greenock we branch left onto the A78, past Inverkip to Skelmorlie, where we park to look at some well-exposed dykes near the sea. I didn't bring my camera from the car. When we return to it (a short muddy walk about a block) Donald astonishes me by opening up the car's hatch to show me inside it a travelling geological library, including Hutton Vols. I and II (facsimiles), and III; The Lost Drawings; the most recent report (by G.Y. Craig) of Hutton's 'Abstract' – which he gives to me, a complete file of my letters to him, guidebooks, maps and more…..."

Dennis Dean is the author of "James Hutton and the History of Geology", 1991 Cornell University. He inscribed a copy of his book: "For Donald B. McIntyre with admiration and gratitude. There is no other Scot now living who has done so much to preserve and honor Hutton's reputation. I shall always regard our days together in Scotland as the most moving geological experience of my life, and my friendship with you as one of its finest ornaments." *He also edited* James Hutton in the Field and in the Study *– a Bicentenary tribute to the Father of Modern Geology, 1997.*

In 1997 Donald had great pleasure in co-operating with Alan McKirdy to write and publish **James Hutton – The Founder of Modern Geology** *– ISBN 978 1 905267 736 This "little book" – as Donald would often speak of it – is available in its third edition from The National Museums of Scotland, Chambers Street, Edinburgh EH1 1JF, Scotland*

On 30th July 1997 Donald was honoured to give the opening address at the International Conference organised by the Edinburgh Geological Society in the bi-centennial year of James Hutton's death.

An expanded version of Donald's talk was published in *Earth Sciences History, Vol.16, No.2, 1997, p.100-157.* Copyright 1997 by HESS .

Here are some glimpses of its content:

James Hutton's Edinburgh – The Historical, Social, and Political Background.

Abstract: James Hutton (1726-1797) was born and bred in Edinburgh. Having decided to be a farmer, he went to Norfolk aged twenty-four to learn new methods of husbandry. From that base, he travelled widely and developed an interest in geology. In 1767 he left his Berwickshire farm and returned to Edinburgh, where he became a valued member of the remarkable group of men who founded the Royal Society of Edinburgh and made the city an unrivalled intellectual centre of the age.

Edinburgh was a capital without the distractions of king and parliament. When the Industrial Revolution began, many disciplines were already represented by men of world-renown who knew each other – many, indeed, were related. There were still no boundaries between narrowly defined disciplines; there was shared interest in all knowledge.

Geological structure had constricted Edinburgh's growth, keeping the compact Old Town on its ancient defensive ridge. The North Bridge, completed soon after Hutton's return to Edinburgh, made possible the planned New Town, in dramatic architectural and intellectual contrast to the mediaeval city. The beauty and interest of Edinburgh's scenery is the result of an active geological past. Consequently, in a small and accessible space, rocks of different character are exposed in a natural geological laboratory.

James Hutton did not live in an ivory tower. War, rebellion, and revolution, both political and industrial, all had their influence. In a turbulent world, a decade of peace (1783-1793) was another factor making possible Hutton's great contribution to modern geology.

This is the story of interrelationships and connections between an extraordinary group of highly intelligent people set against a background – sometimes indeed it becomes the foreground – of national and international events of importance and interest. Hutton was one of the central figures. He was seventy years old when he died, but to understand his environment we must reach back, albeit briefly, to events 200 years before he was born, and allude to happenings almost two decades after his death.

The subject is vast: the *dramatis personae* includes more than 150 remarkable characters; the range of talent is great, and the interconnections are astonishing. We have here pioneers not in geology only; we meet distinguished lawyers, statesmen, soldiers, sailors, historians, scientists, engineers, and literary men. Despite the constraints of time and space, it is hoped that the paper conveys something of the scope and character that Hutton knew.

For example, Donald described and told tales of many different characters among them, John Clerk, the son of Hutton's friend and colleague, John Clerk of Eldin.

John Clerk had a contracted leg, which made him limp. One day he overheard a lady say to her companion, "That's John Clerk, the lame lawyer." he turned round and said, "No, madam, the lame *man* not the lame *lawyer*....Like Hutton, John Clerk spoke broad, Scots: "the powerful direct Scots of the able highly educated man, a speech faded not from human memory." Addressing the House of Lords in London, Clerk argued that "the *watter*" had rin that way for forty years." The Lord Chancellor, much amused, asked: "Mr Clerk, do you spell water in Scotland with two 't's" to which Clerk replied: "Na, my Lord, we dinna spell watter wi' twa 't's but we spell maineers wi' twa ' n's." (Maineers = manners.)

James Hutton with his unique contribution to knowledge of our planet's history, was close to the centre of this community, not only by virtue of his life-span but, thanks to his generous and warm personality, by his friendships with some of the most brilliant men of the age. This paper will have achieved its object if the reader gains a feeling for the broad cultural, social, and political environment in which Hutton lived. If we could reproduce the intellectual climate that made Hutton and his friends possible, we would have found the philosopher's stone.

Afterword

"James Hutton was an accomplished field geologist. He systematically tested his conjectures, and those of others, by seeking new observations which were either consistent with those conjectures or provided reasons for rejecting them." (McIntyre & McKirdy, 1997). Everyone interested in the history of science will agree with Playfair who, in his *Life of Dr Hutton*, wrote: "It would be desirable to trace the progress of an author's mind in the formation of a system where so many new and enlarged views of nature occur, and where so much originality is displayed" (Playfair, 1805, p.55). This was my subject in 1957 at Herbert Evans' History of Science Club in Berkeley (a modern incarnation of the Oyster Club), and also in toasting Hutton at the Banquet of the Geological Society of America in San Diego in March 1961 (McIntyre,1963). Following Tomkieff's example (1948), I tried to see Hutton in his historical context.

Herbert Butterfield's argued that historical understanding is achieved by "making the past our present and attempting to see life with the eyes of another century than our own" (*The Whig interpretation of History*, 1931/1951, p.16). Developing this thesis, Colin Russell declared that it is "perverse to imagine that the practitioners of science operate in a cultural vacuum. They, and we, are affected by the prevailing climate of opinion and this will have a profound effect on how science is perceived" (*Whigs and Professionals, Nature*, 1984, Vol.308, p.777). Nevertheless, Hutton is often presented as if he lived in isolation. It was therefore a pleasure to give the opening address at the Conference in Edinburgh marking the bicentennial of Hutton's death. I attempted to sketch Hutton's Edinburgh – the environment in which Hutton made his great contribution to our understanding of Earth's history.

"Scientists grope their way, seeking to divine where they are going from where they are coming; they reach into the future as well as the past." They think they see networks of concepts extending the tough time: these "are not whiggish sins but the essence of science in action" (*Edward Harrison, Whigs, Prigs and Historians of Science, Nature*, 1987, Vol.329, p. 214). My text was longer than could be accommodated in the Proceedings of the 1997 Hutton Conference, and I am grateful to Earth Sciences History for agreeing to make it available.

Mutual Acquaintance and Antiquarian Company 'The Vestige of a Beginning' to a Friendship

Iain Gordon Brown
formerly Principal Curator of Manuscripts,
National Library of Scotland;
Curator of The Royal Society of Edinburgh

It was the summer of 1976. I was working towards my PhD on the cultural world of the virtuoso Sir John Clerk of Penicuik, and to that end I had been reading through vast quantities of the Clerk Muniments in the old Scottish Record Office at General Register House, Edinburgh. As a very minor contribution to the celebration of the bicentenary of American Independence I published in *The Times Literary Supplement* for 9 July a small documentary discovery recently made in the course of this research. What the manuscript poem in question was about is not now of any great significance, as indeed it was not really to me then, since it was remote in time and subject from what I needed to look at in the Clerk Papers; but it related to aspects of contemporary science, to King George III and to the notion of the American Colonies slipping away.

Knowing his interest in the Clerks and their geological connections, a British friend sent Donald McIntyre a cutting from the *TLS*. On 6 August Donald wrote to me for the first time. How well would I come to know that hand in the years to follow! He explained that, though he had lived and worked in California for twenty-two years, he was 'an Edinburgh product'; that he was a geologist; and that it was from this point of view that he himself had rooted among the Clerk and Adam papers in the SRO some years before. He said that he planned to be in Edinburgh for an extended period the next year, and expressed the hope that we might then meet.

A chain of coincidences had already begun to form and its links would also be those of shared intellectual interest and personal friendship. The first of these coincidences was that on the very day Donald had written to me, Charles Waterston, of the then Royal Scottish Museum, had telephoned to ask whether, in the course of my Clerk researches, I might have gleaned anything that could throw light upon the provenance of John Clerk of Eldin's lost (but by this time found!) drawings for James Hutton's *Theory of the Earth*. These, he told me, were soon to be published, and he was also interested in any other family information I might have come across that would further illuminate the Clerk and Hutton connection.

I have retained, in a yellowing file labelled 'Clerk of Eldin and James Hutton / Theory of the Earth / August 1976', rough copies or drafts of my letters etc – and so I find that I am able to reconstruct these events in order and in detail. (As a comparatively young man I had not by then had enough experience of correspondence with distinguished scholars to become blasé about the fact, and I kept such copies as evidence of what I was, in my vanity, pleased to think of as my own emerging scholarly standing!). On 8 August I wrote a long letter to Charles Waterston giving him many references to and quotations from correspondence and other documents in the Clerk Papers relating to Eldin, Hutton, geology, various scientific enterprises in the Clerk circle, and so on. Looking back now on the matter, I realise that it must have taken quite a bit of weekend work to extract that information from my notes, piece it together in a logical way, and construct an informative letter that might actually have made a small article. But the effort was not in vain. Out of it came a friendship of more than thirty years. From it, too, emerged an intensified and expanded interest in the world of the Scottish Enlightenment. This, though of course pre-existing, was given fresh impetus and new relevance by intimate acquaintance with the unique way that Donald McIntyre blended science, art, literature and learning to give life back to this most vibrant period of Scottish – indeed British and European – cultural history.

My 1976 engagement diary, also retained, tells me that I was at Penicuik House on 10 August. For many weeks that year I had been going through and arranging the contents of the Charter Room at Penicuik, and in the course of this work I had turned up a sketchbook and notes that were clearly of geological interest. These discoveries were not without significance as Elizabeth Clerk, now the Dowager Lady Clerk, had herself turned up the folio containing the 'lost' Clerk of Eldin drawings some years before in that same, remarkable treasure-house of a muniment room, and had taken it to the Royal Scottish Museum for Charles Waterston to inspect. As I learned later, that was a red-letter day in the annals of the history of Scottish science; for at the precise same time, Donald McIntyre, working on the Clerk Muniments at Register House, had chanced upon evidence that connected Eldin and Hutton in their great geological enterprise. Excited, he had rushed up the Bridges to tell Charles Waterston, only to find him in his office spellbound to have on the desk before him the very drawings which had been thought lost to the world and which could now be set in the Clerk-Hutton context revealed by the Penicuik Papers.

Also at Penicuik on 10 August was Charles Waterston, invited in order to get to know me better, and to discuss geology as revealed by the family archives. A major subject of conversation that day was one Donald McIntyre, academic geologist, historian of geology, and fellow digger and delver in the Clerk Muniments.

On 11 August Donald's letter arrived from Claremont. (There is another coincidence in that place-name; for 'Claremont' was one of the 'fancy' monikers with which Sir John Clerk had amused himself in considering as a possible title for any future, grand Clerk seat that might someday be constructed at Penicuik, 'the hill of the cuckoo', where in his time stood the venerable and beloved house known simply (and somewhat inaccurately) as Newbiggin.) I replied immediately, saying that 'by great coincidence' I had heard of my correspondent and his concerns only the previous day. I told him of my own work and of my specific and general Clerk-related and Clerk-centred interests; and that I had given Charles Waterston a good deal of information which he in fact considered (as I told Donald) 'really your department'. I explained that I had sent Charles 'some obscure bits of information gleaned from the Clerk Papers… and one or two amusing quotations… that I thought might be useful if anything is to appear, in the new book [I knew that the work on the lost drawings for Hutton's *Theory of the Earth*, eventually to be published in 1978, was on the stocks], on Clerk of Eldin's scientific and artistic background.'

This, my first letter to him, elicited a response from Donald on 3 September. Here were revealed two vital facts: the enthusiastic, even effervescent, nature of Donald's personality; and the remarkable way in which he blended all human knowledge, refusing to see 'science' as something separate from the society in which it was 'discovered' and reduced to dry, theoretical order. He asked my opinion of the authorship of specific drawings, which he disputed with Charles Waterston and also with Gordon Craig, James Hutton Professor of Geology in the University of Edinburgh.

Immediately I felt involved in Donald's work and in the exciting project about which I had so recently learned something. I felt welcome 'on board'. But what struck me particularly was Donald's evident approach to the study of the past, whether that of 'deep time' itself or that of the age of the great men who first explored the original concept of the real age of the earth. 'During the past week', Donald wrote, 'I have been making slides of Edinburgh portraits and street scenes for a lecture at a conference on the Scottish Enlightenment at Cornell University…This makes me feel that I have recently enjoyed a holiday in Edinburgh!' This lecture was, I suppose, one of those earlier, dress-rehearsal attempts at synthesis and context of which Donald was a master, even to the extent of nearly completely disappearing in a maze of intellectual arguments and a web of social connections akin to the darker and more impenetrable closes of the Old Town. Years later I would hear the never-to-be-forgotten lecture where the audience was introduced to 'McIntyre's red herrings'; and, later still, the intellectual pyrotechnics that constituted the brilliant lecture to the Royal Society of Edinburgh Hutton bicentenary conference in 1997 and which saw the light of published day as the truly remarkable paper on 'James Hutton's Edinburgh; the Historical, Social, and Political Background' in *Earth Sciences History*, vol. 16 (1997). Donald also wrote this in his letter of 3 September: 'Do tell me about the amusing quotations about the Clerks. I am anxious to collect these: they help to bring the people and the times to life again.' Here was a man after my own heart!

A copy of the long and full letter I had sent to Charles Waterston eventually winged its way to Pomona College. On 20 November Donald wrote to express his pleasure: 'The whole subject excites me very much, and I look forward with keen anticipation to meeting you when as I plan, I visit Edinburgh in the Spring... I expect to be in Edinburgh for several months.'

By the time that Donald arrived in 1977 I had joined the staff of the Department of Manuscripts of the National Library of Scotland where, in the course of my early duties, I had already encountered Jean Jones, then working as research assistant to Gordon Craig on the Hutton drawings project. My initial meeting with Donald at the Library was a most agreeable one. It was followed by lunch in the University Staff Club. Many other lunches, dinners and meetings followed over many years. We discovered mutual interests in the world of the 18th-century antiquaries, scientists, historians and philosophers; in the art of Allan Ramsay and Henry Raeburn; in the circle of Sir Walter Scott – whose birthday Donald was so proud to share, and whose manuscripts I came to curate; in the history of the naval and military campaigns of the Napoleonic Wars; and in so much else. It gave me great pleasure and much pride exactly twenty years later to have Donald's name among those of my supporters when I was a candidate for Fellowship of the Royal Society of Edinburgh. On the evening of the ballot Donald, with characteristic kindness and enthusiasm, had made me wait in the George Hotel across the street from the rooms of the RSE, so that he could scurry over and give me the good news (as we hoped – correctly as it turned out) of my election. Dinner followed, my mother and myself as Donald's guests; and, as if that was not enough, there was a most generous present of a handsome book thrown in for no apparent reason and out of no necessity, but merely out of a wish to celebrate.

As a boy I'd had a precocious but not profoundly scientific interest in geology. I have still my copy (bought, and inscribed, 1963) of the Edinburgh Geological Society's excursion guide, *Edinburgh Geology*, with the mud stains upon it resulting from its having been consulted at the Agassiz Rock by Blackford Hill, on the mine dumps at Wanlockhead, and at Hutton's Section of Salisbury Crags, where I seem to remember attempting – scandalously – to chip at the haematite vein in the nearby Hutton's Rock with an ordinary claw hammer and a cold chisel: this before my doting parents, imagining a Nobel prize some long way down the line, bought me a real geological hammer! I collected and catalogued rocks, minerals and fossils avidly for a few years. Getting to know Donald brought some at least of this early interest back into my life, and some long-lapsed knowledge to recollection. In the early 1980s, under his influence, I even bought a used copy of Arthur Holmes's *Principles of Physical Geology* (second edition, 1965), promising myself that I would read it – which I never really did. I recall a magical and inspiring ramble on Arthur's Seat and the Crags one magnificent summer's evening when Donald was staying with me in Great King Street. How fortunate, I thought, to be a Pomona student with such a teacher, whose 'sermons in stones' were so clear and so enthusiastic and so exciting!

During his visit in 1983, I remember, we enjoyed together various events. These included the quarter-centenary celebrations of the foundation of the University of Edinburgh (which we attended with my mother, who had graduated the year Donald went up); and the 350th anniversary parade of The Royal Scots, The Royal Regiment, First of Foot and senior regiment of infantry of the line in the British Army, which Donald the piper will doubtless have witnessed with special attention to the selection of marches played by the regiment's Pipes and Drums.

On another occasion during one of Donald's home visits we explored Midlothian localities near Eldin in pursuit of the erstwhile house and forgotten grave of the great John Clerk, merchant, coal-owner, etcher, scientist and naval tactician. On yet a further exploration around Lasswade and Loanhead we admired the Arcadian landscape at the still-beautiful but sadly desolate and fast-decaying Mavisbank. This was Sir John Clerk's subsidiary seat, a villa which had been the focus for his Roman life of virtuous ease and which had been his great self-indulgence but also his legacy to Scotland: one of the most exquisite architectural creations of the age, the Enlightenment in stone.

Then there were times of celebration. Donald's splendid 70th birthday dinner at magnificent Arthur Lodge, in the Edinburgh suburb of Newington and offering a view of Arthur's Seat, seemed like a gathering of some two hundred years before, with its talk of the great days of Edinburgh as a 'hotbed of genius' and its living connection with that past in the person of Sir John Clerk, FRSE, 10th baronet of Penicuik, heir to a wonderful family tradition of 'hospitality to the mind'. Some six years later, and otherwise occupied elsewhere that night, Donald was able only to look in on my mother's 80th birthday party at the New Club, saying that he would not have missed the 'historic occasion' for the world – something that I managed to work into my speech with the suggestion that it took a geologist fully to understand and celebrate old age. But by the time of her 90th birthday in 2009 Donald himself was too unwell to attend.

With his informed appreciation for in the connection between John Clerk of Eldin's theories of naval tactics and British maritime triumphs of the age of Nelson, Trafalgar Day was for Donald always a time of reflection and remembrance. The date 21 October is special for me in various ways: a day of supreme interest, of course, for an amateur naval historian; but personally significant as the day of my successful job interview for my Assistant Keepership in the National Library and thus the foundation-date of a long career in the service of the national heritage; and very special later on, above all and everything, as the day of my marriage to Patricia Andrew. And it remains special, too, as the day that Donald McIntyre, friend and inspirational mentor for nearly thirty-three years, died in Perthshire – the county in which, at Glen Tilt, John Clerk and James Hutton had made some of the most significant observations in the history of geology.

On the 200th Anniversary of James Hutton's death on 26 March 1997, Donald paid tribute to him at his grave in Greyfriars Kirkyard, Edinburgh

In 1797 people still believed that the Earth was only 6,000 years old, but James Hutton showed its age was far more than that. Measurements possible today prove that the age of the Earth is a million times greater.

Hutton asked: 'How shall we acquire the knowledge of a system calculated for millions, not of years only, nor of the ages of man, but of the races of men, and the succession of empires?' And he answered: 'We must read the transactions of time past in the present state of natural bodies'. We acknowledge the silent testimony of the rocks, knowing, as Hutton taught us, that the Present is the Key to the Past.

Hume, Scott, and Hutton were the three great thinkers of the Enlightenment born and bred in this city. Yet Hutton, beloved by all who knew him, lay here for 150 years in an unmarked grave. Fifty years ago Arthur Holmes, the most distinguished geologist of his time, said: 'To the geologist a rock is a page of the Earth's autobiography with a story to unfold'. Hutton showed how to read it; doing so he disclosed the marvel of deep time: 'We perceive', he said, 'a fabric, erected in wisdom'.

Playfair wrote of his friend: 'With his exquisite relish for whatever is beautiful and sublime in science, we may easily conceive what pleasure he derived from his own geological, speculations. The novelty and grandeur of the objects offered by them to the imagination, the simple and uniform order given to the whole natural history of the Earth, and, above all, the views opened of the wisdom that governs nature, are things to which hardly any man could be insensible; but to him they were matter, not of transient delight, but of solid and permanent happiness.'

Today we have come to know that living creatures evolve, that continents drift, that stars, and galaxies are born, mature, grow old and die. We salute the memory of James Hutton, who opened our minds to these wondrous possibilities."

(In 1997 Donald and Alan McKirdy published *James Hutton – The Founder of Modern Geology* ISBN 978 905267 73 6. The book, in its third edition, is available on Amazon and from The National Museums of Scotland, Chambers Street, Edinburgh, EH1 1JF, Scotland.)

See *The Fabric of Geology* 1963 edited by Claude C. Albritton Jr., which also includes two of Donald's papers: *James Hutton and the Philosophy of Geology* and *Precision and Resolution in Geochronometry*.

Donald's final paper *The Royal Society of Edinburgh, James Hutton, The Clerks of Penicuik and the Igneous Origin of Granite,* was published in the Royal Society of Edinburgh's Earth Sciences 97, Suppl.1-Suppl.15 2008.

In April 2011, copies of this paper were presented to all the guests at the national celebration held in Edinburgh commemorating the opening of The James Hutton Institute, Invergowrie, Angus, Scotland. Copies of that paper may be obtained from Ann McIntyre or from The Journals Officer at Royal Society of Edinburgh, George Street, Edinburgh, Scotland, EH2 2PQ.

"What dust of extinct lions sleeps under our feet everywhere! The soil of this world is made of the dust of Life, the geologists say…." Thomas Carlyle

Chapter 10
Retirement

The Geologist's Wife

*To her husband, Robert Chambers (1802-1871),
upon setting off on an excursion*

*Adieu then, my dear, to the Highlands you go,
Geology calls you, you must not say no:
.Alone in your absence I cannot but mourn,
And yet it were selfish to wish your return.*

*No, come not until you have searched through the gneiss,
And marked all the smoothing: produced by the ice
O'er granite-filled chinks felt Huttonian joy,
And measured the parallel roads of Glenroy.*

*Yet still, as from mountain to mountain you stride,
In visions I'll walk like a shade by your side
Your bag and your hammer I'll carry with glee,
And climb the raised beaches, my own love, with thee.*

*Me, too, you'll remember, for love claims no less,
And all your proceedings a fondness confess
Each level you take, be it not from the sea,
But above the dear place where your Susan may be*

*Let everything mind you of tender relations-
See, even the hard rocks have* their *inclinations!
Oh, let me believe that wherever you roam
The axis of* yours *can be nowhere but home*

*Suppose that you find on the mountains of Lorn,
A boulder that long since from Nevis was torn.
'Twill seem like that fond one who left his own shore.
Perhaps to return to Lochaber no more'.*

And if, in our wanderings, you chance to be led
To Ross-shire or Moray, to see the Old Red,
Oh still, as its mail-covered fishes you view,
Remember the colour is love's proper hue.

Such being our feelings, I'll care not although
You're gone from my side – for a fortnight or so;
But know, if much longer you leave me alone,
You may find, coming back, you have two wives of stone!

> Quoted from *The Story of a Lifetime* (1908) by
> Lady Eliza Priestley, daughter of Robert Chambers,
> one of their family's fourteen children.

There are two copies of this poem among Donald's papers, one of them carefully hand-written by his mother! For my part, along with other Geologist Wives, this poem resonates strongly and evokes feelings of inadequacy – and envy – of Mrs Chambers' geological knowledge and poetic skill. But – and I am not sure whether to be glad or sad – James Secord★★ has advised me that even though, Eliza, the Chambers own daughter, thought this poem had been written by their mother, Anne Kirkwood Chambers, it has come to light that Robert Chambers himself was the poet!

On 2nd September 1846 Robert wrote to his wife from Dunnmor Lodge: "Tomorrow I am off for Glenroy. By the way, I have written the beginning of a song, as addressed by you or Mrs D. Milne to your respective husbands."

The poem was published without attribution in *Chambers's Edinburgh Journal* in September 1846 and is one of the many ways that Robert Chambers played around with anonyms and pseudonyms.

★★Professor James Secord – a student and friend of Donald – graduated from Pomona graduate in the class of 1976. He is now Professor of the History and Philosophy of Science at Cambridge University, England, and Director of the Darwin Correspondence Project. He has edited *Vestiges of the Natural History of Creation and other Evolutionary Writings* (1994) *by Robert Chambers*, and is the author of *Victorian Sensation, The Extraordinary Publication, Reception and Secret Authorship of Vestiges of the Natural History of Creation* – "a major work on Victorian cultural history – brilliantly written, painstakingly researched and beautifully illustrated. Secord makes many provocative and insightful revisions to our understanding of the history of evolutionary thought and how history can be studied through one of the most common yet unappreciated human activities – reading."

Setting the Scene

At the end of June 1989 Donald retired from his duties at Pomona College. We had pondered long and hard about how best to go forward into retirement. Donald wanted to ensure that the Geology Department faculty felt completely at liberty to develop its own style in its new era.

Planning for Ewen's long-term future was of utmost importance, for we knew – despite the challenges for someone in a wheelchair in a less temperate climate – it would be important for Ewen to live within easy hailing distance of our few close relatives in Scotland and to receive support from the then Scottish Council for Spastics. In 1995 it was renamed Capability Scotland – and Donald was a member of that team.

In July 1989, lock stock and barrel, the three of us set off on into our new life accompanied by Matt Mann – Ewen's carer and our ever helpful family friend. We settled into a small rented house in the country town of Blairgowrie. For a month after our arrival it never rained once – what a wonderful welcome home!

We wasted no time in house hunting – and well before Matt had to leave for his missionary parents' home in Thailand – we had bought the very first house that we had looked at: newly built, facing south, mid-way up a hill and with a glorious view over the River Tay. We were warmly welcomed into the little community of neighbours in the hamlet of Kinfauns. We created our own garden on what had recently been farmland – this was a great opportunity for me. Since my father had been a nurseryman, fragments of his knowledge had remained with me. I was hugely delighted to become re-acquainted with trees, shrubs and flowers that were beloved old friends from my childhood.

It didn't take us along to settle in: to befriend the huge Clydesdale horses grazing in the field below our house; to collect mushrooms and watch badgers by the burn (brook), as well as participating in many local activities while both building and renewing many important friendships.

Retired?

It is often stated that "When you retire you will be busier than ever before!" And so it was for Donald – a different environment, different times…and no lounging around in a chaise-longue for Donald. As ever, he didn't let the grass grow under his feet: even if mowing our lawn at Kinfauns was his least favourite chore!

In August 1989, a few weeks after our return to Scotland, we visited Glen Tilt with the Clerk family on a glorious summer day.

At Glen Tilt, August 1989, Sir John Clerk, his son
Robert Clerk, Ian Brown and Donald study John
Clerk of Eldin's geological drawings of 1785.

In every way, Donald knew how important it was for us to integrate as best we could in a very different Scotland from the one we had left in the 1950s. He was soon involved with a local pipe band; and, along with Ewen, we all three attended weekly Scottish Country Dance evenings; we joined the National Trust for Scotland and Historic Scotland and Donald soon became an active member of Perth Burns Club and Perth Civic Trust – which oversees the preservation of local history and buildings.

Involvement with the Perth Civic Trust was helpful and highly relevant as we quickly became involved in helping plan for the future of the little church on the hillside of the Kinfauns a few hundred yards from our new home. The church was closed just weeks before we arrived, and Donald would maintain, jokingly, that had we been in the vicinity a few months sooner and attended services there, the three of us would have doubled the church congregation! How different from Victorian times when that little church played a pivotal role in the local community, with farmers, their families and hired help all trudging across the hillside, without fail, to attend the kirk on Sundays.

We were all fascinated by the gravestones and by two older buildings from medieval times in the church grounds. There were rumours that the church might be demolished or converted into a house. Cheered on by our new neighbours, Donald led a successful campaign to save the little church and, as a side effect, laid the foundations for precious friendships with families who have had long, local and historic connections with the area.

Ever thorough – as part of the campaign to save the church from demolition – Donald studied the history of Kinfauns Church and its graveyard. Donald discussed strategy for this campaign with the neighbours, which led special friendships with local landowners – the Walters and the Lowson family (Sir Denis Lowson, Lord Mayor of London in the 1950s is buried in the graveyard). In due course, on a cold and frosty December morning, the official Reporter from The Scottish Office in Edinburgh came to visit Kinfauns to determine whether the church with its active graveyard should be considered suitable for conversion into a dwelling house.

As Donald left no stone unturned, he had also contacted the descendants of the Gray family – one of the oldest peerages in Scotland dating from the mid 15th century. Their family had built a little chapel in the Kinfauns graveyard, so Lord Gray of modern times, clad in a flowing tweed cape, joined a large contingent of determined local residents. Together we all demonstrated resistance, to the proposal of the church being converted to a house. The reporter did indeed reject that proposal! Alas, in 2013, ever more neglected, the church has seriously deteriorated, the 1991 decision has been overturned and the Scottish Office has decided that the church may, after all, become a dwelling house.

The campaign to save Kinfauns Church and contact with Lord Gray led to another fascinating opportunity. The question was: what had become of the Great Sword that had belonged to Thomas De Longueville who, in 1299, had become a friend and companion to Sir William Wallace and was much "distinguished" by King Robert Bruce. Sir Thomas's sword was said to have been buried at Kinfauns – and to discover its whereabouts thereafter was just the kind of Sherlock Holmes mystery that Donald relished. It transpired that what is believed to be that massive sword is in the safekeeping of the Earl of Moray at Darnaway Castle, Forres in the Scottish Highlands.

Donald and I were honoured to visit the Morays at their home and there to marvel at the famous Great Hall with its 15th-century hammer-beam roof. One of only two medieval halls in Scotland still with its original roof; it is capable of accommodating 1,000 men! We handled the Great Sword there and enjoyed the many fine portraits including that of Cardinal York, younger brother of the Young Pretender, and painted by Blanchet, as well as the 'death portrait' of the second Earl of Moray who was killed in 1591. We heard some of the remarkable family tales including how our host, Douglas, Earl of Moray, came, to his surprise, to inherit that title through the death of a cousin; he learnt this news "by snail mail" while still a schoolboy in South Africa.

Donald had long been interested in the history of the Celtic crosses to be found across Scotland with many of them in Perthshire, more or less on our doorstep. A particularly beautiful one, the Dupplin Cross, of about AD 820, was situated on the hillside high above the village of Dunning, where it had stood over the centuries, battered by the wind and rain of harsh winters. Working with the local minister and others, Donald helped oversee the preservation of the cross which was exhibited in the National Museum of Scotland in Edinburgh and in 2002, in the care of Historic Scotland, was brought to St Serf's Church, Dunning, where the delicate Pictish carvings are protected from further erosion.

By becoming so involved in local affairs, it was perhaps not surprising that Donald was invited to become Chairman of the Perth Civic Trust. He edited their magazine, oversaw the revision the Trust's constitution and enjoyed contacts with the other Trust's Board members. He was invited to open both a private art gallery at Bridgend, Perth, as well as classroom for school natural history study at Rodney Gardens where he planted a tree in honour of the occasion while a plaque on the centre's door commemorated this event. Ewen too is commemorated at the Gardens on one of the modern sculptor pieces that carries hand-prints of local people – a policeman, a councillor and a child along with the handprints of Ewen and one of his friends from Upper Springland!

Ongoing work with Ken Iverson on the development of the J computer language was a source of great satisfaction. Donald and Ken's friendship was particularly special – a meeting of minds in mutual admiration. I often recall how low-key, perhaps in keeping with his Norwegian roots, Ken would twinkle with amused delight when Donald was in full passionate flow over his latest scholarly theory or discovery.

Throughout his retirement there were many opportunities for Donald to contribute to APL and J conferences in Toronto and in the USA. He celebrated his 70th birthday in Canada in 2003 and, it was a great surprise, when a piper played the pipe tune that had just been composed in his honour – *Professor Donald McIntyre* by Norrie Sinclair of Perth.

While travelling in North America, Donald would often spend time with the Iversons at their home – and we enjoyed their several visits to our home at Kinfauns. When Ken died suddenly of a heart attack in 2004, such was the depth of their friendship that Donald grieved continuously for him as for a brother.

There were several return visits to North America – Donald undertook a lecture tour in 1990 and there was the very special expedition in 1993 when Donald and I returned together to Claremont for Donald to receive an Honorary Doctorate of Science from Pomona College.

In Scotland, Donald was appointed a Fellow of both Edinburgh and St Andrews Universities; he taught courses at St Andrews and worked with some high school teachers. Jointly with Alan McKirdy, he wrote a small popular book on his "friend" of many decades: *James Hutton, the Founder of Modern Geology*. In 2012 the book was reprinted its third edition by The National Museum of Scotland and includes an introductory tribute to Donald.

In August 1989, Donald received a warm-welcome-home to Scotland letter from Bill Murray:

Bill Murray's Welcome Home

There arc some rare occasions when one can hardly believe one's eyes. One such was my reading that first sentence of your letter. That you and Ann and Ewen were back in Scotland was the best news I've had this year. The speed with which you've acted is phenomenal. Your lives in the last two months must have been hectic. But to get landed last week with a van – a load of furniture before carpets were down, and maybe with more gear than you'd room for, sounds to me like the culminating nightmare. The one good thing is to be said for a nightmare is that it's soon over. By now you've probably emerged from the tunnel into light. I do hope all went well. Kinfauns sounds a good place.

The Scottish Mountaineering Journal came out last week. I saw in it an obituary by Geoff Dutton on Dick Brown that you used to practice bag-piping in the corridors of the Grant Institute. I had forgotten your piping skills. Have you kept them up? Geoff Dutton also has recently retired and lives close to Blairgowrie at Bridge of Cally. He's had one or two books of poetry published and a book of short stories. Last year he had a bad time with a complicated appendectomy. But he seemed to be recovered at the SMC Centenary Dinner in May.

I'm sorry you missed that dinner. It was at Blair Castle and by a stroke of good luck was the best I've ever known. The castle gave an ideal ambiance in the heart of the hills, in perfect order for all its great age, and since the duke was there we had the advantage of his piper to greet us and an army of kilted gillies to serve the whisky. We dined in the ballroom (which is why we were there, for highland hotels can't seat 250). And although the walls were forested by stags' antlers we had at table the loin of Atholl venison and salmon, both top quality and abundant. I had feared in advance that a centenary dinner would produce dull speeches reciting club history. By a miracle we were spared. The President had had the good sense to lay on as principal speakers Bob Grieve and Robin Campbell. Bob arrived at Bridge of Tilt hotel that late afternoon in a state of consternation – he had left his prepared speech lying on his desk in Edinburgh. When it came to the crunch and he rose to propose The Club, the Muses chose to visit him. We had 20 minutes of Bob at his best. Robin Campbell who had to toast the guests was even better. The Club's tradition here is scurrility with wit. It has been many years (about 50) since I laughed so much.

Kenneth and I left a 3 a.m. while we could still negotiate the mile-long drive without damage to the Duke of Atholl's lime-trees, but the main party lasted beyond dawn.

This has been the best summer in the west for many a long year. June came with a heat-wave, when temps of 80 degrees and more prevailed. Anne was away for a week in Skye at the end of the month, and one morning I thought to cut the grass before the sun got too hot (we have 1,600 sq. yards). I forgot I wasn't still in my 20s. When I'd finished, and sat in a deck-chair to rest, I had a mild stroke i.e. paralysis of the right leg. It lasted just a few minutes. Then I found a way to force myself up. But I was so tottery for a week thereafter and found that there were short spells when I couldn't add or subtract, or put words together on paper, or spell properly, that I rang the local GP who sent me to hospital by ambulance. They discharged me in four days. They said some small clots of blood had lodged in my brain, and then dissolved of their own accord. No permanent harm done. If I was lucky, I'd be ok in a few weeks, or if unlucky, in a few months. The main point is that throughout I feel well and in positive good health. The only trouble as yet is mechanical. Each day I have some dizzy spells of perhaps 30 seconds and have to sit down. My expectation is that in time these too will pass off, and that I'll be able to travel around. I can walk several hundred yards without trouble, but become dizzy thereafter. I get dizzy sometimes if I rise too swiftly out of a chair. But I'm hoping that all will be well before winter. I'm active in the garden – hedge cutting, etc.

As for you, your "so-called" retirement will, I forecast, be the busiest time of your life. Anne and I will have to move out of Loch Goil. The house plus two and a half acres of ground is more than I can manage to maintain in good order. And for Anne especially, it's become too remote. We wish you all good fortune in your new home.

Our Scottish Homes

Donald chose to retire when he reached his sixty-seventh birthday and had completed thirty-four years fulfilling years at Pomona College.

In the spring of 1988 I made an exploratory expedition to Edinburgh to determine what possibilities there might be for Ewen if we were to return to live in Scotland. After discussion with what was then known as The Scottish Council for Spastics, and an exploratory visit to the Upper Springland Centre, it became clear that Perth would have much to offer Ewen and would make a good base for all three of us with Edinburgh, St Andrews and the Highlands – all of them being readily accessible.

In those days prior to the wonders of the Internet, we even tried to buy a house in Perth by fax! But instead, guided by friends, it was much more practical to rent a small house in Blairgowrie. And, to cut a long story short, with the trauma of leaving our beloved Claremont behind us, we arrived in Scotland in mid-July – just a month after Donald had officially retired.

Such speed of action was very much Donald's style – he was determined not to linger in Claremont as he knew from personal experience that the Geology Department would inevitably face change and that in no way did he want to appear to either impede that or to experience too much difference himself.

So here we were. We arrived in the nick of time to attend a young cousin's wedding – a lovely occasion on a beautiful, very hot, July day, with a marquee in the garden of Kilbride Castle – kilted guests, bagpipes, Highland dancing and – as the invitation indicated 'carriages at 11 p.m.' – time to go home! It was a thrill for us all, and perhaps most especially for Matt Mann. He was Ewen's carer, and our dear family friend, who had travelled with us from Claremont and was such a help to us all, by accompanying us, driving us while taking a roundabout route to visit his missionary parents in Thailand. It was a memorable summer in so many ways – and unbelievably, every day was sunny and warm – Scotland at its best!

The day after the wedding we set about house-hunting. We approached the first house on our list by driving on a twisty back road, while admiring the beauty and greenness of the gentle hills, the farmland pastures and woods, and even a field where a pony and a donkey grazed together beside a gaggle of geese – a fairy-tale situation – had we just arrived in heaven? And, just along the road and up the hill from there, we found a newly constructed house. Though not immediately wheelchair accessible, it offered immense potential – and a tiny purple and golden heartsease viola was smiling a welcome to us from the uncultivated land around the house. We visited several other houses that sunny day but none compared favourably with the first that we had seen. Fast forward to September when we were welcomed into the delightful little community of Kinfauns in the nick of time for a splendid neighbourhood party to mark the demise of an old worn-out tree. There were "clootie dumplings" (puddings steamed in a "cloot"/cloth) on the barbeque menu – a Scottish favourite that we had long forgotten.

We immediately felt very much at home; we enjoyed working with local tradesmen who somehow seemed youthful compared with their counterparts in Claremont! We added a wheelchair ramp up to our front door and planned our garden where we planted favourites that I remembered from my childhood. Indeed, my youthful experiences helping at our father's forest tree and rose nursery on the outskirts of

Edinburgh came into their own and through the care and skill of its present owner the Kinfauns garden has matured into a beautiful show-piece place that we love to visit.

Shortly after our arrival we awoke one morning to find giant footprints in the newly planted flower beds. We had had an overnight visit from the local Clydesdale horses who having found their gate wide open and plodded up the hill to investigate the new garden. Their huge hooves only damaged one small shrub!

For nine happy years we enjoyed the beautiful views looking south over the River Tay and on to the hills of Fife. No wonder we chose to call the house "Luachmhor" – Gaelic for a "precious place" as Donald's parents had named their retirement bakery/cottage home in the Highlands. The name is now part of a McIntyre tradition as our nephew Andrew and his wife, Gillian, have chosen "Luachmhor" as the name of their Scottish home – a trio of "very nice places" – and undoubtedly there will be more to come!

In the late nineties, while totally dependent upon owning and ability to drive a car while living the little hamlet of Kinfauns – Donald, with typical foresight for his family's well-being – suggested that we consider moving into the county town of Perth before we were too decrepit to adapt to another new environment. Our timing was fortuitous. In no time at all, we happened upon an empty flat roof-top in the very centre of Perth where a developer had plans to build a roof-top third floor pent-house.

With only a few days grace to decide whether we should purchase this property (which was already on offer, but to Canadian people who were dithering about possible purchase) we were asked to quickly make our minds. Our decision was clinched when I inquired about Ewen's potential safety while living in a flat, when a representative of the local fire service department assured me – "Ma'am …we can get people out of anywhere!"

Working with an accomplished architect, Donald designed a bright and airy home with wide corridors for a wheelchair and which took full advantage of the roof's prescribed area. For Ewen, access to the flat (apartment) is, of course, entirely dependent upon the reliability of the building's lift (elevator) while ambulatory people can access the six different flats/apartments by climbing the 59 step staircase – quite an exercise in keeping fit!.

We are fortunate to overlook and to hear the chimes of St John's Kirk, founded 1242 and from where John Knox first announced the Reformation in 1559. Close at hand, we enjoy the architecture of the picturesque buildings as well as the more distant woods of Kinnoull Hill which remind us of both the changes of the seasons and of ancient glaciation. It is here, high above the shops and cafes, that we, along with the birds and the bees, cherish our little garden patio – an oasis of colour and fragrance all summer long!

Piping in our Homeland

Donald – the piper, 1957

Norrie Sinclair, Donald's bagpipe teacher wrote:

Soon after the family's arrival in Scotland in 1989, Donald came to ask me if I would take him for piping lessons. I agreed and he was with me weekly for three or four years. Donald had played the pipes many years before but throughout his years in America, he never had enough time to practise. So I took him through all the exercises first, then on to "little tunes" progressing to "heavier tunes" when he was ready for them. All this, of course, was on the practice chanter but when he was ready for them, I took him onto the pipes. He was thrilled – I could see it in his face! Donald enjoyed his lessons and I enjoyed teaching him! So keen and enthusiastic!

In 1993 Norrie composed the pipe tune *"Professor Donald McIntyre"* which continues to be played many years on. It has been recorded by dance bands and solo performers and is requested on Scottish music shows.

Donald played some of his favourite pipe tunes on a cold, frosty, misty Armistice Sunday afternoon at Errol Cemetery, Perthshire – November 1996

> *Scotland, my ain hame*
> *Dark Island/Silver Threads*
> *Tumbledown Mountain*
> *Dargfau/Somme*
> *Rowan Tree/Auld Hoose*
> *My Land*
> *Perth in Bloom (composed by Norrie Sinclair)*
> *Green hills/After the battle*
> *My Home/ Highland Cradle Song (Ewen's favourite)*
> *Flower of Scotland*

See also pages 134-5

With incredible patience and attention to detail, Donald transcribed many pibroch bagpipe tunes on to the computer so that others could learn from listening to the world's finest pipers playing this complicated music. Several famous pipers visited our home to fine-tune and advise on these remarkable computer renditions. Our visitors included Andrew Wright, a well-known Scottish piper from the Simon Fraser Pipc Band in Canada. When the computing transcripts were completed, Donald presented them to The Glasgow School of Piping for use by their students.

With his new friend and fellow piper, John Mackay, Donald greatly enjoyed many annual weekend gatherings of the Pibroch Society especially when the annual banquet took place at Stirling Castle.

From over the Garden Wall –
the neighbours' perspective
by Jill & Leslie Hill

It was in August on a hot summer day when we began our journey from Berkshire to Scotland in a car containing one chirping budgerigar, a lively rabbit, squeaking guinea pig and an apprehensive eleven year old daughter. Our destination was an isolated hamlet in Perthshire called Kinfauns, situated on the hillside overlooking the River Tay. We knew no one. However, it was not long before we realised that "there was gold in them thar hills"! Our accents and car registration gave us away as 'foreigners': not Scots.

Ann and Donald and Ewen McIntyre lived only a short walk from our little white cottage with a magnificent view along the Carse of Gowrie, near Perth. Very soon after our arrival a white van pulled alongside us and a cheery voice invited us to take a short lift up to our home. Unless you have ever been a total stranger somewhere, you have no idea how much it means for someone to break through the wall of loneliness that seems to engulf you. So began the journey of friendship with a remarkable family.

You were not in Donald's company long before you realised that you had "struck gold". Donald was a man with an insatiable curiosity about everything, and a generosity of spirit that wanted to share his knowledge in his own inimitable creative and humorous style. On one occasion he invited us to join him for a walk up to the top of Kinnoull Hill. On the way we learned about the topography of the landscape, the geology of the rocks as well as the fact that here was a man older than us and in far better physical shape!

Someone said 'Kindness creates love'. Donald was a man of immense kindness and acceptance that embraced people indiscriminately. One cold 12th November a knock came on the green front door of our home and there stood a bagpiper, resplendent in full Scottish national costume. Donald had discovered that this was Leslie's birthday and having played at the Errol Remembrance service in the morning, he came to play for the birthday boy. Walking up and down he serenaded us with a tune that he had composed. We were so thrilled: what a birthday gift.

Our daughter was struggling with some mathematical concept for homework. Her Dad was not answering her questions to her satisfaction. "Donald would know!" was a hint that her Dad should go and get help. He left the house for the McIntyres at 8:30p.m, and returned at 10:30 p.m. "If it takes Donald and Dad all that time to do homework how do they expect me to do it as well as three other subjects?" she mused. On his arrival her Dad was not only able to answer the question but give the background to the whole topic. Donald had an encyclopaedic knowledge of many things. By chance we got into a conversation about the reason for Scotland having less hours of daylight in the winter than England. Before long Donald was standing us in strategic positions around the room to represent the planets of the solar system, one revolving, one rotating and one moving slowly on an elliptical pathway. What a teacher! We never forgot it.

One winter day we happened to meet Donald and asked him whether he preferred living in America where the weather was more clement. Without a moment's hesitation he replied, "That is like asking me whether I prefer roast beef and vegetables to toast and cereal. I like both and both provide me with a meal but at different times." What a beautiful philosophy!

We enjoyed bantering with him and said that we had some question about how he looked at us when we told him we went to church on Saturday. As a quick as a flash his reply came, "I thought you looked strangely at me when I told you I went on Sunday!" We all went away laughing.

Each winter challenged us to navigate the narrow snow piled lane that led to our cottage by offering snow grips for our tyres. If that failed there was an alternative – leave the car on the McIntyre driveway until the road was clearer.

Donald's generosity showed itself in a very particular way one day when Ann and Donald invited our friends, David and Anita, to afternoon tea. David was researching the origin and practices of early Christianity in these islands. We were about to leave when Leslie asked Donald if he had any books on St Columba. Without hesitation Donald said he had and that David could borrow it. The book on the Life of Columba proved an invaluable resource to David.

March 13, 1996 is a day to be remembered in Scotland for all the wrong reasons. Leslie will not forget the day of the Dunblane School massacre. The news had come over the car radio and he was unsure which school I was working in that day. His first thought was to call on Donald and Ann. As always, he found great comfort in their kindness amid such unspeakable tragedy.

It was a great privilege to be invited by Donald and Ann to attend a lecture by John Polkinghorne at the Royal Society in Edinburgh. We both recall Donald giving us a brief history of that particular area of Edinburgh as well as enjoying rich conversation while travelling in the car.

The day before we left Kinfauns the McIntyre family invited us to a lunch that included delicious artichokes. We remember the feeling of sadness at leaving behind this precious family who were no longer simply neighbours but treasured friends.

"More gold has been mined from the thoughts of men than from the earth." Donald -Thank you for sharing gold with us!

Editor's note: *We all treasure our friendship with the Hills and much enjoy their delightful sense of humour. On one occasion when we were away for the weekend, a flock of sheep escaped from the local farmer's field. They chose to graze on the lush green grass of our unfenced garden bank that sloped down to the little country road leading to the church along from of our house. The Hills captured the invasion on camera and presented us with a collection of photos entitled "Where sheep may safely graze"!*

The Spell of Dunsinane
(In Perthshire, Dunsinane is pronounced as Dun/sin/an)

Shortly after we arrived in Perth in 1989, Donald was anxious to renew his much loved connection with the bagpipes. After some research, he decided to visit the Scone Pipe Band – a very fortuitous decision as it was there that he met John Mackay – piper, pibroch player and historian who became a wonderful, stimulating and faithful friend. At that time John was also a Councillor of Perth & Kinross Council.

So it came about that in 1991, Donald and John's shared love of Scottish history, culture and landscape dove-tailed somewhat dramatically in a campaign to raise awareness of the danger to a site of great historical, archaeological and cultural importance, just north of our home at Kinfauns.

Donald and John went into spirited action on learning of the outrageous plans to extend the activity and scope of Collace Quarry near the site of an early Iron Age fort and the ancient fortress of Macbeth, King of Scots and Thane of Cawdor in the 11th century. John had previously been successful and had managed to persuade the Council to refuse permission, but an appeal had reopened the whole issue. It was at this point that Donald became involved. John worked with the logistics and Donald with the publicity – he enjoyed this role immensely!

The theatrical highlight of the campaign took place on a warm and sunny May day when Donald invited Professor Barrow of Edinburgh University to bring some twenty of his students – along with members of the press – to accompany us up the hill and to a enjoy a picnic lunch at the top.

It was a memorable day and a great learning experience. Professor Barrow had already explained the historical details of the site to the students on their bus journey so Donald was free to point out the geological features of the ascent and to read aloud from Shakespeare's text at the assumed site of Macbeth's castle.

There was a champagne toasting to the success of the campaign on the hill-top and the occasion was further enhanced when pictures of the expedition appeared on television news that evening followed next day by articles in both national and local newspapers!

John describes the final outcome: 'In due course Perth and Kinross District Council signed an agreement with the National Trust for Scotland and with the landowner of Dunsinane. This document states that the Council's application to extract rock over a further 80 metres be granted subject to stringent conditions. The National Trust for Scotland would ensure that the area would be landscaped, fenced off and protected for posterity.'

"So thanks to all at once and to each one!" (Shakespeare's Macbeth)

With gratitude to Meg Cowie who researched the details of this vignette.

Donald's Essay on
The Building Stones of Perth – a geological perspective

As the title implies, the following account is a geologist's view of Perth buildings, and readers must look elsewhere for authoritative architectural and social history. The principal object is to introduce Perth residents and visitors to the local geology, and the emphasis is therefore on locally derived building stones. Artificial building materials are largely ignored.

Because stones are pieces of rock, we need some understanding about different kinds of rocks and how they are made. Unlike the Moon, the Earth is a chemically and physically active body which is constantly changing. In our short lives this may not be obvious, but buildings soon fall into ruin when steps are not taken to maintain them. The same month that this paragraph was written a passer-by was killed by falling masonry from an old building in Edinburgh, and people were narrowly missed by stone falling from two buildings in the centre of Perth. Think, then, of the changes that occur over hundreds, and even thousands, of millions of years! During the vast periods of geological Not only do buildings decay but, during the vast extent of geological time, entire mountain ranges are reduced to sand and mud.

Even when not polluted by human action, Earth's atmosphere is chemically reactive. Oxygen, which is necessary for our survival, is powerful enough to cause iron to decay – we call this rust – and the iron that is a common constituent of rocks is not immune. We would not survive if the amount of oxygen in the atmosphere were much reduced; and a rather small increase in the amount of oxygen could lead to spontaneous combustion of wood. Water, too, can in time destroy even the hardest rock. Wind and rain play their part in the destruction. Water expands on freezing and the process being many times repeated enlarges cracks until pieces of rock break off and fall under gravity. Look up and see that in many buildings in Perth sizeable plants have taken root in crevices. Plants were at least partly responsible for dislodging the masonry that fell from the rooftops.

At the surface of the Earth, rocks breakdown physically into smaller pieces and break down chemically into fine material such as clay and mud. This destructive process is necessary for the production of soil and is therefore essential for our very existence. Under the action of gravity and running water the products of disintegration and decay are carried to lower and lower elevations as boulders, pebbles, sand grains, and flakes of clay, and ultimately deposited as layers of sediment (sand and mud) on the sea floor. On their journey the loose pieces collide with one another and break into smaller pieces. Given enough time all dry land will be destroyed.

Earth's hot and active interior provides the power to move the crustal plates, and when plates collide new mountains are raised from the debris of a former world. During this process the sedimentary debris is solidified by heat and pressure and by deposition of minerals (such as calcium carbonate) from water circulating between the broken grains. Thus sand is converted into sandstone and mud into shale. We make bricks by heating clay in kilns, and nature does something similar. If temperature and pressure are high enough, grains of quartz in sandstone are recrystallised as quartzite; shale is converted into slate or, at even higher temperature and pressure, into glistening mica schist. This is how the rocks of the Highlands were made. We call the process "metamorphism" (i.e. "change of form"). At still higher temperature the rocks melt, and granite forms as the molten rock (magma) slowly cools deep below ground. Crystals of quartz, feldspar, mica, and other minerals grow large enough to become obvious to the naked eye – granite indeed means "grained rock". Sometimes magma erupts from below the Earth's crust, feeding volcanoes and often covering vast areas with great sequences of lava flows. The thickness of the lava flows in this area is over 2400m. [BGS Geology of the Perth & Dundee Area, 1985, p.94] In Scotland these hard, black volcanic rocks (technically andesite, basalt, and dolerite) are often called whinstone.

These processes of erosion and destruction of older rocks, followed by uplift and building of a new land, involve a remarkable recycling of material. The cycle has been repeated over and over again during the 4,500 million years the Earth has been in existence.

These, then, are the origins of our natural building stones. In order of their increasing age, the available building stones in the neighbourhood of Perth are as follows:

- Whinstone: lava flows of andesite and basalt of Lower Devonian age (about 400 million years old).

- Sandstone and conglomerate (puddingstone) of Lower Devonian age (about 400 million years old but younger than the volcanic rocks.

- Dykes of intrusive dolerite (diabase) about 300 million years old.

For more information on their nature and distribution see the British Geological Survey maps 1:50 000 Series, Perth Sheet 48W Solid Edition, 1983, and Drift Edition, 1985; also Geology of the Perth and Dundee District, HMSO, BGS, 1985, 108p.

In the Bridge of Earn area and in the Carse of Gowrie as far as Dundee, sandstones, often red in colour, of Upper Devonian age (i.e. about 360 million years old) have been used for building stone and flagstones for paving the streets. At Clashbenny, east of St Madoes, they have yielded fossil freshwater fish. Late glacial marine clays (about 14,000 years old) are used for brick-making at Erroll.

Metamorphic rocks (about 500 million years old) north of the Highland Boundary fault include slates that were formerly worked at Dunkeld and Logiealmond for roofing in Perth.

Before proceeding to discussion of particular stones and buildings, the following general points should be noted:

- • The sources of stone used even in modern buildings are seldom documented.

- • Names such as "Craigleith" and "Binny" are sometimes used in a generic sense; instead of meaning that a particular stone came from the famous quarry named, it may be that the character of the stone is merely claimed to be similar to the best stone from that particular quarry.

- • Rocks from a single quarry may differ significantly; e.g. the quarry at Locharbriggs (Dumfries) yields excellent white sandstone as well as the uniformly red stone for which it is well known.

- • Through the ages earlier buildings have commonly served as convenient economic sources of stone for new buildings; Hadrian's Wall and St Andrew's Cathedral, for example, were obviously used as quarries. Oliver Cromwell built one of his five great Scottish fortresses in Perth (Leith, Ayr, Inverlochy, and Inverness were the others), and the main reason why Perth has few ancient buildings is that in 1651 Cromwell ruthlessly demolished any that could provide stone for his citadel on the South Inch.

Until the arrival of the railway in 1848, Perth was largely confined to the flood plain of the Tay, of which the North and South Inches are extensions. Maps show that expansion, first to the west from the railway station, and slightly later towards the north of the old town, had taken place by 1893.

An unusually "primitive" wall labelled "Old City Wall" forms the north side of Albert Close, between George Street and the north end of Skinnergate. This wall is on the line of the original defensive wall, which used the city lade as a moat, but the present wall lacks the strength required for a serious defensive structure. The Scottish Urban Archaeology Trust discovered the foundations of the city wall in excavations at the west end of the existing wall. The foundations, faced on the north side with ashlar (dressed rectangular stone blocks), were thicker than the present wall [personal communication, David Bowler, SUAT]. A conspicuous feature of the wall is the variety of rock types used in its construction. Pieces of sandstone in different sizes and shapes are common. Unlike the more massive sandstones common in other Perth buildings, the sandstones in this wall are mainly small slabs split along prominent bedding planes laid horizontally to avoid rapid weathering. The wall also contains rounded boulders of massive sandstone.

Of particular interest are prominent pockets of water-rounded quartzites, green schist, and schist with large crystals of garnet; these rocks have come from the Highlands, They may have been taken from the river, because at low tide the beach at the north end of Friarton (Moncreiffe) island can be seen to be made of pebbles and boulders of similar rocks. I know no other wall within Perth that incorporates Highland rocks – though the wall of the old barn at Muirhall farm contains glacially derived Highland rocks. The history recorded by these strange rocks – strange at least to Perth – is amazing! Once upon a time (as the story goes), about a thousand million years ago, there were mountains, formed no doubt like present-day mountains by plate collisions. Weather and erosion slowly but surely wore away these mountains and the debris of sand and mud was deposited in an ocean that existed then but which has long since vanished. These unusual rocks in Albert Close are relics of this debris, and so tell us something about the otherwise long lost mountains.

Some seven hundred million years after the mountains were formed, the ocean that had received the debris was destroyed by another plate collision; the sediments on the sea floor were squeezed and heated; sand and mud reacted chemically to produce new minerals, such as garnet and mica, stable under the new conditions of high temperature and pressure; the once horizontal layers of sand and mud became contorted layers of schist and quartzite, and were slowly elevated to make high mountains equivalent to the Alps or perhaps even the Himalaya. In subsequent time these "Caledonian" mountains have in their turn been eroded – the Highland hills are all that is left. The Tay and its tributaries continue the work of destruction, and pieces of Highland rock litter the bed of the River as it carries them to a watery grave on the sea floor. Gaze, then, in awe and wonder at the wall in Albert Close!

Without crossing the river, the nearest source of building stone was on the high ground to the west. The ground rises abruptly from the flood plain to the level of the railway station and Whitefriars, where it is underlain by unconsolidated marine strata deposited towards the end of the ice age when the sea stood at higher levels than it does now – Moncreiffe Hill was once an island. Look west across the North or South Inches, or up South street, and notice the marked change in slope that occurs approximately at the line of Methven Street.

Beyond the line of Glover Street and Feus Road the ground rises steeply again. It is underlain there by Old Red Sandstone rocks which extend from Perth north as far as the Highland Line at Birnam and throughout Strathmore, north of the Sidlaws. The sandstones are here largely concealed by debris left by the ice-sheet that once covered Scotland, though sandstone was quarried on the Burghmuir (Newhouse Quarry) within living memory. Many samples seen in old walls (e.g. near Ochil Nursing Home, Ettrick Drive) are rich in flakes of mica which makes them easy to split along the bedding planes. Some large massive sandstone blocks are displayed in the Fittis Road park and on West Mains Avenue near Soutar Crescent. Burghmuir Quarry was a possible source when stone became used in Perth buildings. It was an advantage that transportation was downhill and did not involve crossing the river. Only a little further away was Huntingtower quarry south of the Crieff Road. Most of the stone for St Matthews Church on Tay Street came from this quarry in 1872 (Miss Rhoda Fothergill, personal communication). Being a continuation of the same "horizon" (layer), as at Quarrymill, the two are indistinguishable. Rocks from Burghmuir quarry (Newhouse) were probably also similar. Small outcrops of sandstone on the east side of the river are recorded in the Statistical Account of 1844.

Kinnoull Hill, like most of the Sidlaws and the Ochils, consists of a succession of north-dipping andesite lava-flows (commonly called whinstone or trap), which in the Sidlaws reaches a thickness of about 1,500m. These rocks outcrop in the grounds of Kinnoull Primary School (cement conceals the outcrop on the road has been concealed by cement) and near the toll-house on the Dundee road. There is also a small outcrop opposite 33 Dundee Road. It was formerly quarried south of Scone at Muirhall farm and at a number of smaller sites. The same rock is worked south of Perth at the large Friarton Quarry. Volcanic action was not confined to the Sidlaws and Ochils, but is known to have included the Oban area, Ben Nevis and Glencoe, Blackford Hill and the Pentland Hills (south of Edinburgh), St Abb's Head, and the Cheviot Hills. Today this type of volcanism is associated with "subduction"; i.e. one crustal plate being pushed underneath another. The great volcanoes of the Andes (hence "andesite") are of this type – the Plate under the Pacific is being subducted under South America. Consequently the rocks of Kinnoull Hill are evidence that plate subduction took place in Scotland some 380-400 million years ago.

This black volcanic rock is hard and very tough. It breaks into sharp angular pieces, which make good road metal. It has been used in walls along the Dundee Road between the Smeaton Bridge and Branklyn Garden, though sandstone is used for the high retaining wall of the Garden itself. Here and there surprisingly rectangular blocks are incorporated in the walls along the road, but it has rarely been used for building in Perth. Cottages in the village of Glencarse, however, are almost exclusively built of the volcanic rock, and are well worth examining. Whinstone has also been used for houses in Abernethy, though cornerstones and the surrounds of doors and windows are usually "freestone" – which a mason can work freely in any direction – normally supplies. Excellent examples of freestone can be examined in the south wall of the bridge that carries the Glasgow Road across the railway. Although the blocks are layered (stratified), the shape of individual blocks is independent of the layering.

A small abandoned quarry at Corsiehill, above St Mary's monastery on Kinnoull Hill, is in a volcanic dyke formed when molten rock (magma) erupted from depth through a vertical fissure. Because the magma cooled slowly below ground, the resulting rock (dolerite) is coarser grained than common whinstone. I have not seen any record of how it was used, but having fewer irregular cracks it may have been suitable for making setts for paving streets, or even shaped into rectangular building blocks. Some of the setts in the streets beside St John's Kirk and the City Hall are fine-grained with steam-holes formed by escaping bubbles of gas as the magma reached the surface. Other setts are distinctly crystalline, coming from the centre of a lava flow or dyke where cooling was slow enough to allow crystal growth. A few other setts, such as some of those in Flesher's Vennel and its extension into South St John's Place, are blocks of granite. These granite setts have, of course, been imported, indeed I am informed that the granite setts now being laid on the west pavement of Tay Street came from China! It seems likely that at least some of the setts in the city centre have been brought for re-use from other streets (possibly from other cities).

The 50 million year old Corsiehill dyke is a member of a swarm of east-west dykes. Others of the swarm cut the youngest Carboniferous (coal-bearing) strata between Edinburgh and Glasgow, and must be younger than the volcanic rocks of Kinnoull Hill. As the molten rock was intruded up vertical, east-west trending cracks in the Earth's crust, Scotland at that time must have been stretched and pulled apart by forces directed north and south. Another dyke crosses the Tay at Campsie Linn, and being resistant, creates a waterfall in the river to the delight of canoeists. This dyke has been quarried at Wolfhill, a little more than a kilometre east of the river.

A large east-west dyke crosses the main road from Perth to Stirling about 1km beyond the turnoff to Tibbermore. The dyke is exposed in the road cut [046 208]. Being close to the main road it is difficult and even dangerous to study it. The rock, having cooled slowly from a molten state, consists of a mass of intergrown crystals visible to the naked eye on a freshly broken surface. The Gask road continues west and crosses the same dyke, which is then seen to the north of the road and nearly parallel to it. Because the dyke is more resistant to erosion than the surrounding sandstones it is a conspicuous feature looking like an abandoned railway embankment. The BGS [Geology of Perth and Dundee District, 1985, p95] says that this dyke was quarried at "Lamberkine" [058 208] – although the topographic map shows "Lamberkine" as an area some 2.5km to the NE of this locality.

Records show that Lamberkin quarry was once an important source of building stone. The parking area immediately behind the Sheriff Court building on Tay Street was formerly the site of the County

Prison built from Lamberkin stone [Miss Rhoda Fothergill, personal communication]. The rock, which is preserved in walls adjacent to three sides of the parking area, is probably dolerite, which though black, weathers to a rusty surface.

The Murray Royal Hospital is built of similar rock, though one would assume that in that case the stone would have come from the Muirhall Quarry, only a short distance up the hill. If so its grain size would suggest that the source was one of the thicker lava flows – two flows were formerly exposed in Muirhall Quarry [BGS Geology of Perth & Dundee District, 1985, p.32, 39]. This quarry – like so many others – is now filled in and no specimens are available. Mr John Dow of Muirhall farm is, however, of the opinion that the Murray Royal was not built from Muirhall stone. Whatever its source (Muirhall and Lamberkin have been suggested), the stone of this large building has been carefully trimmed into regular rectangular blocks.

The volcanic rocks forming Kinnoull Hill are in layers, each resulting from an individual volcanic eruption some 400 million years ago. The layered structure can be detected by looking from Perth at the sloping grassy areas on the west side of the hill, and is seen most clearly in the south-facing cliff above West Kinfauns when viewed from beside the well-known tower ("folly") at the top of the cliff. The contrast between the precipitous south side of the hill and the gentle north slope is due to the fact that the sequence of lava flows, originally horizontal, has been tilted towards the north. As a result younger rocks, which originally were deposited on top of the lava flows after volcanic activity ended, are now found in the lower ground north of Kinnoull Hill. The rocks of the Old Red Sandstone extend from New Scone north to the Highland Boundary Fault, which is seen from Perth as a long straight line running from ENE to WSW.

These rather massive sandstones were quarried along the Annaty Burn at the appropriately named Quarrymill. It is said that there were formerly extensive quarries in the Kincarrathie area between the Isla Road and Scone Road, but I have not found any evidence in old maps or in the Statistical Accounts. Moreover the British Geological Survey's map [1984] shows no sites in that area where bedrock has been recognised at or near the surface.

Dr Douglas Simpson's account of St John's Kirk states that in 1328 "King Robert the Bruce asked permission for hewn stones to be taken from the quarries of Kinharrachie [sic] and Balcormac, belonging to the Abbey of Scone for the edification of the Church of Perth [St John's Kirk]" [1958, p.16]. William Barclay's history of the structure of St John's Kirk says that the rebuilding of the nave in the 15th century "was done from the quarry of Kincarrathie under the liberty obtained by Bruce's request to the monks of Scone" [1920, p.10]. The etymology of Kincarrathie is uncertain: perhaps it is related to Ceann ("head" – there is no K in Gaelic) and Carraigeach ("rocky" or "craggy").

A map dated 1792 shows that the Annaty Burn Woodland Park (Quarrymill) lies within the Kincarrathie estate (John Dodds, Factor: personal communication,), and there can be little doubt that this is the quarry that was at one time called "Kincarrathie Quarry". At Kincarrathie House a doocot (dovecote), built of obviously local stone, bears the date 1694; it is less than half a mile (0.7km) from the quarry in Quarrymill Woodland Park.

The Old Red Sandstone (ORS) is so-called because it is older than the strata containing the coal seams, whereas the New Red Sandstone (at Dumfries) is younger than the coals. The red colour is iron oxide (hematite) produced when iron silicates in rocks such as granite are oxidised in contact with the atmosphere. Marine sediments are grey or even greenish – never red. The ORS is the major locally derived building stone in Perth. It varies greatly in quality, but in general it has a pleasant pale purplish colour and an interesting texture. We have already pointed out that it underlies Strathmore between the Sidlaws and the Highland line. Kirriemuir and other Strathmore villages have a richer red stone than Perth, and often an attractive coarser texture. Close to the Highland line the sandstone is replaced by conglomerate (pudding-stone) which is well exposed on the coast at Stonehaven and Dunnottar, and at Cargill's Leap on the River Ericht upstream from Blairgowrie. Some of the boulders exposed south of the harbour at Stonehaven are comparable to boulders in the Colorado River at the bottom of the Grand Canyon, and are witness to the former existence of a great river with its source in the former Caledonian Mountains.

The west abutment of the Smeaton Bridge is the best place to see the local sandstone. Many water-rounded pebbles of older rocks are scattered through the red sandstone. These are typical fluviatile deposits; i.e. the sands accumulated by braided rivers, rather than by deposition on the sea floor free from atmospheric oxygen. The rocks of Smeaton's Bridge have all the characteristics of flash-flood deposits;

they are massive rather than thinly bedded and poorly sorted. Rapidly running water carried the sand and pebbles and then suddenly dispersed and dropping its burden. These are all features of deposits forming today in desert environments as in Death Valley, California.

During the deposition of the Old Red Sandstone, 350-400 million years ago, Scotland was about as far south as Madagascar. It was arid and no land plants protected loose material from erosion. When torrential rains released a flash flood, the water spread on large alluvial fans and petered out on the desert floor as happens today in similar situations. When running water loses energy it drops its load, and in a desert this is likely to happen in a sudden and haphazard way. At its furthest point the muddy water will no longer be carrying boulders or even sand, and finally the water leaves behind a layer of mud which soon dries up with a characteristic pattern of roughly hexagonal mud-cracks. The hot sun dries the platelets of mud which curl up round the edges like sheets of wet paper. When the wind blows, or the next flood arrives, the flakes of dried mud are carried away and dispersed. But sometimes, without being transported more than a short distance, they are covered with fresh sand and gravel.

This explains the stringers of red flakes of dried mud that are sometimes exposed when the masons cut sandstone blocks. These features are common in Perth's older buildings: good examples are visible on the north wall of Oliphant's Vennel; the second buttress from the east end of the exterior north wall of St John's Kirk, and the south-east corner of the base of the great pillar at the north-west corner of the crossing; on the front wall of Kinnoull Primary School; and on the west side of the wall along Platform five – the oldest platform in Perth Railway Station.

It is impossible on lithological evidence alone to say from which quarry or quarries in the Lower Old Red Sandstone these rocks have come, but despite the near five hundred year span of building history, the conditions of deposition of the original sands were very similar. Architects obviously took more care to choose sandstone free of pebbles when stone was selected for an important building like St John's Kirk than for the Smeaton Bridge, but there are nevertheless plenty of examples of pebbles in the exterior walls of the Kirk, and there are even some in the interior walls; e.g. to the left of the door leading from the nave to the Halkerston Tower.

When a small delta is being built, sand grains are carried along the top surface until they tumble down the front slope of the delta. In this way the front of the delta moves forward. As a result the successive former delta fronts will be seen in cross-section as "cross bedding" at a steeper angle than the bed itself. The cross bedding common in Perth's local Old Red Sandstone tends to involve coarse sand and pebbles, showing that deposition was spasmodic.

Evidence provided by the British Geological Survey [Scottish Journal of Geology, 34, 1998, p.145-152] includes petrological descriptions of sandstone from Quarrymill, Lethendy, Huntingtower, Letham House, Crossgates, and Kingoodie (Invergowrie), and is consistent with the suggestion that the famous Stone of Scone (Stone of Destiny) came from Quarrymill [the story of the Stone is given by Pat Gerber in Stone of Destiny. Edinburgh: Canongate, 1997, 204p]. The BGS authors wrote: "A few small old quarries also exist but are in most cases overgrown or infilled. Perth's infilled Burghmuir Quarry and the now poorly exposed Quarrymill/Kincarrathie quarries are the only sandstone workings in the Scone (Perth) area of the appropriate antiquity to have supplied the Stone of Destiny" (p.151). They show Kincarrathie on their map (fig.4) as a place name and not either as a quarry or as a bedrock outcrop.

The authors make the following observations: "It has to be acknowledged that even a close lithological match can only indicate a probable origin, and that comparable rocks may well be present in the ORS [Old Red Sandstone] or in other formations, while features such as colour, porosity and proportion of lithic grains [pieces of rock] may vary over small distances at outcrop. The best that can be hoped for is to be able to state that a particular sample site might have been the source, and to exclude certain other sites" (p.151). For the same reasons any attempt to match building stones with geological sources is uncertain if builders' records are not available – and they seldom are. Most of the walls along the Isla Road between Bridgend and Upper Springland are built of either pale red and poorly sorted sandstones of local origin or of whinstone. The association suggests that the locality is close to the contact between the volcanic rocks and the overlying sandstones.

Stone from Quarrymill was shipped downstream to build Smeaton's Bridge. "The bridge lately built over the Tay is an elegant structure. The stones of which it is chiefly composed are a reddish sand-stone containing in its substance a variety of round polished stones of different kinds and sizes. The quarry from whence the stone was brought, lies about a quarter of a mile farther up the river, and its strata dip obliquely towards the North [D.M. Henderson & J.H. Dickson, *A Naturalist in the Highlands: James Robertson: His Life and Travels in Scotland, 1767-1771*, Scottish Academic Press, 1994, p.151-152 (June 2nd 1771). [I am grateful to Dr Iain Robertson for this reference].

Work began in 1766 and the bridge was completed in 1771 [George Penny. Traditions of Perth, 1836; Statistical Account, 1844]. Although the quarry is now overgrown there are some poor exposures at Quarrymill, the local walls display the nature of the lock rock, and the bridge itself displays magnificent samples to which there is easy access at the west abutment.

St John's Kirk, the oldest building preserved in Perth, was granted to Dunfermline Abbey in 1126, but nothing of the earlier building remains above ground. If the three consecration crosses in the choir are correctly identified, that part of the Kirk had been built before 1242. The stones in the choir are smaller, less regular in shape, and less well finished that those in the nave. All appear, however, to be of local sandstone. In many places in the building – notably between the crossing and the nave – there is evidence that old walls have been modified, patched, and rebuilt, no doubt old stones being reused. The pillars in the nave are noticeably simpler than those in the choir.

About 1400 the Chapel of St James, on the south side of the Kirk, was repaired, and in 1440 funds were assigned for "building the choir and porch of the parish church" [Simpson, p.20]. About the same time the names of Baillie John Fuller and his wife – no doubt donors – were commemorated on the pillar towards the south-east end of the choir, and a reference in 1448 to "the new choir of the parish church" shows that this part of the Kirk was completed by about 1450. Dr Douglas Simpson says that the nave was completed by 1500 and the central tower before 1511 [Simpson, p.20, 39]. He dates the vaulting in the porch of the Halkerston Tower as 15th century [Simpson, between p.22 & 23]. A programme of repairs to the nave began in 1598 [Simpson, p.26], and inspection shows that many walls were modified after they were first built. The north transept was shortened as late as 1823 in order to widen St John's Place, and about the same time the exterior of the choir was refaced [Simpson, p.31-32]. Sir Robert Lorimer was responsible for a major restoration of the Kirk between 1923 and 1926.

A house in the Watergate bears the date 1725, and although commemoration stones of this kind can be reused at later dates, there is no reason to doubt that that this is indeed the construction date. Unfortunately, here, as in a number of other buildings, the walls have been plastered and painted so that the stone work is concealed. The date 1774 is found high on the gable of the first building on the west side of George Street at its junction with the High Street. Once again the stone work is concealed. Uncoursed walls made of random rubble (rough and ready local sandstone of poor quality) can be seen in the backs of some buildings in the city centre; for example, some with frontages on George Street, St John's Street, and St John's Place would do poorly in a moderate earthquake.

With increasing affluence, Perth's builders looked further afield for better quality stone. The earliest record is in 1379 when King Robert II arranged for stone for his own monument to be brought from Holyrood Abbey to Leith and then carried by sea to Perth [Simpson, 1958, p.18]. As the Tay was navigable upstream as far as the High Street, it would have been relatively easy to bring stone from Kingoodie, on the shore of the Tay near Invergowrie (though this is Old Red Sandstone), or from the Lothians.

The New Town of Edinburgh is built of grey sandstones of Carboniferous age (about 350 million years old) from Craigleith, Granton, Hailes, Cramond, Redhall (Slateford), Binny (Uphall), Dalmeny, and other local quarries [For information on these quarries as sources of building stone see Andrew McMillan (Editor): *Building Stones of Edinburgh*, Edinburgh Geological Society, 2nd edition 1999].

The statue of Prince Albert on the North Inch (1864) is carved from Redhall stone (Miss Rhoda Fothergill, personal communication). I do not know the date of the oldest Perth building using imported stone, Tay Street, however, provides many examples of buildings constructed of high quality grey sandstone presumably of Carboniferous age. On the east side of King Street and on Marshall Place, for example, houses with fine facades of grey sandstone have side walls of local red sandstone. It should be mentioned that the dark grey colour is superficial: after buildings in Edinburgh's New Town have been cleaned the exposed colour is often brilliantly white or yellowish. There are places in Perth where corners have recently been damaged and the broken surfaces gleam surprisingly white and sugary in appearance; e.g. the buttresses of the south wall of St Matthews Church on Tay Street and the north west corner of the Pullar Building on Kinnoull Street. It doesn't take long, however, for the accumulation of dirt to darken the rock again.

Unlike the Old Red Sandstone (Devonian age) the sandstones of Carboniferous age (Fife and the Lothians) were deposited in shallow-water marine deltas; this is why they lack the oxidised iron that gives a reddish or purplish colour to Perth's local rocks. Between 1826 and 1873 several enormous fossil tree trunks (up to 14m long and 1.8m thick) were found in Edinburgh's Craigleith quarry, which is now filled in. The trees had apparently been swept into the delta during a flood and buried before the wood had rotted. [see references in *Building Stones of Edinburgh* by McMilllan, Gillanders & Fairhurst, published by The Edinburgh Geological Society]

A characteristic feature of these shallow-water marine sediments is the prevalence of "cross bedding". This is a little different from the typical cross bedding in the Old Red Sandstones. The cross layering within a bed of sandstone is finer and more sigmoid; that is, it begins with a gentle slope, then steepens before flattening out again tangential to the base of the main bed. Moreover the upper part of a cross-bed has often been eroded away before the next bed has been deposited. Consequently the cross bedding is tangential to the base of the bed but is truncated at the top. Observing this one can tell whether a block of cross-bedded sandstone is the "right way up" or whether the builder has turned it upside down. Many of Perth's grey sandstones show these features, but they are particularly obvious on the east and south walls of the Sheriff Court building on Tay Street.

The original grains of sand (mainly quartz) are held together by a cement deposited by percolating water over millions of years. The commonest cement is lime (calcium carbonate), but is sometimes iron carbonate or even silica. The durability of the stone depends very much on the efficiency of the natural cement, silica being the best. One can therefore see considerable differences in the amount of weathering of different stones under nearly the same conditions. Examples of sandstones that are uniformly well cemented and unweathered (though discoloured) freestone can be seen on the capitals at Nos.50-52 and 63-66 (the former museum) Tay Street; the corner of the Old City Chambers at High Street and Tay Street; the High Street façade of the Council Building; and at the SE corner of the High Street and King Edward Street. (The light coloured stone on the Council Building is from Woodburn Quarry, Cumberland: Miss Rhoda Fothergill, personal communication). There are many examples of other grey sandstones that have suffered considerable weathering; e.g. pillars on South Street at Tay Street.

The City Hall is made of uniform, rather fine-grained greyish sandstone with numerous excellent examples of truncated cross bedding and even one or two examples of contorted beds resulting from the escape of water during the compaction of what were once loose sand layers at the bottom of the sea. The best places to look for these sedimentary features are on the south and east walls, especially on the parts of these walls towards the SE corner of the building. The texture and colour of this rock differs from that of the Sheriff Court, or indeed of other buildings on Tay Street. According to The Perthshire Advertiser, 1911, the City Hall is "built of bluish grey stone from Leoch Quarries, Forfarshire." {Miss Rhoda Fothergill, personal communication. The Leoch quarry [NO359361] was still being worked in 1952 [BGS Geology of Perth and Dundee District, 1985, p.94]}

About 250 million years ago Scotland was near the equator and the conditions were like the Sahara today. Some of the great sand dunes from that time are preserved in the New Red Sandstone (Permian) of the Mauchline and Dumfries areas, notably in the Corncockle and Locharbriggs quarries, where many footprints of early reptiles have been found (Robert Boyle, *Trans. Geological Society of Glasgow*, vol.13, 1909, p.344-384; M.E. Brookfield, *Sedimentology*, vol.24, 1977, p.303-332 & *Scottish Journal of Geology*, vol.15, 1979, p.81-96; P.J. McKeever, *Scottish Journal of Geology*, vol.30, 1994, p.11-14). Sand dunes in the desert are constantly changing. The wind sifts the grains and drives them up the gentle slope of the dune. When the sand reaches the summit of the dune it cascades down the steep front, and the dune slowly migrates downwind. This produces dune (aeolian) cross-bedding which is similar to, but not the same as, stream cross-bedding. Unlike sand grains in a river (fluviatile) grains carried by wind are better sorted and, not being buffered by water, are more rounded and have a frosted appearance. Each grain is commonly coated with iron oxide (hematite), which accounts for the uniform red colour of the rock.

The opening of the railway in 1848 opened the possibility – abundantly fulfilled before the end of the century – of transporting the superior Locharbriggs red sandstone from Dumfries (Peter F. Marshall,

The Scottish Central Railway: Perth to Stirling, Usk, Mon: The Oakwood Press, 1998, 248pp. p.94). The red stone, which was used for the steps below the Statue of Liberty in New York, is a conspicuous feature in many parts of Perth: the Sandeman building, and the former Gloag building on Kinnoull Street along to the High Street, and up to Caledonian Road; the Salvation Army building on South Street (another building on South Street, west of Princes Street, has the date 1885?); the buildings on South St. John's Place (one building has the date 1910); South Street the Caledonian Road School; Perth Christian Centre on the Glasgow Road, the former Middle Church on Tay Street (now flats), and some buildings, including the Perth Theatre in the High Street. These are some of the buildings built of stone that was formed in great sand dunes on an arid land. The characteristic desert sand-grains can be seen with a hand-lens – though more easily if a broken piece is available. The pillars of the new flood gates on the North Inch adjacent to the Smeaton Bridge contain beautiful freshly-cut red sandstone very like Locharbriggs [it is from St Bees Quarry: Personal communication: Mr Cowan of Baptie] displaying the fine layering and uniform constitution found in a sand dune. Examples of truncated cross-bedded dune sands are common in many of Perth's red sandstone buildings; see especially the north wall of the Sandeman building, the north side of the High Street immediately east of Methven Street, and the lower part of the wall at Peddie's at the top of the High Street east of Caledonian Road.

If we look around with open eyes and open minds, it is truly marvellous what we can see in old stones. As John Playfair said of a geological field trip he attended in 1788, "The mind seemed to grow giddy by looking into the abyss of time; … we became sensible how much farther reason may sometimes go than imagination can venture to follow."

Donald's 80th Birthday Party.

Chapter 11
Donald, Ann and Ewen

Thanks Robert Frost

Do you have hope for the future?
someone asked Robert Frost, toward the end.
Yes, and even for the past, he replied,
that it will turn out to have been all right
for what it was, something we can accept,
mistakes made by the selves we had to be,
not able to be, perhaps, what we wished,
or what looking back half the time it seems
we could so easily have been, or ought….
The future, yes, and even for the past,
that it will become something we can bear.
And I too, and my children, so I hope,
will recall as not too heavy the tug
of those albatrosses I sadly placed
upon their tender necks. Hope for the past,
yes, old Frost, your words provide that courage,
and it brings strange peace that itself passes
into past, easier to bear because
you said it, rather casually, as snow
went on falling in Vermont years ago.

from "Sam's Book" by David Ray
- with his kind permission.

"Marriage is like a fine wine -
if tended properly it just
gets better with age"

I first knew of Donald when I was about eight years old. His parents had recently come to live in the manse of Morningside High Church at Churchill, Edinburgh. The direct route from the manse to the church, to the main road and tram stop led past my parents' home – a Victorian house where a high wall surrounds both house and garden. Tom-boy that I was, I was often perched atop that wall and from that vantage point, my sister and I would note a serious young man who regularly passed that way – and who, perhaps deliberately, ignored our cheeky presence. Over the years we came to know Donald's parents as good neighbours and I recall my first visit to their home, when, just old enough to vote myself, I was canvassing for the Conservative party in our neighbourhood! It turns out that Donald *had* noted that occasion!

The years flew by – my sister and I enjoyed holidays in Orkney and in Ireland, but it wasn't until 1952 that I was to have my first adventure abroad – a remarkable opportunity to spend some months in Neuchâtel, Switzerland with Monsieur Eugene and Madame Cecile Wegmann.

Some time after Donald had returned from his year's study in Professor Wegmann's Geology Department at the University of Neuchâtel, Madame Wegmann had asked Donald if he might know of a Scottish girl who might like to spend summer months in their home – the Wegmanns had no children of their own. The duties would involve helping "laver les fenêtres", cleaning the parquet floors and generally helping with housework. Claiming that he wasn't qualified to find a someone who might follow through on that opportunity, Donald passed this request on to his mother, and then – in a round-about indirect manner, this remarkable offer chanced to come to my way.

Although I was employed in the Editorial Department of Thomas Nelson & Sons, publishers, my gracious boss, George Dickson, agreed that I might have a three-month leave of absence: and so, innocent, unprepared and with only a superficial knowledge of school-girl French, off I went! I travelled by train; hailed a taxi and spent the night in a somewhat shabby Paris hotel – how I achieved all this I know not! Then next day, I was speeding across France by rail and still recall how entranced I was by the beauty unfolding before me – a memorable glimpse of a fisherman in his tiny boat on a canal; great stretches of flower-filled fields and the transformation to the vine-clad slopes and sparkling waters of Lake Neuchâtel. It was as if living a dream.

I attended L'Ecole de Commerce to augment my scanty knowledge of French and Madame Wegmann would scold me whenever I spent an afternoon with my new English friend Sheila who lived with a family living above the Wegmanns' flat. My memories include collecting the milk delivery each morning just after the milkman had filled our household's family jug (no bottles) at the foot of the long driveway; hard labour house-work using a wire pad underfoot to remove old wax from bare wood floors and – less arduously – applying a new wax coating.

I was included in all the Wegmanns' activities, shopping at the picturesque market with Madame; dining with their visitors – often famous geologists, (though I didn't appreciate that at the time) – laughing at Monsieur Wegmann's corny jokes that I barely understood – the bathroom door was decorated with cartoons – gathering herbs in their little garden, sampling new food including yogurt, which though it is hard to believe, was still unknown, unavailable in Scotland!

And, best of all, very soon after my arrival and with a small group of students, we set off at 5 a.m. one glorious summer morning on a geological trip to southern Switzerland. We travelled by train to Sion, drove up the mountain by bus and finally clambered by foot on a path flanked by deep blue gentians and tiny flowering rhododendron bushes, to a self-catering chalet high on Mont Nouble. Had I arrived in heaven?

The three months flew by so fast and because the Wegmanns were leaving home to attend a geological conference in Denmark, I was able to extend my visit and to stay, until the end of October, with the family of Professor Baer, zoologist: a contact that, in due course, led to my job as translator (1955-57) with the International Union for the Conservation of Nature in Brussels, Belgium.

On my return to Edinburgh after my months in Switzerland I had much to share with Donald and we would occasionally go country dancing together. I admired his nimble foot-work and his elegance in his kilt: but then – all too soon – Donald told me that he was leaving Edinburgh and would be teaching geology in distant California – so that was the end of that.

A year later, ever ready for adventure, I set off to Brussels. For most of those years, prior to moving to my own flat in early 1957, I lived and dined in a lively boarding house run by an Englishman and his Belgian wife. I became a member of the "British/ Belgian Colony" and enjoyed two years of a social whirl Meanwhile, my colleagues in the office, including Madame Caram, a vivacious lady boss from Lebanon, ensured sure that my French improved by leaps and bounds.

As part of my fascinating job, I spent a week camping on the German island of Fehmarn in the Baltic Sea (no tourists around at that time).

There I was the only native English speaker, but because of listening to much "pidgin" English, by the end of that week I was startled to find that I was almost incapable of putting together a coherent English sentence! The following year's adventure took us to a camp in the mountains near Salzburg, Austria, where we all slept in a hay loft and were surrounded by beautiful scenery. To state that my job with IUCN was a jewel, is an under-statement!

And then, to my astonishment, in the spring of 1957, a letter arrived out of the blue from California. Donald wrote: "I am coming to Scotland this summer and hope that I can see you". Problem! On the dates that suited Donald, I was already committed to represent the International Union for the Conservation of Nature at an international youth camp at the Gran Paradiso National Park, north of Aosta, Italy. Though Donald was too "old" to qualify as a "youth member" with the group, after a little diplomatic juggling, he was permitted to join the young people from all over Europe in this idyllic mountain setting. Though this turned out to be a week of Spartan living with a meagre diet – it was an overwhelmingly wonderful way to cement our friendship. (Poor Donald, it was quite an endurance test. When we finally fled from the camp a day or two before it ended, we found a fine restaurant in Aosta. There we ate through its dinner menu – not just once but twice – starting all over again at the beginning to relish another three courses! Donald loved to tell that story.)

Soon after, back in Scotland, Donald presented me with the beautiful blue zircon ring which ever since has only once left my finger. Initially, though I was unaware of it, the ring was too wide for my finger so that, soon after our engagement, it slipped from my finger at my parents' farm and was lost for one terrible night. The shepherd's wife found it next morning on the garage floor.

So it is that zircons have always been extra special for us so that an article in *Science Scotland, Summer 2013* has been of particular interest. Professor Chris Hawkesworth, Deputy Principal of St Andrews University – writes that "when rocks are reworked during periods of Geological changes, the zircon they contain is often durable enough to survive processes such as erosion and even metamorphism, providing a record which pre-dates the rocks they now inhabit. Zircon yields high-precision ages of the zircon's original crystallisation, and these ages have been the cornerstone of establishing the geological time scales, and the ages of events throughout the history of the Earth…. In many ways, zircon is therefore the workhorse of the geological record" – a beautiful symbol of the many different "processes" of our very happy marriage!

> *"If my dear wife should chance to gang*
> *Wi' me to Edinburgh toun,*
> *Into a shop I will her tak,*
> *And buy her a new goun.*
> *But if my dear wife should hain the change,* (hain: spare)
> *As I expect she will,*
> *And if she says, 'the auld will do* (auld: old)
> *By my word, she shall hae her will"*

Old Scottish Ballad

And Donald wrote the following quotation by hand – it states a position with which he strongly identified and adopted! He hated argument and, taking Benson's advice seriously, he would choose to fall silent rather than expend energy trying to convert an "opponent". Nonetheless, as man and wife, inevitably, occasionally, we did argue. I never won. *"The temptation to argue with people of convinced views should be resolutely resisted; argument only strengthens and fortifies the conviction of opponents, and I can honestly say that I have never yet met a man of strong intellectual fibre who was ever converted by argument." From a College Window* – A.C. Benson

"The happy state of matrimony is undoubtedly the surest and most lasting Foundation of Comfort and Love – the Cause of all good Order in the World and what alone preserves it from the Utmost Confusion."

Benjamin Franklin

Setting the Scene

We were fortunate that in December 1959, Donald's parents ventured to sail through the Panama Canal on a small "working" ship – Donald's mother helped paint a deck – in order to visit us in Claremont at our first Christmas in our new home on West Twelfth Street. This was a courageous journey for them, especially as they were no longer young and Donald's father had a heart condition. Sadly In April 1961, Donald's father died in Inverness. Though he knew that our "Baby X" was coming soon, unfortunately Ewen never met his McIntyre grandfather. To commemorate him, Ewen shares his initials – R.E.M.

There are now three generations of Ranalds – Ewen's uncle – Ranald Crawford McIntyre; Ranald Ewen McIntyre himself, and his second cousin Ranald Harding. Early experience in Claremont, California quickly taught us that if Ewen had been addressed as Ranald in America his name would inevitably have been mistaken for Ronald.

On Ewen's birth on 2 July 1961, we dispatched cards announcing the arrival of "The New Boss". In our innocence, we thought that to be something of a joke, but – bossy indeed – fortunately that New Boss quickly came to approve of several quaint McIntyre customs and readily responded to bagpipe music especially when his father, on his chanter, played the tune "My Home" as a lullaby.

The McIntyre motto – *Per Ardua* – would suggest that we are not the first McIntyres of the clan to have met challenges. When he was about nine months old, Ewen's diagnosis of cerebral palsy showed us that, above all, we needed to learn the art of living with patience and in the present moment – not easy for a hyperactive trio! We have never been disappointed – the manner in which doors have opened for us all in perfect timing has been nothing short of miraculous.

Our experience is expressed well in a charming essay, *Welcome to Holland* by Emily Perl Kingsley. She describes the experience of raising a child with a disability and in an endeavour to help people who have not shared that experience, she acknowledges how sometimes life takes off on a different course than the one which new parents may have been expecting. Using the metaphor that instead of symbolically arriving by plane amidst the artistic splendours of Italy, as parents may have been planning, there is also great beauty and joy to be found – albeit perhaps in a simpler form – if your "arrival destination" unexpectedly turns out to be in Holland.

And life "in Holland" has been the making of us all. Indeed as Martin Buber (1878-1965) wrote: "If we could hang all our sorrows on pegs, and were allowed to choose those we liked best, every one of us would take back his own, for all the rest would seem more difficult to bear."

Our Happy Life "in Holland"

Ewen was three years old, a nursery school for children with disabilities opened at Casa Colina Rehabilitation Hospital in Pomona – a mere ten-minute drive from our home but outwith both the college community and the many privileges of Claremont. This real-world experience was rich and timely for us all. The day nursery provided a warm and loving space for approximately a dozen children with special needs and we all remember the love and care of its director, Mrs Robinson. This happy place helped introduce both Ewen and his parents how to really enjoy and be involved in the many good things of the American way of life. National holidays are celebrated so fully and joyfully there, and it didn't take us long to learn that in December "We'd better be good, we'd better not cry for Santa Claus is coming to town!"

When the boys first went to "real" school, both Ewen and our neighbour's son, John Pixley, were enrolled in a special class for disabled children at a state school in the little town of Ontario – some ten miles drive from home. This involved Ewen and John being whisked away by taxi each morning and, off they went for some months with a driver who was so eager to get everyone to school on time that he was arrested for speeding – with our precious children on board –en route to the local freeway!

Such adventures were relatively short lived, for in 1968, Danbury, a new primary school which included a class for children with disabilities, opened its doors – a mere five minutes drive from home! And on one exciting day, Santa Claus himself drove the children to school in the yellow school bus!

And remarkable advantageous happenings have kept on coming ever since! Ewen was part of the very first class for students with disabilities at El Roble, the local junior high school and this, to some extent, prepared him and his class mates to continue on to join the hurly-burly of Claremont High School with its one thousand pupils. On graduating from high school, Ewen attended Citrus College in West Covina – all wonderful worldly experiences all three of us. And it speaks volumes that several of Ewen's able-bodied friends from those early school days went on, in due course, to become physiotherapists.

Horseback riding soon became important for Ewen – both for fun and as therapy. He was introduced to ponies at my parents' farm at Corehead, Moffat, in the Scottish Borders – and in due course, riding opened the door to many adventures. On two summer occasions, we travelled with our group by plane to attend the National Cerebral Palsy Games, first in Michigan and a year later in Texas. Ewen rode on a "cowboy" saddle with a horn (a projection to hold on to at the front of the saddle); he became an expert in guiding his horse through intricate obstacle courses and introduced us to many lovely people.

Ewen has and continues to recieve great benefit from riding over many years. On our return to Scotland, we relished many special week-long holidays at Borlum Farm, Drumnadrochit riding over the fields and hills amidst the spectacular scenery on the shores and hills of Loch Ness – and yet, somehow, the famous Monster always eluded us!

Our summer travels were annual highlights. Not only were they an opportunity for us all to spend time with my parents and with Donald's mother at her home in Nethy Bridge, close to the beloved Cairngorms which Donald knew so well. These were golden days of picnics, walks by the lochs and through the woods. Sometimes Ewen was often perched on his father's back in his "hike-a-poose" or if in his manual wheelchair we would often go off from the beaten track with Donald pushing the chair and Ann pulling from the front like a harnessed pony.

For fifteen years, after these joyous family holiday weeks in Scotland, Ewen and Ann would leave to spend two weeks in London to make a daily pilgrimage to work with Mrs Bobath at the Bobath Centre which offers physical therapy to children with cerebral palsy. And, remarkably, in 2013 we are again in touch and benefiting from Bobath expertise through Bobath Scotland, Glasgow. In 2012, this centre launched a pilot programme to evaluate the importance of physical therapy for adults with cerebral palsy; Ewen is proud to be one of the pioneer older adults taking part in this study. Long after her death, Mrs Bobath continues to be recognised as the world's most expert physiotherapist in her work with people with cerebral palsy – and sobering thought – in 1962, we paid a mere £3.00 for her hour-long session with Ewen.

We were greatly honoured in the early 1970s, when Dr and Mrs Bobath were guests at our home in our home in Claremont. Together we visited the Joshua Tree National Park, where Mrs Bobath, an amateur sculptress, delighted in the shapes and colours of the rock formations. And, later in the week, Ewen participated as her model in a demonstration of her therapy at a hall in Los Angeles.

In London our accommodation was varied. We began by staying with my sister and her family in Maidstone but this involved hour-long train to reach London each day; later on we were welcomed by long suffering friends and family though one year, stayed in the basement of a weird boarding house. And, wherever we went it, it Ewen was carried up and down countless stairs – and without mishap. I think back on all these experiences with incredulity. How ever did we survive – and even thrive?

And how can we ever express our immeasurable gratitude for the tolerance and kindness we received wherever we went – to Jean and Bernard Lefevere; to our wonderful cousins – to our "Cookie" cousins – the Cook family – to the clerical Smith family and the gentle, wise and loving Eileen Waterman. We remember with gratitude too our beloved bachelor doctor/cousin – William Halliday Welsh – whose generosity helped fund these fruitful and extraordinary summer experiences and travels.

We loved the walks on Hampstead Heath where the military bands played on Sunday afternoons; we ambled in Regent Park's rose garden and explored the canals; local shopkeepers became our friends – and we even enjoyed the noisy excitement of hot summer thunder storms! Weekends were a highlight, often spent with family and friends. There were weekends of *"haute cuisine"* with Donald's sister, Sheila, an unstintingly energetic carer to their cousin, Morag; their team work showed us all how to live life to the full despite the many challenges of muscular dystrophy.

From time to time, Donald would join us but, above all, it was fortuitous that he had time to relish some summer freedom – at the libraries in Edinburgh furthering his friendship with James Hutton; John Clerk of Eilden (and with Iain Gordon Brown!); strengthening his understanding of computer languages APL and J in Philadelphia with Ken Iverson; at a piping camp in the Sierra Nevada mountains and – occasionally – quietly at home or with the MacColls at Crestline.

And there were other adventures – a memorable trip to Switzerland to visit Madame Wegmann and the kind Schaer and Portmann geological families before moving on to a holiday in Zermatt where Donald pushed Ewen in his small two-wheeler chair half-way up the Matterhorn! And returning home to California to visit Arizona, the National Parks, and to camp in the Mojave Desert where we slept under the stars.

We were fortunate to be included so generously into the congregation of The Claremont Presbyterian Church. Just five minutes from our home, Ewen and I were at church every Sunday morning, learning from and enjoying Dr Angell's preaching, and cherishing the fellowship and kindness lived out by that Christian community. In due course, Ewen grew to become a member of the church's worship planning committee and, for three full and interesting years, I was their Clerk of Session.

Camping under the stars.

As time went on, it was obvious that we needed extra help with Ewen's care at home: so we built a room onto our house at 625 West Twelfth Street. We offered this space to students rent-free in return for helping Ewen both morning and evenings. What an education and pleasure that turned out to be! We are ever grateful for the many friendships, love, enrichment and learning we all gained from this experience.

Our first live-in helper was Carl from the Deep South, student at the local Theology School. At bedtime Carl would come through to our part of the house to sweep Ewen off to his shower and to pop him into bed – a black potentate resplendent in his deep maroon dressing gown. We learnt a great deal from Carl. In due course, his place was taken by Paramount from Mississippi. His was a sad tale and we often wonder if he were able to fulfil his dream as a psychiatrist to "his own people". Then came Detlef who was writing his PhD theology thesis. Guided into computing by Donald, Detlef now runs his own successful computing firm in northern California. And last, but far from least, California, Rune came from Norway and helped us invaluably as we prepared for what was to be our final year in California. To this day, we so much enjoy his friendship and his visits to us here in Scotland that we look upon him as our dear Norwegian "son" – very much part of our family.

Matt Mann has become another life-long friend and much loved former helper to Ewen. In Claremont, he took Ewen regularly to Saturday horse-riding and joined us on many outings. Then in mid-July 1989 we all travelled together to arrive in Scotland in the nick of time to attend a cousin's very Scottish wedding. On a summer of glorious weather, Matt helped us house-hunt and to generally settle in. Since that wonderful bonding time, we have been honoured to keep in touch with Matt and his wife Lori who together lead a remarkable Christian ministry with the street children of Laos.

Ewen always wants to be involved in useful jobs – "busy work" has no appeal to him. It was a boon that Donald was able to write personal computer programmes which enabled Ewen to have two "real" jobs. The first evolved thanks to Florence Cohn of Family Real Estate. Through using abbreviated codes, Ewen was able to transfer hurriedly pencilled lists of figures into the computer to make an official record of the expenses of the rented properties that Florence managed. This led, in due course, to Ewen being invited to be a volunteer as a record-keeper for Pomona Valley Hospital's Cardiac Department. The hospital found his work so useful and his work practice so good that within a few months, Ewen was promoted to the hospital's official pay roll.

Now, in 2013, fortune paves the way again, and Ewen has a little job making plant labels for a Perth nursery that employs and works with somewhat disadvantaged people – job seekers". And a wonderful bonus from this pleasant work is that he has been appointed an official "buddy" – his dear friend Ali and her family have become his close friends.

Another source of remarkable good fortune and comfort to us all has developed through our friends, Helena, Alex and Lindsay Cant. Lindsay's parents have long hoped that their daughter's future might ensure that Lindsay's experience would as far as possible that of her able-bodied brother – he owns his home, has a car and generally "does his own thing". To that end, Helena, Lindsay's mother established Equal Futures, an organisation which helps families build circle of friends around their loved ones with a disability. Equal Futures is based on the work of PLAN in Vancouver which has operated there for some

25 years. Ewen has just such a circle – ten friends of his/our choice meet with him every few months to ensure that his wishes are being fulfilled and help him to realise dreams. The overall concept is that this splendid circle, one of many now in Scotland, will ensure that when old age catches up with the disabled person's parents and their role is inevitably diminished, the Circle steps into the breach. The existence of Ewen's Circle was a great comfort to Donald as it is to me – and to Ewen. Indeed, Ewen's cousin Andrew – Circle member – describes the meetings as "a form of family gatherings" and we are all so happy that Helena's inspired work has been properly recognised. In the Queen's New Year Honours 2013, Helena received an M.B.E. for services to disabled people.

One of Ewen's dreams has been the possibility of visiting China because of the tales his parents had brought back of their visit there. In present circumstances, alas, this is not a realistic proposition, but The Circle arranged a mini-Chinese experience when we all dined together, Chinese-style at the friendly restaurant immediately below our flat in Perth. A bright Chinese banner festooned the restaurant, while we feasted upon chop suey; vegetable rolls; chicken rice, fortune cookies – and experimented with chopsticks. It was ingenious and satisfying evening in every way!

"Individuation is a work, a life opus, a task that calls upon us not to avoid life's difficulties and dangers, but to perceive the meaning in the pattern of events that form our lives. Life's supreme achievement may be to see the thread that connects together the events, dreams and relationships that have made up the fabric of our existence. Individuation is a search for and discovery of meaning, not a meaning we consciously devise, but the meaning embedded in life itself. It will confront us with many demands, for the unconscious, as Jung once wrote, 'always tries to produce an impossible situation in order to force the individual to bring out his very best' ". C.G.Jung, The interpretation of Visions, Spring 1962, page 154. from *Healing and Wholeness* by John Sanford

Switzerland and The Grand Tour

In the early 1980s Donald, Ewen and I did a Grand European tour. We left from London after Ewen had benefited from his annual week of physiotherapy sessions with Mrs. Bobath. We sailed the Channel from Dover to Calais to travel across France staying overnight in delightful *auberges*. I recall of a Sunday First Communion parade, young people, looking angelic in their white robes and of Ewen comment that he was "tired of all these dead people" – it was easy to appreciate this as we drove mile after mile past rows of staked vines with the countless crosses commemorating the fallen of so many brave soldiers in the First World War.

And what a welcome to Switzerland to happen upon a Swiss *fromagerie* close to the border after leaving France. The wonderful memory of tasting samples from a great wheel of Gruyere cheese lingers with me to this day. Then on to Neuchâtel to a warm welcome from the Schaer family at their home in their vineyard, and, of course, visiting Madame Wegmann and the Portmann family.

Our return journey brought us through Alsace and on to Holland where we visited the wonderful Frans Hals and Van Gogh museums. We particularly enjoyed Vincent Van Gogh's detailed pencil works including *The Rocks,* which shows tilted rocks so dear to a geologist's heart. To this day, we have a framed copy of this picture in Donald's study and it always reminds me of one of Donald's mischievous tales.

When he lectured to lay groups, Donald would often take this pencil drawing as a tool to demonstrate geological principles. At the conclusion of the lecture, he sometimes asked the audience if any of them might be interested in purchasing the picture and how much would they offer for it – with the implication that he himself was its artist! A somewhat embarrassed audience would cast down their eyes. It was only then that Donald would divulge that Vincent Van Gogh was the artist!

Mr Plod the Policeman

In the summer of 1965, after Ewen and I had completed our two week physio-therapy sessions in London, we boarded the plane as usual to fly home to Donald who would meet us in Los Angeles.

The plane took off from Heathrow airport in mid-morning but we were just settling in for the long flight when it was announced that the plane would be returning immediately to London as one of the engines had failed. This meant that the vast amount of fuel on board for the direct flight to Los Angeles had to be ejected for the plane to land safely back in London. It was not exactly reassuring when one of the crew members, peering out of the window across from us and who, on seeing the vast black cloud of fuel emerging into the atmosphere, exclaimed "Oh My God!".

Ambulances and fire engines awaited us at Heathrow and the plane landed safely – phew! We waited all day – not easy for a 4-year old – and though our original flight was to take off again that evening – it was officially agreed that Ewen and I could delay our departure until the next morning. Off we went to a nearby motel. I have no idea of the details of how that day ended other than when I tucked Ewen up in a monstrously big double bed, he was dismayed to find that his beloved hand-puppet and bedtime companion, Mr Plod, the Policeman, of Noddy/Enid Blyton fame, was nowhere to be found.

Next morning we were on our way again and on arriving safely at home, Donald wasted no time in setting up a search party for Mr Plod. It transpired that he had flown all the way to San Francisco on his own on the original plane's second flight and that British Airways were anxious to return him a.s.a.p. to his youthful owner. A phone call or two ascertained that Mr Plod would arrive by helicopter at the local pad and would Donald please go there to meet him. Nearly fifty years on, Mr Plod is still with us – still smiling – if a little smugly.

Mister Rogers – Our Neighbourhood Friend

"I like you as you are; exactly and precisely
I think you turned out nicely
And I like you as you are.
I like you as you are, without a doubt or question, or even a suggestion,
cause I like you as you are.
I like your disposition, your facial composition, and with your kind permission,
I'll shout it to a star.
I like you as are you are, I wouldn't want to change you
or even rearrange you, not by far.
I like you, I "L.I.K.E." Y..O. U..
I like you, yes I do, I like "Y.O.U."

In 1963 when Ewen was two years old, on the recommendation of one of his therapists, we bought our first television set. Needless to say he loved the children's programmes and soon came to look upon Bugs Bunny as a dear friend. Donald and I were less enamoured of this new TV 'toy' until we discovered the wonderful PBS programmes – *The Forsyte Saga*; *Upstairs Downstairs*; the art programmes and the splendid concerts.

And it wasn't long until Ewen gave pride of place to his daily visit with Mister Rogers via his Neighborhood programme – forty minutes with a lovely gentle man, who on entering his room, changed his jacket for a comfortable cardigan – just like Dad at our house! – and chatted with his many friends including Mr McFeely, the delivery man. McFeeley was actually Mister Rogers own middle name. Then we all got aboard the little trolley tram that whisked us all to the Land of Make Believe – there to visit the haughty King Friday, timorous Daniel Striped Tiger and wise Dr Duckbill Platypus and many others – a time for fun, song and useful discussion.

Mister Rogers' tuneful, simple and reassuring songs address many topics that puzzle children ....

> *"You can never go down*
> > *Can never go down*
> *Can never go down the drain.*
>
> *You're bigger than the water.*
> *You're bigger than the soap.*
> *You're much bigger than all the bubbles.*
> *And bigger than your telescope."*
>
> *"When a baby comes to your house*
> *It's a girl or it's a boy,*
> *It's a sister or a brother*
> *But it's never just a toy.*
> *It can cry and it can holler*
> *It can wet and it can coo.*
> *But there's one thing it can never...*
> *It can never be like you."*
>
> *"Sometimes people are Good*
> *and they do just what they should.*
> *But the very same people*
> *who are good sometimes*
> *Are the very same people who are bad sometimes.*
> *It's funny but it's true.*
> *It's the same, isn't it, for*
> *Me and ....?*

We sang – and still sing! – along with Mister Rogers.

"You are special...." with Mister Rogers, 1968

One day when Ewen was seven or eight, PBS (Public Broadcasting Service) television station announced that Mister Rogers would be visiting Los Angeles in February and if children would like to meet him, their parents should phone the PBS number. I dashed to the phone and explained that we would indeed like to come on that Saturday morning and, as Ewen uses a wheelchair, would the meeting place be accessible? "Yes, please do come ....there won't be any problem...we will send you the tickets." And then almost immediately, our phone was ringing: "The children of PBS staff will meet with Mister Rogers on Friday afternoon. Would Ewen like to come at that time, when it will be less crowded than on Saturday morning?"

So off we set – despite the deluging California rain. When we were some miles on our way, at Kellogg Hill, I asked Donald if it was sensible for us to continue our soggy journey. "Of course we're going on!" he retorted....and we duly arrived – but a few minutes late. As we sped Ewen in his wheelchair along the corridor to the studio, a door opened beside us and who should come out – Fred Rogers himself! He stopped in his tracks immediately, kneeling to Ewen's level to say Hello – it was overwhelmingly beautiful.

Later that memorable afternoon Mister Rogers played some of his best loved songs on the piano and he invited Ewen, glowing with joy, to sit beside him. Other children must have been present, but we have no recollection of any them – all these years on – it still seems as if that had been an occasion uniquely for Ewen!

This visit became the prologue to a warm flowing correspondence to and from Pittsburgh with this remarkable kind and gifted man. And then one extraordinary day, while the three of us were lingering over a Sunday lunch on 27 January1985, our doorbell rang and there, on our very own doorstep, was Mister Rogers himself, He explained that while travelling south on the freeway (motorway), he had spotted a sign to "Claremont" and exclaimed "That's where Ewen McIntyre lives!" He was duly driven into town, made inquires at the Congregational Church of the whereabouts of Ewen McIntyre. He "hit the jackpot" and received clear instructions of how to find our house! The four of us spent a magical half hour together – indeed, we still have to pinch ourselves to be sure that visit really happened though we have a photograph of the three of us with Penny dog taken by Mister Rogers himself – so it must be true!.

We are touched that Fred Rogers never forgot his friendship with Ewen; he wrote regularly and surprised us years later when, in 1992, he arranged for his friends – a "voice-over" for one of the puppets of the Neighbourhood – to bring his greetings to Ewen while we were living at our beautiful Scottish home at Kinfauns overlooking the mighty River Tay.

Needless to say, Ewen has been the envy of many of his American peers – a whole generation, many of them college students, who mourned deeply as at the loss of a parent. Mister Rogers died prematurely of cancer in February 2003.

> *"So please don't think it's funny*
> *When you want an extra kiss,*
> *There are lots and lots of people*
> *Who sometimes feel like this.*
> *Please don't think it's funny*
> *When you want the ones you miss,*
> *There are lots and lots of people*
> *Who sometimes feel like this."*

> *"In the daytime,*
> *In the night-time*
> *Any time that you feels*
> *the right time*
> *For a friendship with me*
> *you see*
> *F-R-I-E-N-D special..*
> *You are my friend,*
> *You're special to me.*
> *There's only one in this*
> *Wonderful world:*
> *YOU are special."*

(…All of which rings so true for each and every one of us)

*The Fred Rogers Company grants Ann McIntyre **one-time only permission** to include the words of six songs by Fred Rogers in her book "McIntyre's' Parcel of Fine Red Herrings – A Life of Learning, Love and Laughter – Donald McIntyre (1923-2009)".*

A charming book "The World According to Mister Rogers – Important Things to Remember" was published by Hyperion, New York 2003.

Sabbatical year 1969-1970

"Forsan et haecolim meminisse iuvabit."
"Perhaps someday it will be heart-warming to recall these things."

Vergil, Aeneid, 1.203

Donald's sabbatical year was a wonderful year for all three of us. Donald's mother and my parents were still alive and well. We visited and entertained them frequently and it was a special joy to share Christmas together.

We chose to spend the year in Edinburgh where Donald's mother discovered a lovely ground-floor flat with a garden to rent in a residential area on the south-side of city – close by the area where both Donald and I grew up. It was within easy walking distance of the town centre, libraries, galleries and the hills. We settled in fast, enjoying neighbours who quickly became good friends and, once Donald had mastered the foibles of the stove in the basement, though the house was often chilly by Californian standards, it didn't take us long to adapt to a very different climate and life style.

Donald used the year to great advantage, exploring many matters of great interest to him along with carrying a considerable teaching load at the University's Geology Department at the Grant Institute in Edinburgh.

In his "free time" Donald found a tutor with whom to study Latin – hence forth he often took a Horace ode to study while awaiting dental or doctor appointments. He read and transcribed manuscripts written in ornate script by the Scottish reformer, John Knox (1514-1572); and he developed his theories of how much better it would be if, in Britain our money worked on a decimal scale rather than having twelve pennies to shilling – after all we have just ten fingers. Together we visited and studied Celtic sites and crosses – an interest that continues today.

Ewen made good progress with reading, spelling and counting at Westerlea School, part of what is now Capability Scotland – the organisation which runs the Upper Springland centre place where Ewen lives today, a parent founded organisation which continues to use its unique expertise in caring for people with disabilities.

The friendly neighbourhood, the house and garden overlooking Edinburgh's Blackford Hill was a great joy to us all – a memorable and happy year. We were sad to leave for many reasons and the success of that year back in Scotland greatly influenced our decision to return "home" on Donald's retirement nineteen years later.

Donald wrote to Professor Frank Turner on August 22 1985:

Thirty-two years ago you sent me a letter that changed my life, and I cannot adequately thank you for it. You told me that you had given my name to President Lyon when he was seeking someone to succeed A.O. Woodford as Chairman of Pomona's Geology Department. I remember you urging that I should take such an offer seriously, even if I had not heard of the College; you thought that Pomona and I would be right for one another.

Although, as you know well, leaving one's homeland, where roots are deep, is not done lightly, I took your advice then, as, to my advantage, I have always done. At the age of 62, with the prospect of retirement to be taken seriously, I look back and know how greatly I benefited by what you did for me. My life, I am sure, has been much fuller than it could have been had I stayed in Britain;

Ann, who has supported me all those years so loyally and well, also has no doubt that I made the right decision when I agreed to accept President Lyon's offer.

On his retirement the Lyons moved to be our close neighbours. It will please you to know that they act towards Ewen as if he were their grandson. Unfortunately Dr Lyon's eyesight has failed and he has prematurely aged, but for many years we have enjoyed their company at Christmas and Easter, at birthdays and on many informal gatherings. The admiration and love they have for Ann knows no bounds. I was pleased and honored on July 4th to be asked by Dr and Mrs Lyon to take them to the Claremont parade, at which Dr Lyon was Grand Marshal.

The enclosed cutting from "The Claremont Courier" is the particular reason for my writing to you now. In it you will see that the Council for the Advancement and Support of Education; has named me California Professor of the Year and that I have been chosen as one of ten to be honored by the entire United States.

I cannot think of any fitter testimony than this to the confidence you had in me when you lent me the weight of your own reputation all those years ago.

Ann and I have always deeply valued your affection and trust. That we are sorry Ewen's problem has prevented our seeing you more often is, of course, a gross understatement.

You will be happy to know that Ewen won a gold medal for equitation at the National Cerebral Palsy Games in Michigan two weeks ago. We are proud of him. He said recently: "I am very happy; there is nothing wrong with my life!" Many who know Ann and Ewen have found comfort, strength, and encouragement from their habitual optimism, cheerfulness, resolve, and courage.

In reflecting on what I owe to you, I find all words inadequate. But I know that you will understand the depth of my feeling when I say "Thanks, Frank".

Very Special Friends

"Every time you smile at someone, it is an action of love, a gift to that person – a beautiful thing" – Mother Theresa

Ewen has been – and continues to be – fortunate in enjoying many very beautiful friendships.

Manuel

A wonderful childhood friend was Manuel Dominquez – his father, a self-employed gardener, came to know us on our daily walks with Penny Dog, along the peaceful tree-lined streets of our neighbourhood in Claremont.

It was Mr Dominquez -as we always addressed him – who took the initiative to form our friendship. While tending local lawns and gardens, he would frequently switch off his noisy lawnmower and chat with us as we passed – most Claremont gardens are unfenced so that the lawns directly border the sidewalk/pavement. In due course, not surprisingly, we invited Mr D to be our gardener too, and very soon thereafter he arranged his time of work in our garden so that his 10-year old son, Manuel, could accompany him.

Ewen and Manuel became great pals. Manuel gave Ewen a rabbit – his very first pet. He introduced him to the fun of carving a Halloween pumpkin as well as encouraging him to "crawl" in competition with our tortoise across our "backyard"/garden under the persimmon tree. We were honoured to attend Manuel's his first communion at the local Catholic church.

It was a delight to enjoy Manuel's company on some of our family expeditions. One spring-time, after a heavy rainfall, we visited a local canyon where, to his astonishment, Manuel discovered that river-beds actually carried water and were not permanently dry desert rocky piles. His pleasure and surprise at each new experience was a delight. He was dazzled to see the vast space of the halls and the brilliance of light from the magnificent ceiling-hung chandeliers at the Los Angeles County Museum and was equally delighted when we all got the opportunity to tour the gigantic liner that had brought our Papa "Wegmann" on his long voyage from Europe to Los Angeles harbour.

Manuel and his parents taught us so much. Mr Dominquez was a dedicated member of The Society of Vincent St Paul – whose work is based upon that of St Vincent (1581-1660) and of his friend, St Francis de Sale. These saintly men tried to alleviate some of the terrible suffering of medieval times while preaching a message of hope: "God is a God of gentleness and goodness". It was their passion to transmit the message of God's love to others through their own way of life. Mr Dominquez identified strongly with that message but, alas, although his own heart was certainly one of gold, it wore out all too soon – he died in his late fifties.

Manuel respected his father's deep desire for him to become a priest; however, after two years at seminary and much soul searching, he decided that he would marry and, to the best of my recollection, switched to a career in social work. Unfortunately after we left Claremont, we lost touch with him and his kind, gentle mother.

The Botvins

We have had – and continue to enjoy – the friendship of many good neighbours. On Twelfth Street we enjoyed the company of the Foremans and their four active children – Gail, Scott, Guy and Mark. When they moved away, the Botvin family and Seb, their lovely Alsatian dog, arrived. We rejoiced with them at the birth of each their three beautiful daughters – Tamara, Yael and Michal, and had much pleasure in seeing them grow up.

Each Christmas Eve the girls would come to admire our Christmas tree and our delicate, brightly coloured nativity scene that Donald had found for Ewen in Mexico. And alongside that, each year we place a lovely wooden carving of Mary, Joseph and the infant Jesus which the Botvins brought us from Israel and a wooden camel train from Lebanon to accompany the three kings.

To our surprise, in 1988 – the year before we ourselves left California to return to our homeland – the Botvins set us an example. They uprooted themselves and moved to Jerusalem in Israel. We have kept in touch with them ever since – weeping with them when the girls' father Mel died in his early fifties, and again just a few years later, when we learnt that their middle daughter, Yael, a teenager shopping for her school equipment at a local mall, had been killed by a suicide bomber. They bear these tragedies with bravery and without bitterness. We often wing special thoughts to their family – especially at each Christmas and Hannukah.

The Christies

The Christie family play an important role in all our lives, not only through Donald and John's long professional connections but also through our shared Scottish heritage. Helen and John's presence with us in Claremont made a huge personal difference to both Donald – and perhaps even more so – to me! After a mere six months in California, while Donald was away on the Clearwater Lake summer expedition, I popped in to our local market one afternoon to be greeted by the butcher: "Your sister has just been in!" And what a wonderful "near" sister Helen is to me! Our marriages had taken place just six months apart and their daughter Catherine is just a week older than our Ewen! And it wasn't long before their two younger children – Donald and Ann! – came along to join the fun.

Despite the Christies move to Santa Monica, we continued enjoying frequent "family" visits and adventures together – one of my first camping experiences sleeping under the stars in the desert, was with them – and ever since, we have rejoiced in all that we share and enjoy together. Even now, Helen makes annual visits to Mima, her real sister in Invergowrie – a half-hour bus journey from our home in Perth! Californian connections continue to be strong and to cover the three generations.

Florence Cohn

Florence is a wonderful character, larger than life – bubbling with energy, creativity and kindness. Donald came to know Florence in 1959 when she was recommended to help prepare our annual tax forms. One evening, shortly after the initial contact, Donald gathered up all our financial papers and set off Florence's home to seek her advice. He came home late and chuckling at the experience of the carefree turmoil at her home with her five boisterous youngsters.

From then on, Florence became a firm friend and also our expert business adviser; and the years rolled by while Florence delighted us, not only with practical help but also with laughter. When Florence learnt that Ewen was using the computer with considerable success, she ventured to ask if he might help her by recording the routine data of accounts for the rented homes that she managed. As Ewen likes to be doing "real work", Donald immediately designed a simple computer programme so that he could take up this challenge. This all worked really well and led, in due course, to Ewen having a small paid computing job in the Cardiac Department of Pomona Valley Hospital! Ewen's reference from the hospital states that the example of Ewen's diligence even encouraged the other office workers to apply themselves a little harder!

Wherever Florence goes she dreams up projects to help others. She loves the high desert of New Mexico and built an isolated house-in-the-round high on the plain, in the heart of North American cowboy/Indian country. We enjoyed three summer holidays there in the sagebrush and with a herd of llamas for company! Ever thoughtful of neighbours, Florence launched and has sustained a Claremont Christmas project to collect toys and bicycles as gifts to American-Indian children of impoverished families.

The McCullohs

Yet another geological link that has brought enduring and important family connections is with the McCulloh family – Thane, Mary-Anne; and their children – Thayne (spelt differently from his father's name); Paul and Anne-Marie.

Anne-Marie has become a Carmelite nun and as Sister Joseph-Marie is a prayerful, long-distance/corresponding member of Ewen's Equal Futures Circle of Friends. Thayne is President of Gonzaga University in Spokane, Washington.

The Mitescus

We have long enjoyed friendship with Catalin Mitescu, professor of Physics at Pomona College so that when his young Canadian wife joined him after their marriage in the 1970s, Nicole and I became good and bonded friends. We have shared so much with the four generations of Mitescus as Anna, Natalie and Emilie grew up and blossomed. And thanks to Nicole's several visits to Perth and to the gift of e-mail, I continue to cherish their friendship and that of their now far-flung and gifted family.

W.H. Murray

On 25 April 1994, Bill Murray wrote to Ewen:

"It is nearly two years since I met you at your home in Kinfauns. I used to climb mountains with your father before you all lived in California and I was delighted when you came back to Scotland. In fact the first time I ever met you was in the Cairngorms when you were a baby and you were carried by Donald and Ann over the very top of Cairn Gorm (above 4,000 feet). (*This is not quite accurate – the three of us climbed the small hill by Loch an Eilean with Bill and his wife Anne*). So I was very happy to meet you again after 32 years! (My own job since has been writing books).

Donald and Ann tell me that you are now living at Springland and are enjoying life there. I was especially glad to hear that you are still riding; horses – that was long one of my youthful ambitions – but the chance never came – I think horses are the most beautiful of all the animals. The only animal I've ever ridden was a camel in Egypt – ironic, because it must be one of the ugliest and certainly the most uncomfortable to ride. Its back gives a peculiar jerk at every step.

I write just to say how happy I am that all goes well with you. I wish you good fortune in the years ahead."

Stanley and Rhoda Sapon

We came to know Stanley and Rhoda Sapon through our friend, Bob Segalman – all three of them were Jewish, which, in itself, was a wonderful learning experience for us. We were privileged that the Sapons came to be such brilliantly lively, loving and special friends and helpers to us all over many years.

In the 1970s Stan and his wife, Rhoda, spent a sabbatical year in California and after Bob's introduction we made several pilgrimages to Santa Monica so that Ewen might benefit from speech therapy lessons from this lovely, deeply caring man. For twenty five years Stan was a pioneer Professor of Psycholinguistics and Director of the Verbal Behaviour Laboratory at the University of Rochester – and Ewen was certainly fortunate to reap benefit from his important research and unique skills.

Stan and Rhoda were involved in many fields and passionate about every one of them. From the 1970s they followed a strict vegan diet (see Stan's website www.veganvalues.org) and were both strong advocates of animal rights. As a young man Stan had worked in a candy-making factory. Though gluttony there had made him sick, his sweet tooth never left him and he loved to reminisce about that time.

Donald visited them at their home in Rochester, New York and 1998 they visited our home at Kinfauns for memorable days of fun and laughter. The days flew by as we endlessly exchanged stories – their tales were unique, always humorous and full of interest and insight. They gave Ewen a copy of *The Phantom Tollbooth* by Norton Juster – a wise and witty fantasy…. very "Sapon-ish"!

Stan and Rhoda would tell us how they would argue with each other at least once every single day – and enjoyed so doing, for as they explained, their arguments always came around to the pleasure of a "making-up" process before the sun went down! Although not big in stature, they were "big, broad-minded" people in so many lovely ways.

Because we had such good Jewish friends – including our neighbours on West Twelfth Street – by domino effect, I was especially glad to help found Claremont Presbyterian Church's annual exchange of pulpits, baby-sitting and friendship with the congregation of the local Temple Beth Israel. Now, some 35 years on, this successful program is said to be the longest Protestant/Jewish exchange in USA!

After Rhoda died in 2008 and Donald in 2009, Stan and I continued to treasure poignant phone conversations almost to his last days; his old sparkle would often surface during these chats, and he told me of how touched he was (although he had not been a practising Jew) when he was widowed, the local synagogue in Florida took him under their wing, looked out for him and even arranged a special birthday party. Stan died aged 86 in December 2010.

John Pixley

.....More remarkable coincidences – John Pixley and his family became our neighbours when the Ewen was three, He is a year older than Ewen, his father professor of mathematics at Harvey Mudd College and his mother, Jean, a primary school teacher. John, bright, brainy and into everything, battles through life triumphantly, as does Ewen, despite both of them challenged by severe disability from cerebral palsy.

John contributes a regular column to the local newspaper, The Claremont Courier. *Here are extracts from his article of 2 March 2010 after my visit to Claremont for the Annual Eckis/Hilll Geology dinner which, on that occasion, honoured Donald's memory.*

John wrote:.

"Ewen was my best friend when I was growing up. The McIntyres lived just around the corner, and I always loved going over there for afternoon tea. Even when it was quite simple, I thought it was very grown-up and sophisticated. Later, I was fascinated by how to make shortbread and how to get it better and better, and I still use Ann's recipe.

I didn't see Donald nearly as much as Ann and Ewen, but when I did, he was always very nice, although a bit quiet. I remember being surprised, because he seemed so shy but then would tell interesting and often quite amusing stories. His face would light up, and he would become quite animated. He was like one of those boys in high school who are painfully shy but end up stealing scenes in the school play.

It never surprised me to hear that he was a very popular and good professor. Although I never saw Donald teach, it was easy to imagine that he brought a great, infectious enthusiasm to the classroom as well as the office. My mother, who taught fifth grade, appreciated his help when she was citing earth matters.

I also remember Mr McIntyre wearing a kilt and playing the bagpipes. For a long time, I didn't enjoy the bagpipe-playing because they were so loud. It was not until much later that I realized how beautiful they are – at least from afar – and how hard they are to play.

Donald became quite interested in computers and, I think, ultimately focused his work on them. He was particularly pleased about helping Ewen, who is disabled, use them to get work done and to communicate.

Ewen and I grew apart. Perhaps this was inevitable, especially when I left for college and then, all the more so, when he moved to Scotland with his parents. Still, I have always felt that my life was enriched greatly by having not only a friend who was disabled like me but also his wonderful and wonderfully interesting parents, bringing another world with them, so close by.

Yes, there were lots of nice things that I, as well as my family, did with the McIntyres – we even got together with their relatives when we lived in England for a year – but at least as significant was that they were a big part of my growing up in Claremont – a part of Claremont when I was growing up. In a very real sense, the McIntyres are still a part of Claremont and my life.

I think it says a lot that I learned of Donald McIntyre's death when I was talking with someone at a concert at the Colleges. He had just died the previous week. Twenty years after they had moved to a place far, far away, news of the McIntyres, travelling fast, was important.

While the family were still here, sometimes people meeting me would mistake me for Ewen. Sure, I can be cynical and say that this was an instance of people thinking that people in wheelchairs all look alike, but it also showed how much Ewen and I had become part of, ingrained in, Claremont.

And it wasn't just because we were in the Fourth of July parade one year, with our chairs decorated and our dads pushing us and how they would pretend that, since Ewen's birthday was on July 2; that the parade was in his honor.

I was thinking about such things when watching a programme on T.V. about Huell Howser visiting Red Rock Canyon State Park – a place, I was sure that Donald McIntyre would love. But I wasn't thinking that I would be hearing Ann McIntyre on my answering machine. And I definitely wasn't thinking that she'd be calling from right here in Claremont.

She was in town for a week. The Pomona College geology department was holding a dinner in Donald's honor. Clearly Donald is still a part of Pomona College.

Ann had a very busy week here, with lots and lots of people to see. She was, as always, trying to do too much, and I only had a brief visit with her. But it was a delight to see her and to notice that she is in at least as good, if not better, health and vivacious spirits as ever.

I will probably never see Ann McIntyre, or Ewen, again – and I will never see Donald again. But the McIntyres will always be a part of my life."

Equal Futures

Since 2004 Ewen has enjoyed an official "Circle of Friends". This has been established and is supported by Equal Futures, a family-led Scottish organisation whose aim is to help create a good life, both for the present and for the long-term future , for people with disabilities. To that end, Equal Futures employs Community Connectors to help build and maintain lifelong circles of support around a person with a disability. It knows that it is uncertainty, exclusion and isolation caused by lack of relationships, which is the real disability and that "Planning for tomorrow changes today". Indeed, Ewen's cousin, **Andrew McIntyre,** a key Circle member and tower of strength, compares the joyful spirit of Ewen's Circle meetings to those of a happy family gathering.

To add to the pleasure, three of the Circle members regularly visit to work and play with Ewen. He greatly enjoys and benefits from his times with his enthusiastic Circle Co-ordinator, **Fiona Wilkie;** his very special computer teacher, **Sheila Mackay,** with the unique and remarkable **Ali Richards** who joins him in making plant labels for a local nursery and takes time to expand both his vocabulary and his awareness of nature. **Jean and Arthur Bruce,** who are core members and who, thanks to their loving care and patience , have made possible many memorable, wonderful holidays for us -north, south, and east in Scotland. Each Circle member is unique and special – **Katie Elliot; Tori Graham; Marg Meade; Scott Meredith, Magdalene Sacranie and Peter Upton** – they all keep in touch with Ewen, send him postcards and generally cheer him on..

Amazing Grace – Jean Vanier

In 1997 it was a "wow!" moment when I spotted a notice announcing that Jean Vanier, known for his life work with people with learning disabilities, was coming on a weekend visit to Scotland. I had read about Jean's remarkable work in his book, *The Broken Body.*

The weekend gathering in Glasgow was scheduled for a time when Donald was away from home but I was eager that, by hook or by crook, Ewen and I would be there. So we began to research the possibilities, only to find that the chosen venue was inaccessible for people in wheelchairs. Since this was an opportunity not to be missed, we worked it out that I was able to be there for most of the weekend while Ewen joined in on Sunday. (And every cloud has a silver lining for, as a result of our family's access problem on this occasion, it has now become a high priority that all L'Arche and Faith & Light national meetings take place in buildings with wheelchair access.)

In Glasgow, a whole new world awaited me. It was an enlightening and entrancing introduction to L'Arche, an international network of communities, which Jean Vanier founded in 1964 when he invited two people with developmental disabilities to share his home. From this tiny beginning, there are now 150 L'Arche homes in 40 countries and on six continents where a small group of intellectually disabled people and those who assist them, share their lives together.

We arrived at what seemed like a "family" gathering where people with severe intellectual disabilities and their assistants welcomed us with a warmth and love as if by Jesus himself. Jean's talks – gentle, profound and beautiful – amazed me, even as he blended the interruptions and distractions from "the little ones" into a talk of wisdom, humour and care. I wondered if I perhaps I had arrived in heaven!

We all have so much to learn – how to live in the present moment, how best to share life along with to those who struggle with mental and physical problems and to fully appreciate the transforming powers of reciprocal love, compassion and care. We become aware of the need to simplify our lives, to try to discard ambition and competition in a world that sometimes seems only to revere "climbing the ladder" to achieve so-called worldly success. That was in 1997, and perhaps by now, sixteen years later, Jean Vanier's message of compassion and community along with his stress on the dignity and value of human life, is just beginning to strike a universal chord. To that end, I especially recommend one of Vanier's books *Becoming Human – D.L.T 1999* and its many reprints.

Since that moving introduction, Ewen, Donald and I have joined others in cherishing every opportunity to be with Jean. On a visit to Perth in 2000, we were honoured to have Jean dine at our home prior to his inspiring talk at St Matthew's Church – a church is so close to our home that we look out upon it from our roof-top flat/apartment and sometimes can even see a peregrine falcon circle its tall spire. On that special evening, a fellow guest set off with Jean to accompany him to the church. Fortunately – for time was of the essence – Donald left home just a few minutes after the others had set out, and, in the nick of time, was able to redirect the speaker and his friend as they headed off in quite the wrong direction! Shortly after that memorable evening, Jean wrote to Donald thanking him especially for the 1955 St Emilion wine from Donald's "cellar" that graced our dinner.

So great has been Jean's influence for good – truly understanding the wealth that evolves from sharing life with vulnerable people, its beauty and its joy – that in 1998, together with my friend Margaret Meade – a Canadian whom I met at a L'Arche meeting – we have established a Faith & Light local community: a non residential "sister" group to L'Arche. Fifteen years on, our little group of disabled people, along with their families and friends, meets together each month and continues to flourish. Faith & Light was founded by Jean Vanier along with Marie-Helene Matthies in 1966. It is both humbling and enriching to know that we are one tiny part of 1,600 Faith & Light communities world-wide – we sing the same songs, act out the same Bible passages as do others, for example, in Malawi, Malaysia and Morocco, and we all cherish the unfailing joy, love, friendship and support that comes through our local gatherings as well at national and international gatherings.

Jean Vanier writes: *"In discovering the beauty and light hidden in those who are weak, the strong begin to discover the beauty and delight in their own weakness......We need to be ourselves, with our gifts and abilities, our capacity for communion and co-operation. This is the way to be happy."*

Jean Vanier – Essential Writings – Darton, Longman and Todd, 2008

"If you seek today to live peace, to be peace-makers, to help create communities of peace, it is not just to seek success. If we find peace, live and work for peace, even if we see no tangible results, we can become fully human beings, walking together on the road of kindness, compassion and peace. New hope is born." From *Finding Peace* – House of Anansi Press, Toronto, Canada, 2003.

And, while we were still living in California, we knew of and pondered upon the courageous life of Etty Hillesum, a Dutch Jewish woman of Amsterdam who died in the Nazis' Auschwitz camp in 1943. It touches me deeply to discover that Jean Vanier constantly speaks and writes of Etty's extraordinary maturity into a life of hope, care, compassion and love of God. When she and her family were transported from the Westerbork deportation camp on one of the inhumanly crowded trains that carried a thousand Jews at a time to Auschwitz, Etty managed to throw a letter through a crack in the wall of the cattle truck. This note was found by a Dutch farmer. It included the words: "We left the camp singing".

I commend the book of Etty's Letters and *Etty Hillesum – A Life Transformed* by Patrick Woodhouse.

A Selection of Donald's Addresses and Talks

Over the years and across the globe, Donald was honored and grateful for the opportunity to give many major addresses and speeches

Footprints on the Sands

Address at the Opening Convocation of Pomona College's Centennial Year
September 3, 1987
Footprints on the Sands

President Alexander, President Lyon, Members of the Board of Trustees, Professors Emeritae et Emeriti, the Faculty of Pomona College, new and returning students, ladies and gentlemen:

We are entering our second Centennial, and the College has introduced a new course, required for all Freshmen; it is called "Critical Inquiry". We are to take nothing for granted. On the contrary, we will use our intellectual microscopes to scrutinize all statements and conclusions; we will become expert at distinguishing true gems from imitations; we will pan gold and assay its fineness. In this spirit of inquiry, it is, I believe, appropriate for a geologist to ask: Why, on Earth, should we celebrate Pomona's Centennial? "A question not to be asked", as Falstaff said to Prince Hal.

As everyone knows, Copernicus showed we had made a grievous error in thinking the Earth to be the center about which the Universe revolves. After 1543 it should no longer have seemed obvious that the Universe was made for Man; the Earth is not in a specially favored position. The cosmologist, Sir Hermann Bondi, called this the "Copernican Principle". Moreover, in 1918, after an ingenious investigation of variable stars in globular clusters, Harlow Shapley, at the Mount Wilson observatory, found that the Sun is not the center of the Universe; we are, indeed some 27,000 light years from the galactic center. Seven years later Edwin Hubble, again at Mount Wilson, demonstrated that our galaxy is an island in a universe of galaxies – as William Herschel had thought as early as 1785. In 1929 Hubble made the momentous discovery that the Universe is expanding.

Bondi therefore expanded the scope of the "Copernican Principle", reviving an old idea and calling it the "Perfect Cosmological Principle". It asserts that the universe is homogeneous and stationary in its large-scale appearance, as well as in its physical laws. My mathematics professor, Sir Edmund Whittaker, expressed it simply: 'it is impossible to tell where one is in the Universe" – a statement that attracted attention as a rarity; namely a definition of the impossible – a postulate of impotence. Another example is that it is impossible to know at any time where an electron is within an atom.

It was, of course, Kepler who took the next step after Copernicus. Following years of calculations, he found that the Earth's orbit – though nearly circular – is in fact an ellipse. He also discovered that the period of each planet – the length of its year – depends on its distance from the Sun; in fact the square of the period is proportional to the cube of the average distance, a result published in 1619 in his book *The Harmonics of the Universe*.

Kepler thus gave science its first laws. As Arthur Koestler put it: "Although (owing to the peculiarities of our educational system), a person may never have heard of Kepler's Laws, his thinking has nevertheless been molded by them without his knowledge; they are the invisible foundation of a whole edifice of thought."

The problem was then to derive Kepler's laws from simpler, presumably more fundamental, assumptions, and in this Newton succeeded. By accepting the laws of motion and gravity as axioms, true for every body in the Universe, Newton demonstrated that Kepler's laws necessarily follow. He inaugurated modern science in a book acclaimed as the most extraordinary production of the human mind. The force acting on the falling apple is the same one that holds the Moon in its orbit round the Earth, and the Earth in its orbit round the Sun. There is only one science of Physics, and its laws are truly universal.

Believing that rocks increase in density with depth in a mine, Newton computed the average density of the Earth by extrapolation. As available data were then hopelessly inadequate, perhaps he really got his figure another way, but the fact remains that for a century there was no improvement upon his result. Newton used it to compute the mass of the Sun and the densities of Jupiter and its satellites. His prediction that the Earth was flattened at the poles was confirmed long afterwards by scientific expeditions comparable in effort, resources, and results to the space programs of our own day.

In 1987 we celebrate the fact that, since the College's foundation, our planet has revolved around the Sun a hundred times. How doubly arbitrary a measure! After all, the Earth would have gone round more often had it been closer; and had it been further away we would have waited longer for our Centennial.

Because life, as we know it, survives only within a narrow temperature range, the distance from the Sun (and hence the frequency of Centennials) is critical. Variation in the seasons, moreover, depends on both the ellipticity of the Earth's orbit and the tilt of its axis; if either were much greater there might be nobody to celebrate a Centennial.

A contemporary of Newton's believed, indeed, that the equable conditions of Eden ended because the Earth's tilt changed – perhaps as a result of the Flood. The heat generated by radioactivity within the Earth depends on the Earth's size. Were it significantly different, the planet would either be lifeless – like the Moon – or earthquakes and volcanoes would be more frequent and violent, and the atmosphere unfavorable to life.

The fitness of the environment for the support of life is, indeed, remarkable. But thinking of the widespread ignorance about such matters, I am reminded of William Moon's pessimistic comment: "To live so uninformed before such grandeur is the hallmark of a true native son".

In recognizing a Centennial we emphasize that we have two hands, each with five fingers – for the words "five" and "finger" have the same root. But the thumb's special role enabled man to distinguish himself as a tool-using animal; as Carlyle observed, "Without tools he is nothing, with tools he is all!" Why are we still enthralled by a decimal number system? We could have adopted base 8, because a "digit" is a "finger" – literally a "pointing thing", which nowadays doesn't usually include the thumb, except for hitchhikers.

Computer users avoid the word "digit" because it suggests a base 10 system. They invent, instead, words like "bits", "bytes", and "nibbles". Multiplication and division by shifting the point is not, of course, peculiar to base 10 – as Napier knew very well when he introduced what we call the "decimal point" 370 years ago. Twelve is a much better base, for the reason that 12 is an "abundant" number – it has more factors than any smaller number. Twelve is divisible by 2, 3, 4, and 6; ten only by 2 and 5. No wonder eggs and beer come in dozens and sixpacks!

At a College with Pomona's heritage I need not dwell on the fact that Jesus chose 12 apostles and 6 times this number of disciples, sending them out, as St Luke observed, in binary – two by two. Although mathematicians, such as Laplace and Lagrange, recognized the advantage of base 12, political considerations prevailed, and in 1795 the French revolutionary government imposed decimal currency.

According to that perceptive and readable historian George Bernard Shaw, when Sir Isaac Newton's housekeeper was checking her laundry bill, she was heard to say: "Three sixpences make one and sixpence, and three eightpences make two shillings: they always do. But three sevenpences. I give it up. I'll ask Mr Newton. He'll know, if anyone will." Mistress Basham – like everyone else in England – could think in base 12, and because a pound contained 240 pence, she could compute in base 240 as well. Consider stock-market prices; they often involve eighths or even sixteenths – fractions clumsy in base 10, but represented by whole numbers of pennies.

When Britain entered the European Common Market, it was tragic that the investment of a nation in a superior numeric system was swept away by poverty-stricken 10, despite the arguments of some of the best mathematicians. Such was the effect of the French Revolution in our own time!

Pomona College is now 100 years old, and I have been here for a third of its history; but a hundred cannot be divided neatly even by so simple an integer as 3. So, although I appreciate the opportunity to reflect on Pomona's place in time, I would like even better to participate in the College's 144th year. Acknowledging the realities of the occasion, however, I commend to your attention the scientific Centennials of 1687, 1787, and 1887.

In 1687, the year before the Glorious Revolution that brought William of Orange to the throne of England, the Royal Society published Newton's "Principia".

Newton's mathematics and physics guide our spacecraft; the telescopes that probe the furthest reaches of space are built to his design; his research on the colors of the rainbow led to our knowledge of the composition of the stars, the velocities of distant galaxies, and the rate of expansion of the Universe.

"Nature and Nature's laws lay hid in night, / God said, 'Let Newton be!' and all was light."

Newton found the Universe to be marvellously ordered; a vast and complex machine, so intricate that it couldn't be produced by chance. "This most beautiful system of the sun, planets, and comets," he wrote, "could only proceed from the counsel and dominion of an intelligent and powerful Being." This is the Design Argument for the existence of God; Newton was persuaded by it, and – to this day – he succeeds in convincing others. Science, it would seem, supported theology.

Despite Newton's scientific triumphs, the major physical concept lacking in 1687 was the extent of time. Only a month ago the age of the Universe was estimated anew: it is now between 10 and 12 billion years. Although Newton knew that a red hot Earth wouldn't cool in 50,000 years, as an authority on Biblical chronology he was convinced that the year of creation was 3998 BC. His estimate was a million times too small.

Lord Macaulay said Newton's name is "pronounced beyond the Ganges and [beyond] the Mississippi with reverence exceeding that which is paid to the greatest warriors and rulers". But a century passed before anyone recognized the depth of geological time – time so long that (in the words of George Wald – Nobel prizeman and once Robbins Lecturer at Pomona) "not only living organisms but stars and galaxies, are born, mature, grow old, and die".

In 1787, James Hutton recognized the immensity of geologic time, discovering an unconformity on the island of Arran. As he had predicted, one set of strata lay across the eroded edges of another. It was the year the Constitutional Convention met in Philadelphia.

Hutton, born in Edinburgh the year Newton died, earned his doctorate in Medicine at Lyden; was both a farmer and an industrial chemist; and enjoyed close friendship with men like Joseph Black, James Watt, and Adam Smith. Noticing that soil forms by weathering of solid rock, he concluded that even the highest mountain would, in time, be worn away. But he also observed that the present land is made of debris from an older one. The process is cyclic and the span of time required must far exceed anything previously imagined. Hutton's paper marks the beginning of modern Geology.

In 1969 I had the good fortune to discover the field notebooks of Hutton's friend and companion, John Clerk. Reporting on this, the President of the Geological Society of London wrote: "This unexpected and magnificent publication reminds us that from time to time miracles can still happen. Miraculous, because drawings known to have been made on the spot during some of the most momentous geological excursions of all time, but lost for nearly 200 years, have come to light." Last year, I was honored to speak to the Royal Society of Edinburgh in commemoration of the Bicentennial of the address Hutton gave to that Society.

Last May the present Sir John Clerk visited Pomona College en route to Hawaii to represent his distinguished family when the Duke of Edinburgh dedicated the infra-red telescope on Mauna Kea to the memory of the great physicist, James Clerk Maxwell. On that occasion Sir John gave me this drawing, made, two centuries ago, when his namesake was in the field with Hutton. It shows a boulder containing three rock-types, from whose cross-cutting relations Hutton determined an age sequence. This is the original record of one of the most important observations ever made in the history of science – a priceless addition to Pomona's magnificent library of rare geological books.

Like Newton, Hutton accepted the Design argument: "In nature", he said, "there is wisdom, system, and consistency. For having, in the natural history of this earth, seen a succession of worlds, we may from this conclude that there is a system in nature; in like manner as, from seeing revolutions of the planets, it is concluded that there is a system by which they are intended to continue those revolutions." David Hume, a member of Hutton's Edinburgh circle, attacked this logic In his *Dialogues Concerning Natural Religion*. It is interesting that while Hutton ignored Hume, he used some of the very words Hume had taken from Colin Maclaurin's *Newton's Philosophical Discoveries* – especially when we know that Hutton was a pupil of Maclaurin's, and that Maclaurin had been appointed to his Edinburgh Chair – "Newtone ipse suadente" (as his tombstone in the church of the Greyfriars records).

In one of his last essays, Mark Twain addressed the question whether the World was made for Man. "The geological evidence", he said, "is not all in, yet. It is coming in, hourly, daily, coming in all the time, but naturally it comes with geological carefulness and deliberation, and we must not be impatient, we must not get excited, we must be calm, and wait. To lose our tranquility", said Twain, "will not hurry geology; nothing hurries geology."

Geologists appreciate what Carlyle called "The loom of time". As Hutton's friend, John Playfair, wrote: "Amid all the revolutions of the globe the economy of Nature has been uniform, and her laws are the only things that have resisted the general movement. The rivers and the rocks, the seas and the continents have been changed in all their parts; but the laws which direct those changes, and the rules to which they are subject, have remained invariably the same."

Charles Lyell put that quotation on the title page of his influential book, *Principles of Geology*. It was published just in time for Darwin to take with him on the voyage of the Beagle, during which many of his Ideas took shape. Darwin was later to say: "I always feel as if my books come half out of Lyell's brain, and that I never acknowledge this sufficiently". The line of descent is clear; from Hutton it goes, through Playfair and Lyell, to Charles Darwin.

In 1887, a century after Hutton, Albert Michelson conducted one of the most significant experiments of all time. Using measurements good to one part in a billion, he showed there was no evidence for the Earth's motion relative to absolute space. It was the year Pomona College was founded.

Michelson's negative experiment marks the birth of Physics In America, and for it Michelson became the first American scientist to receive the Nobel Prize. According to Einstein, Michelson's "marvellous experimental work paved the way for the Theory of Relativity".

Forty years later Michelson came here to southern California to measure the velocity of light, one of the fundamental constants of the Universe. For this experiment, the 22 mile distance between Mount Wilson and San Antonio Peak (otherwise Mount Baldy) was measured to an accuracy of two-tenths of an inch – the most accurate length ever surveyed by triangulation.

Now, in 1987, relative motion of the plates of the Earth's crust has been measured directly for the first time.

Signals from beyond our galaxy – which have travelled with the speed of light for five billion years – arrive at Hawaii and Japan a fraction of a second apart. From measurements of such astonishing accuracy, by an extension of Michelson's methods, distances on the Earth can now be determined with unprecedented precision. These distances are changing; at this moment, Hawaii, on the Pacific plate is moving towards Asia at the incredibly fast speed of 3 inches a year – a rate about equal to the growth of a fingernail.

The most recent issue of *Science* reports that the measured value of the Newtonian gravitational constant changes with depth in a mine – a result compatible with the possibility that a "fifth force" – suspected but undiscovered – Interferes with the force of gravity. As we look back at Centennials past, a new Centennial has already dawned. Our celebration is but an instant in time. The future is exciting.

One of our duties and opportunities at a liberal arts College Is to look at familiar things In new ways. Think, for example, of Samuel Butler's aphorism: "A hen is only the egg's way of making another egg". Are you and I merely vehicles for transmitting genetic information? More recently George Wald said: "It would be a poor thing to be an atom in a universe without physicists. And physicists are made of atoms. A physicist is (indeed) the atom's way of knowing about atoms".

Richard Dawkins begins his book *The Selfish Gene* with the thought-provoking sentence: "Intelligent life on a planet comes of age when it first works out the reason for its own existence". In *The Tempest*, Prospero asked Miranda: "What sees't thou else in the dark backward and abysme of time?" Today's variant is: "Why is the Universe 10 billion years old?" And science's non-trivial answer is: "Because it took that long to ask the question". Our Sun, you see, is not a first generation star. The atoms we are made of were created inside an older star – one that had run the gamut of stellar birth to death. That process took 5 billion years. Allow a billion more for the crucial emergence of carbon-based life from our silicon based ancestors – crystals of clay – and add 4 billion for Darwinian evolution. Carlyle was right when he urged: "Despise not the rag from which man makes Paper, or the litter from which the Earth makes Corn"; but he was wrong in thinking that science destroys wonder.

Stephen Hawking, one of the greatest and most courageous of scientists, now occupies Newton's chair at Cambridge. This "totally cerebral man" was in his wheelchair while a student presented his inaugural lecture for him. Hawking asked, "Why is the universe as we observe it?" And he answered that "if it were otherwise, there wouldn't anyone to ask the question". Our Universe has remarkable properties. Had any one of a large number of them been slightly different, life would have been impossible.

In 1973, at the Cracow symposium celebrating the Quincentennial of the birth of Copernicus, Brandon Carter (a colleague of Hawking) proposed the term "Anthropic Principle" for the idea that "Things are as they are because we are"; the only constraint on a theory of the Big Bang is that the conditions were such that (in Wald's words) "life might eventually evolve scientists who could cast back upon the history that produced them, and could begin to understand it; through whose knowing the Universe could come to know itself".

Perhaps intelligent life must arise, because a universe without an observer is not a universe at all. The idea is a novel application of the Huttonian dictum: the Present is the Key to the Past.

Newton, paraphrasing the 12th Century Bernard of Chartres, said: "If I have seen further [than other men), it is by standing upon the shoulders of Giants". It Is particularly fitting in a Centennial year that we cast back upon the history that produced us, and remember in gratitude those who founded and nurtured this College. Honor them by dedicating yourselves to the ideals of Liberal Education; acquire the knowledge and skills that, literally, are "worthy of free men and women"; cherish the intellectual freedom itself, which the Liberal Arts support and from which they derive.

Until the Fire Marshall perceived danger, Founders Day was the College's principal fall event, when, during the ceremony of the flame, from initial darkness, light passed from candle to candle. Thirty-three years ago, I represented the new members of the Faculty, and received the flame from President Lyon (whom we salute today), and from members of both the first and the third of Pomona's graduating classes. I would like to pass on that flame to the faculty and students who are new. I trust they will find as many benefits as I have enjoyed from the precious tradition of learning and inquiry fostered at Pomona. We need all to take seriously President Blaisdell's well known words: "They only are loyal to this College who departing bear their added riches in trust for mankind."

"Hast thou ever contemplated in thy soul the thing called Time, and yet sayest thou that the age of Miracles has ceased?"

Remembering Pomona's Benefactor – Frank R.Seaver
November 1964.

As Daniel Webster said of his Alma Mater: "It is, sirs, a lit small college/and yet there are those who love it". No-one loved Pomona more than did Frank Seaver, whose memory we are gathered to honor in this week of Thanksgiving. But Mr. Seaver was an eminently practical man and he demonstrated his affection in a most effective manner.

Every one of us knows about the magnificent gift of the Seaver Science Center; few know of all the many contributions to Pomona through the years. But l have no doubt that, above all, we are in Mr. Seaver's debt because he saw the strategic necessity for these things. Eight years ago he had the vision to realize that a great scientific and technical revolution was changing our world; that in a liberal arts college this fact had to be reflected in the existence of strong science departments; and that the very future of the College was at stake. His judgment and timing were masterly and his generosity beyond compare.

It's a human failing to take for granted whatever good things have been provided by the toil of others. But where would Pomona have been today if it weren't for Frank Seaver? How many of us would be in Claremont now? The plain truth is that Pomona would have fallen so far behind the accelerating frontiers that it is difficult to imagine how the gap would ever have been closed.

Instead of being in that desperate position, Pomona has set standards which others, throughout the nation and even abroad, are proud to emulate. Mr. Seaver has changed my life, and if you have anything to do with Pomona College, he has probably changed your life too.

Amongst many accomplishments Mr. Seaver was a lawyer, and that he was a good one I know from personal experience. To be cross-examined by him was to have one's mind purged as if by fire. Woolly thoughts evaporated instantly.

I shall never forget the impression his thoroughness made on me. One day, in asking for justification of an important piece of equipment, he found me inadequately briefed on the financial status of the manufacturer. It was a salutary lesson, and I didn't return to see Mr. Seaver until I had studied the balance sheet and interviewed the president of the company.

His shrewdness and practical good sense were well evident in his attention to detail in the design and construction of our magnificent science buildings. From a roof which will require no maintenance to the means of sewage ejection from the basement in case of emergency, he had to be satisfied that everything was first-class.

In 1752 Lord Chesterfield wrote to his son:' "Learning is acquired by reading books; but the much more necessary learning, the knowledge of the world, is only to be acquired by reading men and studying the various editions of them". In this Frank Seaver was a connoisseur. When he came to see the spectacular equipment he had provided, what he wanted to know was not how it worked, but whether the person showing him around knew how it worked. And he had a wonderful Puckish sense of humor, so that you were never quite certain when your leg was being pulled.

Mr. Seaver loathed waste, even of words, and I think his motto was one word: QUALITY. No one persuaded Mr. Seaver to give these gifts to the College. Indeed the problem for most of us – and fortunately Mr. Seaver understood better than we did -was to recognize how high Mr. Seaver wanted our sights to be.

For him, nothing but the best was good enough for Pomona. Once, we made the mistake of asking a distinguished colleague in a famous University to examine our proposed list of equipment. He cut out one item. Mr. Seaver insisted that it be put back and he reminded us that his instructions had been to include all the equipment we thought appropriate for a first-class undergraduate college.

He knew that "Without laboratories men of science are soldiers without arms". The result is that the Seaver Science Center provides the finest environment for science instruction in the country. Several members of the National Academy of Science have remarked to me, after visiting the department: "What I need to do is to enrol as a student at Pomona – if I could get in".

Mr. Seaver must have remembered Pasteur's exhortation: "Take interest, I implore you, in the sacred dwellings which one designates by the expressive term: laboratories. Demand that they be multiplied, that they be adorned. These are the temples of the future -- temples of well-being and happiness. There it is that humanity grows greater, stronger, better".

The world thinks of Mr. Seaver as a successful industrialist. I think of him as a great educator. To plan for and work with the new equipment was and is like attending a super graduate school, and I truly believe that Mr. Seaver caused me to learn more than I ever I did from my official teachers. We miss him now; but we value as a high honor the privilege that we enjoyed his friendship, shared in some of his counsels; and continue to be inspired by his ideals.

Remembering President E. Wilson Lyon
May 12 1989.

Elijah Wilson Lyon was inaugurated as the sixth President of Pomona College on October 18th 1941, our 54th Founder's Day celebration. He was 37 years old. In his tenure of 28 years, Dr Lyon presided over this College during some of its most critical years – periods of the greatest danger both physical and moral: and of the greatest challenge, both financial and intellectual.

Elijah Wilson Lyon was born in Jasper County, Mississippi in 1904. In the tradition of the time he was named for his grandparents: Wilson was his mother's family name; his first name and initials were those of his paternal grandfather, Elijah Washington Lyon. Despite its association, President Lyon did not care for the name Elijah, though it was – in abbreviated form ('Eli' or 'Lige') – the name he was known by in Oxford.

His mother called him "EW". After his retirement he asked me to call him Wilson; but I think this was the only thing I refused him. With the deepest affection and friendship I called him President Lyon – or in later years Dr. Lyon. In this I was true to my own tradition; and he understood and respected that.

At the outbreak of the Civil War, Elijah Washington Lyon, then a medical student, enlisted in the Confederate army. On being captured and imprisoned in Chicago, he agreed to serve as a physician with the Union army – but not against his own people – and was sent to Colorado. Later he became a country doctor with a remarkable interest in learning, and it was to him that Wilson Lyon owed his abiding love of history. President Lyon's library included his grandfather's copies of classics like *The Decline and Fall of the Roman Empire* and he was especially proud of an early edition of Darwin's *Origin of Species*.

Wilson Lyon's father, Rufus Lyon, an only child, inherited the family farm, but, unlike Wilson's grandfather, he was not intellectually and academically directed. Rufus Lyon was a witty raconteur; like his son, he had a remarkable memory. Although he possessed a fine sense of humor, he was not altogether a happy man: he experienced the burden of readjustment that came to the generation in Mississippi after the Civil War. He felt trapped and frustrated in an agricultural economy that had known so profound a change.

Wilson Lyon's mother, Willia Wilson, had been an elementary schoolteacher, and while her son attended the village school, she acted as his devoted tutor. He used to tell how he often carried to school a cold, baked sweet-potato in his lunchpail! Life could not have been easy. There were few amenities in the small agricultural community, where the dirt roads were almost impassable in winter. His mother began married life in her father-in-law's home; he ending his days in hers, where she lovingly also cared for her handicapped daughter, Wilson's sister, Josephine.

Having completed eighth grade, and the local educational opportunities, Wilson Lyon transferred to Jones County Agricultural High School, where many of the remarkable qualities for which we remember him were nurtured. He derived enormous benefit from dedicated teachers who urged their pupils to continue further education beyond high school, and most of them did indeed go on to College. Because the school was residential, he met his teachers in the dining hall and in social situations, as well as in the classroom, and they gave time generously to their pupils. How excellent a preparation for the future President of Pomona College! With the encouragement he received in that rich soil, Wilson Lyon blossomed, holding first place throughout his three years there.

Although claiming to have had little mechanical instruction or ability, he was an active member of the 4H Club, sponsored by the Department of Agriculture to promote Head, Heart, Hands, and Health. His love and understanding of the soil was one of the deep satisfactions of his life, and many of us know of the enjoyment he and Mrs. Lyon shared in their gardens, first at the President's house, and after retirement, at their home on Twelfth Street. It was therefore particularly appropriate that, on President Lyon's retirement, Pomona should name a garden – the Carolyn Bartel Lyon garden – in honor of Mrs. Lyon.

We all appreciate how, as Pomona's President, he chose his faculty with skill and shrewdness, but few know that in his senior year at high school he was a member of the livestock judging team that won the State Championship.

It was fortunate that at his high school graduation, in 1921, the Commencement speaker was Dean of the College of Liberal Arts at the University of Mississippi, for this convinced him to go to "Ole Miss" in Oxford. It is difficult to realize that the University had then little more than half the enrolment that Pomona does today. As a student Wilson Lyon led an active life: as a freshman he began work for *The Mississippian*, and became editor-in-chief in his junior year. His earnings as a journalist for newspapers in Jackson and Memphis were sufficient to cover his expenses during his last two years on campus.

In 1925, upon graduating from the University of Mississippi, Wilson Lyon entered St. John's College, Oxford, as a Rhodes Scholar. He studied Modern History with W.C. Costin as his tutor, and subsequently wrote a thesis, supervised by Professor R.B. Mowat, on The Sale of Louisiana to the United States. He left Oxford in 1928 with two degrees: a B.A. and a B.Litt. in Modern History.

The Oxford experience was a crucial one in Wilson Lyon's life, and certainly prepared him well for the presidency of Pomona, the oldest member of the Claremont Colleges. As this Faculty knows, President Blaisdell's plan was modelled on the organization of the Oxford Colleges and much influenced by *The Idea of a University'* written by John Henry Newman, both an Oxford scholar and a Cardinal.

For many years President Lyon edited 'The American Oxonian' here in Claremont, and in 1964, in recognition of his unfailing support, Her Majesty the Queen appointed him Honorary Commander of the Host Excellent Order of the British Empire.

Today the Rhodes program for the United States is administered in Sumner Hall. Louisiana Polytechnic Institute gave Wilson Lyon his first teaching position, and he appreciated the considerable freedom he was allowed in organizing his courses. He taught 12 hours in the first semester and 15 hours in the second. After a year there, through the recommendation of a Canadian Rhodes Scholar, he was appointed Assistant Professor of History at Colgate University in Hamilton, New York. Although for historic reasons Colgate was styled a University, at that time it was only three-quarters the size of Pomona today. Spending the next three summers at the University of Chicago, in 1932 he received his Ph.D. degree in Modern European History.

While at Colgate, Dr. Lyon published two books on Louisiana and French Diplomacy. He was promoted to a professorship and chairmanship of the Department of History in 1934, and played a prominent part in the extensive reorganization of the Colgate curriculum.

At Chicago he was fortunate to meet Carolyn Bartel, a Wellesley graduate with an H.A. from Chicago, who was then an editorial assistant on 'The Journal of Modern History' and other publications of the University of Chicago. They were married in 1933. When Carolyn and Wilson arrived in Claremont in 1941, their family consisted of two children, Elizabeth, who was five, and John, who was two. During his long tenure as President of Pomona, Wilson Lyon was supported by a devoted wife. We cannot think of one without thinking of the other; they were partners working as a team for the same goals.

Knowing of his ideal preparation one can hardly be surprised that when President Edmunds reached retirement age in 1941, Pomona's Board of Trustees, under the Chairmanship of Frank H. Harwood, invited Dr. Lyon to assume the presidency. The inauguration of the new president took place on October 18th, being Founders Day at Pomona – an occasion always marked by a formal convocation during Dr. Lyon's presidency. At the ceremony President Lyon spoke on The Role of the Liberal Arts College in our Generation, characteristically taking the broad view, calling for a re-appraisal of our political and economic institutions, and an understanding of the place of the United States in world affairs. We have watched, he said, Central Europe, Spain, Norway, the Low Countries, and finally France fall beneath their totalitarian conquerors – showing us how much we accepted our liberties without ever thinking they could be endangered. 'No person or institution can plan effectively as long as the shadow of armed conflict continues to spread over the earth.'

How terrifyingly right he was! On December 7th, as President Lyon arrived in La Jolla to discuss a proposed new dormitory building, he heard on the radio that the Japanese had attacked Pearl Harbor. Less than two months after his inauguration our new President saw the United States plunged into the global conflict; many thought that California would be bombed – possibly even invaded; and, before long, half the student body, and a large part of the Faculty, had left to serve their country.

All of his administrative skills were required to keep the College alive during the war years. He instituted an accelerated calendar, and arranged that the army should have a pre-meteorology program and the Army Specialized Training Program on campus.

In his inaugural address in 1941, President Lyon had said: 'If we place the test first upon accomplishment, support will come in one way or another. On this score I have no fear for the future of Pomona.' And at the conclusion of the war he acted with vigor, on this principle, to rebuild his Faculty. The strength of the Faculty was his first concern.

But before long, President Lyon, along with every other College and University administrator, was faced with a challenge from an altogether new quarter. Beginning in 1950, Senator Joseph McCarthy waged his own war – what Dr Lyon called a 'near reign of terror' – against honourable citizens who were branded as communist sympathisers.

Not until December 1954, during my own first semester at Pomona, did the /senate censure McCarthy and put an end to shameful persecution. As Dr Lyon has said: in those years 'free speech and free thought were in jeopardy, and individual Faculty members were often the targets of unfair criticism.'

On the retirement and death of Frank Harwood, Rudolph J Wig became Chairman of the Board in 1948, bringing a new style of operation in which individual Trustees were to intervene ore directly in the affairs of the College. Academic freedom was in danger. The Board of Trustees were divided, and the President faced sharp criticism from some members. But he kept constantly in mind that at his inauguration he had received this charge: 'to be unswerving in your devotion to the cause of truth; that you be the active enemy of prejudice and intolerance; that you inculcate the youth of this College with a love of clear and precise thinking and of orderly knowledge; that you tech them both by precept and example to abhor mediocrity and sham, and to be ever loyal to the spirit of service to all mankind as well as to their immediate fellows; that you keep our shield unsullied and hold our banner high.'

President Lyon bore the heavy pressures alone. His own record is that: 'Objectively and patiently the president talked with individual trustees, committees and the Board, taking care never to be personal and always leaving a conversation so it could be resumed without rancor.'

His interest in the College was paramount. There are still those who remember that in the Year of the Oath he said to the Pomona Faculty: We see the smoke from a fire on a distant hill. We must deal with this rationally and intelligently, without emotion, so that it does not become a political problem. But be assured that, should it be necessary, I will stand between you and danger. The young untenured faculty especially needed this assurance, and they had absolute confidence in their President, never doubting that he would hold fast to his principles. For this alone the College owes him a great debt. In retrospect President Lyon felt that one of his greatest services to Pomona had been the guiding of the College through the 1950s. He succeeded in preventing a confrontation that would have irrevocably damaged the College. Good relations between Faculty and Trustees were further promoted by Mr Wig's generous funding of the retreats that began in 1951 and still continue.

The 1950s were difficult years of cold war; they were also exciting days for science, for it was in this period that the foundations for many later revolutionary advances were laid. In April 953, Crick and Watson discovered the remarkable structure of DNA and recognized that it could replicate genetic information. In 1960 Runcorn confirmed that America and Europe had moved apart to form the Atlantic Ocean. On October 4th 1957, the Russians startled the western world by launching Sputnik, Earth's first artificial satellite; in 1969, a few weeks after President Lyon's retirement, American astronauts landed on the Moon; and in 1976 Pomona became the first undergraduate college to have field stations on another planet. President Lyon recognized that the changes from the pre-war period were so vast as to constitute a scientific revolution, and he worked untiringly to recruit appropriate faculty members.

It was during this period of the 50s that President Lyon supported and gave every encouragement to his Faculty members who worked directly with Mr. Wig and Mr. Seaver in building the Seaver Science Center that has meant so much to this College.

The appointment of faculty was the function of the presidency which he considered of highest importance. In his latest Convocation Address he said: 'I have given more time to the selection, promotion, and encouragement of faculty than to any other duty of my office.' He felt that it was the only way to build a sense of community and mutual responsibility – a sense of concern for the whole College. He was personally involved in the selection of new faculty, and whenever possible he interviewed each candidate himself. He was therefore well known as a visitor to the top graduate schools. His travel schedule – long before jet airplane – was legendary. He described how he sought men and women of character, teaching ability, and scholarly interest; how he looked primarily for young people who appreciated the special values of the residential liberal arts college, believing that the development which he foresaw would lead such young faculty members to remain for long periods of service. He sought good people, and then he trusted them.

President Lyon asked me to meet him in Oxford in the summer of 1953, when the Lyons were there for the Fiftieth Reunion of Rhodes Scholars. Scotland was then a long way from California, and I had not previously heard of Pomona College, but the impression its President made on me was such that I did not hesitate to give up my considerable investment in research – for Geology is based on local knowledge – to accept his invitation to come to Claremont and lead the Geology Department. A few weeks ago Professor Poland recounted his similar experience. I am reminded of the way the disciples were recruited: "And they straightway left their nets, and followed him."

President Lyon was not a colorful personality, and there are few anecdotes about him. Moreover he would not want it said that he did any more than his duty to this place. He was, as each of us must be, a man of his time: although the bitterness of the late 1960s distressed him, he knew it was not directed against him or against the College; he was puzzled by the moral void that is now so evident, and I know it pained him deeply.

President Lyon was a model of southern graciousness; his manner was formal, but genuine; his courtesy was unbounded, and he bestowed it with perfect sincerity on each person he encountered; he addressed everyone as an equal; although a shy and modest man, he was truly interested in the welfare of each person he knew; he worked hard to know the name of every student, but it was a labor of love; many alumni have been astonished and pleased at his power of recall.

President Lyon was a man of extraordinary integrity, honesty, and incorruptibility; he was humble, generous, and scrupulously fair; he was patient and immensely tolerant – even of angry dissent; because he lived always true to the highest of principles, he was immune to the slings and arrows of this world; he could be disappointed, but he could not possibly take offense; he could be indignant, but his indignation was always under control; no one ever saw him lose his temper.

President Lyon combined a sense of learning, wisdom, and business acumen; his was an unswerving devotion to the ideal of the liberal arts college and to Pomona College most especially. He had a deep and abiding religious faith and belief in the goodness of man and the future of mankind; he never doubted man's ability to guide his destiny. This faith made possible his resilient optimism. As his old friend Professor W.T. Jones said so well, this optimism elicited a response in those with whom he dealt – people acted more rationally, more responsibly, because he expected them to do so – one would have been ashamed to let him down.

Such unbelievable, unshakable, and sometimes even unfounded, optimism made possible his great contributions to this College.

President Lyon endured a long debilitating illness with the nobility, gentleness, and great courage which he displayed throughout his life. Up to the very end, even when his eyesight had almost gone, nothing pleased him more than to tour this campus, to recount stories associated with each building, and to ask questions about Pomona's present welfare. He died on March 3rd and is buried in the Oak Park cemetery of Claremont. His simple tombstone is inscribed:

Elijah Wilson Lyon
1904-1989
President, Pomona College
1941-1969
Wilson Lyon's character is summed up in the words of Horace:
Integer vitae scelerisque purus
The man whose way of life is characterized by moral integrity,
and whose heart is pure,
needs not the weapons of lesser mortals ...
Over the interior of the North door of Saint Paul's Cathedral in London
there is this inscription:
Si monumentum requiris, circumspice
If you seek his monument, look around.

"Nothing that is worth doing
      Can be achieved in our lifetime;
      Therefore we must be saved by hope

Nothing which is true or beautiful or good makes
      complete sense in any immediate context of history; .
      therefore we must be saved by faith.

Nothing we do, however virtuous, can be
      Accomplished alone;
      Therefore we are saved by love."

Reinhold Niebuhr, from
"The Irony of American History"

Quoted by Dr Homer Henderson at the Memorial Convocation for E. Wilson Lyon, Pomona College, 1989.

Remembering R. Nelson Smith
Bridges Hall of Music, February 28, 1984.

The last time I spoke in this beautiful place on such an occasion, I paid tribute to Frank Roger Seaver, a giant with whom Nelson Smith shared much. I can still see Nelson sitting near the front, encouraging me (in his inimitable and customary way) as I faced the difficult task of impressing the magnitude of Pomona's debt to that very remarkable, loyal, and generous alumnus.

Nelson Smith and Frank Seaver were both perfectionists, even in little things, and both sought the ultimate in excellence for Pomona College. Frank Seaver had absolute confidence in Nelson Smith, and I remember Mrs. Seaver, after Mr. Seaver's death, saying that she looked on Nelson as a trustee for her husband's concerns at the College.

Nelson lived in several worlds, which seemed hardly to overlap. Rather than eat at the Faculty House, he preferred to share his lunch-time with old friends amongst Claremont's businessmen. He led hard-working construction crews (sometimes, I think, of one person) at Mount Baldy village; but he talked to us of Pomona College, chemistry and computers, seldom of philosophy, religion, or politics.

Nelson's integrity and transparent honesty were obvious to all who knew him. He treated everyone alike and, to a remarkable degree, he gave undivided attention to whatever matter was laid before him. Little wonder is it that so many loved him. Our custodians told me that on learning of his death, they wept like children.

When offering personal advice, as he frequently did, Nelson seemed embarrassed to be so involved in another's affairs. He would say: "I have absolutely no business to be interfering like this" – but he did his best to influence you to take the wise and proper course when you were at a crossroads. Nelson was a wonderful ally: a colleague in the truest and finest sense. He knew instinctively when help and moral support were needed and how to give them. I can still hear him say: "You can't do that. You mustn't do it. You won't really do it, will you?"

Nelson was my best and closest friend, and I know that others will say the same thing of him. Only a few months ago he said, with the characteristic look of admonition that mixed seriousness and humor: "Now, remember! You better see to it that there is no memorial service for me." Yet here we are, gathered as a college community to pay our tribute and express our appreciation for the life of a colleague that meant so much to our enterprise, and to renew our determination to follow his example of selfless dedication and evolution to whatever is noblest in education and scholarship at Pomona College.

There is, of course, a risk in defying so expert a practical joker; if I find my car in the foyer, should a flight of doves be released from the ceiling, or should a bucket of water fall on my head, we will know who is responsible.

I remember Nelson: tall, spare and bald; with a smile, a mischievous smile, often accompanying a wry remark that challenged you to rethink a position you had already taken; not muscular, but with the strength of a tungsten wire. His toughness came all from the mind. 'Moral fiber' was more evident in Nelson Smith than in anyone else I ever knew. He had indomitable courage and persistence, sometimes interpreted, I am afraid, as rebelliousness and obstinacy.

I remember Nelson: in a white shirt; short sleeves, and with his long, skinny, unorthodox, custom-home-made tie that served as a heraldic device.

Nelson's classes were big: in fact he taught more students than anyone else in the entire history of Pomona College. But I remember Nelson tutoring one freshman chemistry student; sitting at the round table in the corner of his office. The table was too low; his long legs couldn't possibly fit underneath it. He nursed his right arm, massaging the elbow with his left hand; his back bent and his neck twisted so that he was near the student and the work in front of them. Chin, knees, and bare elbows, all close together in an angular bundle. The model of a patient teacher. Perhaps he would have been happier on a mountainside, sitting at one end of a pine log with the student at the other, like the proverbial Mark Hopkins.

I remember Nelson: using his acetylene-torch to light 250 candles on the cake at the Geology Department's celebration of James Hutton's 250th birthday. His welder's helmet made him look like an astronaut, but impaired his vision so that he nearly set fire to the Faculty House drapes. If you haven't tried to light that many candles at one time, you can't appreciate the skill it takes. With a flame 18 inches long, anyone else would have severed both candles and cake, but the master glassblower's hand was sure and the applause deafening.

Nelson loved excitement and the spice of danger. Even on hiking trips into wilderness areas, he adamantly refused to comply with the official rule to report where he was going. It was characteristic of him that he came to his class even though the mountain was burning. There was no turning back once flaming branches were falling on his car. It was more than a circus act, and I think he loved it.

It is the more curious that as a teacher or public speaker he was not in the least flamboyant; in fact he spoke very quietly, almost with diffidence, as if to an individual. His effectiveness came from his extraordinary frankness, directness, and sincerity. He so obviously cared.

I remember Nelson: walking beside me, up and down the basement corridor in Mason Hall, while I played the bagpipes. He tried so hard to make me laugh. I remember Nelson's extraordinary gait. His long legs could take immense strides, which he sometimes exaggerated so that his whole body rose and fell like a weight on a spring. He could walk like a Scottish hill shepherd or a Swiss Alpine guide. His motion was purposeful and controlled; I thought he would go on tirelessly forever.

I remember Nelson: Nelson's part in my inaugural lecture to the beginning geology class of 1954. Woody (whose 94th birthday we celebrated yesterday, and who is here this morning) was seated prominently with members of the Geological Survey, distinguished alumni, and others whom I did not yet know. After I got into my subject, I detected the faint sound of distant bagpipe music; before long the volume increased, and soon I could scarcely make myself heard. Nelson had piped in sound effects through the air conditioning.

I remember Nelson: Nelson whose voice could carry for miles. In the old days, when football was played on Alumni Field on sunny Saturday afternoons, the games were enlivened by Nelson's comments aimed at some player, doubtless a student of his, but appreciated by everyone in the bleachers. Even recently I heard him hurl a pungent remark after someone a block away on College Avenue.

I remember Nelson: Nelson, who, always intensely practical, was doing the work of the Plant Department, making a cabinet or putting up shelves. As he pounded the nails, Mason Hall reverberated with his piercing shrieks and cries of "Let me out! Let me out!" as if some unfortunate were being imprisoned. Unknown to Nelson, someone enlisted the willing help of Dean Iredell, who pretended to reprimand him for disrupting a funeral service in the church opposite.

I remember Nelson: Nelson, late at night, cleaning the still in the attic of Mason Hall. Who else, I ask you, would have thought of doing such a thing at any hour of day or night? But there was Nelson, inside the still, doing his duty for Pomona College. We found him when John Christie showed our new colleague, Gerhard Oertel, and his wife, the curiosities of our work place. Around the still the remains of the old Anthropological Museum were scattered in disarray; an African chief's hut stood there along with spears, instruments of torture, and a witch doctor's regalia.

Nelson's pants, which he had removed in order to perform the messy task, were beyond his reach, and we stood in a circle exchanging pleasantries and eyeing the tools left by the anthropologists. John was in favor of lighting the burner under his captive, but in the end spared him by departing, with the dignity and deference of a British valet, taking Nelson's pants with him. He promised Nelson would find them on Marston Quadrangle, safely at the top of the flagpole.

It says much for Nelson's fantastic sense of humor that he and John remained the best of friends. Indeed he later sponsored John's fiancée when she applied for a visa to come to the United States, and he gave the bride away at the wedding.

I remember Nelson: Nelson, on a Sunday afternoon, at work on the plans for a new chemistry building. Mr. and Mrs. Seaver had come to our home for lunch, and Mr. Seaver wanted to inspect the Seaver Laboratory, where geology had moved from Mason Hall. Our conversation came around to the needs of the Chemistry Department, and I proposed that we go to Mason Hall and see Nelson's plans. Mr. Seaver was in excellent humor, and Nelson delightedly seized the opportunity to explain the need for the new building and share his enthusiasm for the project. I believe that was the moment when the idea of Mr. Seaver's support for what came to be Seaver North crystallized.

Nelson, like Frank Seaver, had the vision to know what things were necessary to make this College first class, and he worked untiringly to achieve them. In 1964, when he heard IBM's announcement of a new generation of computers, the general purpose System 360, he saw to it that an order was placed as a line-item in the Chemistry Department's budget. As everyone knows, Pomona received the first 360 delivered to a customer. Its successor, which Nelson worked for in its turn, is used by every department in the College.

I remember Nelson: Nelson the catalyst (and often the target) of so many practical jokes. I think his greatest pleasure came from his ability to outfox those who tried to play pranks on him. When his door was sealed with cemented concrete blocks, he managed, despite the watchers, to clear everything away singlehandedly in the depth of the night. In the morning he denied that there had ever been anything unusual. He was a veritable Houdini as an escape artist. I remember Nelson: Nelson, fiercely independent and determined not to take time from anyone else, though he seemed oblivious to what he himself gave away so generously. When in place of the chair at his desk he found a toilet seat, fastened to the floor by bolts sealed with molten lead and covered with reinforced concrete, the only help he would accept was the loan of a sledge hammer.

Nelson loved this College with an intensity I think unequalled even among so many dedicated supporters. His devotion was not to his own area alone; the breadth of his concern was altogether extraordinary.

His sense of responsibility and duty was infectious. For all the years I knew him he was the conscience of the College. The files in Sumner Hall must bulge with memoranda from Nelson with suggestions for improving and strengthening Pomona. It was Nelson, for example, who first conceived and then conducted the campaign inviting faculty members to contribute to the College's fund drive, believing that our contributions, of whatever size, would greatly hearten and encourage others who could give more.

It was Nelson's ingenious mind that invented the remarkable program of Seaver Research Grants, and it was his persuasive powers that caused the setting up of this fund, which now provides such generous financial support to science faculty when traditional sources are unavailable. He continued to coordinate this important activity even after retirement, and he wrote a paper to bring this uniquely Pomonan scheme to the attention of other colleges.

Nelson delighted in accepting challenges. If he had been a gambler, he would have been deadly; but Nelson's challenges came from solving scientific problems (his Chemistry Workbook swept all others from the field), from helping students and colleagues, and from surviving in the rugged terrain where he chose to live. Only two weeks after he and Nancy had moved to their home perched above Mount Baldy village, their next-door neighbor was washed away. Even this was nothing new for Nelson. As a child in Fontana he had himself barely escaped drowning during a rainstorm.

In recent years his eyesight deteriorated, and he needed to wear glasses for reading. How often have we seen him working intently on the finances of the Seaver Science Center, looking up now and then to peer at us over the top of his half-lenses and make a humorous but telling comment. Only a month before his fatal accident, he fell while crossing a stream; he missed his footing and got soaking wet. He blamed the mishap on failing eyesight, and commented that perhaps he needed new glasses.

He loved the hills and the mountains, perhaps as much as he loved Pomona College. In the end Mount Baldy claimed him, though Nelson could not have grown old any more than Peter Pan.

In theory Nelson had retired, but in practice he didn't consider his duty done. He still worked long days, and even became anxious about the interruptions that slowed his pace. We must all face the fact that the tasks we set ourselves will remain unfinished. Let our tribute to Nelson be the resolve to strive while we are able towards the heights of integrity, friendship, and cooperation that he exemplified, and towards the ideal of excellence that was his dream, for his family, his many friends, and for Pomona College, its teachers and its students.

I have not lost the magic of long days:
I live them, dream them still.
Still am I master of the starry ways,
and freeman of the hill.
Shattered my glass, ere all the sands had run,
I hold the heights, I hold the heights I won.

Mine still the hope that hailed me from each height,
mine the unresting flame.
With dreams I charmed each doing to delight;
I charm my rest the same.
Severed my skein, ere all the strands were spun,
I keep the dreams, I keep the dreams I won.

Remembering Harry Carroll, Professor of Classics
at the Faculty Meeting, Pomona College
September 2, 1983.

Mr President:

Our colleague Harry Carroll, Edwin C. Norton Professor of Classics, died on Wednesday, August 17, early in the morning. Treated with radiation and chemotherapy for cancer of the oesophagus, he had fought back with the courage that was characteristic of him, and we enjoyed his lively conversation and keen wit at the Faculty House less than three weeks before his death. His last outing was there, before spending his seven final days in hospital.

Harry Joseph Carroll Jr. was born on January 14, 1920, in Akron, Ohio, where his father was a manager with the Goodyear Tire and Rubber Company, and where Harry was educated at Akron Central High School. He received his BA from the University of Akron in 1941, graduating with distinction in History, having fallen under the influence of Newton Sappington, the head of the Department.

After completing his MA under Professor Sterling Dow at Harvard in 1942, he enlisted in the U.S. Army, serving until 1946 as a footslogging soldier in an armored unit, the 71st Cavalry Reconnaissance Troup. He was promoted Sergeant, and was awarded the Bronze Star and a Unit Citation.

Harry often said facetiously: "For those of us who still remember the Peloponnesian War ...", and those who listened would smile, supposing that this was the only war he knew about. How greatly were they deceived! Harry was an active combatant, taking part in the Sieges of Nantes, Metz, Trier, Hainz, and on into Austria. In the words of his beloved Pindar: "War is sweet to those who have not tried it. The experienced man is frightened at the heart to see it advancing". Harry knew very well what he was talking about, and he spoke with genuine feeling and from deep conviction (as indeed was his constant habit) when he lectured to us in 1981 on "Girls and Gatling Guns, or Why Liberate Aspasia", a lecture that I think upset some of his scholarly audience.

On April 29, 1945, he arrived some 10 miles from Munich, where his unit was the first to enter the town of Dachau and liberate about 32,000 prisoners from the vile and infamous Nazi extermination camp in which brutal so-called "medical" experiments had been performed on more than 3,500 persons, and where thousands more had joined these wretched victims in death. Harry (who one must remember was only 25 when he reached Dachau) did not often talk about this moving experience, but the sight of these miserable survivors from man's inhumanity affected him profoundly, and I am sure steeled his unflinching commitment to the ideals of freedom and democracy, the virtues of ancient Greece.

In the words of Gilbert Murray, Regius Professor of Greek at the University of Oxford: "If the value of man's life on earth is to be measured in dollars and miles and horse-power, ancient Greece must count as a poverty-stricken and a minute territory. ... The conception of Freedom and Justice, freedom in body, in speech and in mind, justice between the strong and the weak, the rich and the poor, penetrates the whole of Greek political thought, and was, amid obvious flaws, actually realized to a remarkable degree in the best Greek communities. ... Greece realized soon after the Persian war that she had a mission to the world: that Hellenism stood for the higher life of man as against barbarism, for excellence as against the mere effortless average."

We who knew Harry can recognize how his experience of the horror of war, and the unspeakable barbarity of the Nazis, must have stood in stark contrast to the pursuit of Truth, Freedom, Beauty, and Excellence, that he had learned from his study of Greece. We who have been spared such searing experience must learn from his, and resolve to strengthen our stand for the Liberal Arts now that he is no longer here to conduct his accustomed, spirited defence of what education at Pomona ought to be.

Is it any wonder that Harry may, at times, seemed to have bridled too easily or appeared too testy and sensitive? The fault may, I think, have been in us, or at least in our more naive and sheltered experience.

In the summer of 1945, while waiting for his formal discharge from the army, Harry studied classics at the Sorbonne in Paris. He then returned to Harvard, where he was a teaching assistant in Greek and Roman History from 1946 to 1948.

In 1947 he married Olive Bowersox of Oar Harbor, Ohio. Mrs Carroll is a graduate of Howling Green State University. She has a Master's degree in English from Columbia University and a degree in Library Science from Western Reserve, Cleveland. In all the programs in Greece that Harry was later to organize and lead, Olive invariably served as librarian. In 1964, as Special Collections Librarian, she arranged the Honnold Library's exhibit commemorating the 400th Anniversary of the birth of William Shakespeare.

The study of Classics was languishing at Pomona College in 1948, and President Lyon searched intensively for a teacher who could breathe new life into the department and its related course offerings in Ancient Civilizations and save it from extinction.

President Lyon travelled to Princeton and Harvard, the two principal centers of Classical Studies in the United States, and through his old friend, a former Rhodes Scholar, Professor Mason Hammond, he met Harry Carroll in Harvard [President Lyon, Personal Communication, 8/26/83]. But Harry had just received the prestigious Charles Eliot Norton Travelling Fellowship for one year's study and research at the American School for Classical Studies at Athens. With characteristic acumen, President Lyon made an offer that Harry could not resist, granting a year's leave of absence before beginning teaching, and Harry's appointment as Instructor in Classics was announced in June, 1948, although he was to take up active teaching at Pomona in September, 1949.

Thus Harry's first year at Pomona was spent in Greece. He was always grateful to President Lyon for this early opportunity to know Greece at first hand, and we should be too; he might otherwise have waited seven years for a sabbatical before making his first pilgrimage to that land he was to love and come to know so well, and the College would have been the poorer.

In Athens he conducted research connected with his thesis on Greek inscriptions, and he travelled to acquaint himself with the historical and cultural remains of Ancient Greece and the Aegean Islands, and to prepare for his teaching duties at Pomona. Harry came to Pomona filled with enthusiasm for Athens: "city of singing, stanchion of Hellas, glorious Athens, citadel full of divinity".

But from 1947 to 1949 bloody civil war between communists and nationalists raged in Greece. What, we must ask ourselves, was Harry's reaction to this struggle for freedom, so bitterly fought, in the Greece he loved so much? It must, I think, have served to deepen his feelings about the tyranny of the Nazis, the result of which he had seen for himself, and promote his devotion to the cause of Civil Liberties and the ancient tradition of Greek democracy. Those who are young need to reflect that barely one month before Harry started teaching on this campus, the Russians detonated their first atomic bomb.

When, at the age of 29, Harry Carroll came to Claremont, and for many years later, we taught on Friday afternoon and Saturday morning, and the standard course load was heavy. In his first year, Harry taught Elementary Greek, Elementary Latin, Classical Civilization and the Western Heritage, Survey of Latin Literature, Ancient Art and

Archaeology, and the History of Greece and Rome, all these being year-long courses. In our time, when the week is shorter and the course load lighter, Harry continued to carry these almost unbelievable loads. Indeed it may be impossible to persuade anyone to undertake the task that he had set for himself this year.

But these formal course listings represent only part of his commitment. He willingly and even gladly agreed to teach individual students over and beyond his scheduled classes. A student wishing to learn New Testament Greek before going to theological school would find Harry ready to teach a special class. If there was any hope of saving the college career of a student in academic trouble, Harry was the man to try. He knew how to temper the wind to the shorn lamb, and I suspect that he was willing to place his careful judgement ahead of rigid adherence to letter of the law; and if he did so, l am sure that he spared the anguish of Deans and Registrars by not publicizing the good works he did.

When Harry came to Pomona in 1949, he was the only member of our Classics Department, but Harry, together with Bob Palmer (who, arriving the same year, taught Latin at Scripps), gave the Claremont Colleges a superb and well—rounded program in classics. Indeed I believe that for a long time, this was the only effective joint program in Claremont. Harry was later to welcome as a colleague at Pitzer his own former student, Steve Glass, of the class of '57, and it was Steve who gave the well-received toast at the surprise dinner on the evening of Alumni Day 1979, marking Harry's thirtieth anniversary of service to the College.

In addition to being Chairman of the Classics Department from his arrival in 1949 until June 1981 (a period of 32 years), Harry was an active member of the History Department and he not only taught courses in the Art Department, but was Chairman of that Department in 1958-59.

On completing his Ph.D. at Harvard in 1952, Harry was promoted Assistant Professor. He became Associate Professor in 1956 and Full Professor in 1962. It was singularly appropriate that the Chair he occupied was named for Edwin Clarence Norton, Pomona's original Professor of Classics, because Norton was the College's first truly great teacher. In their profound influence on a large body of students, Dean Norton, Ralph H. Lyman, and A.O. Woodford are possibly the only teachers who, in the entire history of this College, could compare with Harry Carroll.

Harry had the extraordinary honor of receiving the Wig Distinguished Professorship in 1967, 1974, 1977, and 1981, which is very close to the maximum frequency permitted by the rules governing the award.

Harry collaborated with his former student Dr Knox Mellon, Jr, class of 1950, in the publication of three textbooks on the development of civilization. His archaeological and epigraphical research on the inscriptions from the Agora of ancient Athens were supported by Harvard University, a Fulbright award, the American Council of Learned Societies, and fellowships from the Ford Foundation and the American School of Classical Studies in Athens, with which he was closely associated for 35 years.

From his study of the fragmentary inscriptions, he was able to " throw light on Athenian democracy from the fourth century BC to the second century AD, and he expected to publish a magnum opus on this subject in collaboration with W. Kendrick Pritchett, Emeritus Professor of Classics at Berkeley, and John T. Traill, Professor of Classical Archaeology at the University of British Columbia. Another research interest was on the influence of the performance of military service, and the prevailing means of warfare, on the development of civil rights in ancient Greek and Roman society. It was his genius to be able to show us, in his own inimitable and dramatic fashion, the lessons of contemporary significance that are to be learned from these antique and apparently impractical studies.

In 1963, with the help of a Fulbright grant, Harry planned an eight-week seminar in Greece for 20 College and Secondary School Teachers studying ancient history. The program was sponsored in 1964 by the U.S. Educational Foundation in Greece in cooperation with the American School of Classical Studies in Athens. It was the first step in what became a tradition that has provided rich benefits to many Pomona students.

In later years Harry's program in Greece became a recognized and immensely popular part of Pomona's curriculum. Comments like "Dr Carroll is a truly excellent professor and a wonderful man" and "his enthusiasm and love for all the sites we visited were infectious and inspiring" are standard responses from his delighted students. One, when asked "What do you like best about Pomona's Study Abroad Program?" answered in two words: "Harry Carroll".

In addition to providing the spirit and leadership for these visits to Greece, Harry devoted great energy-to the planning that must go into a successful program, and for many years he was a member of the Managing Committee of the American School of Classical Studies in Athens, and he became a Trustee of "College Year In Athens", the organization through which the College works in placing our students.

Demand from the Alumni was met by a Tour in 1977, with the title "Pomona Among the Ruins". So great was the response that it had to be repeated. A third tour for Alumni again with overflow participation, followed in 1982. One eager and thoughtful alumna advised that "for a Harry Carroll tour, participants should go into physical training two months ahead of time! Forewarned by the 1977 tour, I did", she continued, "and was better prepared for the rigorous schedule".

Harry was devoted to the Alumni, and many of us have heard him say: "There is nothing that I would not do for the Alumni." He cared more, I think, for the programs of study in Greece than for almost anything else, and he had a burning desire to help Pomona students know and appreciate Greece, its culture, and high ideals. He was remarkably successful.

To be healthy, any College needs a few "characters" in its Faculty. Without these distinctive individuals we are a dull and torpid lot, no matter how many degrees we have between us, or how many papers we publish in our narrow learned journals. Harry Carroll was one of these necessary and liberating adjuncts; his humor and lively intellect, his directness and candor, his patent honesty and sincerity, the opinions expressed with passion, indeed his anger, drove us from our complacent and convenient trains of thought, even when we disagreed with him. We are in the shadow of this man, and I wonder how long we must wait to find another like him.

In an address to the Alumni Council in 1978, Harry made this characteristically provocative declaration:

"I have opposed every Academic and Social change that has come to Pomona in the last 30 years:

1. I opposed abandoning the Seven Pillars of Wisdom.

2. I thought a five course program better than a four course. I still do.

3. I dislike Independent Studies.

4. I am appalled by Pass/No Credit offerings.

5. I think co-ed dormitories are sinful, the Counseling Center too large, the dormitory hours far too liberal, the dress of women and men too casual, the social mores and the standards of courtesy execrable, and the "liberated" language vulgarean.

6. I am against air-conditioning, don't think we should have closed College Way, don't like the architecture of the Science Buildings, Thatcher Building, the new Art galleries, and the Oldenborg Center, and I cannot abide the Dober plan. I like formal dances, served dinners, banner springs, freshman rivalry, and strict hours for Pomona women."

"I believe we have to be as careful about the maintenance of an educational atmosphere at Pomona which encourages contemplation, appreciation, and enjoyment as we do an educational atmosphere which encourages action and worldly success."

We remember Harry. He walked with purpose; it was very obvious that he was going somewhere. Yet he could always find time for a cheery greeting or a telling and amusing anecdote, even if he had to pirouette once or twice to recount it before hastening on his way. With his cap, his suit, his bowtie, all perhaps a little awry, and the folder of papers that he would be clutching with both hands, he seemed the very model of an antique absent-minded professor as he scurried along with curious gait. As I saw him cross Marston Quadrangle en route to the Administration Committee, he sometimes made me think of the white rabbit in "Alice in Wonderland". But the appearance was highly deceptive. He was a marvellously organized man, and, however familiar he certainly was with antiquity, he lived in Los Angeles County in 1983 and he knew much better than most of us exactly what was going on. He had read the latest books, was a regular patron of modern theater, and he followed in detail the fortunes of Ohio State, the Indians, and the Dodgers. One of the few Republicans on the Faculty, current politics were of very serious concern to him, and woe betide you if you jested at the wrong time or place.

Harry was eminently a man of principle. Do not ask whether he was liberal or conservative; Harry did not believe in labels. In some ways he was an arch-conservative, but he was also Chairman of the local chapter of the American Civil Liberties Union. The well-known words attributed to Voltaire were certainly true for Harry Carroll: "I disapprove of what you say, but I will defend to the death your right to say it." He believed with all his Hellenic soul in the importance of maintaining individual liberties. If he found it necessary to speak out, he feared no man; there was no pussyfooting. How often have we heard him say, with feeling: "I am sorry, Mr X, BUT...", whether Mr X was the President of the College, a distinguished visitor, or a first- semester freshman. For each would be accorded the same 'courtesy and formality. He invariably showed the same gallantry to men and women alike.

Ever loyal to his democratic principles, on his first visit to Greece, and much to the disappointment of Olive, he declined an invitation to meet King Paul and Queen Fredericka, despite his general approval of their position.

He believed in decorum, in good manners and propriety, and he believed that as a teacher, and he was an inspired one, it was his duty to instil such behavior in his pupils both by precept and example. Louis Agassiz, the great scientist of Switzerland and the United States, used this designation in his will: "Louis Agassiz, Teacher". If we were to raise a monument to our colleague, "Harry Carroll, Teacher" would be a suitable inscription.

Instruction in Latin and Greek has been considered by many generations of scholars to be the most dismal task performed in the schoolroom. Pope, referring to Bishop Bentley, spoke of the "mighty Scholiast, whose unweary'd pains made Horace dull; and Byron recalls "The drill'd dull lesson, forced down word by word in my repugnant youth ... Then farewell Horace; whom I hated so."

As we well know, this was not the style of Harry Carroll's teaching. He had a profound knowledge of the diverse subjects he taught; and he had a reverence for the antique world, its beauties and its values. For many years he had to stand alone in carrying the banner that displayed the place of Classics in liberal arts. He was in very truth Defender of the Faith, for if he had failed, the existence of his department would have been most seriously in question.

But he took delight in his work, and his greatest satisfaction was to have his students share in the pleasure. Like Chaucer's Clerk of Oxford: "Gladly would he lerne, and gladly teache".

He loved his students as if they were his family, and he had real concern for their welfare. They in turn loved him. The Metate of 1955 carries these words: "In appreciation of his invaluable contribution to the College and the campus through his varied roles as teacher, friend and individualist, the editors of the 1955 Metate gratefully and humbly dedicate this product of their labors to Dr Harry J. Carroll, Jr." This Metate has a photograph of the Harry Carroll we never knew; he wears a steel helmet.

Parties at the Carrolls' home were proverbial; for their various houses were never large enough to contain everyone, and the overflow spread into the street. For years Harry was Advisor to the Phi Delta Theta fraternity. He advised students in his office and in his home. He was tender-hearted towards the down-trodden, and was always available and easy to talk to.

But this teacher knew the bounds of the frame, even if the pupil did not. He was very wary about the access of students to "power" in the institution. There are areas that are simply "not the students' business". There is such a thing, he maintained in a somewhat old-fashioned way, as "appropriateness" in College affairs, and indeed in life. His task was to teach and theirs to learn. Pity, then, the unfortunate Pitzer student, who as a member of the College's Committee on Appointment and Tenure, was delegated to interview Professor Carroll on the merits and failings of a Faculty colleague!

In one of his famous public lectures (which invariably drew overflow crowds), Harry, quoting from the remarks of Phoinix to his pupil Achilles, said: "The toil will be long for both of us, but in the end it is my tears and not yours that count. I weep for your failures, but you weep only when I am forcing you to succeed."

There were sacred subjects that students learned were areas where the wise would tread with caution. Patriotism, Loyalty, and Excellence, for example, were topics that would produce a sudden seriousness in marked contrast with the humor and gaiety that had gone before.

Harry was a wonderful raconteur; he had a zest for story-telling. His knowledge was extraordinary, and he seemed to have total recall. He loved to talk: about anything, everything – and could make any experience, even the most trivial, entertaining and fascinating. He talked with joyous abandon, pouring out a continuous stream of opinions and ideas. Martha Andresen, who taught a course jointly with Harry, tells me that even at 7:30 in the morning he was overflowing with humor, energy, and good spirits. He was ready and eager, as she put it, to "begin the good fight and engage in his new day".

Martha also pointed out how tremendous was his command of detail, and yet how easily he portrayed the overall picture, to the great advantage of his students. "He had", she said "the historian's eye and memory for detail, and the raconteur's sense of drama, color, and timing". But, in addition, he was an excellent listener, and he had the habit of repeating the last word or two of any story you told, as if he was savoring it like a connoisseur rolling wine round his mouth to bring out the spectrum of flavours and bouquet. Indeed his habit has reminded me of our former colleague, Edward Weismiller, who told us that he did just that when reading poetry in order to taste the words.

Harry loved life and wanted to share it generously. I think I will always remember him laughing. His was a hearty laugh, with head thrown back, and an invitation to join in; as if to say, in Shakespeare's words: Here's "to the world's pleasure and the increase of laughter".

In 1953, Mortar Board, then a women's organization, sponsored a series of Special Lectures, in which the speaker was asked to imagine that this was his last lecture. The first Last Lecture was given by Harry Carroll at Mudd Parlor on February 11, 1953.

It would be appropriate today. Its curious title was De Satyri Pedis Digito: Exhortatio [On the Satyr's Toe: an Exhortation] which is explained when I tell you that he had in mind an Attic vase painting of the god Dionysos flanked by two ecstatic satyrs who dance to the very edge of the frame but no further. "The dancing satyr's toe", said Harry, "the pointed abandoned free toe given fully to the joy of actuality points the warning in man's capacity for freedom. It dances ever so slightly over the frame ". And from this image Harry taught a lesson that needs to be learned by each generation. You cannot hear Harry's inimitable delivery, but you can read his words, and I urge you to do so.

This Last Lecture (delivered more than 30 years ago) pivots on an ode of Pindar's that Vincent Learnihan read so movingly at Harry's grave:

> *"Creature of a day, what is he?*
> *What is he not? Man is the dream of a shadow;*
> *But, when god-given glory comes*
> *'A bright light shines upon us and life is sweet."*

In 1969 a new series of Last Lectures was organized, and not surprisingly, Harry Carroll was asked to begin it. Thus it was that in Holmes Hall on April 22, 1969, he addressed the College on "The Satyr's Second Toe: A Conservative Reaction", being a Second First

Last Lecture. This lecture was published in "Pomona Today", but it would, I think, be appropriate to reprint both of Harry's "Last Lectures", so that yet new generations may learn from his wisdom.

To those of you who do read "The Satyr's Second Toe", but whose memory of Pomona does not extend to 1969, I must say that, less than two months before Harry gave this lecture, bombs were exploded simultaneously in a women's rest room at Scripps College and in the foyer of the ground floor in the Carnegie building at Pomona. The satyrs had indeed danced out of the frame into chaos, and Harry's reference to boobytraps on the Pomona campus, in his lecture to the Alumni Council in 1978, is to be taken quite literally.

Concern in Claremont was real, and the ROTC had retreated to Claremont Men's College, leaving space in Crookshank for Classics. "The space", Harry wrote, "had been offered to numerous – not to be mentioned – but less courageous departments who were afraid to take it on the grounds that whoever was in it might shortly be bombed or boobytrapped by protestors who had not bothered to ascertain the immediate whereabouts of the hated military."

Harry, who had seen the United States Army put an end to the horrors of Dachau and give freedom to cities across Europe, could not understand the sickness of a time when that same Army was attacked by "protestors" who owed their own freedom to its strength. The age of terrorism, with ruthless attack on innocent victims had begun.

Harry knew for some months that his death was to come soon. With the stoicism of a Greek and the fortitude of a Roman he was not going to cry about it. Before Socrates drank the poison that had been given to him, he is reputed to have said: "I owe a cock to Asclepius; will you remember to pay the debt?" Harry was determined to fulfil every obligation to the goddess Pomona.

After his death, the "Journal of Higher Education" announced that enquiries concerning the vacant position in Classics at Pomona College were to be addressed to him.

During the summer, he led alumni on a tour to the Getty Museum, and because 300 were turned away, he led a second party even though the cancer in his throat seriously troubled him. Yet all who attended were thrilled with his style and brilliance; no one present knew the extent of what he had given.

Harry Carroll was selfless. He thought always of others, and never of himself. Harry helped me with a translation of Erasmus that I wanted for a lecture I gave in Edinburgh in July, marking the Quatercentenary of the University. He brought it to me at my home to save me trouble.

I had hoped that Harry and Olive would be at my 60th birthday dinner on the 15th of August, but he was taken to hospital. Though so ill he relayed a most cordial greeting, and, in the early hours of the 17th, he died.

As I remember his sprightly conversations at lunch during the past months, and the calm acceptance of his fate, I think of Pindar's Ode, written more than 2400 years ago: "Pursuing the delight of the day, in peace of mind shall I walk softly to meet the time of death. For we all perish, though our luck varies."

R.W.B. Burton, of Oriel College, Oxford, closed his book of *"Essays on Pindar's Odes"* with that quotation and with these words: "The very heart of Classical Greek spirit: the contemplation of the god-given gleam, and the calm acceptance of man's impermanence. It is indeed a "sundown, splendid and serene'."

We can recognize that this is indeed the noble spirit that Harry embodied. He was still teaching as he fronted death itself.

Harry applied for tickets to attend the Olympic Games next summer, knowing full well that he would not attend. But the symbolism of the Olympics gave him strength to look out. He particularly wished to be at the closing event and see the Marathon runner finish the course.

Horace knew that he had immortality through his poetry. Harry knew that he would find his through what he had given to his students.

> *Completed is my memorial:*
> *it will outlast bronze, it is taller than the royal pyramids;*
> *no rain or smog, no raging Northwind*
> *can tear it down, nor years unnumbered*
> *nor all the flight of ages.*
> *I will not wholly die: the greater part of me shall escape death.*
> *I will grow on, kept alive by posterity's praise.*
> *Non omnis moriar*

I close with the words of Catullus:

> *I come, my brother, to present you with*
> *the last guerdon of death,*
> *and speak, though in vain, to your silent ashes,*
> *since fortune has taken your own self away from me —*
> *alas, my brother, so cruelly torn from me!*
> *Take this sorrowful tribute*
> *for a funeral sacrifice;*
> *take it with a brother's many tears*
> *and for ever, Hail and Farewell!*
> *Ave atque vale*

Mr President:

I had intended to end here, but when I shared this thought with Olive, she showed me two slips of paper that she had newly found on Harry's desk. They had been turned over, so that she had not realized at first that they were written on. They are his last words, and though their meaning is not altogether clear to me, perhaps he was trying to say something to all of us at Pomona.

Let Harry have the last word:

> *Don't have to say*
> *Ave atque vale to either*
> *of you but as the Greeks*
> *put it, Cronia pola, many years to you;*
> *may they be happy and prosperous,*
> *and may all of us continue to enjoy the pleasure of your company*
> *Lost and wandering souls who*
> *had only found limbo in*
> *Claremont's groves of Academe.*

Dark Backward and Abysm of Time: A Case Study of Creativity
on the occasion of the first Honors Convocation
The University of Idaho. April 11, 1986

1543 is a milestone in the progress of ideas because that year saw the publication of two books of first importance: *The Fabric of the Human Body* by Vesalius, and *The Revolutions of the Celestial Spheres* by

Copernicus. They mark the beginnings of modern Anatomy and Astronomy. There are, however, great differences between them: one emphasizes detailed observation and experiment; the other shows that facts long taken for granted can be interpreted in an entirely new way. Vesalius supplied a wealth of fresh knowledge, but Copernicus contributed no new data at all; the crucial observations in astronomy were made later, by Brahe and Kepler. Copernicus didn't even offer a physical theory: Newton provided that nearly 150 years later. Although Copernicus believed his system to be simpler than the long accepted Ptolemaic one, he couldn't demonstrate that it was so, and its advantages were far from self evident.

It is important to note that Copernicus' title is not `The Revolution of the Celestial ' but `The Revolutions of the Celestial'. Everyone knew that the stars were not independent. You can see that they move together round a single axis, and the simplest way to explain this was to suppose that they were fixed to a sphere revolving once every 24 hours. Because the Sun, the Moon, and the planets move in similar ways, presumably they too must be fixed each on its own sphere. The evidence is so straightforward, and its interpretation had been so long accepted, that to question the conclusion seemed absurd. What Copernicus did – despite the title of his book – was take the movements away from the heavenly bodies and put them in the moving planet Earth. Even if the stars were at different distances from the Earth, everything would still appear the same as long as all of them were sufficiently far away. Copernicus banished the Earth from its central position, but just as importantly, he removed the basis for postulating the existence of the spheres. Perhaps he didn't fully realize it, but in one stroke he demolished the finite physical boundary of the universe.

In the 16th century the implications of Copernican theory struck at almost every aspect of human thought, from Astronomy and Physics to Theology and the interpretation of God's purpose. Today knowledge is so specialized that a change in one area can leave others untouched, and a revolution in world-view comparable to that wrought by Copernicus is unlikely to happen again. The discovery of the immensity of space, which was one consequence, rightly receives an important place in any intellectual history. The `discovery of time', on the other hand, has been curiously neglected by philosophers and historians of science.

My title, "What see'st thou else in the dark-backward and Abisme of Time?" is from Shakespeare's `Tempest': Prospero asks his daughter,

Miranda, what she remembers from her infancy, before she came to her island home. Like so many of Shakespeare's words, these have echoed down the ages, even when their source is forgotten. Milton, for example, speaks of "the dark unbottom'd infinite abyss", and Wordsworth of "Nature's dark abyss". Abysmal, incidentally, simply means unfathomable, as the bottomless pit.

A recent book, *The Dark Abyss of Time*, credits the phrase to Buffon. In his *Natural History*, published in 1779, Buffon wrote, with obvious emotion:

"What profound obscurity surrounds the time preceding written tradition! And even written history has transmitted only the chronicles of a few nations, the acts of a tiny part of the human race; the rest of mankind has become nothing for us or for posterity; they have passed like shadows which leave no trace behind; and how one wishes that the names of those would-be heroes, whose crimes or bloody glory we have remembered, had equally been entombed in the night of oblivion!"

[How reminiscent of Macbeth: "Out, out, brief candle! Life's but a walking shadow, a poor player, That struts and frets his hour upon the stage, And then is heard no more; it is a tale Told by an idiot, full of sound and fury, Signifying nothing."]

"We must pierce the night of time", said Buffon. "Only from knowledge of what is present can we establish those things that existed in ancient times but are now gone. In Civil History, we determine the epochs by consulting documents and deciphering old inscriptions; so, in Natural History, we must dig through the World's archives and extract ancient records from the bowels of the Earth. This is the only way that we can fix a few points in the immensity of space, and place some milestones along time's eternal road. The past is like distance: our view of it would shrink, and even vanish, if history and chronology hadn't placed lanterns or torches at the darkest points."

Thomas Carlyle, no scientist, but a genius at breathing life into the past, used some of the same images:

"So many things are hidden in that dead abyss of Past Time; only here and there a glimpse of actuality recoverable from the devouring night. And of these few the meaning and meanings are so hard to seize! A little row of Naphtha-lamps, with its line of Naphtha-light, burns clear and holy through the dead Night of the Past: they who are gone are still there; though hidden they are revealed, though dead they yet speak.

There it shines, that little miraculously lamp lit Pathway; shedding its feebler and feebler twilight into the boundless dark oblivion."

In classical times it was common knowledge that well-preserved marine shells could be found far from the shore, and many drew the obvious conclusion that much of what is now land had once been covered by the sea. This of course implied that the age of the Earth must be much greater than the extent of human history. Each person was at liberty to hold and express whatever views he chose. Geikie called this the "speculative freedom of the ancients". But that freedom ended when the Bible was interpreted as an accurate historical record. The earliest churchman to construct a Biblical time-scale was Eusebius, Bishop of Caesarea, who, sitting at the right hand of the Emperor Constantine, delivered the opening address at the Council of Nicaea in the year 325. Using the Biblical genealogies, he and St Jerome created a time-scale back to Adam.

In 1593 John More placed the birth of Christ at the year 3929 reckoning from Creation. In 1642 John Lightfoot, distinguished Hebrew scholar and Vice-Chancellor of Cambridge, computed that Creation began at `9 o'clock in the morning on September seventeenth'. But the best remembered authority is Archbishop James Ussher, Primate of Ireland, who in 1658★★ fixed the time as `the entrance of night' preceding the 23rd of October, 4004 B.C., and this date was introduced by Bishop Lloyd into his edition of the Authorized Version of the Bible in 1707. (★★*Ed. Note – this is the year of publication of the English translation of Ussher's famous Chronology, translated after his death.*)

During the Middle Ages it was believed that all history would consist of a `cosmic week', in which each `day' was a millennium, or 1,000 years, and that the last millennium would begin in the year 2000; so that, to quote Shakespeare's Rosalind, "The poor world is almost 6,000 years old". Scientists as well as theologians and poets believed this chronology. Kepler's acceptance of such an estimate for the age of the Earth is shown by his exclamation, in reference to his own work: `God has waited 6,000 years for an observer'. Indeed from his study of eclipses, Kepler concluded that there was an error of 4 years in the Biblical dating of the crucifixion, and this is why the date of Creation was subsequently taken as 4004 B.C.

Based on a passage in his *Novum Organum* of 1620, the claim is made that because Francis Bacon recognized similarities between Africa and

South America he conceived the modern theory of Continental Drift. But even Bacon was a prisoner in his own intellectual environment. If you know that the Earth is only a few thousand years old, you cannot conceive that the Atlantic could have opened – a process we now know took 200 million years.

Having observed that "a globe of iron an inch in diameter, exposed red-hot to the open air, will scarcely lose all its heat in an hour's time", Newton calculated that "a globe of iron equal to our Earth would scarcely cool in above 50,000 years". But despite this astute reasoning, even he accepted Hebrew chronology. In fact Newton's last work, on which he devoted great labor, was his *Chronology of the Ancient Kingdoms Amended*, published posthumously in 1728.

In 1779 Buffon, after repeating Newton's experiments, concluded that the Earth had taken 75,000 years to cool from a molten condition, and he expressed his belief that `the more we extend time, the closer we shall be to the truth'.

But it was James Hutton who finally broke the `time barrier'. In 1788, the year of Buffon's death, Hutton's *Theory of the Earth* was published by the Royal Society of Edinburgh. Three years earlier, because Hutton was ill, Joseph Black, read the paper to the Society for him. Black was both Professor of Chemistry and a practicing medical doctor. By discovering carbon dioxide he was the first to show that air is not an element, and his recognition of latent heat helped James Watt inaugurate the Industrial Revolution.

Black's opinion of Hutton's Theory is therefore of especial interest:

"In Dr Hutton's system", he said, "there is a grandeur and sublimity by which it far surpasses any that has been offered. The boundless pre-existence of time and of the operations of Nature which he brings into our View strikes us with astonishment. The mind is expanded in contemplating so great an Idea and the length of time which the Change thus imagined (I may say demonstrated) must have required; The short-lived bustle of Man's remotest reach of History or tradition appear as nothing when compared with an object so great."

Hutton's observations had convinced him that the present land had been built by processes that acted very slowly, and that operations now in action must ultimately destroy it. He recognized that an immense time was required for the total destruction of the land, but "Time", he said, "which is often deficient to our schemes, is to nature endless and as nothing."

Between the presentation of his paper in 1785 and its publication in 1788, Hutton collected crucial field evidence designed to test his Theory. At Siccar Point he found horizontal sandstones resting on the eroded edges of older upturned strata, exactly as he had predicted. His friend, John Playfair, Professor of Mathematics and Physics, who was with him, gives this vivid account of the Discovery of Time:

"On us who saw these phenomena for the first time, the impression made will not easily be forgotten. The palpable evidence presented to us, of one of the most extraordinary and important facts in the natural history of the earth, gave a reality and substance to those theoretical speculations, which, however probable, had never till now been directly authenticated by the testimony of the senses. We often said to ourselves, What clearer evidence could we have had of the different formation of these rocks, and of the long interval which separated their formation, had we actually seen them emerging from the bosom of the deep? We felt ourselves necessarily carried back to the time when the schistus on which we stood was yet at the bottom of the sea, and when the sandstone before us was only beginning to be deposited, in the shape of sand or mud, from the waters of a superincumbent ocean. An epoch still more remote presented itself, when even the most ancient of these rocks, instead of standing upright in vertical beds, lay in horizontal planes at the bottom of the sea, and was not yet disturbed by that immeasurable force which has burst asunder the solid pavement of the globe. Revolutions still more remote appeared in the distance of this extraordinary perspective. The mind seemed to grow giddy by looking so far into the abyss of time; and while we listened with earnestness and admiration to the philosopher who was now unfolding to us the order and series of these wonderful events, we became sensible how much further reason may sometimes go than imagination may venture to follow."

"Hutton's genius", according to Zittel, "first gave to geology the conception of calm, inexorable nature working little by little – by the rain-drop, by the stream, by insidious decay, by slow waste, by the life and death of organized creatures, and eventually accomplishing surface transformations on a scale more gigantic than was ever imagined in the philosophy of the ancients or the learning of the Schools. And it is not too much to say that the Huttonian principle of the value of small increments of change has had a beneficial, suggestive, and far-reaching influence not only on geology but on all the natural sciences. The generation after Hutton applied it to palaeontology, and thus paved the way for Darwin's still broader, biological conceptions upon the same basis."

Sir Charles Lyell, born the year that Hutton died, recognized that "Hutton laboured to give fixed principles to geology, as Newton had succeeded in doing for astronomy", and Lyell expressed his own indebtedness by placing the following quotation from Playfair's `Illustrations of the Huttonian Theory' on the title page of his immensely influential book, *The Principles of Geology* in 1830:

"Amid all the revolutions of the globe the economy of Nature has been uniform, and her laws are the only things that have resisted the general movement. The rivers and the rocks, the seas and the continents have been changed in all their parts; but the laws which direct those changes, and the rules to which they are subject, have remained invariably the same."

This remarkable statement is a definition of uniformitarianism, a concept often misinterpreted. Geology was the first historical science; biology, thanks to Darwin, was the second; and atomic theory followed after the demonstration of radioactive transmutations. Now it is commonplace to talk about the relative ages and evolutionary sequence of the stars. But Physics, with its fundamental constants and rigorous laws, seemed to stand apart.

Roemer determined the first universal constant, the velocity of light, in 1676 by timing the occultations of the satellites of Jupiter. The second was the gravitational constant (not measured for a century after Newton defined it). The charge and mass of the electron, and Planck's constant are among the others. In 1937, however, Paul Dirac argued that the so-called `constant' of gravity must decrease with time, and Toulmin and Goodfield have pointed out that if Planck's constant increased with time the famous `red-shift' could be accounted for, and the apparent recession of the galaxies would be an illusion. Perhaps only the form of the `laws' resists the general change!

The lucid expositions of Playfair and Lyell popularized Hutton's discovery of the magnitude of time. Geikie said, "Astronomy had made known the immeasurable fields of space; the new science of geology seemed now to reveal boundless distances of time". Carlyle's friend John Sterling expressed it more emotionally: "Lyell's Geology gives one the same sort of bewildering view of the abysmal extent of Time that

Astronomy does of Space". But Hutton himself had written: "The abyss from which the man of science should recoil is that of ignorance."

The first volume of Lyell's `Principles' appeared in time for Darwin to take a copy on the Voyage of the Beagle, during which many of his ideas took shape. Darwin said later: "I always feel as if my books come half out of Lyell's brain, and that I never acknowledge this sufficiently".

As this, the concept of evolution in the organic world was preceded by its demonstration in the physical. Lyell's `Principles' begins with this definition:

"Geology is the science which investigates the successive changes that have taken place in the organic and inorganic kingdoms of nature; it inquires into the causes of these changes, and the influence which they have exerted in modifying the surface and external structure of our planet".

Darwin's tribute in the *Origin of Species* of 1859 is simple and direct:

"He who can read Sir Charles Lyell's grand work on the Principles of Geology, which the future historian will recognize as having produced a revolution in natural science, and yet does not admit how vast have been the periods of time, may at once close this volume."

Today, when even children learn that the age of the Earth is measured in billions of years, it takes mental effort to realize how great was the genius of Hutton, who 200 years ago saw clearly that this "living Earth" has a history long enough for mountains to be worn away by the weather, and slowly raised again, forming what he called "a succession of worlds". Stephen Jay Gould put it well when he said:

"Geology has no more important lesson to teach than the vastness of time. We have no trouble getting across our conclusions intellectually – 4.5 billion years rolls easily off the tongue as an age for the earth. But intellectual knowledge and gut reaction are very different things."

James Hutton was born in Edinburgh, where he spent most of his life, and where he died. It was a small and rather isolated city, with a population of about 60,000, but its inhabitants included men of great breadth of interest, who were able, moreover, to learn from one another. Hutton was an innovative farmer, who wrote a textbook on the principles of agriculture. He was an industrial chemist, the first commercial producer of ammonium chloride in Europe. He took an active part in the project of constructing a canal between the cities of

Edinburgh and Glasgow. He wrote on meteorology and philosophy, on the Chinese language and the economics of coal. His closest friends included the chemist Joseph Black (who was acknowledged as `master' by Lavoisier) and Adam Smith, (Professor of Literature, Commissioner of the Excise, and founder of Economics). Black and Hutton were Adam Smith's trustees, just as Smith and Black had been the trustees of their friend, the philosopher and historian, David Hume.

Other friends included: Adam Ferguson, chaplain to the Black Watch regiment at the Battle of Fontenoy, Professor of Philosophy and Professor of Physics, who wrote `The History of Civil Society' – one of the first building stones of Sociology; Daniel Rutherford, Sir Walter Scott's father-in-law, and Professor of Botany, who discovered nitrogen; William Robertson, Principal of the University for 30 of its most distinguished years, and minister of the Church, who was acknowledged by Edward Gibbon as one of the most eminent of historians; and John Clerk, whose essay on Naval Tactics changed world history when Nelson put its principles to practice at the battle of Trafalgar.

In his biography of Hutton, Playfair tells us:

Dr Hutton "used regularly to unbend himself with a few friends, in the little society usually known by the name of the Oyster Club. The original members of it were Mr Smith, Dr Black, and Dr Hutton, and round them was soon formed a knot of those who knew how to value the familiar and social converse of these illustrious men. As all the three possessed great talents, enlarged views, and extensive information, without any of the stateliness and formality which men of letters think it sometimes necessary to affect; as they were all three easily amused; were equally prepared to speak and to listen; and as the sincerity of their friendship had never been darkened by the least shade of envy; it would be hard to find an example, where every thing favourable to good society was more perfectly united, and every thing adverse more entirely excluded. The conversation was always free, often scientific, but never didactic or disputatious; and as this club was much the resort of the strangers who visited Edinburgh, from any object connected with art or with science, it derived from thence an extraordinary degree of variety and interest."

The University Honors Program on this campus claims to offer the following benefits to those who participate in it:

The challenge of broadening one's intellectual horizons.

Small classes taught in discussion format by specially selected faculty members.

A chance to make friends and exchange ideas with talented peers.

I have described Hutton's fertile intellectual environment so that you may recognize similarities between it and the Program that is the reason we are called together today.

Playfair remarked: "It would be desirable to trace the progress of Dr Hutton's mind in the formation of a system where so many new and enlarged views of nature occur, and where so much originality is displayed." But how can anyone hope to follow the sequence of ideas that unconsciously have been at work in a creative mind? The classic answer was given by John Livingston Lowes in his study of the process of creation in the mind of Coleridge. Taking advantage of a notebook in which Coleridge had recorded whatever caught his attention; Lowes followed him through his reading, so "retracing the obliterated vestiges of creation". The origin of almost every phrase and metaphor is identified; and the sources form quite an assortment.

Many readers have smiled at Coleridge's ignorance of astronomy, so flagrantly displayed in this stanza from the `Ancient Mariner', published in 1798:

> *From the sails the dew did drip –*
> *Till clomb above the eastern bar*
> *The horned Moon, with one bright star*
> *Within the nether tip.*

Frederick Pottle, for instance, referred to "the horror of that moon with its impossible star". But in a paper published by the Royal Society, Coleridge had read that "a Star appear'd below the Body of the Moon within the Horns of it". Another paper with the memorable title "The appearance of light, like a star, seen in the dark part of the Moon", was published only four years before the `Ancient Mariner' by no less a person than the Astronomer Royal. And in 1787 the renowned astronomer William Herschel, fresh from his discovery of the planet Uranus, published an account of what appeared to be three active volcanoes in the Moon. The number of papers being published on what are now called `Transient Lunar Phenomena' shows that the subject is still of great interest.

Coleridge himself was well aware of the creative process: "the imagination, the true inward creatrix", constantly working on the "shattered fragments of memory, dissolves, diffuses, dissipates, in order to recreate." He wrote elsewhere that the "hooks-and-eyes of memory permit a confluence of our recollections." His analogy parallels Poincare's image of mathematical discovery, in which he pictures ideas as hooked atoms ploughing through space like molecules in the kinetic theory of gases. The number of possible combinations is so vast that even in a lifetime they couldn't all be examined, and Poincare concluded that esthetic sensibility, the appreciation of the beauty of an elegant solution, acts in the subconscious like a delicate sieve to catch the combinations worthy of the attention of the conscious mind. Thus the creation of a poem and the discovery of a mathematical law may have much in common. Perhaps a geological theory is born in the same manner.

A century ago that giant of American geology, Grove Karl Gilbert, elaborated this theme in two masterly presidential addresses: *The Inculcation of Scientific Method by Example* and *The Origin of Hypotheses*. He wrote:

"Just as in the domain of matter nothing is created from nothing, just as in the domain of life there is no spontaneous generation, so in the domain of mind there are no ideas which do not owe their existence to antecedent ideas which stand in the relation of parent to child. It is only because our mental processes are largely conducted outside of consciousness that the lineage of ideas is difficult to trace. To explain the origin of hypotheses," wrote Gilbert, "I have a hypothesis to present. It is that hypotheses are always suggested through analogy. Consequential relations of nature are infinite in variety, and he who is acquainted with the largest number has the broadest base for the analogic suggestion of hypotheses."

To devise a hypothesis one needs: an excellent memory, and an extensive knowledge of the relevant material; the ability to form associations of ideas, and to reason by analogy; and the possession of an unusually high degree of esthetic feeling for an elegant solution, and a burning enthusiasm for the subject.

Hutton, we are told, possessed "the experienced eye, the power of perceiving the minute differences and fine analogies which discriminate or unite the objects of science, and the readiness of comparing new phenomena with others already treasured up in the mind." His M.D. thesis was on 'The Circulation of the Blood in the Microcosm'; his contribution to Geology was the demonstration of circulation of matter in the macrocosm.

"A circumstance which greatly distinguished his intellectual character", said Playfair, "was an uncommon activity and ardour of mind, upheld by the greatest admiration of whatever in science was new, beautiful, or sublime." Hutton and Black were both "formed with minds inventive and fertile in new combinations".

These are qualities apparently essential to creative genius. Is it not our duty to cultivate them through liberal education?

In his book the *Firmament of Time*, Loren Eisley gave his evaluation of Hutton:

"Time and raindrops! It took enormous effort to discover the potentialities of both those forces. It took centuries before the faint trickling from cottage eaves and gutters caught the ear of some inquiring scholar. Men who could visualize readily the horrors of a universal Flood were deaf to the roar of an invisible Niagara falling into the rain barrel outside their window. They couldn't hear it because they lived in a time span so short that the only way geological change could be effected was by the convulsions of earthquakes, or the forty torrential days and nights that brought the Biblical Deluge. James Hutton had come upon the secret of the relatively perpetual youth of the planet."

With the development of the new paradigm of plate tectonics it has become common to display a certain arrogance and belittle the contributions of Hutton and other pioneers. The last sentences of a new book, *The Dark Side of the Earth*, are these:

"What Earth scientist would wish to spend years compiling an accurate and detailed map of one small region? Yet just as Natural History continued to survive after Darwin, so parts of the old Geology no longer considered suitably scientific will be sustained through the amateur. The creation of the Earth Sciences has broken the pattern that allowed Geology to survive informal and unhurried for more than a century. With the loss of the older science there will also go the expert whose knowledge consists of the ability to name a plethora of fossils, minerals, and identify the stratal age; all these skills are denigrated in the new overviews of the Earth scientist involved in laboratory work or indirect geophysical mapping. Thus as the science gains a greater appreciation of the whole planet so it loses the joyous intimacy with the landscape that came from the purposelessness of summer fieldwork and winter walks along the seashore, an intimacy that lies at the very heart of Hutton's philosophy of Geology. It is the passing of an era: through becoming scientific, the old Geology, that was so framed according to the poetic and irrational measure of man, is now, in the new technological Earth Sciences, in danger of losing its soul."

Unlike that writer, I see Geophysics and Geochemistry only as tools for the study of the composition and structure of the Earth, and for helping us understand its evolution. Hutton, more than anyone else, convinced us that small causes and slow movements, continuing over immense periods of time, can produce great effects. Hutton's Theory has withstood the test of time; it is essential to the paradigm of plate tectonics.

I close with these words from Carlyle's *Historical Sketches*:

"The loom of time: O, though cultivated reader, hast thou ever contemplated in thy soul the thing called Time, and yet sayest thou that the age of Miracles has ceased?"

Dedication of the
Timken Science Library
The College of Wooster, Ohio
October 17, 1998

President Hales, Members of the Board of Trustees, Faculty, Staff, and Friends of the College of Wooster: It is a privilege and great pleasure to join with you in dedicating the Timken Science Library – the oldest and newest building on campus. The heart of a College is its Library; there we store a rich treasury of accumulated knowledge, making it available to successive generations.

The *New Yorker* recently conveyed the excitement of one of the world's greatest libraries. The Vatican collection was started in 1451 by a Pope who believed that "reviving classical antiquity would usher in a golden age". He attempted "to buy, copy, or even steal" every manuscript that had survived the Dark Ages.

We, too, have the duty to build and preserve our collections. To do this, co-operation may be essential. An early President of Pomona

College envisioned a group of Colleges sharing library resources, and I congratulate Wooster on uniting the catalog of its library with those of several neighbors. From my home in Scotland I found your Consort system superior to online catalogs of many better known libraries.

Facts! To build a house, one must first provide bricks; and with so many wonderful facts to discover, why waste time on fiction? As a student at Edinburgh University, I learned *facts*. The curriculum was so prescribed that science students weren't admitted even to classes in the history or philosophy of science. My first year was Mathematics, Physics, and Chemistry to be the foundation for all that followed. The next three years were devoted to Chemistry along with Geology, a novel subject suggested by a fellow student. We learned more facts.

One day I asked the geology instructor a question. Although the question is long-forgotten, I will always remember the answer: "What", he asked, "do *you* think?" I learned later that two short words encapsulate the Enlightenment: sapere aude – "dare to think".

Laboratory experiments are done under controlled conditions: we maintain constant temperature or use platinum crucibles that won't take part in the reactions. But Nature doesn't simplify, and laymen ask questions that professional geologists can't answer. This world is full of questions waiting to be asked!

Years later, on inheriting my father's books, I remembered long-ignored advice: "If you don't read when you are young, you won't be able to re-read favorites when you are older". My attention was first taken by Saintsbury's introductions to his 1893 edition of Fielding's novels. Saintsbury said *Tom Jones* is "the science of life … As you turn the pages, the long silent world becomes alive again". I learned that the characters in these novels are not less real because they are fictional; skilfully dissecting their brains and hearts, Fielding shows us their hidden workings.

Through Saintsbury, too, I met Edward Gibbon, whose fact-filled *Decline and Fall of the Roman Empire* was published in that eventful year 1776. Gibbon declared: "The Romance of Tom Jones, that exquisite picture of human nature, will outlive the palace of the Spanish kings and the Imperial Eagle of the House of Austria". Gibbon was right: Tom Jones has indeed outlived both! Pity, then, the Duke of Gloucester, whose fame rests on these immortal words: "Another damned, thick, square book! Always scribble, scribble, scribble! Eh! Mr Gibbon".

Do you know Jocelin of Brakelond? Unlike Tom Jones, Jocelin was a real person of flesh and blood, with human feelings and sense of humor. In his diary, the monk Jocelin tells us how King John, who signed Magna Charta, visited the Abbey of St Edmundsbury – the King passed so close that Jocelin almost touched him! Jocelin tells us about the intrigue, lobbying, and rumour attendant on the appointment of a new Abbot. Here, if anywhere, are authentic, first-hand *facts* recorded 700 years ago. Yet "Jocelin recounts what interests *him*; [he is] entirely deaf to *us*".

You can read his diary – in its original Latin with English translation on facing pages, or in Thomas Carlyle's inspired account in *The Ancient Monk*, where Jocelin seems to live again – speaking to us over the centuries. Better still make a pilgrimage, as I did, to the once great Abbey and read Jocelin's words within its ruins.

And who can forget the opening chapter of *Barchester Towers*? The Archdeacon kneels at the dying Bishop's bed, knowing that his chance of being appointed successor depends on whether the old man dies before the imminent assumption of power by a new Government. Trollope makes us kneel and experience the Archdeacon's anguish.

I remember how, some years ago, Pomona College appointed a new Dean and then a new President. Having read Jocelin on the election of an Abbot, Trollope on the appointment of a Bishop, and C.P. Snow on the election of the Master of a College, I was better prepared to understand how people react at such times; human nature changes little over the centuries.

Dickens put the first words of *Hard Times* into the mouth of Mr Thomas Gradgrind: "Now, what I want is Facts. Teach these boys and girls nothing but Facts. Facts alone are wanted in life". But Dickens knew that every so-called historical "fact" has been selected by passage through successive filters. The other day I wrote to an old friend, reminding him of happy experiences shared in Edinburgh fifty years ago. But, quoting from his contemporary diary, my friend showed that my recollected chronology was incorrect. In order to spend several months in Scotland, immediately after the War, he had been forced to leave his wife and new-born daughter at home in Germany; in many ways his retrospective view differed from mine. If we can be in error about events personally experienced, what confidence should we have in records passed to us by others whose motives are unknown?

How, then, can we possibly know what happened before there were observers to leave records? The unexpected answer is that the Earth has written its own biography – selective, of course, and with gaps in the story.

Rocks exposed to the atmosphere disintegrate and decompose, and under the ever-present action of gravity, the waste is carried to lower levels, to accumulate, layer upon layer, as stratified rocks like sandstone and limestone. Once consolidated, these rocks are uplifted by forces within the Earth to form new land. Like detectives, we decipher the history of our planet from the nature of the rocks and their superposed sequence.

A year ago I helped celebrate James Hutton's life on the bicentennial of his death. Hutton, more than anyone else, laid the foundation of geology by showing how to read Earth's autobiography. It had been thought that the Earth was a few thousand years old, but Hutton opened our eyes to the fact that it was a million times older than that! Geology was the first historical science, and Hutton's understanding of 'deep time' allowed his successors to discover that, in the words of Nobel laureate George Wald: "We live in a historical universe, one in which not only living organisms but stars and galaxies are born, mature, grow old and die".

When I was young, a controversy, fuelled by the inadequacy of facts, raged about the origin of granite. I was therefore despatched to Switzerland to spend a year with Professor Wegmann, a respected authority. That he refused even to discuss the subject proved a blessing in disguise; for his publications were all collected in the library, and studying them, I discovered that his work stood on a foundation inherited from his teacher and predecessor, Emile Argand, whose publications were also there. Argand's papers in turn led me to the publications of his teacher, Maurice Lugeon, whose papers, also conveniently collected, included his classic monograph of 1900 on the structure of the Alps. So I returned to Scotland ignorant about granite but ready to advance the study of the structure of the Scottish Highlands.

More importantly, I had learned a new way of research, which I have used and advocated ever since. When plate tectonics was first debated, I encouraged students to study key papers as if the authors were present for cross-examination. When these authorities quoted assertions of others, our motto was, as Dickens put it: "What the soldier said is not evidence". These secondary and tertiary sources were summoned from the library for examination.

To this procedure I owe appointments to National Lectureships so diverse as on plate tectonics for the American Association of Petroleum Geologists; on X-ray fluorescence and Martian rocks for Sigma Xi; and on language as a tool of thought for the Association for Computing Machinery.

Today I want to emphasize the importance of understanding the historical *context* before making *judgements*; and for this the library is likely to be our first and principal resource. The journal *Isis* is devoted to the history and cultural influences of science. I would rather refer to the influence of cultural background *on* science.

Sir Hermann Bondi, is a practical man: Chief Scientific Adviser to the Ministry of Defence, Chief Scientist of the Department of Energy, and Master of Churchill College. He advocates that science should be taught as a liberal arts subject, not as the entry to a profession.

Celebrating the 300th anniversary of the *Principia*'s publication, Bondi argued that Newton's genius was his selection of *solvable* problems. Newton solved the two-body problem: the gravitational interaction between the Sun and a planet. The three-body problem (Sun, Earth, Jupiter) can be solved only by computer simulation. Because Newton believed that the cosmic time-scale was only a few thousand years, he ignored the possibility of collisions resulting from perturbations of planetary orbits over millions of years. We, however, were privileged to witness a comet collide with Jupiter in 1994.

Changing the angle that Earth's axis is tilted from the plane of Earth's orbit would catastrophically alter the seasons, and we know today that over periods of time inconceivable to Newton, the obliquities of the planets do undergo chaotic (i.e. unpredictable) changes. The large size of the Moon has, fortunately for us, stabilized Earth's tilt at a convenient angle!

A century ago Lord Kelvin made a gigantic error in underestimating the Earth's age. From experiments on the cooling of hot spheres, Kelvin concluded that the Earth was fifty thousand years old. But Darwin and other geologists, following Hutton, argued that the evidence of rocks and fossils showed that Kelvin's figure was far too small. Kelvin challenged anyone to find an error in his arithmetic, but his error was assuming that the Earth had no internal source of heat. He hadn't allowed for radioactivity, which Becquerel discovered in 1896! Poor Kelvin!

It was not until 1904, however, that it was known that radioactivity generates heat. Moreover, such a distinguished physicist as Sir William Crookes believed, wrongly, not only that pressure within the Earth would prevent radioactive decay, but that the radioactivity of rocks is only surface fallout from the Sun. In 1907, the year before Kelvin's death, it was proved that radioactive elements were indeed original constituents of the rocks in which they are found. Don't blame Kelvin for ignoring facts that weren't yet known!

For Hutton's bicentennial, I wrote an essay on his *Historical, Social, and Political Background*. In it, I correct revisionists who mistakenly claim that Hutton was an impractical theorist, more influenced by religion than by observation of rocks. Hutton was Adam Smith's friend and executor, and one of the principal figures of the Scottish Enlightenment. To treat him narrowly as a geologist is a gross distortion. Just a week ago, the Principal of a Scottish University commented on my essay approvingly: "Science", he said "has a human face if only scientists were not so shy or fixated on objectivity to show it. The Age of Reason and Enlightenment was a wonderful thing. It is a pity that in the end it solidified into a reductionist view of the world, including us. So now I campaign", he said, as Hutton did, "for the holistic view of the world".

Scientia et Religio: Ex Uno Fonte – Knowledge and Reverence come from a common source. The College motto could have been Hutton's. God looked at the Earth and saw that it was good. Hutton agreed. "It would be absurd", he said, "to suppose anything but wisdom could have designed this system of the Earth".

Revisionists, of course, condemn Hutton for appealing to the *Argument from Design* when he wrote: "the matter of this active world is perpetually moved, in that salutary circulation by which provision is so wisely made for the growth and prosperity of plants, and for the life and comfort of its various animals". Newton, however, viewed the machinery of the Solar System in much the same way that Hutton did the Earth: "This most beautiful system of the sun, planets, and comets," Newton wrote, "could only proceed from the counsel and dominion of an intelligent and powerful Being".

It is increasingly recognised by scientists that life on Earth is possible only because of the coincidence of many apparently unrelated facts – too many to recount here. Most of the chemical elements making up our bodies and the rocks we live upon are star dust, produced in the death throes of a star a generation older than the Sun. The Universe's vast size and age are prerequisites for our being here.

Cosmologists have concluded that the existence of life has required the Universe to be "fine tuned" in astonishing detail. For example, had the expansion rate been either faster or slower than by a decimal point followed by 60 zeroes and a 1, then galaxies would not have formed. Recognition of coincidences like this fascinates professional cosmologists and philosophers, such as the authors of *The Accidental Universe*, *Cosmic Coincidences*, and *The Anthropic Cosmological Principle* all here in our library. Although only proponents of the strong form of the anthropic principle argue that these coincidences are evidence of a purposeful designer, the theme is of great interest, as shown by titles like *God and the New Physics*, *The Mind of God*, and *Cosmos & Theos*.

In the past month two new publications focus directly on the connection between cosmology and religion: *Conversations with Religious Cosmologists,* from the California Academy of Sciences; and *The exhilarating connection between Science & Religion*, reviewed in *Science* by Mark Richardson of the Berkeley Center for Theology and the Natural Sciences. We should hesitate before dismissing Hutton, who, 200 years ago, described the Earth as "a world contrived in consummate wisdom; a world peculiarly adapted to the purposes of man".

I adhere to the view that science is an education of the mind rather than a professional training. Like the late, often misunderstood Enoch Powell, I deplore the heresy that education must be useful, with its evil corollary that education is to be judged by the economic well-being it produces, or even by the number of published papers that result.

With those who have given this splendid science library to the College of Wooster, I share the belief that "Education is a Good Thing because man has an insatiable appetite to learn and to understand, and because prominent among the joys that console him on his earthly journey is the joy of communicating to others, and especially to the young, what he has learned and understood, and, even more, how he managed to come by that learning and understanding. Like all things joyous, beautiful and good, education is self-justified."

May all who support and use this Library share that joy, combining Reverence and Knowledge.

The Immortal Memory
honouring Robert Burns, (1759-1796)
Scotland's national poet.
at St John's Kirk's Burns Supper, January, 1994.

Auld Acquaintance is not forgotten at St John's Kirk! Our family remembers how you carried Ewen, in his wheelchair, up to Kirk House in 1990; and we are grateful that you have invited us back each year since then.

During the War, and in its aftermath, there were no Burns Suppers. The first I attended was at the Perth Burns Club in 1990, when the Immortal Memory was proposed by that master orator and poet, our friend David Ogston. His theme, and I shall long remember it, was *The Twa Dogs*. He captivated our attention by his sensitive appreciation of this, the first poem in the Kilmarnock Edition.

Following in his footsteps I could take the second Kilmarnock poem – a Scottish paraphrase of a text from Proverbs 31. In the Version authorized by James VI:

7. Give strong drink unto him that is ready to perish, and wine unto those that be of heavy hearts.

8. Let him drink and forget his poverty, and remember his misery no more.

However, in Perth there are others better qualified to speak on this text!

In *The Art of Reading*, Sir Arthur Quiller-Couch wrote: "My first piece of advice on reading the Bible is that you do it."

I am reminded of Dr Johnson's reflection: "Let every man be sensible how small a part of his time is employed in talking – or thinking – about any of the most celebrated men that have ever lived. Let this be extracted and compressed; into what a narrow space will it go!"

Now nothing would please me more than to think you might leave tonight wanting to re-read Burns for yourselves. I am grateful that David Ogston did that for me in 1990!

Let's begin with a poem Burns wrote in 1775, when he was 16. Just some verses; for tonight time won't allow complete poems!

Note how he makes single adjectives conjure up such vivid images.

> *Now westlin winds and slaught'ring guns*
> *Bring Autumn's pleasant weather;*
> *The moorcock springs on whirring wings*
> *Amang the blooming heather:*
> *Now waving grain, wide oer the plain,*
> *Delights the weary farmer;*
> *An the moon shines bright, as I rove by night,*
> *To muse upon my charmer.*
>
> *The paitrick lo'es the fruitfu fells,*
> *The plover lo'es the mountains:*
> *The woodcock haunts the lonely dells,*
> *The soaring hern the fountains:*
> *Thro lofty groves the cushat roves,*
> *The path o man to shun it;*
> *The hazel bush o'erhangs the thrush,*
> *The spreading thorn the linnet.*
>
> *Thus evry kind their pleasures find,*
> *The savage and the tender;*
> *Some social join, and leagues combine,*
> *Some solitary wander:*
> *Avaunt, away, the cruel sway!*
> *Tyrannic man's dominion!*
> *The sportsman's joy, the murd'ring cry,*
> *The fluttring, gory pinion!*
> *The fluttring, gory pinion!*

What economy of expression in the double adjectives of the last line! What depth of sympathy for the falling bird!

It was Carlyle's opinion that "No poet of any age or nation is more graphic than Burns – three lines from his hand, and we have a likeness." (p.15)

His feeling for unfortunate fellow-creatures is seen again in The Wounded Hare:

Inhuman man! curse on thy barb'rous art,
And, blasted by thy murder-aiming eye,
May never pity soothe thee with a sigh,
Nor never pleasure glad thy cruel heart!

Go live, poor wanderer of the wood and field,
   The bitter little of life that remains!
   No more the thickening brakes and verdant plains
To thee shall home, or food, or pastime yield.

Seek, mangled wretch, some place of wonted rest,
   No more of rest, but now thy dying-bed!
   The sheltering rushes whistling o'er thy head,
The cold earth with thy bloody bosom prest.

Oft as by winding Nith, I, musing, wait
   The sober eve, or hail the cheerful dawn,
   I'll miss thee sporting o'er the dewy lawn,
And curse the ruffian's aim, and mourn thy hapless fate.

"*The Wounded Hare*", said Carlyle, "has not perished without its memorial; a balm of mercy yet breaths on us from its dumb agonies, because a poet was there." (p.14)

On a Winter Night he thinks of the ourie cattle and the silly sheep, suffering in the storm (Carlyle, p.20).

When biting Boreas, fell and doure,
Sharp shivers thro the leafless bow'r;
When Phoebus gies a short-liv'd glow'r
   Far south the lift,
Dim-dark'ning thro the flaky show'r
   Or whirling drift.

I thought me on the ourie cattle,
Or silly sheep, wha bide this brattle
   O winter war,
And thro the drift, deep-lairing, sprattle
   Beneath a scaur.

Ilk happing bird, – wee helpless thing! -
That in the merry months o spring,
Delighted me to hear thee sing,
   What comes o thee?
Whare wilt thou cow'r thy chittering wing,
   An close thy e'e?

A single word in the *Epistle to William Simpson* paints a bloody picture of horror and carnage as our fathers fought for their freedom, and ours. (Carlyle, p.17)

> *At Wallace' name, what Scottish blood*
> *But boils up in a spring-tide flood?*
> *Oft have our fearless fathers strode*
> > *By Wallace' side*
> *Still pressing onward, red-wat-shod,*
> > *Or gloriously dy'd!*

Asked in what the excellence of Burns consisted, Carlyle answered: "His Sincerity, his indisputable air of Truth gives him the power of making all subjects interesting" (p.9). So kind and warm a soul; so full of love to all living and lifeless things! His heart flows out in sympathy over Universal nature; and in her bleakest provinces discerns a beauty and a meaning! (p.7)

Think of *To a Mouse*; *To a Mountain Daisy*; and the *Address to the Deil* – all in the Kilmarnock Edition. "The very Devil he cannot hate with right orthodoxy!" (p.20)

Observe him chiefly as he mingles with his brother men! In 1786 Burns met the 23-year old Lord Daer, second son of the Earl of Selkirk, at Professor Dugald Stewart's country home near Mauchline.

> *This wot ye all whom it concerns:*
> *I Rhymer Rab, alias Burns,*
> > *October twenty-third,*
> *A ne'er-to-be-forgotten day,*
> *Sae far I sprackld up the brae,*
> > *I dinnerd wi a Lord.*
>
> *I watchd [for] the symptoms o the Great -*
> *The gentle pride, the lordly state,*
> > *The arrogant assuming:*
> *The fient a pride, nae pride had he,*
> *Nor sauce, nor state, that I could see,*
> > *Mair than an honest ploughman!*
>
> *Then from his Lordship I shall learn,*
> *Henceforth to meet with unconcern*
> > *One rank as weel's another;*
> *Nae honest, worthy man need care*
> *To meet with noble, youthfu Daer,*
> > *For he but meets a brother.*
>
> . . . . .

For a' that, an a' that,
The man o independent mind,
He looks an laughs at a' that.

The Epistle to Dr. Blacklock:

I hae a wife and twa wee laddies;
They maun hae brose and brats o duddies:
Ye ken yoursels my heart right proud is -
I need na vaunt -
But I'll sned bisoms, thraw saugh woodies,
Before they want.

Lord help me thro this warld o care!
I'm weary-sick o't late and air!
Not but I hae a richer share
Than monie ithers;
But why should ae man better fare,
An a' men brithers?

. . .

To make a happy fireside clime
To weans and wife,
That's the true pathos and sublime
Of human life.

He tells James Smith he thinks of publishing:

Just now I've taen the fit o rhyme,
My barmie noddle's working prime,
My fancy yerkit up sublime,
Wi hasty summon:
Hae ye a leisure-moment's time
To hear what's comin?

Some rhyme a neebor's name to lash,
Some rhyme (vain thought!) for needfu cash;
Some rhyme to court the countra clash,
An raise a din;
For me, an aim I never fash:
I rhyme for fun.

This while my notion's taen a sklent,
To try my fate in guid, black prent.

When the Kilmarnock Edition was published in 1786, Burns was in desperate straits – he was forced to hide from the bloodhounds of the law that James Armour had set upon him. But Professor Dugald Stewart's reception and Dr Blacklock's response to the Kilmarnock edition encouraged him to go to Edinburgh in the hope of publishing an expanded edition of his poems.

Burns arrived in Edinburgh just a month after meeting Lord Daer. His conversation and manly bearing took the city by storm. Nine days later he wrote:

"I am in a fair way of becoming as eminent as Thomas Aquinas or John Bunyan; and you may expect henceforth to see my birthday inserted among the wonderful events in the Almanac. The Earl of Glencairn and Mr Henry Erskine have taken me under their wing; and by all probability I shall soon be the 10th Worthy and the 8th Wise man of the World."

The Earl's brother was married to Lady Isabella, whose brothers were the Earl of Buchan, Henry Erskine (Leader of the Scottish Bar and Master of Canongate Kilwinning Lodge) and Tom Erskine (Lord Chancellor and Leader of the English Bar). Henry Erskine introduced Burns to notables such as the Judge Lord Monboddo, and the Duchess of Gordon. Burns was immediately received into the hearts of every level of Society.

William Creech, who had been tutor to the Earl of Glencairn invited subscriptions for the new edition – which he published in April 1787, and the Members of the Caledonian Hunt, "one and all", subscribed. Henry Mackenzie, to whom Scott later dedicated Waverley called him "this heaven-taught ploughman".

In 1788 there was a sensation in Edinburgh when it was discovered that Deacon Brodie, one of its most prominent citizens, led a dual life being a burglar by night. He is the original of Stevenson's Dr Jekyll and Mr Hyde.

Henry Erskine, who defended him, objected to a witness being called; a man already convicted of a felony in England. When the Prosecution produced a Royal pardon, Henry Erskine made the following statement – duly recorded by William Creech (Burns' publisher), who was a member of the Jury, and who quickly published an account of the trial:

"It appears a most extraordinary doctrine: that the King's pardon restored the credibility of the person pardoned. I have heard that the

King could create a Peer, but that he could not create a Gentleman; much less could he make a hardened villain an honest man."

> *For a' that, an a' that,*
> > *Our toils obscure, an a' that,*
> *The rank is but the guinea's stamp, -*
> > *The man's the gowd for a' that.*

> *A prince can mak a belted knight,*
> > *A marquis, duke, and a' that!*
> *But an honest man's aboon his might -*
> > *Guid faith, he mauna fa' that!*

In 1789 Burns wrote to Dr. Blacklock telling him that he had become an Exciseman:

> *But what d'ye think, my trusty fier?*
> *I'm turn'd a gauger – Peace be here!*
> *Parnassian queires, I fear, I fear,*
> > *Ye'll now disdain me,*
> *And then my fifty pounds a year*
> > *Will little gain me!*

That July the Bastille fell. The French Revolution had begun, and the watchwords were Liberty, Equality, and Fraternity!

Thomas Paine (another Exciseman) published *The Rights of Man* in 1791 and 1792. Although defended by Tom Erskine, he was convicted of high treason. Burns wrote:

> *While Europe's eye is fix'd on mighty things,*
> *The fate of empires and the fall of kings:*
> *While quacks of State must each produce his plan,*
> *And even children lisp the Rights of Man;*
> *Amid this mighty fuss just let me mention,*
> *The Rights of Woman merit some attention.*

The poem was published in the Edinburgh Gazeteer, whose editor and printer were afterwards imprisoned. Burns could have been in trouble!

In December (1792) the Convention of The Friends of the People met in Edinburgh, calling for "A full, free, and equal representation of the people." And the vote for all males over the age of 21!

The delegates called each other Citizen, and the proceedings closed with the oath "to live free or die". As Burns put it: Let us do, or dee!

Burns was dangerously Politically Incorrect, giving extempore toasts that often had ambiguous or seditious overtones:

Freedom, Reform, and the People.

The last verse of the last chapter of the last book of Kings:

The King: His private worth it is altogether impossible such a man as I can appreciate.

May our success in the present war be equal to the justice of our cause.

He sent four carronades (from a smugglers ship) to Paris, but they were impounded at Dover and an enquiry into his loyalty began!

A month later, 1 February 1793, France declared War, and repressive trials for sedition began in Edinburgh.

Thomas Muir had distributed Thomas Paine's The Rights of Man – as in fact Burns was doing in Dumfries! He received 14 years Penal Servitude in Botany Bay. Fysche Palmer was convicted in Perth and given 7 years.

In 1794 Maurice Margarot, was arrested for attempting to carry a Tree of Liberty across Edinburgh's North Bridge. He and William Skirving were given 14 years. Yet Burns had published *The Tree of Liberty*!

> *Syne let us pray, auld England may*
> *Sure plant this far-famed tree, man:*
> *And blythe we'll sing, and hail the day*
> *That gave us liberty, man*

Joseph Gerrald, who likewise was given 14 years, objected to the presence of William Creech and Peter Hill on the Jury – Burns' friend and publisher and one of his printers. Burns might easily have become Australia's National Bard!

Robert Watt was publicly beheaded outside St Giles, the executioner holding up the severed head with the words: "Here is the head of a traitor". Walter Scott had come to Edinburgh expressly to attend the trial and witness the execution.

The madness was no laughing matter for Mrs Archibald Fletcher, an Edinburgh lady who had expressed her sympathy for parliamentary reform. She was accused of using a small guillotine and practising on chickens and mice!

It happened that Burns was at Gatehouse in Galloway on the very day that Thomas Muir, in irons, passed through the village on his way to stand trial in Edinburgh. On that day Burns gave the *Selkirk Grace* at dinner with Lord Daer's father, and composed *Scots Wha Hae*, which has a deeper meaning than you may have recognised!

> *By Oppression's woes and pains,*
> *By your sons in servile chains,*
> *We will drain your dearest veins,*
> > *But they shall be free!*
>
> *Lay the proud usurpers low!*
> *Tyrants fall in every foe!*
> *Liberty's in every blow! –*
> > *Let us do, or dee!*

It is little wonder that, with invasion threatening, Robert Burns became a founding member of the Dumfries Volunteers, which he did on 31st January 1795.

How many people remember today that in Scotland coal miners were bought and sold with the mines until freed by Act of Parliament in 1799 – 3 years after Burns' death?

Scotland owes an immense debt to Robert Burns for collecting, improving, and writing so many of our best loved songs and ballads, yet he received not a penny for providing this priceless heritage. Note the repetitions and conciseness of the ballad:

> *Curs'd be the hand that shot the shot,*
> *An curs'd the gun that gave the crack!*
> *Into my arms bird Helen lap,*
> > *And died for sake o me!*
>
> *I lighted down, my sword did draw,*
> *I cutted him in pieces sma'*
> *I cutted him in pieces sma'*
> > *On fair Kirkconnel lee.*
>
> *I wish I were where Helen lies!*
> *Night and day on me she cries:*
> *O that I were where Helen lies*
> > *On fair Kirkconnel lee.*

Burns' last song was for Jessie Lewars, aged 17, who nursed him during his final illness, and took care of his four sons after his death. It has a ballad-like quality.

> *O, wert thou in the cauld blast*
> *On yonder lea, on yonder lea,*
> *My plaidie to the angry airt,*
> *I'd shelter thee, I'd shelter thee;*
> *Or did Misfortune's bitter storms*
> *Around thee blaw, around thee blaw,*
> *Thy bield should be my bosom,*
> *To share it a', to share it a'.*
>
> *Or were I in the wildest waste,*
> *Sae black and bare, sae black and bare,*
> *The desert were a Paradise,*
> *If thou wert there, if thou wert there.*
> *Or were I monarch o the globe,*
> *Wi thee to reign, wi thee to reign,*
> *The brightest jewel in my crown*
> *Wad be my queen, wad be my queen.*

"He died, in the prime of his manhood, miserable and neglected."

"This was he for whom the world found no fitter business than quarrelling with smugglers and vintners, computing excise-dues upon tallow, and gauging ale-barrels. In such toils was that mighty Spirit sorrowfully wasted: and hundreds of years may pass, before another such is given us to waste." (Carlyle, p.8)

Burns' voice is "The Voice of a Nation and the Voice of Humanity itself. He is a writer who belongs not to Scotland only, but to the whole world." (Thomas Crawford, p. 343)

> *Then let us pray that come it may*
> *(As come it will for a' that),*
> *That Sense and Worth o'er a' the Earth,*
> *Shall bear the gree an a' that.*
>
> *For a' that, an a' that,*
> *It's comin yet for a' that,*
> *That man to man, the warld o'er*
> *Shall brithers be for a' that*

Tributes to Donald

An Obituary from The Royal Society of Edinburgh
by Professor Gordon Craig, and Dr Charles Waterston.
Published in The Royal Society of Edinburgh
Review of the Session 2010-2011,
pages 347-352 and reprinted here with kind permission.

Donald Bertram McIntyre was born at Edinburgh on 15th August 1923, the second child and elder son of Rev. Robert Edmond McIntyre MA, then minister of Orchardhill, Giffnock. His mother was Mary, daughter of Dr Thomas Brown Darling and Jessie Walker. The family moved to Edinburgh on R.E. McIntyre's translation to the High Church, Morningside in 1935. Having started his schooling in Giffnock, Donald moved to Watson's College Edinburgh and in 1939 was evacuated to Grantown-on-Spey where he became Dux of the grammar school in 1941.

He entered Edinburgh University to major in chemistry and was sufficiently enthralled (and competent) while an undergraduate to collaborate with Dr Arnold Beevers of that Department to examine the crystallography of fluor-apatite in relation to tooth and bone structure. Some twenty years later McIntyre's interest in X-Ray fluorescence was rekindled when a machine was purchased by Pomona College for the chemical analyses of granite under Dr A.K. Baird, one of his staff. In 1967 the Pomona team of Baird, McIntyre and Welday analysed the geochemistry and structure of a granite batholith in California. They carried out over 1000 XRF analyses and using 1960s 'high-speed computers', trend surface and vector analyses, processed and interpreted their data. McIntyre and his small team added computing and more rigorous statistical and sampling techniques to their armoury and Professor Bernard Leake has told us that Pomona became the leading laboratory in the world for the XRF analysis of granitic rocks from Mars.

Dr Robert Campbell, McIntyre's Director of Studies at Edinburgh, persuaded him to change his degree course from Chemistry to that of geology and he graduated with First Class Honours in 1945. The Grant Institute of Geology at that time was a hotbed of 'granitisation', the much criticised theory by which granitic rocks are formed by metamorphism rather than by the intrusion of molten magma. Under supervision of the shy but brilliant Professor Arthur Holmes and egged on by the professor's exuberant wife, Dr Doris Reynolds, McIntyre mapped the Loch Doon granite in the Southern Uplands of Scotland and was awarded a PhD in 1947. Later that summer, with the help of a Cross Research Fellowship, he travelled to Neuchâtel to work under Professor Wegmann, the leading structural geologist in Switzerland. That year abroad, doubtless organized by Holmes with a view to giving his gifted student a better understanding of the structural implications of granitization, gave McIntyre an insight into the world of structural geology, Alpine-style, with its emphasis on fold-axes, stereographic projections and petrofabrics. McIntyre returned to the Grant Institute in 1948 as Lecturer in Economic Geology and, as a round peg in a square hole, relished the opportunity to learn blowpipe analysis and adapt his expertise in stereographic projection to the needs of mining surveyors. In 1949 he presented the results of his research on the Loch Doon granite to the Geological Society of London where he argued that the apparently intrusive granodiorite and granite were transformed country rock. He met strong opposition from the petrologica establishment including Drs A.G. McGregor, Deer and Nockolds. However Dr J. Phemister was pleased to find a rising generation of petrologists at once so enthusiastic and. eloquent. Five years later the Publications Committee of that Society was still requiring changes to the submitted paper but McIntyre by this time was heading for a new life in California. His Loch Doon work remains unpublished.

McIntyre had other geological interests besides granite. Using his new Alpine techniques he mapped fold structures in Highland rocks in Strathspey and presented the results to another meeting in the Geological Society in 1951. He was able to project folds seen at the surface to depths of eight miles and received warm plaudits in the ensuing discussion. This time his paper was published. In the same year he and was awarded the Daniel Pigeon Fund from the Geological Society for the promotion of original research. In 1951 he was appointed Secretary of Section C (Geology) when the British Association for the Advancement of Science held its annual meeting in Edinburgh. At the end of the meeting he led a party to the Scottish

Highlands to look at geological structures. There he met and attracted the attention of Professor Frank Turner of the University of California who invited him to spend the summer of 1952 at the Geology Department at Berkeley. McIntyre brought with him deformed marbles from Strathspey and during that summer discovered some of the complexities of the deformation of quartz and calcite crystals in both field and laboratory.

Outside geology Donald's zest for life was boundless. He became President of the Edinburgh University Mountaineering Club and in 1946 a member of Lord Malcolm's Douglas-Hamilton's ATC mountain training team which included the Everest climber and geologist N.E. Odell. He learned to play the bagpipes, initially in the basement of the Grant Institute of Geology, but was banished to the relative isolation of Craigmillar Quarry. His year in Neuchâtel (1947-48) gave him an appreciation of wine which, on his return to Edinburgh, led him to found the Oenological Club the rules of which were so bibulous that the club did not survive beyond its inaugural meeting!

McIntyre quickly became known to academia in the States through the networking of Dr Frank Turner. Donald's personality and scientific work attracted the attention of Pomona College, a small liberal arts institute at Claremont, California where Dr Woodford, Head of the Department of Geology was about to retire. So in 1954 McIntyre left his cold but stable Scotland for an associate professor appointment at Pomona in warm unstable California surrounded by powerful earthquakes, growing mountains – and a department of two staff. He left Scotland in the midst of controversy about the structure of Ben Lui which he claimed was not a recumbent fold as described by Sir Edward Bailey. Ben Lui is now known to be a large-scale recumbent syncline: and yet McIntyre was not wrong in his detailed analysis of the fold. Controversy on folds in the Highlands of Scotland continued in the American Journal of Geology. Dr Mike Johnson has reminded us that McIntyre is now remembered as a pioneer in the use of structural analysis and petrofabrics in the Highlands of Scotland, built on his Swiss experience.

Donald returned to Scotland in 1957, a visit which culminated in his marriage to Ann Alexander of Edinburgh and Moffat in December of that year. Their son Ewen, whose happy nature and special needs because of cerebral palsy have had a profound influence on the family and all who know him, was born in 1961.

Pomona is a college with generous donors, including Mr and Mrs Seaver. The Seaver Science Centre for Geology and Biology was opened in 1959 just five years after McIntyre had been appointed. In 1964 a state of the art IBM 360 computer was bought. As Donald said later 'Mrs Seaver insisted that I must have one of my own'. Indeed McIntyre drove to the IBM centre in Riverside to place the order at a cost of $268,000 on the very day that the new computer was publicly announced. He already had access to the Physics Department's Clary DE-60 for use in crystallography and geochronometry. Shortly afterwards McIntyre was appointed first Director of the Pomona Computer Centre. He became adept at using the IBM 360 to plot contour maps showing not only elevation, but also population density and mineral content. Other applications followed including the analysis of poetry. Help with computerizing finance and other business matters was soon requested by the Registrar's office. McIntyre was so adept at the uses of the machine that he became more expert than the IBM systems engineer assigned to Pomona. McIntyre's early and enthusiastic exposure to the world of computing brought him into contact with gifted mathematicians. Kenneth Iverson, who developed APL (A Programming language) became a close friend. McIntyre learned APL and its derivative language J and in 1994 received the Kenneth E Iverson award for his outstanding contribution to the development and application of APL. Today APL and J are no longer mainstream languages.

The 75th anniversary of the foundation of the Geological Society of America gave McIntyre the opportunity to show his diverse talents at the conference and in the subsequent celebratory book (1963), firstly as a historian of geology, with Hutton at the centre and secondly as a self-taught statistician investigating precision in the age-dating of rocks. Surprisingly Arthur Holmes, his mentor and internationally renowned as the Father of Age Dating, was not mentioned. McIntyre's contribution to this volume *James Hutton and the Philosophy of Geology* was his first published work on the history of science. It was an appropriate debut for McIntyre who had walked the same streets as had Hutton; was a Fellow of this Society of which Hutton was a founding Fellow, and had graduated from the Department of the University of Edinburgh which had counted among its professors Sir Archibald Geikie who revived Hutton's right to be regarded as the Founder of

Modern Geology. In this paper McIntyre brought to the notice of a North American readership the dispute over Hutton's possible debt to the writings of G H Toulmin or, as appears more probable, the reverse, which had been revived or perhaps initiated by S I Tomkieff. Tomkieff's work had remained unnoticed until the publication of McIntyre's paper who gladly acknowledged his debt to Tomkieff. In 1970 McIntyre received a Guggenheim Fellowship to revisit Edinburgh to research *The Rise of Scottish Geology,* an ambitious task which occupied his thoughts for the rest of his life.

In his address at the Opening Convocation of the Centennial Year of Pomona College in 1987, McIntyre invited his audience to set out on a "Critical Inquiry" in which "We are to take nothing for granted. On the contrary, we will use our intellectual microscopes to scrutinize all statements and conclusions..." Such a historical approach had long been applied in Scottish law and became the metaphysical basis of Scottish science in the Enlightenment. Donald McIntyre was not merely a scholar of that Enlightenment but a product and embodiment of it. *James Hutton's Edinburgh: The Historical, Social, and Political Background* the subject of McIntyre's address to the Hutton bicentennial meeting organised by this Society was a *tour de force* in this approach. This extraordinary mélange of dates and relationships proved to be a revelation to many unfamiliar with Scottish history.

McIntyre's research on Hutton and Clerk of Eldin as field geologists will probably be recognised as his most important historical contribution. When the text of the third volume of Hutton's *Theory of the Earth with Proofs and Illustrations* edited by Sir Archibald Geikie was published in 1899 it revealed much about the excursions which Hutton had undertaken with his friends in search of proofs of his theory in the field. In particular it was known that many of these geological proofs had been drawn by John Clerk of Eldin but their whereabouts was not known and substitute illustrations had to be made for Geikie's edition. As we have seen McIntyre was interested in the genesis of Hutton's ideas and as part of his research he studied the background and interests of Hutton's friends. Search in the Scottish Record Office revealed several small diaries in which Clerk of Eldin wrote details of his travels in Galloway with Hutton and of his geological observations. By happenstance, while McIntyre was so engaged a folio of drawings was found at Penicuik House which Lady Clerk and their daughter Honor brought to The Royal Scottish Museum where they were recognised as

"The Lost Drawings" of Clerk of Eldin and those of Arran by his son Lord Eldin. This led to their publication in 1978 together with an explanatory book of which McIntyre was a co-author. He was also co-author with A McKirdy of an excellent popular account of Hutton published in 1997.

McIntyre's last published work, *The Royal Society of Edinburgh, James Hutton, the Clerks of Penicuik and the Igneous Origin of Granite,* shows that his interest in Hutton and his contemporaries remained as lively as ever. The gem contained in this paper is McIntyre's recognition and proof that certain boulders collected by Hutton to illustrate the relationship of the Athol granite with the schistus into which it was intruded and of subsequent vein intrusions were, as Hutton wrote in the third volume of the Treatise, from Glen Tarf. Clerk of Eldin had mistakenly written below his drawings of them that they were from Glen Tilt, a neighbouring locality from which other illustrative boulders had been collected.

McIntyre was perhaps happier with the spoken rather than the written word and was a brilliant speaker and inspirational teacher. His exceptional talent was recognised in 1985 by his election from some 5,000 eligible professors as California's Professor of the Year. In the same year he was awarded the Medal of the Geological Society of China following a lecture course there on computers. Four years later he left Pomona and, with his family, settled in Perthshire. He immediately campaigned against what he regarded as the desecration of the Kinfauns churchyard and later against the quarrying of Dunsinane Hill. His enthusiasm for the worth of the environment soon led to his appointment as Chairman of Perth Civic Trust. He was a member of the Piobaireachd Society and his understanding of the great music led him to play it not only on his pipes but on his computer and his programme is used as a teaching tool at the College of Piping in Glasgow. Tribute to Donald as a piper has been paid by his friend Norrie Sinclair's tune *"Professor Donald McIntyre"*. Donald bravely fought the onset of Parkinson's Disease from which he died on 21st October 2009.

Tribute from David Alexander, President Emeritus of Pomona College
October 2009

In the history of Pomona College, Donald McIntyre stands among the titans of its leadership. His uncountable contributions to the life and program of the College as a member of the faculty from 1954 to his retirement in 1989 admit him to the company of those heroic persons who have created and sustained the College's excellence. As a geologist, he was a superb teacher whose students have themselves become leaders in academic geology and its practical applications. As a professor, he extended his classroom to encompass all who would learn from his vast erudition. As a visionary, he and his colleagues Nelson Smith and Charles Fowler impressed Frank Seaver to the extent that Mr. Seaver's philanthropy was enthusiastic and bountiful. Indeed, it is said that whenever the three professors expressed some concern that their plans for the science buildings might be unrealistically expensive, Mr. Seaver, who trusted them completely and admired their sense of thrift, would chide them for not asking for the best and most comprehensive building designs and for equipment of the highest standard as he presented his larger and larger checks to Pomona College. Mere words cannot adequately describe the extent of Donald McIntyre's influence in the development of the Seaver Science Center and the College's program in the sciences.

Donald McIntyre's scholarly attainments were not confined to his successful career as a geologist. His boundless creative energy and broad competence brought him national recognition as a pioneer in developing new programs in computing, and he was a central figure in the development of computing and computer programming at Pomona College. His love of history and his deep professional knowledge of the history of geology eminently qualified him to become widely recognized as an intellectual historian of the Scottish Enlightenment. His research into the life of James Hutton added new information not only about the origins of modern geology but also about Hutton's pivotal role in the Enlightenment. Hutton and his friends Adam Smith and Joseph Black founded the Oyster Club, which drew the best thinkers of the day to Edinburgh, and Donald McIntyre's accounts of Hutton's life emphasize the extent to which this congregation of learned men changed the world.

Being in the presence of Donald McIntyre was like, one imagines, being in the presence of an intellectual nuclear reactor. Learning radiated from him. One always learned something from his agile and ever inquisitive mind. Moreover, he was a pleasure to be around: a loving husband and father, a caring friend, and an upright man of a palpable personal integrity. Having known him leaves an indelible mark on one's life.

In his 1997 paper on "James Hutton's Edinburgh: The Historical, Social, and Political Background", Donald McIntyre quotes Thomas Carlyle: "What dust of extinct lions sleeps under our feet everywhere." One such lion rests here in Claremont as well as in his native Scotland, but not extinct in one sense, to be sure, for as long as Pomona College flourishes, it will celebrate Professor Donald McIntyre's life and career.

Tribute from James C. Kelley (Pomona Class of 1963), President of the Board of Trustees, California Academy of Sciences
November 2009

It is hard to express how much Donald meant to all his former students and colleagues. He was, without any doubt, the most important person in my own intellectual evolution. He always had time, or would always make time to explain, always from first principles, how a problem could be addressed and solved.

I have many memories of times when I interrupted Donald when he was extremely busy and he would always take the time to help. Once he was trying to decipher an octal core dump from WDPC in the days when our input device to UCLA was the U.S. Postal Service and turnaround time was one week. It was a very challenging problem, but he looked up and gave me that look which said, "Can't you see that I am very busy?" but then immediately dropped the printout sheet and answered my probably trivial question. He once took hours to explain to me, alone, the principles and operation of a petrographic microscope. When Donald was your mentor, you always knew that he deeply believed you were capable of learning and understanding the most complex concepts and he kept at you until you proved him right. I never, in my entire academic career, met anyone with both his unmatched intellectual ability and his dedication to imparting his immense store of knowledge to anyone who would listen. Donald deeply believed that if you asked him a question, you really wanted to know the answer – it never occurred to him that it could be otherwise.

He was without any doubt, the most important person in my own intellectual evolution. He always had time, or would always make time to explain, always from first principles, how a problem could be addressed and solved. When Donald was your mentor, you always knew that he deeply believed you were capable of learning and understanding the most complex concepts and he kept at you until you proved him right.

Donald was simply the most intellectually challenging and inspirational person I have ever known. I often wonder where this knowledge came from in all of its ramifications and subtleties and I cannot imagine where I would be today if I had not known Donald. Every day, as I follow my own intellectual pursuits I feel as if Donald is looking over my shoulder to be sure that I don't leave anything out, that I have understood all aspects of the subject at hand and that I am being as honest as possible in my assessments. Now, he truly is looking over my shoulder. He will be for the rest of my life, and until we are all together again.

Ann, I have so many wonderful memories of our times together in Scotland. Carrying Ewen on my back as we visited castles and field sites, with Donald reciting Robert Burns poetry as we crossed the field where famous Scots had fought famous battles. Just sitting up with you in the evening over a whisky, listening to his stories of his boyhood in the Highlands was true bliss. I remember the evening in 1969 when I was visiting you in Edinburgh when Donald was on his Guggenheim sabbatical year, and two of your uncles, I think they were, were talking about their deep Scottish roots, and Donald told the story of his father ministering to his flock in the Highlands. He had one parishioner who was an old lady (*of the McIntyre clan*) and he got who her to read her Gaelic Bible. Donald pointed out that "Mc" means "son of" in Gaelic and that "Intyre" means "carpenter" and so with all the references in the Gaelic bible to "Jesus McIntyre" he didn't want to push the point as to who could trace their roots back the farthest. I'm sure you have heard these stories many times, but to me they were truly wonderful and so characteristic of Donald's incredibly subtle and sophisticated sense of humor.

Ann, I miss him very much. I know you and Ewen must be devastated. But we were so fortunate to have known him for as long as we did. There will never be another like him. His shadow is long indeed and his intellectual influence and impact was vast and profound.

Tribute from David D. Pollard,
(Pomona Class of 1968) –
Professor of Geology, Stanford, University, CA

November 2009

The following are my thoughts about Donald, in part taken from something I wrote in December 1990 at the time of his retirement from Pomona College. Now, nearly 20 years later, the memories are more distant, but the emotion is more intense.

I believe that virtually every student who participated in one of Donald's classes, and certainly every student who majored in geology during Donald's tenure at Pomona, remembers his contribution to their education and the pleasure it was to attend his lectures. For many of us he personified the best in a college professor – full of enthusiasm for his chosen subject, completely absorbed in its intricacies, and eager to share its beauty and depth with all who cared to listen.

At the same time Donald personified the kind of educator who defines what is special about a liberal arts institution. At the slightest provocation his lecture or discussion on geology would turn to poetry, history, statistics, unblended Scotch whisky, geography, algebra, naval battles, art, computer science, the bagpipes, philosophy, the history of science and countless other topics to both delight and enthral the students. Even among the outstanding educators at Pomona, there is no doubt that Donald was unique and gifted.

For some of us Donald's gift was not limited to those few hours in the classroom, illuminated by his breadth of knowledge, or those precious moments on a field trip, many years ago. For us, his spark of enthusiasm for a newly found fossil or strangely contorted fold kindled a fire that still burns; his gift permeates our careers and continues to emerge in many unexpected ways. Our daily work is an ever present reminder of those moments, but our sense of gratitude extends beyond fleeting recollections. For us, those experiences at Pomona were a singular turning point, one of only a handful that each of us can recount about our lives which, in this case, launched careers in the profession called geology. Donald touched our lives and made a real difference.

Since leaving Pomona, my professional life has developed along a conventional path, characterized by a narrowing of focus and the increasing refinement of technical skills. This specialization has led to contributions in the form of new data, concepts, and understanding in the field of structural geology. But looking back at my undergraduate experience at Pomona, I can only marvel at Donald's ability to be equally at home turning the U-stage of a petrographic microscope, measuring a fold axis with a Brunton Compass, contouring the spatial distribution of chemical elements determined by XRF, explaining the geometry of the Helvetic Nappes, developing a new algorithm in APL, expounding on the statistical analysis of radiometric ages, plotting crystallographic data on a stereographic projection, or determining the focal mechanism of an earthquake. Almost regardless of a student's predilection within the diverse subject matter of geology, Donald was always ready to plant the potent seeds of curiosity and wonder, backed by solid facts and technical skills. Donald's contribution to the careers of the graduates of the Geology Department at Pomona was as varied as these examples.

In this short statement I cannot hope to express the extent of my gratitude, nor can I adequately express the range or depth of my feelings. Still, I am compelled to write this as a small token of my thanks for the gifts I received as one of Donald's students.

In Loving Remembrance
of Donald McIntyre
Martha Andresen, Professor of
English Emerita, Pomona College
October 2009

Some months ago, during our last conversation together, I shared with Donald words spoken by a luminous woman of many years: "Our memories must be sufficient to the beauties we have seen."

Despite the ravages of illness and his difficulty in speaking, Donald, for a time, regained strength and joy in his response to this lovely turn of a phrase, this timely affirmation of the sufficiency that memory can and must be. For a brief moment, we recalled the friendship we had shared, a friendship of many years. Long ago, at Pomona College, he was my colleague in Geology; I was his colleague in English. But we met as kindred spirits and we remained kindred spirits, our association and collaboration vastly enriched by sharing our families as well as our professions, a sharing that spanned time and distance, that encompassed many occasions and every turn in our lives. And now too, his passing.

How abundant, in my memory, are the beauties we have seen. Forever alive are the beauties of Donald's brilliancy; a brilliancy manifest in every encounter we shared. An incandescent, kinetic, irrepressibly passionate and generous brilliancy. A brilliancy of mind, character, knowledge, values, vision, and vocation. A vocation, within and beyond the classroom, to teach and transform us, to open our own minds and hearts to the wonders he ceaselessly embraced and fathomed. Wonders of time and creation, cosmic, planetary, and human, and wonders of origin and connection, a matrix of structural, mathematical, and conceptual relationships, a web of historical significance, a patterning of landscape sublimity and literary splendor.

In such encounters with Donald and his family too, such beauties are attached to the person and to a place. To many places, near and far, each a brave new world, illuminated by his brilliancy, transfigured by his family's love.

Now, in my memory, I am with him in a lecture hall at Pomona College, where he teaches us what computers are and can be and what geology reveals to us. Here too he pays tribute to departed colleagues, capturing their unique and enduring gifts within the history of our college and a liberal arts tradition. Now I am with him in a classroom, co-teaching the art and science of Coleridge's *Rime of the Ancient Mariner*. Now I am with his family in Scotland, at the ruins of Smailholm Tower, where the lame boy Walter Scott once dreamt of Border history and where Donald now recites to us his "The Eve of St John." Now we visit the ruins of Melrose Abbey, the glories of Roslin Chapel, the magic of the Eildon Hills, the warmth of the Inn at Tibby Shiels, at St. Mary's Loch, where we listen to present-day local shepherds singing their border lays. Now I walk the streets of Edinburgh, with Donald at my side, and he recalls each figure of the Scottish Enlightenment, and each legacy of transcendent genius. Now I am with Donald, Ann, and Ewen in a hospital room back home, where they greet my new born baby girl, and present her with a treasure, Ewen's blue-coated, gold-buttoned Peter Rabbit doll. Now I am at their Claremont home, enjoying a holiday feast and recreating for my young child the drama of the first Christmas. Now I am seated in our Pomona College Hall of Music, listening to Donald's ringing centennial oration, "Footprints on the Sands of Time." Now I am at the Faculty House, paying tribute to Donald on the occasion of his retirement and departure for Scotland. Now I am toasting a fond farewell with a bottle of the finest wine, kept for years by Donald and Ann for such a momentous occasion. Now I am at my home in Claremont, far from Scotland and my friends, but welcoming their phone calls and mailings. Here I find family news as well as newspaper cuttings of book reviews and Shakespeare plays. I find too Ann's words of inspiration and comfort and an array of Donald's extraordinary essays and scholarly papers; among them, his magisterial portraits of the historical figures and places he so loved.

And now I speak with Donald for the last time, and we recall many joys.

And now Ann calls to tell me that Donald has passed away. He is at peace at last.

And now Ann calls to say that she is among their circle of loving friends who enfold her in mourning and celebration. And in such welcome company, glorious stories are being exchanged, often with great joy and abundant laughter. Her dear words give me comfort: "Now Donald, as he was, is resurrected among us."

And now, on the occasion at St. Johns' Kirk and forever after, may our beloved friend Donald McIntyre live in our joy and gratitude. May our memories be sufficient to the beauties we have seen.

Editorial footnote: In 1981, during one of our summer visits, Martha spent a few days in Scotland visiting literary sites with Donald and concluding with an expedition to the Scottish Borders. All four of us were engrossed by Donald's readings from The Border Ballads on the very turf which they described. On Saturday evening we stayed at Tibbie Shiels Inn by St Mary's Loch, famous for its connections with both Robert Burns and James Hogg. To our great delight, a local sheep farmer and his daughter, in her twenties, came to the inn and under that low beamed ceiling there – with passion and with joy and long into the night – they both recited poems by Robert Burns. Next morning we saw that same young woman/shepherdess striding over the fields in her heavy boots and, with her black-and-white collie dog, hard at work gathering in the sheep. This was of special interest and amusement to Shakespearean scholar – Martha – who for decades had always associated and taught of the shepherdess in "As you like it" as a dainty feminine figure in frilly dress and little mutch cap!

Remembering Donald
Virginia Crosby, Professor of French Emerita, Pomona College
March 2012

Man is most nearly himself when he achieves the seriousness of a child at play. –
Heraclitus (500 BCE)

Time plays hob with Memory, encouraging her capriciousness. Keys to locked doors in her storeroom go missing, others gape, some spring open at a touch.

Writing this just now opens such a door onto a gallery of images: A family dinner at the house on Twelfth Street, Ewen's endearing smile, the evening's bright and welcoming warmth; Donald, joining Vincent Learnihan's lunchtime table at the Faculty House with only a moment to spare for a cup of hot water; eager to share news of a development in APL, or a fresh *aperçu* into the life of James Hutton, his constant companion on walks in 18th century Edinburgh; Donald perched on the edge of a stage at a Trustee Faculty Retreat, his audience captivated by knowledge so gracefully laced with wit and the joyful love of his subject
.

One image carrying an echo of Highland music, is drawn from hearsay. It is the evening of the traditional dinner in Frary Hall given by President and Mrs. Lyon to open the School Year. I see Donald, kilt rhythmically swaying, piping faculty, spouses, trustees and guests in to dinner. Solemn yet stirring music to lead forward symbolically as well. This now legendary story was part of my introduction when I arrived at Pomona College in 1963, and I was thrilled. My Southern California college had its own piper!

Much has been written and said about Donald's brilliant mind, of his professional achievements, superb teaching, his vast range of interests from vineyards to mountains – Donald, as easily at home with a Roman poet or a medieval Islamic scientist. What Memory privileges me to keep and hold as Donald's most inspiring and inexhaustible gift is the joy he found in life itself, in all of its infinite manifestations in nature; the wonder of the ongoing creative energy revealed in the study so dear to his heart. As my daughter, one of his innumerable grateful students put it—in the irreverent yet telling vernacular of today: "Geology rocks."

Memories of a Meeting of Minds
Colin Nowell, The McIntyre's
IT Guru in Scotland
February 2013

How does anyone begin to relate the unique effect Dr. Donald B. McIntyre has had on their life? My earliest memory of Donald was on a car journey in 1990 – not the journey driving myself to meet him for the first time but another later that day.

Having already met his brother Ranald, via a mutual friend Alastair (also of the McIntyre Clan), I had spent a pleasant time driving north into the heart of Perthshire to arrive at Kinfauns where I was to come face to face with – as it was to turn out – one of the most significant mentors of my life. The premise of the visit was to help Donald manage his personal computing needs at that prolific stage of his productive life. If it had been that simple … but, as I was soon to learn, meeting Donald was never "that simple"!

Even as an accomplished, professional IT Specialist (as I thought of myself at that time of my professional life) imagine how astonished and overwhelmed I felt when, after the initial pleasantries of meeting Donald, Ann and Ewen at their wonderful home, he and I immediately plunged into in an intense conversation about his involvement in the early IBM machines – the grandparents of modern day personal computing devices! Suddenly here was a man telling me that he had been at the forefront of modern day computing technology – and yet he felt intimidated by his own PC! … And, by the way, would I mind taking care of his personal computing needs?

At that point, he invited me to accompany him on an errand in Perth. So off we went into town and back driven by Donald in his own car. What was particularly memorable about that short journey was how, even before we had arrived at our destination, Donald had managed to explain to me the unusual structure of bagpipe pibroch music and of the geological origin of the building stones of Perth! Intense? You bet! Yes, it was… but my goodness, it was then that I discovered that every conversation with Donald, no matter how informal, would be equally animated!

Donald's enthusiasm for all things was very striking. The subject matter, in a way, was largely irrelevant. That intense enthusiasm was always there in every interaction – indeed that is my abiding memory of Donald of every conversation that we shared, no matter what the topic, whether spending a pleasant time at a family dinner or on a brisk walk along the North Inch on the banks of the River Tay with Ann and Ewen – the effect was the same – always enthralling, always stretching the mind....yet always enjoyable! I think I can safely say that I learnt more about the important aspects of life in the 20 years that I had the privilege of knowing Donald than I had learned in the preceding 40 years of my own life. For that, I will be forever grateful.

In his own fields of geology and computer languages, Donald was undoubtedly one of the leaders and innovators of his era. He never stopped giving of his own time and experience unselfishly and unconditionally, to the very end of his days to anyone who crossed his path. I am proud to say that not only did I have the privilege to meeting and, in a sense, understanding Donald, but also of coming to know him as a close friend and valued companion. Thank you Donald, you will always be there in spirit for me.

Reminiscences of Donald B. McIntyre
Norman Butcher
Staff Tutor in Earth Sciences, Scotland 1971-1992, The Open University

I first came aware of Donald McIntyre on 2 July 1954 when he read a paper on the Moine Thrust in N.W.Q. Scotland to The Geologists' Association in Burlington House in Piccadilly, London. Asked at the end by someone in the audience what was the age of the Moine Thrust, Donald replied, quick as a flash: "Well, we know it's older than the peat."

This was typical of Donald's style, his intellectual brilliance shone through in everything he did. He was quite simply a delightful colleague and companion and I was to benefit from this once he retired from Pomona College in California and moved back to Scotland in 1989.

In 1971, to mark the Centenary of the founding of the Regius Chair of Geology in the University of Edinburgh, Donald was one of only two Edinburgh alumni to give a keynote address in the large George Square lecture theatre. The other was Lionel .E.Weiss of Berkeley, California. Donald was the first to speak on the Thursday morning. As he rose to his feet, it soon became clear that he had problems. First he removed his jacket, sat down, then got up and changing tack completely, proceeded to deliver an amazing discourse on all the wonderful Raeburn portraits to be seen in Edinburgh and beyond.

Whilst at Pomona College in California, Donald used often to spend time in the summers visiting Edinburgh. His mother lived in Eglinton Crescent at the West End. He would spend time in the then Scottish Record Office working on the Clerk of Penicuik papers. He developed a close interest in the work of James Hutton (1726-1797).

Having had intermittent contact with Donald on his visits to Edinburgh, I finally got the chance to visit him at Pomona College in California in November 1987. I was on study leave from the Open University in Scotland, which I helped set up from nothing at the beginning of 1971. I recall flying to Boston on 11 November 1987, visiting Harvard, Yale (where I met the renowned John Rodgers), New York; Philadelphia, Washington (visiting the Smithsonian); Reston in Virginia for a US Geological Society (USGS) meeting and then flying to Ontario near Los Angeles where I was met by Donald on 22 November, just in time to celebrate Thanksgiving.

I stayed with Donald, Ann and Ewen at their home and experienced two earthquakes – the first at 6 p.m. on Monday 23 November whilst Donald and I were walking past the seismograph in the Geology Department corridor; the second at 5:20 when I was asleep in Donald's study at his home. That week I also stayed at The Athenaeum, Pasadena, visited the geologist, Stanton Hill and met Lee Silver at the drill site in Cajon Pass in the San Andreas Fault Zone. It was quite a week! I was back in the Open University office in Edinburgh by 2 p.m. on 1 December!

In 1995 having discovered the site of James Hutton's house at St John's Hill in Edinburgh, I announced this at a special meeting in New Orleans at a November gathering to mark the bicentenary of the publication of Hutton's "Theory of the Earth" in 1795. Realising that 1997 would probably the single most important anniversary in the history of British geology – the death of James Hutton and the birth of Charles Lyall, I put the idea of a major commemorative meeting to Professor Fred Last, Convenor of Meetings for the Royal Society of Edinburgh. A committee was set up with both Donald and myself upon it. At one of the Committee's business meetings, Donald arrived late. As he crossed the room to take a seat at the far side of the table, the

Chairman, Gordon Craig, exclaimed "You're wearing a suit"; Donald stopped dead in his tracks, turned around and said: "Now I know what I have been doing wrong all these years!"

On a wet and windy 26 March 1997 Donald delivered an eulogy to James Hutton in the Greyfriars Kirkyard in Edinburgh when we placed a wreath on Hutton's grave. Donald had been much influenced by a lecture on Hutton by Professor S.I.Tomkieff of Newcastle University the year that the then Lord Provost of Edinburgh, Sir John Falconer, proclaimed Hutton as the Founder of Modern Geology.

On Thursday 3 July 1997, Donald and I went up Glen Tilt to identify suitable material to bring to Edinburgh for the proposed Garden at St John's Hill. We had a wonderful day out together, and this is how I shall always remember him as a great field geologist.

★★★★★

Among Donald's papers there is a faded newspaper cutting from The Strathspey Herald of 25 January 1952.

"Hugh Alexander Barrie M.A. lost his life with his friend Thomas Baird M.A. on 2nd January 1928 while climbing these hills."

"Find me a windswept boulder for a bier."

When I am Dead

When I am dead
And this strange spark of life that in me lies
Is fled to join the great white core of life
That surely flames beyond eternities,
And all I ever thought of as myself
Is mouldering to dust and cold death ash,
This pride of nerve and muscle – merest dross,
This joy of brain and eye and touch but trash,
Bury me not, I pray thee
In the dark earth where comes not any ray
Of light or warmth or aught that make life dear;
But take my whitened bones far, far away
Out of the hum and turmoil of the town,
Find me a wind-swept boulder for a bier
And on it lay me down
Where far beneath drops sheer the rocky ridge

Down to the gloomy valley, and the streams
Fall foaming white against black beetling rocks:
Where the sun's kindly radiance seldom gleams:
Where some tall peak, defiant, steadfast mocks
The passing gods: and all that was of men
Forgotten.

So I may know
Even in that death which comes to everything
The swiftly silent swish of hurrying snow;
The lash of rain; the savage bellowing
Of stags; the bitter keen-knife – edge embrace of the rushing
wind: and the still tremulous dawn
Will touch the eyeless sockets of my face;
And I shall see the sunset and anon
Shall know the velvet kindness of the night
And see the stars.

Hugh Alexander Barrie.

On the glorious golden autumnal of Saturday, 9th October 2010, Ranald and Andrew McIntyre, Ewen and I and our good friends Arthur and Jean Bruce, scattered Donald's ashes by his favourite boulder at Glen Tilt.

★★★★★

Inscription in "Great Souls at Prayer"- a little red leather bound book – a gift from Donald's parents on our engagement:.

Ann
- to commemorate 25th August 1957

"O Lord God, when Thou givest to Thy servants to endeavour any great matter, grant us also to know that it is not the beginning, but the continuing of the same, until it be thoroughly finished, which yieldeth the true glory; through Him that for the finishing of Thy work laid down His life, our Redeemer, Jesus Christ. Amen" – Francis Drake before Cadiz.

★★★★★

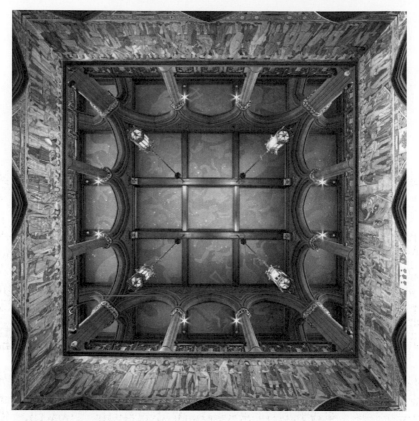

The ceiling of the Great Hall in the Scottish National Portrait gallery, Edinburgh, is made up of 30 panels representing the constellations in the Zodiac, exquisitely painted by William Hole. A star in the constellation of Taurus is dedicated to Donald, in the square by the lantern at the bottom left corner of the ceiling. There is a half circle at the top left corner of the square and the shape of the bull's head and forelegs on its right-hand side.

Permissions and Acknowledgements

Text copyright: Careful and comprehensive efforts have been made to source copyright holders and to secure these permissions. My efforts have not always been successful and if I have infringed copyright in anyway, on being notified, I will gladly correct any errors or omissions in future editions.

Photo copyright: Unfortunately, it has not been possible to trace the identity of the owner of many of the photographs and to request permission to include their work in this book. I am grateful to all the contributors and, on hearing from them, will acknowledge them in future edition of the book. The photographs are put forward for historical purposes only.

Cover design: Thanks to Gilbert and Johanna Summers for designing the cover and the frontispiece of this book. The front cover incorporates the following photographs: Donald on Dunsinane Hill, Perthshire, Scotland; Pomona College's Seaver Science Building, Claremont, California, U.S.A.; Gilbert Summers' photograph of Siccar Point, Berwickshire, Scotland and, on the back cover, Meg Cowie's photo of Ann.

Note: This book would not have become a reality without the patience, experience and guidance of Gilbert Summers, my coordinating editor. I am deeply grateful.

Also with gratitude to the following:

Armour, Richard – *Academic Procession, Pomona College.*

The Edinburgh Geological Society – *McIntyre's Red Herrings* from *The Edinburgh Geologist*, Issue no.40, Spring 2003.

Graham, Harry – poems from *Ruthless Rhymes*, Sheldrake Press, London with permission

Henley, William Ernst – *From a Window in Princes Street"*

Henderson, Henry – The Bard of Reay – *We shall remember* – an original poem

Hiles, Marvin and Nancy – founders of the Iona Center Community, Healdsburgh, California – *An Almanac of the Soul, 2008* and the Daybook

– *All the Days of my life,* whose anthologies of prose and poetry have introduced our family to a treasure trove of great beauty and wisdom. *An Almanac of the Soul* has introduced me to many of the poems and authors that I have quoted.

Hopkins, Gerald Manley – *Inversnaid,* from *Poems of Gerard Manley Hopkins,* Oxford University Press

Killen, John – *When on a trip to Southern Isles,* Baja California

Mackenzie, David – *Man! what a burst o' high elation…."*

Madsen, Stan – Baja California article

Mayne, Michael, excerpt from *Learning to Dance*, Darton, Long and Todd, London 2001.

Morgan Edwin *Theory of the Earth* from *Collected Poems,* Carcanet Press Limited, Manchester, U.K. used by permission of the poet.

Murray, W.H. Quotations from *Undiscovered Scotland,* J.M. Dent & Sons Ltd. first published 1951, used by permission of Anne Murray; and an excerpt from *The Scottish Himalayan Expedition (*London: J.M.Dent, 1951*)*

Perth Mountaineering Club Journal, 2000. *The Magic of the Mountain –* with permission.

Pomona College songs, Claremont, California, USA – used with permission from Pomona College, Alumni Office

Ray, David *Thanks Robert Frost* from *Sam's Book*, Wesleyan University Press 1987 used by permission of the poet

Robertson, James Logie -.*Non Semper Imbres*

Rogers, Fred – *Mister Rogers Songs* – The Fred Rogers Company, Pittsburgh, Pennsylvania, USA – used by one-time permission to include the words of songs by Fred Rogers.

Royal Society of Edinburgh – Obituary of Donald B. McIntyre R.S.E. from The Royal Society of Edinburgh's Review of the session 2010-2011 used with permission.

Saroyan, William "I am not going to try to comfort you…" from *The Human Comedy* Dell Publishing, 1966.

Scottish Mountaineerng Club – Donald's aricle *Winter on Bidean nam Bian*, from their magazine, May 1948

Stevenson, Robert Louis – *When swallows fly*.

Vanier, Jean – quotations from *Our Journey Home – Rediscovering a Common Humanity beyond our Differences,* Novalis 1997 and from *Finding Peace,* House of Anansi Press, Toronto, 2003.

Wheelock, John Hall – excerpt (15 lines) from *Dear Men and Women (in memory of Van Wyck Brooks* from *By Daylight and in Dream: New and*

Collected Poems 1904-1970 by John Hall Wheelock. All rights reserved. Copyright 1966 by John Hall Wheelock. Copyright renewed 1994 by Sally Wheelock Brayton. Reprinted with permission of Scribner, an imprint of Simon & Schuster Adult Publishing Group.
Worden Alfred M. *Hello Earth* from *Hello Earth – Greetings from Endeavour,* Nash Publishing. 1974 used with permission of the poet
Wordsworth, William, *The Alps* from *Descriptive Sketches*
Young, Geoffrey Winthrop from *The Collected Poems of Geoffrey Winthrop Young,* Methuen Co, 1936

★★★★★

Photograph of Benjamin Peach and John Horne used with permission from the British Geological Survey, all rights reserved.
Photograph of Donald at Glen Tilt, 1970 by James Secord, with permission
Photograph of Glen Tilt, 2012 by Arthur Bruce, with permission
Scottish National Portrait Gallery, Edinburgh, to reproduce photograph of the Star Ceiling of the Great Hall, painted by William Hole, with permission.
Scottish National Portrait Gallery, Edinburgh, photograph of the Star Ceiling of the Great Hall, painted by William Hole, with permission.